T0311805

Preface *to* Social Economics

Preface *to* Social Economics

Economic Theory and Social Problems

John Maurice Clark

Moses Abramovitz and Eli Ginzberg, editors

Routledge
Taylor & Francis Group

LONDON AND NEW YORK

First published 1936 by Transaction Publishers

Published 2017 by Routledge
2 Park Square, Milton Park, Abingdon, Oxon OX14 4RN
711 Third Avenue, New York, NY 10017, USA

Routledge is an imprint of the Taylor & Francis Group, an informa business

Copyright © 1936 by John Maurice Clark.

All rights reserved. No part of this book may be reprinted or reproduced or utilised in any form or by any electronic, mechanical, or other means, now known or hereafter invented, including photocopying and recording, or in any information storage or retrieval system, without permission in writing from the publishers.

Notice:
Product or corporate names may be trademarks or registered trademarks, and are used only for identification and explanation without intent to infringe.

Library of Congress Catalog Number: 2009002371

Library of Congress Cataloging-in-Publication Data

Clark, John Maurice, 1884-1963.
  Preface to social economics : economic theory and social problems / John Maurice Clark ; Moses Abramovitz and Eli Ginzberg, editors.
    p. cm.
  Originally published: New York : Farrar & Rinehart, incorporated, [c1936]
  ISBN 978-1-4128-0998-6
  1. Economics. 2. Social problems. I. Abramovitz, Moses. II. Ginzberg, Eli, 1911- III. Title.

HB171.C595 2009
330.1—dc22   2009002371

ISBN 13: 978-1-4128-0998-6 (pbk)

FOREWORD

During the summer of 1935, we were both engaged in reading widely in the works of our teacher Professor John Maurice Clark. At that time we became impressed with the large number of highly significant but inaccessible essays and so conceived the idea of collecting the most important for publication in book form.

In the fall of the year we informed Professor Clark of our plan and asked his indulgence. This he was kind enough to grant. While engaged in the selection of the essays, their arrangement, the search for titles, and other technical problems preparatory to printing, we were fortunate in having the counsel and advice of Professor Clark. Final responsibility, however, rests definitely with us. That we alone must be held accountable for the Introduction hardly needs emphasis; nobody, least of all Professor Clark, is implicated in our interpretation—or misinterpretation—of economics, pre-Clarkian and Clarkian.

The essays, with the exception of "Toward a Concept of Social Value," have been previously published either in learned journals or in scientific compendia; "Long-Range Planning" appeared as a special supplement to an issue of *The New Republic*. They are here reprinted practically without change. At the conclusion of "Business Acceleration and the Law of Demand," Professor Clark has added a note, several pages in length, in which he reviews the more recent discussions of this problem, especially those precipitated by his own treatment.

The division of the essays into Parts I and II is best explained by the half titles. In Part I the arrangement is chronological except for the first essay which usurped that position by virtue of its materials and composition. In Part II, the order represents a compromise between chronology and subject matter; the four essays on business cycles are placed together. The concluding contribution to the volume finds itself in Part II more for reasons of form than of logic: the most recent of Professor Clark's writings, it is also, in many respects, the most comprehensive.

We gratefully acknowledge indebtedness for permission to republish various selections in this volume to The Macmillan Company of New York; F. S. Crofts & Co.; Columbia University Press; The University of Chicago Press; and to the editors of the *Journal of Political Economy*, *The American Economic Review*, *The Quarterly Journal of Economics*, and *The New Republic*.

MOSES ABRAMOVITZ
ELI GINZBERG

Columbia University
June, 1936

Table of Contents

INTRODUCTION

Economic conditions change and these changes alter the adequacy of social policies. Economic theory, with its necessarily abstract propositions, also changes. This, however, is not a phenomenon to be expected, but rather one to be explained. For an economic law, like any scientific proposition, states a relation which is true only under certain conditions. If these conditions are correctly stated, why need economic laws change their form?

The explanation of these developments is, perhaps, the keynote of Professor John Maurice Clark's method of writing and of interpreting economics. The chief phenomena of economic life are the products of a bewildering complex of forces, many of them interacting in a confusing fashion. Propositions to be completely accurate descriptions or explanations would have to apply either to such a limited range of data as to be of little help in organizing one's thinking, or else to apply to such a mass of data as to fit any behavior whatever. A significant proposition must fall between. It must describe the important factors determining a broad range of data and abstract from the remainder. Ideally, one ought also to handle the forces abstracted from; but the task is too complicated, both for the student to present and for the reader to use.

But what is "important"? Economists' evaluations of the important is largely conditioned by their deductions about the potentialities of reform. This is natural, for the practical issues of a day determine the problems to be studied; and since problems are also human issues, the important forces are those which are amenable to control.

If this be true, economics must be concerned with social values, embryonic as well as adult. It must recognize new possibilities for reform which new situations suggest, and also problems, new and old, which the new conditions have heightened. Thus, forces previously neglected must be placed in the center of the stage; forces previously emphasized may be accorded less prominent roles or even dropped from the cast.

While these considerations offer a simple explanation for the substitution of one group of theorems for another, it must not be assumed that the process of transition is itself simple. On the contrary, students engaged therein find the process one of great difficulty. The validity of new evaluations and the selection of new forces do not stand out clearly, in part, merely because they are new. Their importance has not yet impressed itself upon our system of thinking. Hence they can be defended only with great effort against older concepts which have all the strength of habits.

Since the established theories of an era largely secure their acceptance because of their appropriateness for the issues of the time, at first little pressure exists for an exact statement of the conditions under which these theories are valid. A concept when first propounded tends to be assigned a wider applicability than is its due. Qualifications are not, at the time, important. Hence, it becomes difficult to recognize the existence of other factors and, if they are recognized, to evaluate them critically. A newer theory, in its turn, arrogates to itself a wider validity than it deserves and is pressed back within its true bounds only by the effort of according recognition to still other neglected factors. Thus, critical reasoning in scientific work is a part—a difficult part—of constructive effort.

When Professor Clark started his work, the dominant economics stressed what he has happily called *the assumptions of contentment*. Supply and demand tend to equality; resources tend to be fully utilized. The demands of consumers in the market represent in fair fashion their real wants, and the expenses of producers represent the real costs to society of furnishing consumers with what they demand. The pressure of competition tends to carry the production of every article to the point at which its cost is as great as the amount people are willing to pay. The practical conclusion for social policy is, in the main, *laissez faire.*

Properly qualified and limited, these statements are true. But modern economies suffer from unutilized resources of machines and men; empty factories and unemployed men are all too common. On the other hand, fluctuations in the rate of consumption sometimes carry market demand beyond the point at which it can be easily satisfied with existing resources. And we find important exceptions to the propositions that market demand is a good representative of consumers' wants and that producers' expenses are good representatives of social costs.

Against these classical and neoclassical theorems dissenting voices had already begun to be heard at the turn of the century. Davenport had declared that money demands and money expenses were only market phenomena; they told us nothing of social wants and social costs—a rigid negative which was due for correction. Veblen had stressed the importance of alternating periods of strained activity and wasteful idleness; and, reversing the classical formula, he had found competition but an imperfect and unimportant check on the normal tendency of private business to exploit consumer and laborer. Moreover, Veblen undertook the first important studies of forces which did not appear to be self-limiting. These were the so-called *institutions*—the legal system and the industrial arts. The impact of these institutions upon our thinking and acting is pronounced, sufficiently so in fact to lead to a transformation of the institutions themselves. A process of cumulative change is discernible, and Veblen's analysis centered attention upon the process rather than upon the culmination of change.

Of great significance also was a movement within the classical ranks. Represented in America chiefly by John Bates Clark, the father of Professor Clark, this school had pushed to the fore this question: Precisely what are the conditions under which the classical propositions are true? The answers emphasized the drastic nature of the assumptions which were necessary. These assumptions had always been implicit in the older theories and had even been more or less consciously recognized, but they had generally been judged to be less important than the forces which were isolated for study. The effort to give a greater scientific validity to classical doctrines drew attention to elements which had been until then neglected. The change in the conditions of economic life offers an explanation both for this revaluation of the established doctrines and the focus of the newer approaches.

These facts of the day and these threads of developing thought were caught by Professor Clark, subjected to the test of evidence, criticized in the light of his own philosophical and historical background, and developed. Pressed on by emerging problems and political possibilities, by the unrest and aspirations of our time, he has given us three constructive treatises. These are his *Studies in the Economics of Overhead Costs, Strategic Factors in Business Cycles* (the logical sequel of the first), and *The Social Control of*

Business. They treat the problems he has held to be of greatest importance and present us with new abstractions better adapted, we think, to bear the burden of social policy in the times in which we live.

Our object is neither to summarize nor to criticize these positive efforts of Professor Clark. Our only hope is to give some indication of the place his essays fill in the development of his work, and of their significance for the future development of economics. This, however, makes it necessary to strike the contrast between the chief propositions of the older economics and the main conclusions of Professor Clark's approach. The dichotomy may most easily be observed by studying two important theses of classical economics: the tendency of supply and demand, and of price and cost, to equality; and the adequacy of producers' expenses and market demands as representatives of social costs and satisfactions.

Professor Clark, concentrating upon our experience with business cycles, counters the classical theorem that demand and supply (interpreted as capacity to produce) tend to equality. Altho the sum of forces responsible for business cycles at times causes demand to outrun our capacity to produce, yet its more typical result is to leave industry with idle capacity in men and machines.

The last point contradicts the classical proposition that economic changes generally impinge on a situation in which resources are fully employed. But if they are not, the problem of overhead costs becomes vital. Machines cost both business and society substantially the same amount whether they are running or idle. The result is that additional output would increase the expenses of business only by the cost of labor, materials, and power. And much of the cost of materials and power to one businessman is itself represented

by expenses to other businessmen which are relatively independent of their production. Although one manufacturer
may decrease his expenses by refusing to buy materials, this
does not represent a net saving to all businessmen. For his
erstwhile supplier must bear the cost of his idle plant. This
discrepancy, between the bookkeeping of one businessman
and a broader accounting which would consolidate the operations of all producers, arises in large part from the fact that
in times of serious depression, businessmen do not compete
so fiercely that prices are reduced to out-of-pocket expenses.
Thus the price of goods to one man is something more than
its specific cost to another.

Of equal importance is the fact that to society, its human
resources are a constant cost. We do not, so we hope, allow
our unemployed to starve. Hence, there exists a twofold discrepancy between private and social accounting. The price
consumers are willing to pay for additional goods is greater
than the specific cost of these goods to businessmen. And
subtracting the expense of maintaining workers in idleness,
the specific cost to businessmen is greater than that to society.

Thus price is not equal to cost; and given business cycles,
a condition of inequality may continue to persist so that the
discrepancy will not be relieved. Moreover, this is a situation which the individual businessman is almost powerless to
fight. To control the business cycle will necessitate state
action, or action by industrial associations far larger than
even our largest corporations.

We must turn now to the second problem. If demands in
the market are a good index of consumers' wants and the
expenses of production a good index of social cost, then a
market in which price equals the cost of additional production may be said to satisfy our wants wherever these are
great enough to justify the cost. Against this thesis, Pro-

fessor Clark has urged exceptions, in part unrecognized, in part underemphasized by his predecessors. These exceptions appear to him to cause a substantial reduction in efficiency, so great in fact that without corrective action by the community, the shortcomings of a system of private enterprise may outweigh the advantages.

For instance, market demand is held to be inadequate as a criterion of consumers' wants in the case of individuals of low mentality, or where people act in the interests of others. The modern corporation with its separation of management and ownership emphasizes the importance of this exception. Generally, if the decision to be made is very complex, involving many elements of value, demand is a poor index of wants. This is especially true whenever the purchaser cannot canvass a wide range of alternatives. This problem applies to many cases in the market for consumption goods, but its most important application is in the labor market. The importance to the laborer of safety, sanitation, and security can hardly be said to be well expressed in the unemployed worker's search for a job.

These faulty expressions of wants in market demand reach their height whenever irrevocable choices have to be made. Typical are decisions relating to the choice of a profession or trade and decisions relating to the sacrifices incurred in securing work when once the choice has been made. The results of mistaken judgments range all the way from the destruction of one's future bargaining power to the reduction of industrial morale and the stunting of talents and abilities which should have been developed.

Likewise, expenses of production are frequently inaccurate measures of social costs. This may be the case whenever people are unable to assess the costs to themselves, or where they cannot insist upon payment. In the labor market, workers underestimate the cost to them of injury, disease, and unemployment. In the real-estate market, one man's operations may do substantial damage to the value of neighboring property, but the injured owners may have no legal recourse. Again, there are many expenses of production which neutralize one another, producing no additional value to the consumer: competitive advertising, the expenses of bargaining, cross-shipments of freight. A third instance is furnished by cases of unutilized resources. It has already been shown that when men and machines stand idle, a wide discrepancy may result between the price of additional goods and their real cost to society.

These considerations create a prima-facie case for corrective action on the part of individuals, of groups, and of the state. Their importance derives from the fact that they suggest problems worthy of solution, for such solutions may lead to significant reforms. Nevertheless, the economics of a day is far from being merely a tract for the times. For in the logical development of a science ideas have a life of their own. And if new ideas are to be assimilated, they must meet and settle accounts with those of old in open combat in which logic and evidence are important weapons. Thus while a new approach to partially old material will secure its greatest acceptance, even with specialists, from its practical utility, yet students dealing consciously with the material will desire a reasoned defense.

The older economics, the so-called *classical* or *static* theory, with which Professor Clark had to work when he began his studies, denies expression to the facts and forces which Professor Clark's own work interprets. Thus we have, at first glance, two systems of thought whose chief propositions are seriously at variance. A student will demand either that one be proven false or that the two be reconciled. But classical economists have constructed a powerful defense by delimiting their subject matter, by rigorously isolating for study the forces operating in the adaptation of people to an unchanging situation, and finally, by offering evidence for the substantial truth of their principal assumptions.

To progress logically from these studies to a more comprehensive view of economic problems and forces is a critical task of immense difficulty. It demands that the evidence for the truth of the typical classical assumptions be recognized as inadequate. It involves an exposure of the futility of a descriptive economics so severely limited that it is nothing but a formal mechanics which any real behavior would fit. Finally, it requires an answer to the question of how one can use the severely limited static theories in studies less abstract.

This task is not directly undertaken by Professor Clark in the works which present his chief constructive contributions. On the other hand, this is the chief burden of his essays. They form the bridge in Professor Clark's thinking connecting the economics in which he was educated to the treatises which have been his positive offering.

Thus the essays deal in summary fashion with the leading features of the older economics, indicating its shortcomings, its relative falsity, and also its virtues, its relative truth. The attempt to use static economics in the development of a more adequate theoretical structure throws light upon both the virtues and the defects of the older economics. For example, the classical propositions that market demands and producers' expenses may be taken as accurate representations of consumers' wants and social costs are false as simple descriptions of reality. They are true as a provisional standard from which to measure known divergences, especially in the absence of any better criterion. To regard such a standard as provisional, however, points to the need for psychological and legal studies which may reveal specific instances in which the standard is not reached.

Again, the assumption that economic changes generally impinge on a situation in which resources are fully utilized fails us when we attack the business cycle and the stabilization of industry. For such problems, the initial assumptions, from which analysis must start, are excess capacity and prices higher than the costs of additional output. But when the question concerns the forces which distribute our resources among different industries, general movements in business are to a large extent beside the point, and *statics* therefore remains an indispensable point of departure. As long as this problem of distribution retains interest, *statics* will continue to play an important role.

In addition, where the older economics is inadequate even as a provisional statement of the facts—as in the study of business cycles—it may still be useful as a point of departure. If we can state the result of *static* forces and if the concrete data differ, we know where *not* to look for an explanation. Hence, the analysis of the divergences is suggested. For our problem is not the simple one of explaining why static results do not occur but rather of describing what actually occurs. The negative is easy; any one factor may be sufficient. To interpret the entire complex is another matter.

Thus, these essays are an attempt, in part by way of criticism of older theories, in part by the fashioning of new tools of analysis to attack the economic problems which are judged to be of greatest importance in our own day. Further, in selecting new economic problems for study, they have done much to force economic theory into a new mold. An economic problem arises when evils are recognized and when methods to overcome the evils suggest themselves. Evils which cannot be controlled raise insoluble problems. They are taken for granted—like bad weather. We must look for the change in our problems, therefore, in two directions: to the emergence of evils requiring remedies, and to the growth of knowledge which makes remedies possible for evils both old and new.

In pursuance of this thought, the essays present, at diverse points, thumbnail sketches indicating the growth of our problems over the past century. In this regard, the fundamental difference between the present century and the last is seen in the deterministic bent of the modern mind. The development of the sciences, both natural and social, has made us aware of many factors governing our behavior. Before, the blame and the burden were assigned to the individual, but with the discovery of controllable external causes, the responsibility was shifted from the individual to the group. Studies of industrial accidents indicate that the number of injuries per hour increases with the length of the working day and with the absence of mechanical safeguards. This leads to a demand for shorter hours, safety laws, and compulsory accident insurance. As we begin to understand the connection between the number of unemployed men, and the rate of interest or building booms, unemployment ceases to be a matter of individual responsibility and becomes a problem for business and society. The eradication of enforced idleness is a social problem. Thus our growing knowledge, in illuminating controllable causes of evils, increases our problems. Needless to say, such a creation represents progress, not the reverse, for we are brought nearer to solutions.

Further, with the spread of the machine and factory technique, certain evils have grown more serious. First and foremost is the crude fact of unemployment. While it is debatable whether the average volume of unemployment has grown during the last quarter-century, its consequences are assuredly more serious. We no longer live in a rapidly growing world in which new opportunities crowd quickly upon the man who has lost his livelihood. Europe passed beyond that stage of expansion many years ago. In this country, we are only beginning to realize the implications of the transition. Moreover, the technical possibilities of machine production have become more prominent, and to leave these possibilities unused in the face of a still poverty-stricken world is the most serious indictment of an economic system whose *raison d'être* is the efficient exploitation of resources.

Side by side with these gross evils go the more subtle effects of mass production which condition our lives and warp our natures in myriad ways, enhancing the role of the expert, but eliminating the need for intelligent co-operation by the rank and file. To an automaton, food is but fuel; consumption but makes room for more fuel. Men have other purposes and other standards. To them the getting of income is much of life and the spending thereof has values other than the maintenance of efficiency. If the getting be routinized and exhausting, the spending will not be other than unintelligent, even degrading. Yet our machines drive us in this direction, silently but continuously.

Today, economics faces these problems and their existence furnishes the chief need for a revision of economic theory. This accounts for the sense of urgency which marks Professor Clark's writing.

While students ponder, the world does not wait. A regime of private enterprise protects many social values we should otherwise not retain. But it must realize a tolerable proportion of its technical possibilities, and it must give the ordinary man an interesting part to play in the process. If not, the ordinary man will seek abundance by revolution, and in the violence of an overturn, the initiative which can give him dignity. The success of such a venture is uncertain, but the cost will be written in suffering and injustice. Only if scientific imagination can offer us satisfactory alternatives, and only if political organization can realize them quickly, will this suffering be avoided.

M. A.
E. G.

PART I

Economic Theory and Social Problems

THE SOCIALIZING OF
THEORETICAL ECONOMICS*†

INTRODUCTION

I. DESCRIPTION VS. EVALUATION

ECONOMICS inevitably involves two things: a description of the way economic forces work, and a study of the economic efficiency—or inefficiency—which results. These two have probably never been wholly separated, for various reasons which will appear as the argument proceeds, and it is a debatable question how far it is possible or desirable to attempt to separate them. This question will ultimately be answered, not by *a priori* argument, but by the test of doing—by testing different theoretical methods in terms of their results. Hence there is no need to settle it here and now, and we may go on to examine the theory of economic efficiency.

Is there any such thing as an ideal or standard of economic efficiency, apart from our ultimate ideals of what is good? Can the theory of economic efficiency stop short of the whole problem of ideals of good conduct and welfare; in short, of morals and ethics? Certain limitations have been

* Reprinted from the *Trend of Economics*, edited by Rexford G. Tugwell, by permission of F. S. Crofts & Co.

† This essay contains some material originally embodied in two papers read before the American Economic Association; "Economic Theory in an Era of Social Readjustment," *Amer. Econ. Rev.* ix, Supp. 280, Mar., 1919 and "Soundings in Non-Euclidean Economics," *Amer. Econ. Rev.* xi, Supp., 132-47, Mar. 1921. The material is here worked over, with the kind permission of the editors of the *Amer. Econ. Rev.*

tried and discarded. First was the conception of the production of material wealth, excluding intangible services. This has given way, for better or for worse, to the broader conception of the production of "utilities" at the cost of "disutilities," so that economic efficiency has become, at bottom, a psychological conception. It is a matter now of human values, and their organization.

But this, of course, is the whole problem of the modern pragmatic ethics. Can the field be divided, so as to mark off one part as the realm of economics? A division can be made, but *it cannot be done without introducing a bias*. The economic standard of judgment will become a standard which, from the broader social point of view, is limited or warped, either by excluding certain values (for instance, those on which the market sets no value which their creator can collect) or by accepting certain partial or imperfect judgments of value (for instance, the judgment of the laborer as to the fatigues and other sacrifices of production). This raises questions which, again, will only be answered by the test of doing something about them and seeing how it works, but it is evident at the start that so far as economics is inevitably a theory of efficiency, a biassed theory is inevitably a lame and halting instrument.

2. SCIENTIFIC STANDARDS

Standards of scientific procedure may be divided into different grades, which may be roughly designated as strategy and tactics. Strategy is concerned with the choosing of problems and deciding what ranges of evidence to admit. Tactics is concerned with the use of the evidence in attacking the problems chosen. Tactics should clearly be governed by strategy rather than the reverse. The evidence should be handled with the utmost possible scientific accuracy, but the choice of the problem should be governed by the need for light rather than by the amenability of the materials to workmanlike manipulation. If a white light is needed, the availability of petroleum does not justify the use of oil lamps.

But the effect of the scientific "instinct of workmanship" is persistently in the other direction, choosing problems for whose solution there are available materials which will satisfy canons of accuracy and demonstrability. This has its value as a deliberate and methodical approach toward the citadel of knowledge, but in the social sciences humanity demands that we arrive at something, even if it be not ultimate truth. It wants results of some sort, for the help of the generation now upon the earth, on questions which cannot be conquered by such siege-tactics. Moreover, humanity will derive answers to its practical problems from the work of the economists, whether the work of the economists is intended for that purpose or not.

What if economics as a theory of efficiency opens up problems requiring evidence not amenable to academic canons of accurate and absolute demonstration? What does scientific procedure demand? Scientific tactics says: "Limit the study to evidence about which absolute and accurate statements can be made." But scientific strategy says: "It is unscientific to exclude any evidence relevant to the problem in hand." *This comprehensiveness is scientific,* even if it involves some sacrifice of other qualities for which science likes to strive.

The intellectual "instinct of workmanship" has resulted in the development of techniques, with characteristic limitations. First came the "deductive" technique, characteristically limited to studying the results of rationalized human nature working under artificially simplified conditions. The limitations of this method have been sufficiently exposed by modern critics—overexposed perhaps. Deductive study is discredited as belonging to the pre-scientific era and induction is set up as the only scientific procedure, with the result that economics frequently seems to be doing its best to become a Description of Economic Behavior and nothing else. And yet even a judgment of cause and effect requires something more than this: it commonly requires insight as to *what might have been,* had conditions been different.

So far as definiteness and accuracy is concerned, induction leaves a vast deal to be desired; its greatest triumph is the unearthing of a prevailing tendency, admitting of many exceptions. In social data, a coefficient of correlation of 1 is virtually unknown. Induction does, however, rest upon observable evidence, and its propositions can be supported or overthrown by observing how facts behave. Moreover, it gives us facts to deal with, and the human mind is quite irrepressible in dealing with facts. Its formal methods are not adequate to give proven results when dealing with difficult material. Yet it is probably impossible to invent a system of logic so tautologically sterile, or a behaviorism so aridly descriptive, as wholly to prevent the human mind from getting at the inner significance of facts. It has ways of dealing with them which it cannot explain satisfactorily, but which serve to extract meaning from data, if only the data can be had.

And so we come back to the proposition that the core of scientific method lies, not in induction nor in deduction, but in taking account of all relevant facts and excluding none.

3. THE NEW PLACE OF THEORY

This principle of comprehensiveness, however, places an impossible burden upon that section of economic study which is known as "economic theory." The growth of inductive economic study is enormous; general works cannot cover it or even give an adequate idea of its content. Moreover, the general work is fallen from its one-time place of dignity. When deductive methods prevailed, the general work was the source of truth and fountain-head of economic law, and special studies were subordinate exercises in "applied economics." With the supremacy of inductive methods the special studies assume the position of scientific authority and the author of the general treatise ought, properly, to make his pilgrimage to all the shrines and master all the special fields before presuming to set pen to paper, preferably verifying all the original data used in all these fields. As this is obviously out of the question, something else must happen.

There is need, great need, for a common discipline which shall animate these special studies, co-ordinate them and interpret them to each other, and to the intelligent reading public as well. And there are at least four distinguishable services which such a discipline can render. It can furnish a common background of ideas of scientific procedure including both the tactics and the strategy of scientific method: both accuracy of process and comprehensiveness of data. It can furnish tools of thought in the shape of hypotheses, grounded in experience, and available as guides to further study and bases for verification. It can summarize the most important results of inductive study and generalize them; always keeping clear the difference between completely verified results and tentative generalizations which are subject to further verification. And finally, it can present an orienting interpretation of economic life which will have an important pragmatic bearing, governing the kind of opinion and action on practical issues which is likely to grow out of it. This pragmatic bearing is something economic theory cannot escape if it would; it attaches not merely to theories of efficiency but to purely descriptive statements. It is one of the most important qualities of any economic theory, and it is the chief concern of this present paper.

4. INDUCTION AND HYPOTHESIS

So far as economic theories are to serve as hypotheses for inductive studies to verify, it follows that these hypotheses must be such as the workers in the field will use. They must be verifiable; which means that they must call for a definite kind of behavior under given conditions, so that if that kind of behavior is found, they will be proved; and if not, they will be disproved. This rules out certain kinds of propositions of the deductive economics: namely, those which insist on being universally true, with the result that they become tautologies, so that any kind of observed behavior will fit them as well as any other kind. For such statements an inductive economic theory can have no active use, and the more closely economic theory gets in touch with inductive studies, the more will its statements take on new forms, becoming less tautological and more quantitative.

For instance, the "marginal producer" is being translated into the "bulk-line" producer as figures of costs of production make inductive studies possible. We used to be told: "Price is governed by the cost of production of the marginal producer." Who is he? "He is the producer who makes no profit: that is, whose cost of production is equal to the price." Such a statement needs no verification and tells nothing which could be verified. In place of this, inductive studies make their statements in some such form as this: "Price is commonly such that from ten to fifteen per cent of the output is produced at greater cost and the rest at less." [1]

Or, we are told that price is fixed at the point where supply and demand become equal. Supply turns out to mean the volume of goods that holders are willing to sell at any given price (implying a demand at that price) and demand is the volume of goods that buyers are willing to take, if offered at a given price (implying that someone is willing to sell that much at that price; in other words, implying a "supply" equal to the "demand"). Such a proposition is self-evident, and of no use for purposes either of prediction or verification. It is only as common sense or induction adds descriptions of the behavior of "supply" and "demand" that the proposition has meaning attached to it, by a sort of associative process, and becomes a vehicle or symbol of truths which its literal formulation does not categorically denote.

Some forms of the doctrine of marginal utility are even more clearly tautological. Our old friend, the "economic man," is becoming very self-conscious and bafflingly non-committal. Instead of introducing himself to his readers with his old time freedom, he says: "I may behave one way and I may behave another, but what is that to you? You must take my choices as you find them: I choose as I choose and that is all you really need to know." The poor thing has been told that his psychology is all wrong, and he is gamely trying to get on without any and still perform as many as possible of his accustomed tasks. He has become a symbol, rather than a means of description or explanation. Yet this noncommittal treatment of economic

[1] This concept is developed in articles by Taussig, "Price Fixing as Seen by a Price Fixer," *Quart. Jour. Econ.* Feb., 1918; "Price Fixing and the Theory of Profit," *Quart. Jour. Econ.* Nov., 1919 and by Kemper Simpson, *Quart. Jour. Econ.* Feb., 1921, and May, 1923.

choices seems to be of immense import to those who have become accustomed to attach much of their thinking to this symbol.

Human behavior in economic life is so many-sided that if we insist on summing it up under simple formulas and also insist that these formulas shall always be one hundred per cent accurate, the only ones that can satisfy these requirements are in the form "whatever is, is"; preferably camouflaged into a semblance of meaning. A letter-perfect description of the economic world is impossible.

And not only that: it would also be largely useless as a form of general economics, because it would not generalize enough to assist the mind to an understanding. General economics must simplify in order to interpret; otherwise its description will be just as unwieldly and baffling as the world itself. Thus theoretical economics must steer a course somewhere between what is futile and what is impossible. It will be a never-ending search for generalizations that are significantly true, and for that very reason are often neither 100 per cent accurate, nor universally applicable.

A PRAGMATIC VIEW OF ECONOMIC TRUTH

I. SELECTION AND EMPHASIS

This simplification lays upon the theorist a great burden of responsibility for the character and influence of the kind of selection he sees fit to make. It robs him of his defense of scholarly detachment, when critics assail him, for instance, on the ground that his doctrines are out of touch with movements of reform and surgings of unrest. He may answer that he is not supposed to be in touch with them, in his capacity as a scientist; he is supposed merely to furnish a wholly objective description of things as they are. But he is open to the rejoinder that, so far as his description is selective, it is not wholly objective. He selects things that are significant, and significance is at bottom a matter of some underlying purpose.

Some things are significant for one purpose, and some for another. A careful thinker always wants to know for what purpose a definition is to be used before he will admit that it expresses the essential and significant features of the thing that is to be talked about. "Value" (as actually used) means one thing for purposes of taxation and another thing for purposes of regulation, and there are similar varieties of meaning covered by the terms cost, wealth, capital and income. Each term covers a related family of ideas, so that it comes to be of the essence of sound method to choose the particular idea that is appropriate to the purpose in hand, and to avoid all conclusions based on a merging of this idea with others in the same family.

This sort of selection is guided by something different from the abstract and disinterested search for pure truth or pure accuracy of description, which so many theorists would like, in the interests of scientific standing, to achieve. There are always vastly more aspects capable of analysis, vastly more distinctions capable of being used as the basis of reasoning, than the theorist can possibly organize into a systematic body of thought, and more than the hearers can grasp as a connected whole.

In living economic theory the investigators find that their best possible efforts cannot exhaust the material that is of vital importance in its effect on the issues of their time and the needs of their age, and they tend to concentrate upon these aspects of things, not because other aspects do not exist, but because they appear less important. In an economic theory that is not living, this selection is governed by tradition, by professionally vested interest in an existing stock of doctrines and methods, and sometimes by the line of least resistance toward deductive studies, because they yield definite results more readily than inductive, and with less labor of gathering data. But the selection is never governed by the sheer search for truth, for the search for truth is not a principle on which one may decide what parts of truth to include and what parts to leave out. Thus the "realistic" painter who paints life in terms of dung-heaps is selecting; life has other things in it than dung-heaps. He may select the dung-heaps because he is disgusted with the other artists who insist on leaving them out. In that case his selection is governed not by what his subject matter is, but by what the other artists have painted, or said, or written, about it.

Take the statement that men seek their strongest interests, combined with a definition which says that men's strongest interests are whatever things they seek. When we come to put this statement in a form that has some meaning, as for example, when one says that every man is a better judge of his own interests than anyone else can be for him, we are instantly faced by the fact that this is not always true, but that the opposite is true in some cases. Now, as far as the practical usefulness of theory is concerned, the important thing is whether or not a generalization like this is likely to be used in cases to which it does not properly apply, or only in cases in which it is true. Such a statement may be safe-guarded in two ways. It may be carefully qualified, or the situation may be such that qualification is not necessary.

2. THE IMPORTANCE OF TIME AND PLACE

If all the doubtful issues of the time and place are of such a sort that they can best be settled by assuming that each

individual is always the best judge of his own interests, or
vice versa, then, *so far as that time and place are concerned,*
one of these sweeping generalizations is wholly true and
needs no safeguarding other than the fact that in that time
and place only one kind of issue is present. This happy
state of things never really comes to pass, but something
fairly close to it sometimes is true of the watchwords of
strenuous fighting movements. If the existing order is biassed
so far in one direction that all that can be accomplished in
the other direction will not restore the balance, the party of
protest will adopt as a watchword a strong and sweeping
statement of the opposite principle, without weakening it
by cautious delineations, stating just how far it can properly
be carried and what concessions will have to be made.
"Men do not follow an uncertain sound into battle."

On the other hand, the existing order always has some
value, if only by the fact that we are used to it, and if the
question at issue is whether the existing order shall or shall
not be wholly discarded in favor of some untried invention
sure to entail enormous injustice and suffering, and uncertain of ultimate success; then sweeping dogmas of a conservative sort come naturally into use. In a way, this is
proper as it is natural. So far as concerns the issue raised
by a party of wholesale revolution, the most important truth
about the existing order may consist, not in minor defects
and abuses, and not even in the fact that the best possible
system would be very different from the system as it stands,
but rather in the fact that it does harness and utilize some
very powerful forces and get some very valuable results,
and that these would be destroyed by the proposed revolution. The real truth in the defense of the existing order
may be, not that this order is ideal, but that the counter
proposition would be still worse. Thus Adam Smith did not

claim that free enterprise worked perfect results, but rather that the worst evils sprang, not from free enterprise but from the mistakes of governmental interference. Hence the significant truth of a proposition about the existing order depends, not on that order alone, but on the character of the substitutes which political organization, scientific knowledge and human imagination place within the bounds of serious possibility.

It is probably true that economic conceptions have mostly been framed with reference to particular errors or evils which they might serve to combat. This obviously is true of the myths and slogans that animate fighting parties, but it is no less true of the most carefully qualified abstractions. The qualifications recognize passively the existence of facts and forces which the abstraction does not actively interpret.

For that reason new issues must bring forth new selections of significant material embodied in new myths, new fighting slogans and new abstractions. It is this which determines the range of the broader generalizations in the "social science of business." Each generation of economists succeeds to a new assortment of practical problems to which its doctrines are to be applied.

It would be vastly interesting, did space permit, to apply this method of interpretation to the ideas of Medieval economists, Physiocrats and Mercantilists. To one who has been trained to regard these ideas merely as examples of the perverse errors of the unenlightened human mind, their appropriateness to their particular environments comes as a startling revelation, tending at once to lessen one's disrespect for these "fallacies" and to weaken one's trust in the absolute verity or eternal adequacy of the doctrines which the peculiar environment of the nineteenth century has brought into a dominant position in economics.

3. THE ENGLISH TRADITION

We inherit the tradition of Adam Smith and Ricardo, representing the birth and early infancy of the industrial revolution, when the forces latent in this new economic system were struggling for room to develop, and had hardly begun to foreshadow the miracles they would ultimately bring to pass. For the beneficiary control of these forces, class interests and social systems were already struggling; the combat lying broadly between liberal and humanitarian notions of popular welfare on the one hand, and the landed, mercantile and militaristic interests on the other, by whom the poor were more or less frankly regarded as instruments of production and "food for powder."

The first combat was against the national restrictions of the mercantile systems, together with local and craft restrictions surviving from the smaller-scale medieval economy. Here a group of abstractions were developed, serving the ends of economic freedom, such as the idea that both sides gain in an exchange, that consumable goods are the end of the economic system, that the consumer can exercise the best discipline over the producer, and the tacit assumption that demand in the market is an index of social need and economic worth.

The idea of mutual gain serves to combat the medieval notion of exchange of absolute values, wherein one side gains only as the other loses. Mercantile notions of foreign trade carried this same assumption: one nation gained only as another lost, and a balance of trade favorable to one must be unfavorable to the other. The conception of consumable goods as the end of production served to combat the warped notion of exports as a national gain and imports as a national loss, which went with the doctrine of the balance of trade. The idea of the consumer as the best source of trade discipline was urged, not as against social humanitarian policies, but against gild privileges and gild restrictions of an essentially monopolistic character. And the idea of demand as a measure of economic worth, warped as it is when judged by humanitarian standards, served in this period to combat standards which were in every respect farther from the truth. It left ample room for such "non-economic" values as national defense, but served very effectually to puncture the sophisms used to mask the economic burdens of protection.

As over against the chief doctrines they had, at the time, to combat, these classical assumptions were true. If they had been surrendered, it would not have been in favor of modern policies of social welfare and democratic solidarity, for such did not exist at the time. They would have yielded the field to the interests and sophisms of class exploitation; and they retain essential truth to just the extent that these interests and sophisms retain a dangerous degree of vitality. But these early assumptions of liberalism ignore many democratic and human values which are now striving for practical recognition, and the adjustment between these limited truths and others less limited is one of the central conflicts of modern economic thought.

Another conception is the production of "utilities of form, time and place." This expresses a truth as over against the idea that only the creation of material goods is productive. It is, however, only the beginning of an analysis of production from the standpoint of utility. Akin to this is the concept of marginal utility, which was bound to come from the moment the early economists compared gold and iron, or coal and diamonds, and concluded that value and utility were not quantitatively related. This drew attention to an unsolved problem and made some solution inevitable. As against the older blank negative, the doctrine of marginal utility expresses a truth, partial, and expressed with a mathematical exactness not found in nature, but nevertheless important.

The doctrine that "industry is limited by capital" served to emphasize the contention that industries created by protection are not a net addition to the productive forces of the nation.[2] It is valuable for this purpose, even though not unqualifiedly true, but it becomes a stumblingblock when we come to the business cycle, where varying rates of exploitation are of the essence of the problem. The pragmatic bearing of the Marxian "surplus value" theory need not be pointed out, nor the fact that the Ricardian statements which formed its logical basis would have been modified and safeguarded if Ricardo had foreseen to what use Marx would put them. No less obvious is the appropriateness of the "marginal productivity" theory as an answer to Marx on the one side, and to wage-fund extremists on the other.[3]

Adam Smith was born into a world whose official economics was utterly distrustful of free exchange, at a time when free exchange was demonstrating its ability to rise superior to the crude and misdirected forms of regulation then prevailing. He became aware of the wonder of unintentional co-operation in which the frankest selfishness yields surprisingly tolerable results through the efficient but unplanned organization which the system of exchange carries with it. He noted the genuine service rendered by the price that equates supply and demand, chiefly by noting its su-

[2] John Stuart Mill specifically makes this use of the doctrine: *Principles of Political Economy*, Book I, chap. V, § I, 64, Ashley ed.

[3] Since writing the above, I note that Fetter explains the development of the marginal-subjective doctrine as a conscious reply to Marx. See *Jour. Pol. Econ.* xxxi, 602-5, Oct., 1923.

periority to those crude attempts at regulation which furnished his standard of comparison. He grasped the element of mutual aid running through exchange, saw its organizing possibilities and contrasted these with the crippling effects of contemporary sorts of interference. Given all this, the message he had to convey to an unseeing world, and the dominant abstractions of his system—suited to convey this message—were foregone conclusions. The validity of price as an economic organizing force is his contribution, not its imperfections.

The most one-sided parts of such a message are not the parts that deal consciously with the question whether private enterprise is better than public enterprise in any given case, but rather the parts where the writer feels himself to be abstractly and impartially describing the economic system "as it is." For here he is not on his guard as to the use or abuse that may be made of his doctrines. One of the best examples of this unconscious attitude may be found in Smart's *Second Thoughts of an Economist* where he says:

"What I, for my part, found in Political Economy was a science whose main object was *not* defence of any particular system, *but explanation of how men, consciously and unconsciously, work into one another's hands,* and get and give each his daily bread. I saw it analysing what we do in the every-day life of making an income and spending it; gathering up facts into categories and generalisations; drawing deductions of what men in general will do in the future from observation of what they have done in the past. All this seemed to me as impersonal as anatomy, as the writing of history, as the observation of the tides—and as necessary."

In other words, political economy does not defend the existing system but it explains the elements of co-operation in it; which are the elements everybody approves of. It is in fact a highly selective and partial theory which Smart seems to have found as impersonal as anatomy, and it does credit to his saving sense of relevance to the needs of humanity that he felt something lacking in this theory and was moved to step outside of its limitations in his last book.

These limitations are chiefly the work of later writers than Adam Smith, who seldom allowed his thinking to be cramped by its own machinery. But such conceptions become more formalized and crystallized with the passage of time, and structures of deduction are increased upon them, becoming ever more elaborate and more brittle. This happened to the free-trade economics, long after its chief active purpose had been attained in the freeing of trade from mercantilist shackles, and it had subsided into the more passive rôle of furnishing a *prima facie* case for the competitive order—now the established order—as over against projects of revolution or of fundamental reform. Meanwhile the new generations were arising.

4. MODERN ANTITHESIS OF THE ENGLISH TRADITION

What is their vision? The marvel of spontaneous co-operation is no marvel to them. Their textbooks have presented them with its concentrated essence in a purity more or less frankly unreal. This furnishes their intellectual point of departure. The direction in which the world about them departs from this formula is toward apparent variations from type, which fail to produce the expected efficiency and instead cause waste and social loss rather than pure mutual gain in the process of free exchange. The older student was interested primarily in the fact that prices do reach an approximate equilibrium. The newer is interested in their erratic and unruly movements—also in the bad quality of housing accommodations as a disastrous and unnecessary phase of *laissez-faire,* in the effects of seasonal fluctuations of industry as an imperfectly compensated cost of production, in the wastes of competition and in methods of diminishing them.

The older theorist had written down as his "balance carried forward" a theory of the pernicious effects of free enterprise and such tolerably good tendencies as he discovered were clear gain. The modern theorist carries forward a theory of 100 per cent efficiency for competitive institutions and is alert to all shortages, for they appear as a clear deficit. Thus it is the most natural thing in the world that Veblen should reverse the classifications of "orthodox" economics, finding the normal workings of business enterprise in those things which the older economists classed as disturbing elements causing departures from normal.

Orthodox economics undertakes to interpret equilibrium: Veblen undertakes to interpret progressive change. And in the social world this is much the same as saying that orthodox economics studies the assumptions of contentment while Veblen studies the assumptions of discontent; both of which are undeniable facts. Since undeniable facts are difficult to ignore, the net result is very largely to call them by different names.

So when Veblen says that the inherent nature of business is parasitism and that any modicum of service rendered is rendered incidentally and in spite of the inherent nature of business; and when orthodox economics says that the inherent nature of business is service, and that any modicum of parasitism that may remain is an incidental perversion of the true spirit of the institution—they are not so much contradicting each other as selecting different things to talk about. Veblen is talking about the nature of the pursuit of profits; and the beneficial effects of competition, where competition works beneficially, are an incidental and very partial check (and possibly a temporary one) on the natural tactics of the pursuit of gain. Orthodox economics is talking about the nature of competition (or rather of an "ideal" form of competition) as a check on human selfishness in the pursuit of profits and to them any failures of competition to produce its full effects appear as incidental disturbances. In a general way most economists admit the same general mass of facts, but pick out different ones as the central axioms of their systematic economic theorizing.

While Veblen admits a modicum of serviceability under private enterprise, he does not seriously undertake to explain how this perversion of the essentially parasitic nature of business enterprise comes about. He does not focus attention on the nature of the checks on selfish exploitation, embodied in customs, morals, rights of property and person with the negative and positive duties they involve, and in that complex, self-contradictory but very real institution of economic competition.

On the other hand, the older economics more or less tacitly assumes that these checks do their work perfectly, and its conception of competition may be characterized as a simplified and unattainable ideal. Thus we have two antithetical doctrines, both at least partially true. The synthesis which can unite them lies largely in the realistic study of the social checks on private self-interest; their nature, adequacy and inadequacy, success and failure, actualities and potentialities.

Can it be that human nature is so built that it demands the clash of opposing half-truths in order to raise the issues from which it may work out a closer approximation to the truth? In that case, the only truths we can ever arrive at consist of these half-truths; and even ostensibly contradictory propositions might both be "true," in this provisional fashion, which is the only fashion of truth we can attain.

A half-truth outgrown becomes an error; till then it was truth. Or, as dirt is only matter out of place, so error is only truth out of place—one of these human half-truths out of its appropriate environment and application.

NON-EUCLIDEAN ECONOMICS: AN EXPERIMENT IN THE SIMULTANEOUS TRUTH OF OPPOSITES

From the foregoing it appears that there are systems of economics with axioms as far removed from each other as the geometry of Euclid and the non-Euclideans; perhaps as far apart as the conventional physics and Einstein. As abstract systems, they describe different worlds, and Veblen's theory of invidious prestige might be called a theory of economic relativity.

Just what is meant by "non-Euclidean economics" in the present instance? The question can be best answered by taking eight axioms which represent in a general way the traditional position on a number of central points, and inverting them. This is done with no idea of denying the truth of these propositions, but it does raise the question whether their antitheses do not contain a more urgent and vital truth for the present generation. This is not a mere game of logical gymnastics; it is the natural result of studying those facts of human existence which Euclid, as represented by these eight axioms, somehow fails to interpret. Probably none of this matter is new; but, after all, economic theory consists largely in organizing and interpreting known facts rather than in the independent discovery of raw facts hitherto unknown.

1. Economics is the science of wealth, and wealth consists of things (a) useful (b) limited in supply (c) exchangeable (d) appropriable.

2. Consumption is the end of economic activity and production is a means to that end.

3. The standard of economic service is the gratification of human wants through the increase of marketable goods and services.

4. A bargain between two persons concerns primarily those two persons, and only incidentally, under special conditions, becomes "affected with a public interest."

5. As a general rule, cost varies in proportion to output: "overhead costs" which are independent of output are the exception and arise in connection with large fixed capital outlay. This proposition is not definitely stated so much as implied in the typical treatment of the laws of price, where overhead costs are treated as a disturbing factor in special cases which Mill, for instance, speaks of as "rare and peculiar."

6. Private enterprise is necessary and efficient because people will work and sacrifice for their individual ends where they reap the fruits themselves, and will not work as well for a collective end.

7. The rational foresight of individuals is at the basis of individualistic economics.

8. Capital, including machinery, consists of instruments of production utilized by human beings for the production of wealth.

Let us examine these eminently respectable propositions from a pragmatic standpoint, *via* their antitheses. Space permits little more than mention of the first six, and a very brief development of the last two.

Proposition 1. Economics is the science of wealth, and wealth consists of things (a) useful (b) limited in supply (c) exchangeable (d) appropriable.

The alternative proposition is that the most important

subjects of economic study, while useful and limited in supply, are not appropriable and not fully exchangeable, and thus are not wealth in the full sense.[4] For instance, the morale of labor constitutes today one of the most vital of economic problems, but it is not exchangeable wealth. Industrial knowledge is not fully appropriable, while that broader body of social-economic customs by virtue of which the average individual is enabled to go his way without meeting economic calamity at every street-corner—this vital community asset is suffering serious obsolescence as the result of industrial "progress." This cost of industry is not compensated, the necessary rehabilitation demands the best thought and effort of our generation, but this is not exchangeable wealth. Wealth as property consists of a bundle of "rights"—i.e., interests protected by society—but there are many interests unprotected today which are asking protection and which may be protected tomorrow.[5] Tomorrow, then, they will be appropriable wealth, but not today!

Since the consequences of this have been developed by a number of writers, I will merely mention one very interesting corollary: namely, that in the marginal-productivity economics power to produce cannot exist apart from power to withhold. Many things may be useful and limited in supply, but only those which the owner has the option of withholding have a marketable marginal product. What is marginal productivity? It is essentially the power to make a differential addition to the income of an enterprise. (This means to make this income greater if one grants the enterprise the

[4] The germ of this proposition is at least as old as John Stuart Mill (*Principles of Political Economy*, Book V, chap. XI, sec. 14); Sidgwick also develops it (*Principles of Political Economy*, Macmillan ed., 404ff.) and it plays an important part in J. B. Clark's *Philosophy of Wealth* as the "theory of inappropriables."

[5] See Ely, *Property and Contract*, also the writings of Roscoe Pound.

use of the productive factor he controls than it would be if one withheld this productive factor.) In this sense an invention, once made public, is not "productive," and the inventor is not a productive factor, with respect to any past invention, except as he keeps patent rights which enable him to withhold it from the market, and hence to bestow it on the market. He cannot freely bestow it if he cannot also freely withhold it. Thus the meaning of "productiveness" is to some extent governed by the system of legal rights, and may be changed by a change in this legal framework within which economic life is set. Other applications of this proposition are interesting, but we must pass on.

Proposition 2. Consumption is the end of economic activity and production is a means to that end.

This proposition may be broadened; increased productive power is used to make working hours shorter and to some extent to make work easier and more pleasant. This is in general harmony with the proposition that production is looked on as a necessary evil and a means to an end: the less time we spend at it the better. The general proposition seems obvious, and is obvious from the point of view of the individual. When it comes to society's interest, the question is not so clear. Society's purposes are supposed to have something ethical about them. To take consumption as the end of all things corresponds to hedonistic ethics, whose standard is the receipt of pleasurable sensations, but the more modern ethics emphasizes rather the well-rounded development and use of human faculties. It is an active and not a passive standard, a standard of output of energy and not of receipt of sensation.

This makes it seem that our activities are more important than the passive pleasures we receive, and the activities that really develop us most are those where we are faced with the biggest difficulties. This means, commonly, things we would not voluntarily do simply for the fun of doing them. It means work, in one form or another, rather than play. The conclusion is that the quality of the activity involved in work is more important as a positive social value than the quantity or quality of consumption.[6]

There is a twofold need: for work of a sort which, if a man gives his best to it, will develop and not crush him; and for incentives that will make him give his best. And the two needs are more nearly one than economic theory is accustomed to assume. Starvation, poverty, and perhaps even ambition for increased wealth have successively worked themselves past the point of diminishing return as incentives for the mass of labor, and the search for new incentives must focus on other things than wage scales. In this respect, the worst evil is to deny those incentives which represent what man recognizes as best in him. If selfish incentives cease to work, that is a failure: if unselfish incentives have no opportunity to work, that is a tragedy. The partial breakdown of the traditional selfish incentives in industry, which is now disturbing many minds, may prove a blessing in disguise, and one of the greatest of social opportunities.

Proposition 3. The standard of economic service is the gratification of human wants through the increase of marketable goods and services.

This does not intend to deny that the development of good types of human beings is a more important thing, but it singles out increased wealth as the economic way of making possible the development of the best human type, leav-

---

[6] This idea, again, is not new. It goes back to Ruskin and William Morris, and back of them to the Greeks, who graded occupations according as the kind of activity involved was or was not consistent with the "good life" as they saw it. Modern studies of human nature are trying to give us more scientific standards of judgment in these matters, and the results so far are promising and valuable.

ing humanity to use its power as its wisdom or folly may suggest.

In this matter economics has tried to keep itself separate from ethics and to take the attitude that it is not concerned, as economics, with the wisdom of the use men make of wealth. Its ideal is well expressed in the maxim of Francis Bacon, quoted by Jevons in the introduction to his *Theory of Political Economy:* "While philosophers are disputing whether virtue or pleasure be the proper aim of life, do you provide yourself with the instrument of either." [7]

It has, then, as an ideal, a sort of undifferentiated power over nature which man is to secure, and which he can then put to any use, good or bad. The increase of this power is economic gain: the quality of the use made of it is a separate question and not an economic one. This is a very natural position, but there is one trouble with it. The methods of production which increase our power have in themselves qualitative effects on human living of a very direct sort, some of which have already been mentioned. And these effects on the quality of life are not marketable commodities capable of being weighed in the same financial scale with the increased supply of commodities which modern industry furnishes.

Moreover, it may be argued that the tendency of population to increase has the effect of neutralizing the greater part of man's increased productive power, so that by far the greater part of it goes in maintaining increased numbers in the face of the principle of diminishing returns, and the increase in per capita wealth is but a small fraction of the percentage of increase in our essential power over nature. One might go farther and say that it is a positive injury for

[7] This is the concluding sentence of Jevons' "Introduction" (4th ed., Macmillan, 27).

humanity to learn enough about the arts of production to use up all the best of the earth's limited natural resources and occupy all the available territory, until they have learned how to put them to some better use than, for example, they have been making of them in the past nine years.

I am not advocating inefficiency, though there are some sorts of inefficiency for which a good deal might be said. So long as war exists, any civilization that systematically practiced inefficiency for the good of future generations would be speedily displaced by one with less refined ideals and more immediate horsepower. Efficiency is inevitable and, in moderation, not undesirable. But what I am suggesting is that, instead of taking the quality of man for granted and focussing attention on quantity output, it may be more pertinent for the social student to take quantity output for granted—business will not neglect that—and direct his chief attention to the qualitative effects on humanity of the things they do in their inevitable (but largely self-defeating) striving after increased per capita wealth.

One might suggest that in the economy of nature and of her creatures means and ends are reversed: that the creature's ends are nature's means of gaining her ends, and the activities which serve the creature as means of attaining his ends are the things nature is really after.[8] Primitive man is interested in stilling his hunger and to get food he endures enormous fatigues, taxes his rudimentary ingenuity, and perhaps makes a minute improvement in the stone axe or the bow. Nature is not interested in stilling his hunger; in fact,

[8] If this figurative personification of nature appears unscientific, nature's purposes with man may be translated as the requirements of man's biological development, which undoubtedly contain a sounder standard of human welfare than the gratification of his immediate conscious desires. Adam Smith held that nature implanted in man instincts which were wiser, for the good of the race as a whole, than his reason. See *Theory of Moral Sentiments*, Part II, sec. I, ch. V, note, and elsewhere.

she takes very effective measures to see to it that he shall be chronically hungry in order that he may continue to endure fatigues, to tax his ingenuity, to struggle, and as a result to develop biologically into a type with higher faculties. Now that we have supplanted nature's jungle with our man-made jungle of mines, factories, railroads, hotels, jails, hospitals, almshouses and what not; who is strong enough to do what the older jungle did for our ancestors—overrule our purposes for our own good and save us from the danger and possible biological disaster of getting what we think we want?

Proposition 4. A bargain between two persons concerns primarily those two persons, and only incidentally, under special conditions, becomes "affected with a public interest."

The antithesis to this proposition is clearly involved in what has already been said. The most important effects of private bargains consist in the part they play in the qualitative evolution of the personal characteristics and social relations of the human race at large. Their immediate direct effects on appropriable goods and services may well be regarded as things requiring secondary attention from economists in the present stage of human history. Even to increase tangible wealth the prime requisite is to control the business cycle—clearly a community problem—and to improve the relation of labor to industry. *All industry and trade is primarily affected with a public interest,* and only certain phases of it may be regarded as of purely private concern.

Private contract is good, not because it deals with things of purely private concern, but because there is no sure social judgment on these matters. Society does not know what it wants, and private contract furnishes an elastic method of experiment which has many advantages over political tinkering. Its greatest present task is to remake the constitution of industry in a tentative and voluntary fashion. A society formed by "social compact" is possible in the economic realm, grounded upon a social organization developed in other ways, and this social compact is the most significant form and aspect of "private bargaining" at the present time.

Proposition 5. As a general rule, cost varies in proportion to output: "overhead costs" which are independent of output are the exception and arise in connection with large fixed capital outlay.

As an alternative, consider the proposition that overhead costs are not merely the general rule but are universal, and that the costs that are "direct," or "variable" or "prime costs" from the standpoint of the employer are overhead costs from the point of view of society. Every laborer is his own "overhead" and has his constant costs to meet, whether he is working or not. Society has so much productive power. It cannot avoid the cost of either (1) maintaining this productive power, including the human beings who compose most of it, or (2) seeing it depreciate. The power of the entrepreneur to reduce expenses by ceasing to buy materials and reducing his working force, where this means unemployment, is for the most part a financial illusion arising out of the fact that the individual employer does not have to pay the constant costs of the industries that make his materials, or of the labor he turns off.[9]

This principle has many possible applications, largely in the direction of placing the burden of labor's overhead cost on those bearing chief responsibility for the industrial cycle, and where it will have the greatest effect in stimulating people to do things to relieve the irregularities. It is one

[9] This general point has been developed by G. P. Watkins, "A Third Factor in the Variation of Productivity," *Amer. Econ. Rev.*, v, 753, 770-77. The present writer has developed it further in a paper entitled "Some Social Aspects of Overhead Cost," *Amer. Econ. Rev.* xiii, *Supp.*, 50-59, Mar., 1923.

tremendously important instance in which social accounting and business accounting diverge and in which the social accounting is not yet organized and explicit.

Proposition 6. Private enterprise is necessary and efficient because people will work and sacrifice for their individual ends better than for a collective end.

For an antithesis to this, one need not deny individual selfishness. But private enterprise no longer depends on it in the old simple way. One need only remember that the dominant economic personalities today are corporations and labor unions—both types of collective personality. Even the entrepreneur function has become split up into a large group of functions, shared by different persons and even by different corporate entities—for example, the banks. The older proposition is still true, in that the employees of these corporations do not work as hard nor as faithfully as a man "working for himself." Nevertheless the advantages of large scale production have outweighed this handicap and falsified the earlier prophecies as to the limited scope of corporations in economic life.

But these associated personalities act through real persons, and in order that the corporation should act selfishly, following its corporate interests, the real persons composing it must act loyally in the interest of the collective whole. This loyalty has, indeed, become a dominant quality of the modern economic man, vitally necessary to the continued truth of "individualistic" economics. The ability of corporate organizations to stimulate loyalty, or to make loyal behavior the best policy, or both, is the vital necessity of private enterprise. We have now to compare, not private selfishness with collective loyalty, but the business versus the political methods of securing this loyalty, which is equally necessary for private or public enterprise.

Proposition 7. The rational foresight of individuals is at the basis of individualistic economics.

In particular: business men know the "best combination of factors" and the marginal productive worth of different factors, and on this the efficiency of individualism depends. The question at issue is not whether people in general and business men in particular are thus intelligent, but whether an economics founded on the idea that they are is really a sound basis for individualism.

Let us study for a moment a hypothetical society made up of individuals gifted with this degree of intelligence and foresight. Would this be peculiarly favorable to individualism? Business would be highly efficient, it is true, but there is serious question how long beings with this much foresight would continue to compete. Such beings would not let the coal business run in the present wasteful fashion. They would long since have integrated the industry to a point where wagon-mines and backyard wheelbarrow mines could not offer serious competition to the organized large-scale producers. And there would be a Federal Commission.

Perhaps in this hypothetical society employers and employees in, let us say, the building trades, might both get tired of the competitive struggle and unite to assist each other in excluding competitors. If they were very foresightful they might cover up their tracks so well that even Mr. Untermyer might have difficulty in getting evidence enough to make a case. The "best combination of factors" in this case would consist in putting some of the very best brains to work on covering up tracks, and the marginal worth of highgrade brains in this occupation would be extremely high. Since the employers would know all this, highgrade brains would be so employed and lavishly rewarded. On the other hand, the marginal worth of brains spent in detecting such conspiracies would also be very high, and government would know this (by hypothesis) and would bid against private enterprise for the same grade of brains. Thus a large part of society's ability would be devoted to this interesting game of hide-and-seek; to making and contesting valuations of properties; to checking up accounts, inspecting products to enforce standards of quality and service, and many other similiar occupations; and their pay would absorb a considerable part of the national income.

Meanwhile, if people in general could choose intelligently for the future they could and would vote intelligently and select able and honest officers of government, and government departments would be very efficiently run because their heads would know the "best combination of factors," and the "marginal worth" of talent, and would be able to get appropriations that would enable them to bid for it. Their budget system, based on knowledge of the relative marginal worth of different lines of public expenditure, would furnish something society has long needed—a system of social accounting in terms of national welfare.

Thus we should have on the one hand enormous waste in the attempt to control private industry, and on the other hand government departments quite as efficient as private concerns and able to avoid the wastes and duplications either of competition or of regulation. Under these conditions any people with such intelligent foresight as we have assumed could not fail to see the obvious advantages of national collectivism, and we might expect to see it adopted as rapidly as an efficient government bureau could handle the necessary accounting.

But suppose, on the other hand, we assume a population of little foresight, who therefore cannot safely depart far from custom, who are governed much by imitation and suggestion from their fellows, who learn only by making mistakes and being hurt, and who do not know the "best combination of factors" nor the marginal worth of different factors of production. In such an imaginary society, private production would not be very efficient, judged by absolute standards of what is technically possible. On the other hand, a considerable amount of competition would survive for a long time, perhaps indefinitely; partly because it is customary, partly because competitors do not look far ahead, and partly because they are influenced by the suggestive force of a moral code which considers monopoly as contrary to the public interest.

With competition, however, goes a weeding out of the least efficient, which means eliminating the widest departures from the "best combination of factors" and from the systems of paying factors of production according to their marginal worth to the employer, and placing them in industry on the same principle. The survivors would be those who, by luck or intuition, came nearest behaving as they would if they had known what the "best combination" was and what the marginal worth of productive factors was. The force of competition would put pressure on business to install cost accounting systems in order to lessen its ignorance of how much productive factors are worth, and to employ engineers and efficiency experts who, although they may not know the absolute "best combination," may at least be able to devise ways of improving the combination that exists. Thus there would be forces working in the general direction of efficiency and of a rough approximation to an organization on the basis of marginal productivity.[10]

[10] Professor J. B. Clark has, in lectures, made the point that the marginal productivity theory does not require perfect knowledge on the part of business men of what "marginal products" are; but that the force of competitive selection works in this direction automatically.

On the other hand, government departments would not only suffer from not knowing what "the best combination of factors" was, but they would lack the saving grace of competitive elimination to work automatically in that direction, or to put pressure on their administrative heads to install efficient systems of accounting and research. In such a purely hypothetical society, we might expect that the accounting systems of government departments would be far inferior to those of private business; and would be, in fact, inadequate to show how much public services cost, let alone the marginal worth of different productive factors taking part in those services.

Not knowing how much factors of production were worth, government would tend to underpay the highest employees and fail to secure the highest talents in competition with private industry. Moreover, a people of this mental type would be less able to vote intelligently than to buy goods intelligently, since voting makes peculiar demands on the powers of foresight, while the buying of goods can be much less wastefully done by the method of trial and error. Most marketable commodities are renewed far oftener than is the incumbent of a political office, and of those that are not, few commodities are selected without more intelligent study of values than the average voter makes of the average candidate on the average American long ballot.[11] Thus in this hypothetical society there would be less chance of getting able public officers than able business men. And though the absolute efficiency of private enterprise would be far less than in our first hypothetical society, that of public enter-

[11] Cf. T. N. Carver's suggestive comparison of political and economic competition in his *Principles of Political Economy*, 328, and in his *Essays in Social Justice*, 111-125.

prise would suffer still more. In the second society, private enterprise would be more efficient than public.

The tendency to combination would undoubtedly appear, though restrained by the custom of competition and the moral mandate for it. The attempts of government to curb combination would be largely abortive, but the people might still prefer a moderate degree of exploitation to the inefficiency of government operation, or to the effort and uncertainty of conceiving and working out some other substitute for individualism. After some trying experiences, business would probably learn to keep its exploitation within the limits of the people's toleration, not so much from shrewd calculation as from natural hesitation to break with custom and morals, and from the habit of feeling one's way in any new policy. And thus individualism might continue.

Thus it appears plausible that the strongest basis for individualism is not the intelligence of individuals and their irrevocable devotion to the pursuit of their own self-interest, but rather their stupidity and their susceptibility to moral suggestion. Individualism may be regarded, not so much as the system calculated to get the utmost out of a people of extremely high intelligence as the system in which human stupidity can do the least harm. All of which is not so very new, but is more akin to the general trend of Adam Smith's economics than to the Austrian school, and really harks back from marginal utility economics to the earlier classical proposition that individuals can choose for themselves—not with absolute accuracy—but better than any government agent can do it for them. This is a theory of relativity rather than one of the absolute efficiency of individualism as a system by itself.

After all, at the present time one of the most important facts concerns, not the general level of intelligence, high or low, but the differing degrees of training and special information on different topics; the extent to which the specialist in this age of specialists has information beyond the unspecialized man in the street, and the ability of the unspecialized "people" to cope with the specialist who has his axe to grind. This is one of the very large problems for the "economic man" of the twentieth century.

Proposition 8. Capital, including machinery, consists of instruments of production utilized by human beings for the production of wealth.

Let me suggest the alternative proposition that human beings are instruments of production utilized by machines for the machines' increase and biological development. This is not a new idea. Samuel Butler carried it to the point of suggesting that machines might develop consciousness and thus enslave mankind, though in these days of behaviorist psychology the question whether the ruling race possesses consciousness or not bids fair to become obsolete. A more real question is: how many and how important and far-reaching are the things the machines have done to us which we did not intend nor foresee, compared to the things we specifically employed them to do? On this point, some things have already been said (sections 2 and 3 above).

Among economists and social scientists, Veblen has described how machines train and educate human beings.[12] A. S. Johnson has pointed out how the nominal captain of industry is ruled by the processes he presides over.[13] Cooley has asserted the existence of impersonal forms of life with life-processes independent of those of the human beings who impinge on them and further their growth, and he mentions

[12] *The Instinct of Workmanship,* 311-27.
[13] "The Soul of Capitalism," *Unpopular Review,* April-June, 1914, 230-1.

industrialism as one of these forms of life.[14] The Economic Interpretation of History implies that the machines control human life and organization in its highest forms.

Machines may be conceived as making bargains with man in which they offer him things he very much desires, and in exchange bind him to serve and maintain them, to eliminate the unfit among them and promote their racial progress, and to alter his own social and political arrangements in whatever ways may be necessary in keeping pace with the increasingly complex social organization of the machines themselves, and in keeping the children of man faithful to the service the machines require. The full nature of the terms of these bargains are not revealed to man until he is so fully committed that it is too late to turn back, and thus the machines outwit him. For example, they took Adam Smith into their confidence, but only so far as suited their purposes. By such methods they have succeeded in imposing on man many things he never bargained for, some of which he finds extremely unwelcome.

Some might think this shows a low standard of honesty on the part of the machines, but we must remember that honesty is the morality of equals toward equals, not of superior to inferior races, and that our own conduct toward inferior races will hardly stand a critical examination. At least machines have not forced their culture upon us by armed violence. Among their own kind, they show a sense of the superior importance of biological progress to immediate gratification and a subordination of the interests of the individual machine to the progress of the race, which demonstrate a clear moral superiority. Seldom or never, as in Arnold Bennett's *Milestones*, does the older generation cramp the development of the younger. They give way with-

[14] *Social Process*, 6-26.

out complaint, youth is served, and the interests of mechanical posterity are paramount.

The machines appear to have kind intentions toward man, but to lack understanding of many of his feelings and needs; as is frequently the case with ruling and subject races. They have revolutionized both work and product, taking the element of universal individual initiative out of both. They have given man unnatural working conditions which are now leading to incipient revolt, and living conditions that go far to defeat democracy. They are responsible for the "industrial cycle," and as long as their own overhead costs are covered in periods of depression, they have not assumed full responsibility for the corresponding overhead costs of human beings. They have largely taken over the drama without caring to preserve what human beings regard as the highest standards of taste, and they have, intentionally or unintentionally, gone far to undermine the church and even religion itself. They have incontinently switched us from a paternalistic to a *laissez-faire* type of government and are now busily switching us back again, according to the temporary needs of the stage of development they have reached. These are merely examples.

As for their methods of maintaining control: some classes they bribe with large rewards, other classes, largely technicians, and technical-scientists, do not need to be bribed: their minds are captured by the material they work in. And the unspecialized "ruling classes," voters or congressmen or others, cannot cope with these specialists, who are left to do more and more of the governing in the shape of the actual working out of things. The ordinary man cannot even speak the dialect in terms of which many of these issues are settled; for example, the accounting language used in settling the justice of street-car fares.

The machines have cleverly limited human co-operation by splitting human language up into many dialects of many specialist groups, so that the highest common factor of intelligibility, so to speak, for humanity as a whole, consists of relatively simple ideas, largely obsolete in the sense of not actively gripping the newer issues. Among these ideas might be mentioned the simple ideas of public and private ownership. As men become more dependent on machines, the latter become able to rule by penalties as well as by rewards; witness our late heatless Mondays and other penalties imposed by failure to develop our railroad system to a continually increasing size and complexity of articulation. Thus mankind moves in directions it never intended, getting largely things it never definitely wanted as the unexpected result of engaging the services of unexpectedly powerful instruments.

What I have called Euclidean Economics, in general, serves the interests of the machines. It directs attention to the bribe they offer, and away from the conditions they exact. It has countenanced the machines in neglecting to assume the burden of human overhead costs, and in this, as in other matters, by insisting on putting man on a higher level than machines in respect to freedom, it has sometimes put him on a lower level in respect to care for his material needs. This has its fine side, but by teaching man that he is the end of all things, when he is not, his subjection is concealed and thus perhaps perpetuated.

I do not advocate revolting against the machines and abolishing or subjugating them: all I aspire to is a reasonable degree of racial equality. This would make for more friendly relations and would help to allay the distrust of the purposes of the machines which now prevents us from getting all the benefits which they are able and willing to give us. This is peculiarly true of labor, but not of labor alone. We must become far better informed and surer of our own intentions before our dealings with the machine can be characterized by that confidence which marks the bargaining of equals. To attain this we must not merely develop the ability to rise superior, if necessary, to the immediate bribe that is offered us; we must become competent to bargain, as the machines do, with an intelligent eye to our long-run racial and social interests.

These interests are most seriously threatened in the case of labor. The machines tend to confine discretion in industry to the few whom they take into their confidence, while the bulk of labor has largely lost the power to make any constructive contribution to the technique of industry. The job belongs to the machine, and labor feels little responsibility for it. Labor's state of mind and conduct shows the consequences of this, and many laborers appear to alternate between the slave-morality of getting as much as possible and giving as little, and the spasmodic need of exerting power of some sort. Under the circumstances this can only be power to interfere with the orderly progress of industry by strikes or sabotage, since power to improve on the operations laid down by the machines appears to be largely beyond labor's present reach, either for lack of competence, ambition, or opportunity. Racial equality can never be established so long as the bulk of mankind are in this position of undignified and passive inferiority.

The situation demands social organizations capable of exerting the force of constructive human will, enlightened by collective intelligence, *at the point where things are being decided, in the processes of industry itself*, rather than waiting till the decision is made and then, through our "political" machinery, taking belated and purely defensive action.

MATERIALS OF SOCIAL ECONOMICS

Granted that these two types of economics both contain vital truth: can they be synthesized? In present treatises we find these two currents of thought, but in more or less thought-tight compartments. Alongside of Euclidean Economics is another large body of ideas, which some writers distinguish as the "art" of political economy, or "applied economics," in spite of the fact that it is chiefly other principles than those of the economic Euclid which are here applied. It may broadly be called "social economics" as distinct from the deductive, static economics of price, exchange value and distribution. Sidgwick's *Art of Political Economy* is a most valuable contribution in this field. John Stuart Mill enters it in his discussions of property and communism, land tenures and the sphere of government, and in his Essay on Liberty. Adam Smith's treatment of public expenditures belongs here, also a large part of J. B. Clark's *Philosophy of Wealth*, Carver's *Essays in Social Justice* and the writings of Veblen and Hobson.

Far removed as these are from each other, something approaching a synthesis may be possible, on two conditions. One is that description and judgment be kept distinct, with the result that descriptive economics may be free to describe what it pleases without the need of adopting a final yardstick with which to measure all the conflicting values it finds. Under these conditions, the values the market measures need not be the sole material of economics, nor price the sole recognized measure. Another condition is that selective generalizations be recognized and used as *tools of analysis*, and means of approach to truth, rather than as embodiments of ultimate and absolute verity. The marginal method, as a tool of analysis, is invaluable; but as the sole source of truth it is woefully inadequate.

The progress of inductive study is in a fair way to give us truly descriptive statements about prices and other tangible economic quantities in purely behavioristic terms. This should have the result of freeing the "laws of price" from dependence on generalities bound up with connotations of approval or disapproval. On these terms, inductive study may be allowed to range farther afield and gather materials for more fruitful generalizations on social economics than have yet been made.

However, we shall never be free from the need to use constructive scientific imagination. We may describe existing institutions, but we cannot know their effects on man without knowing what alternative institutions would be like. Since the experimental method has such limited possibilities in the field of large-scale human organization, creative conjecture will always play a most important part. Even Veblen has descended to it in his book *The Engineers and the Price System*, taking up the burden of visualizing a possible change in the existing order.

As for final valuations, in which we shall decide which human values are most important and which are not worth what they cost, these cannot be set up in advance, for they will evolve endlessly, as more and more light is thrown on the effects of industrialism; showing us what values it furthers and what values it defeats. We used to have a quantitative economics of social efficiency in purely abstract terms. We can still have a quantitative economics which describes objective phenomena, but the economics of efficiency cannot be quantitative in the sense of having a pre-existing measure of quantities. It must form its measure as it goes along.

II

TOWARD A CONCEPT OF
SOCIAL VALUE*

THE search for standards of social value in the economic realm is a baffling task, yet far from an unprofitable one. We shall presumably never discover a definite yardstick of social value comparable to the dollar yardstick of exchange values; but we may find standards by which those of the market may be revised, or in some instances replaced. An economist should be prepared to face such a search, with all its difficulties, if he accepts three basic propositions.

One is that the problem of the collective efficiency of private enterprise involves quantities and qualities, of which actual market prices are not the only measure, and, I would add, some of which command no market price at all under present conditions,[1] although with changes in law and custom they might perhaps come to command one. Another is that measures of value which may be less exact than those of the market are also much more fundamental. And a third is that our most fundamental concepts should be independent of institutions of competitive exchange; they should be such as would hold even in a socialistic state.

This independent basis is necessary if there is to be any common meeting-ground for debate between socialists, radicals, and conservatives. It is necessary if we are to have any

* This essay, hitherto unpublished, is the non-controversial portion of a projected enlargement of my rejoinder to B. M. Anderson's criticism of my essay, *The Concept of Value*. The latter, with Anderson's criticism and my original rejoinder, appeared in the Quarterly Journal of Economics, August, 1915.
[1] Cf. J. B. Clark, *Philosophy of Wealth*, p. 215 ff.

standard of judgment on economic reforms which are continually overruling the valuations of the market. It is necessary even in the process of describing the workings of competition under different institutions of property, contract and social control, which we recognize as infinitely varied and ever changing. The competitive product of capital does not mean the same thing in two societies with different institutions of inheritance and bequest and different laws and customs in the matter of unfair competition.

Or, let us take the statement that the rental value of land tends to equal the excess of the (competitive valuation of the) goods and services produced upon it above the (competitive) expenses of production. This becomes quite indefinite the moment we realize that the net product in question may or may not include robbing the neighbors of their light and air, obstructing the streets, fouling streams, increasing or destroying the beauty of the landscape or the business character of the neighborhood, admitting tenants whose very presence destroys the value of other real estate in the adjoining blocks, etc., etc.[2] There are as many different kinds of competitive products of land as there are regulations governing these matters, and merely to describe the differences, without passing any sort of judgment on them, we must use terms that go behind the competitive value of the exchangeable product.

The world is full of unpaid costs and unappropriated services.[3] In proportion as we rise above bare material necessities we reach intangible utilities that are harder and harder to appropriate, such as knowledge and personal privacy. The age of material power is the age when these higher and more elusive utilities come increasingly into the

[2] Cf. Ely, *Property and Contract, passim.*
[3] Cf. *Philosophy of Wealth, op. cit.*

focus of social attention. The age of the railroad and the interlocking credit system is an age when business transactions have more far-reaching effects than ever before, and more than can ever be bought and sold directly. The age of researches in bacteriology and environmental determinism is an age when innumerable effects, always in existence, are being discovered and valued as never before. The age of democracy is an age when everyone can exercise to the full the two great social impulses: the impulse to be like one's fellows and the impulse to be different, to be distinguished. But these emulative and especially these invidious utilities are in a peculiar way the ones in which one man's gain is another's loss: they eat each other up, and the resultant is a social utility far different from the sum of its individually appropriable parts.

To illustrate, patents and copyrights are enforced, sometimes very imperfectly, and books are bought and sold, but can we imagine Darwin attempting to collect toll from all who used the ideas and proofs contained in "The Origin of Species"? Or even a weather bureau supporting itself by selling its reports? A photographer once sold a woman's picture to be used in advertising a toilet preparation. The woman objected, but in this case the court asked, not whether she had suffered, but merely whether the negative was the property of the photographer. This led to the passage of a state statute protecting this right, and progressive courts in other states might now rule differently.[4] Thus the scope of appropriable rights changes, by legislation or judicial evolution, and the meaning of a system of free exchange changes with it.

Early railroads were estimated to have increased the value

[4] This sentence was inserted in final revision, 1936. Cf. *Social Control of Business* (1926), pp. 109-110.

of neighboring lands by an amount five times their own cost. How much the western roads subtracted from land values in New England and New York will probably never be known with enough exactness to enable us to compare the gain and the loss. In the panic of 1873 the more conservative banks of New York City were called on to contribute from their funds to relieve the less provident banks from the consequences of their lack of caution. For the soundest bank must suspend if the others do. A few city banks had made profits by bidding for the deposits of country bankers and then, when called on for cash, fell back for support on those who had strengthened themselves by refraining from this extra-hazardous class of business. It was only natural that, in later panics, support was less freely given. It is hardly a blessing to the morale of a system of wholly independent banks to know that the careful ones must bear a part of the cost of others' carelessness, and that careless banks can often benefit by the preparedness of their neighbors, on the ground that all are "in the same boat" and that the soundest institution will suffer if others suspend, and will suffer more seriously if failures of others shake public confidence.

Careful sanitation, even more than sound banking, renders services to the general public which cannot well be appropriated and bought or sold in private bargains, and the result is the socializing of preventive medicine, just as the prevention of epidemics in banking is socialized, and for a similar reason. The stableman who has just screened his premises might, to be sure, try to collect compensation. One can almost see him going around selling safety from fly-borne contagions, so much to one man for one dollar, half as much to another for fifty cents and none to the man who will not buy. Or if we look at the matter in another light, and con-

sider the danger of spreading disease as one of the costs of
the livery business, what law of free exchange would force
the manager of the stable to pay either the expense of reasonable precautions or full compensation for the consequences of neglect?

Again, how shall we compare, socially, the products of
two factories one of which is built with an eye to such
beauty as circumstances permit and operated so as to give
the workers an opportunity for growth, while the other
furnishes an environment of unrelieved ugliness and a large
percentage of "dead-end jobs?"

Part of the value of things that are sold today consists
in taking away value from things that were sold last December. The utility of some women's gowns is being constantly attacked from two sides. To those whose clothes
must be a mark of distinction and the latest thing, their
value is gone as soon as they are imitated by too many people, or people not of the right sort, or as soon as fashion
makes its next move. The fraternities at a certain college
are satisfied to be housed in frame dwellings until one or
two build handsome edifices of brick and stone. The others
must then follow suit or be handicapped in the competition
for the most eligible neophytes. Until Smith bought a Pierce
Arrow, Jones and Brown were happy with their Fords.
What is the net social utility of a new gown, a new house,
a new automobile?

The legal doctrine of *dammum absque injuria* covers a
multitude of such unpaid costs, and the unearned increment
is a great catch-all of unappropriated services. Viewed as a
study of individual utilities and not of organic social values,[5]

---

[5] These two classes of value cannot, of course, be treated as if wholly
separate from each other. The "good of the greatest number" is of great importance to society as a whole.

a theory of inappropriables is merely a tracing of such products and costs as law and custom do not yet recognize and a
revealing of responsibilities which have not yet been brought
home effectively in markets or in courts. Thus the net economic value of a given service may be considered to include
(1) potentially exchangeable by-products in the way of service or damage, valued at the price they would presumably
command in exchange; (2) unmarketables measured by a
standard derived from market price.

We may go farther than this, if we are studying such
fundamental values as might prevail in a Socialist state as
well as in our own. We may value things by other standards
than that of competitive exchange, especially if those other
standards are already effective in society or may reasonably
be expected to become so. Thus the old "rich-man-poor-man
complication" may emerge from the thought-tight compartment in which it has been more or less successfully interned,
and demand a place in the sun, for there is ample proof that
society does not wholly acquiesce in the idea that the desires
of rich and poor should all have economic weight in proportion to the respective purchasing powers of these classes as
they stand under the present distribution of incomes.

Here we have a truly organic social valuation. The theory
of social value does not stop with the theory of inappropriables, which is merely an unusually complete summing up
of individual values, utilities and costs, though this of itself
is highly important to society as an organism. The ultimate
question is: what is the value to society of these utilities consumed by individuals, or the cost to society of these costs
which individuals bear?

Does the enjoyment of an inherited estate by the heir
have a social value adequately measured by its present sell-

ing price? Certainly not if a Lloyd George succeeds in making another estimate effective.

Society weighs men by different standards, varying all the way from the humanitarian standard of equality to that of the most extreme apostles of the superman. Does anyone really accept the scale of the competitive market? We shall have found such a man, when we have found one who honestly approves of existing conditions of poverty: not one who is resigned to them as an inevitable evil, but one who would not lessen them if he could. So long as this does not represent the prevailing sentiment, so long it will be impossible to say that market value measures "social value" in the sense of "value to society." Where society does not even acquiesce in these evils, market values are "social" only in the sense of occurring in an organic social situation, through processes of an organic social character.[6] The prevailing standards are mostly much nearer the humanitarian, and this fact is ever coming to the surface where men are deliberately following a common policy, or wherever some emergency breaks through the superstructure of convention and throws us back upon first principles and elemental needs.

A ticket to the Yale-Harvard game may be cheap enough to be sold for $2 and too valuable to be bought for $10, and the principle of this paradox applies to public land under the homestead act and land-rushes in Oklahoma, to bread in Germany, to train accommodations sold to war refugees by a relief committee, to the administration of justice (though all too imperfectly), and to public education. An allied principle governs poor-relief, minimum wage laws, etc., etc.

---

[6] J. B. Clark's concept of "social effective utility" clearly has this latter meaning combined with expressions pointing less certainly toward the former. *Distribution of Wealth*, Chap. XVI.

When some necessary article sells for a high price in the market, the result is that those who need it most cannot get it, and there are some things so very valuable that this exclusion of the poor cannot be allowed. Mention has been made of the American Homestead Acts, under which a price is demanded for the land, often a very high price, though not in money, and a price which the poor can pay readily while the rich cannot afford it. Where the price is chiefly personal trouble and sacrifice, the work of occupying and improving the land, it is quite effective in preserving the land for those who need it most. The rich may hire dummies and so evade the price, but they will not pay it, for it calls for too high a sacrifice of what they already enjoy, a sacrifice which their desire is not great enough to outweigh.

It is a commonplace of economic writers that our free land while it lasted saved us from many economic ills against which we must now be on our guard. Would it be equally commonplace to say that an economic system which weighs men's wants according to their financial purchasing power under the competitive regime has been saved from some of its worst consequences by having as a safety-valve a frontier where that standard has been overruled in favor of equality between man and man? It is, of course, not a matter of chance that the commodity sold in this unbusinesslike way is no finished product but raw land; the mere opportunity to produce.

Equality of opportunity, then, is what "free land" secures, and this is very far from being the same thing as equality of reward. Therefore it may be claimed that we shall never sell potatoes on the same equalitarian plan, or that if we do, we shall no longer be following the rule of equal opportunity, but shall be undertaking to nullify differences in reward.

This objection would have had more force, some years ago, than at present when governments are beginning to act on the assumption that the opportunity to be productive includes such food, clothes, shelter, and even amusement, as are necessary to maintain physical and mental health and efficiency. We are continually enlarging our conception of what is necessary to an efficient life, at the same time that we have come to emphasize more and more the effect of environment in determining the character and powers of men. It is easy to carry this latter principle to unwholesome extremes; indeed one of the gravest questions now confronting us is how to draw the line between the use and abuse of this most potent charge of intellectual dynamite. At any rate, it is conceivable that in a world wholly committed to the philosophy of determinism, "Equality of opportunity" might come to mean nothing short of equal environments for all. As this is impossible so long as homes and family life survive, it is little more than a bogey to conjure with. We are concerned here only with a tendency of thought which is having a very definite effect on men's attitude toward the present distribution of incomes.

Enough instances could be easily cited to show the all-pervading economic influence of standards of value contrary to those of the free market. Now unless economics can take and use such standards in advance of their becoming effective in the market place, it misses by so much its chances to contribute scientifically to economic reform. As a matter of fact, economists do use these standards constantly in their practical thinking on matters of public policy. Every time an economist supports an ordinance limiting the height of buildings or a bill for industrial insurance he is applying the theory of unpaid costs. When he votes for subsidizing a pioneer railroad he is paying for inappropriable services. When he urges a minimum wage law he is recording a social estimate of the value of a certain standard of living for the poor; an estimate different from that which the forces of free exchange could make effective. Every measure of economic reform on which he expresses an opinion represents an estimate of a social value of one sort or another, different from that of the market. And every debate with opponents of the present order, and every passage in a text book which discusses the justification of private property,[7] assumes standards of judgment, vague or inexact perhaps, yet standards of a truly economic sort, by which the valuations of the market, as products of the present order, are to be criticised and upheld or condemned.

But of all this working philosophy, scarcely a breath penetrates to the rarified atmosphere of technical discussions of the theory of value and distribution. Here the economist holds aloof from the implications of his own thought and actions. He either accepts the market value of a product as measuring the social value produced, or he gives up the idea of social value and treats prices and products as purely individualistic things, measuring comparative and not absolute utilities. On this latter basis we may conclude that unless the utility of a pair of shoes to any individual is greater than any other utility which he must sacrifice to get the shoes, he

[7] Cf. also the distinction made by Hadley between the social product of capital, which is held to explain the maintenance of the system of interest, and the private earning-power which is one of the forces determining the interest *rate*. This passage is so brief as to be sometimes misconstrued, and may perhaps be criticized as somewhat overemphasizing the element of rational calculation in a matter like the maintaining of a long standing custom, and also for omitting to develop the very real connection between increase of private earnings and increase of public wealth. A. T. Hadley, *Economics*, p. 268-269.

will not buy them. And by carrying the argument a trifle
farther we may gain, as a basis for judging the worth of our
institutions, the doctrine that they afford John Doe an opportunity to do as well by himself as he is, under those institutions, able to do.

He does this by rendering other people services whose
utility to them is at least as great as the estimated utility
to them of anything they were willing to go without in
order to buy John Doe's services. Either party to an exchange may be in an economy of keen pleasure or in a
"pain economy" of the most hopeless sort. If, under institutions less humane than ours, a man were to sell himself into
slavery, through pressure of sheer present starvation, such a
theory might comment that even in his case gain was in
excess of cost, since the utility of food to a starving man is
infinite! Or if a laborer is forced to enter a health-destroy-
ing trade to keep his family out of the poorhouse, why, the
keeping of one's family out of the poorhouse has extremely
high utility, and the balance of marginal utilities and marginal costs remains intact. If these be the limits of economic
science, then it simply does not lay hold on the deepest
economic issues of our time. Economists may deal with these
issues in a practical way, but the theory of value and distribution will remain insulated.

However, if we can develop a concept of economic value
and valuation with reference to society as a whole, independent of market valuations and capable of scientific
application to concrete cases, we shall have an intellectual
instrument that will pierce the insulation and establish a
connection with the ideas that are making things happen.

It is a substantial gain to regard a price as the resultant of
conflicts of many kinds of values, positive and negative, in-

dividual and social.[8] But if economics merely accepts and records the outcome as representing the effective social importance of that particular commodity, there is still something lacking. Many a commodity commands a price merely because its negative social value is less than the costs involved in suppressing its use utterly.

Whiskey has at once positive and negative social value and motivates prohibitionists to much expenditure of time, effort and money. Yet this negative "power in motivation" has no effect on the price until it actually prevails in a prohibition law. And then—the price goes higher and not lower,[9] and the outlawed trade becomes more profitable financially than ever before.

The idea of a strong positive value to a minority, in marginal equilibrium with a weak negative value to a majority,[10] does not seem adequately to represent the case. Certainly the price does not express any such equilibrium, but only one side of it. Exchange value will remain positive till the negative social value accumulates such overwhelming momentum as to stamp out the trade entirely. What balances the majority's disapproval is not the desire of the minority, but the whole cost of making the majority will effective. There is no marginal equality of effort between policemen and the customers of an illicit drinking-place. Moreover other values than that of temperance itself may be affected in the attempt to stamp out illicit sales.

The positive value of freedom may deter us from prohibiting the sale of many quack remedies, or outlawing many

[8] Cf. B. M. Anderson, *Social Value*, Chap. XIII. "Social value" can evidently mean more than one thing. Personal utilities and exchange values are of course social in the sense that they exist in society and result from the play of social forces.

[9] Certainly if quality is considered!

[10] Cf. *Social Value*, p. 151.

questionable business practices, which predominant social judgment and sentiment oppose.[11] Or if society were willing to make a sacrifice of freedom in one case, the question of consistency might arise. The negative value of class-legislation has prevented many weaker values from reaching effective expression. The social value of the constitution, or rather, of the traditional interpretation of the bill of rights, has played a decisive part in determining many market prices. Here we have what may be called organic social values playing a part in the field of commerce.

Such values are, of course, all-pervading. Let us take again the case of the distribution of public lands to homesteaders. The value of the land to individuals is one thing, and that of itself has a value to society in that it has weight in determining social choices. But the value to society of a general condition of widely distributed landholding is more than the direct utility which the individuals buy with their quarter-sections, and more than the increase in the values of other property which result from the pioneer settlements. It comes to the settlers, but it benefits others as well, in many intangible ways which lead us to speak of it as an organic social value. (Always remembering that there is no such thing apart from the individuals of which society is composed.)

When men strive for mere superiority over one another, the net sum of all their strivings may be nil, if we look merely at the individual gains and losses in the prestige for which they are contending. Is there no social value here at all? Yes, there is, but it is not the kind of value which individuals are so busy pursuing. It is rather the general

[11] In all this my view is quite like Professor Anderson's, and I gladly acknowledge indebtedness to his writings. It is hardly necessary to add that my greater indebtedness is to our common source, the *Philosophy of Wealth*.

social value that goes with free opportunity to pursue one's desires and impulses and to be responsible for one's destiny. These have very high social value, although other competing values have for some time been gaining as the cult of individualism has weakened. In the eye of society, the absurdities of fashion and the rivalries of hostesses are not so much value in themselves as almost negligible by-products of freedom, which is itself so valuable that it is hardly worth asking whether these particular results are plus or minus.

Again, inheritance is maintained for many reasons, first among which comes the fact that property owners and potential property owners want it. This includes the man who regards an income of a quarter of a million as genteel poverty, although as this class provokes most of the hostility that is felt nowadays toward inheritance, we can hardly say that their enjoyment of their ancestral fortunes is a net addition to the social value of the institution. More important are the mass of smaller property owners and potential property owners who also want to be able to hand on their property to their families. The institution is also upheld as a stimulus to the saving of capital, but most of all perhaps it is borne along by the inertia of immemorial custom.

All of these facts represent, and very properly, strong social values, but not the same social value as that of the millionaire's enjoyment of his fifth country estate, which may be a positive source of weakness. And for that very reason it is entirely out of place to assume that everything which heirs buy with their money has social value proportionate to the price paid. Any system of private inheritance means a certain sacrifice of the ideal of equal opportunity, and this sacrifice is a social cost. If some heirs are vicious spendthrifts, the damage they do is a further cost incurred in attaining a definite social end.

What is the conclusion to which these somewhat obvious illustrations point? Simply this: that if we consider the social value of everything to be represented by its normal exchange value or price, we are really ascribing to a commodity as that commodity's social value the whole resultant of those broader forces and values to which it may stand in the relationship of an insignificant or unwelcome by-product, or even in that of a cost of production.[12] It is the freedom which has social value and not the nostrums or the products of sharp practices which may shelter under its wing. Freedom may be an end in itself like any other utility which affects economic values, and it may also take effect in increasing the output of goods in general. Neither fact can elevate its incidental abuses, recognized as such, to the rank of social utilities or values. The net social value of the latter is negative, not positive,[13] and men in touch with live issues will not long be satisfied with any theory bearing the name of social value which does not embody this principle so unmistakably that he who runs may read.

It is so simple! The marvel is that such an obvious statement of fact could be considered to constitute an economic heresy in any school of thought. The distinction may make little difference in static theory, which ignores institutional changes and rules out as dynamic or abnormal most of the sources of abuse, though it would at least reveal some very significant and unexpected assumptions which have lain implicit in the static hypothesis. But into the dynamic study

[12] May not this be a necessary condition of a really vital connection between economics and sociology?

[13] This conception is ethically neutral, accepting whatever standards are in force, and merely insists on distinguishing clearly (as the other concept does not do) *to what it is that the accepted standards are attached.*

of the actual world the static hypothesis must not be carried. Here abuses are normal and institutions are active forces campaigning against them, with constant changes of plan and shifts of fortune. Wasteful advertising is waste, not social product, though we may not know how to get rid of it without sacrificing more than we should gain. The wasteful consumption of inherited wealth is a social cost incurred in producing whatever values are attached to the institution of inheritance. If static doctrine is to be adapted to deal with dynamic facts, it is at this point, in the concept of value itself, that the modification must begin.

One further result may be noted. If things may have exchange value when their social value is a minus quantity, how shall we say of things which have positive social value that the exchange value, actual or normal, gives a correct measure of their relative social importance? The simplest exchange is not free from these complex relationships which we have been discussing. Each one is a unit in a great social joint product. Thus the theory of social value is anti-marginal in the sense that the part—say the single commodity— takes its price from the value of the whole rather than the whole getting its price from the utility of the marginal part. In a similar way railway rates cannot be fixed by the marginal cost of separate services without running the whole road into bankruptcy.

These, then, are some of the elements which must count in a theory of social value. The theory of inappropriables, the conscious social weighting of men and their desires on different scales from that of free exchange, the insistence that institutional valuations and commodity valuations be distinguished and not both attributed to single commodities, and the readiness on occasion to reverse the marginal method of analysis; all have their place in the interpretation. Such studies can be vitally useful, even if they never reach the exactness of a yardstick.

Indeed, some will probably say that this discussion has been carried into fields which lie outside the realm of economics altogether. If this criticism rests on an unshakable conviction that economics is limited to the subject of exchange values, there is little more to be said, save that exchange value described in terms of itself is meaningless. Our traditional description runs in terms of psychological premises, and therefore goes beyond the boundaries of the world of exchange values: but no one has objected on the score of transgressing the bounds of economics. One might explain this on the ground that this school of economics did not go far into psychology—not far enough, in fact, to secure an adequate and sound equipment of psychological assumptions. But was that a virtue? This paper aims to study, not exchange values in a vacuum, but their relation to human motives and desires, and the reader may judge if the purpose has been maintained. In the course of the study, enough has been said to show many matters truly economic which cannot be contained in the pigeon-hole of exchange value. It is highly probable that the study of economics would still have a separate existence even in a socialistic state.

What, then, are the proper boundaries of economic science? Unless they have been finally and authoritatively established in some writing which has escaped my notice, I feel free to contend that it is less important to keep inside any traditional limits than to follow our natural questionings wherever they may lead, and do whatever work we are specially fitted for and find undone.

In doing this we should accept the authoritative results of

other specialists in the field of psychology, sociology and ethics. We should certainly not ignore their work where it touches our problems, and the last thing we should do is to set up premises of our own in these matters which are at war with the generally accepted conclusions of those best fitted to know. It would be a strangely futile state of things in which the proper premises of two sciences should contradict each other, and a still more futile state in which economists might not either justify or criticise the economic system without being accused of going outside the field about which they are supposed to know.

Economics can certainly not follow a policy of Jeffersonian nonintercourse toward other fields of knowledge. The ultimate problems in which humanity is interested are not those of social value in the sense of "value in society" as registered by market standards. Men are interested in the values of things *to* society, and they rightly demand that economics should contribute to the solution of these problems. Our studies of exchange values are destined to be judged by this broader criterion, and we might as well prepare them with this in mind. To do this it is not enough to study the causes of exchange values, seeing personal utilities as the results of social suggestion and market values as conditioned by social habits and laws. We must study results as well as causes if we are to find what function values perform in the life of society, for this function does not stop with the fixing of a market price. Moreover we cannot be satisfied to take institutions for granted as if they were complete ends in themselves independent of the transactions of the market in which they take effect. If we cannot understand the social value of goods sold under a franchise without reference to the Dartmouth College Case, neither can we understand the social value of the Bill of Rights without reference to its effect on two-cent fare laws. A legal economic institution existing somewhere without reference to individual economic acts is something disembodied, unthinkable.

This view of institutions as independent and inscrutable entities may spring from an overworking of the analogy between social organization and biological organisms, under which human institutions are regarded as the outgrowth of quasi-biological laws, inscrutable to the economist and independent of the desires that clash in the market. To use this premise is to enter the realm of sociology, only the doctrine selected happens to be discredited among sociologists.

So far as laws are the embodiment of custom we need only ask "How did the custom grow?" Out of separate acts, mostly acts of free choice, gradually hardening into a habit, and becoming recognized by law. The habit is the decisive thing, for without it the law quickly becomes a dead letter. This means that an institution, to continue, must rest on masses of individual acts and choices. It is not independent of them. Such habits represent the fact that the cost, effort and risk of deciding each choice on its separate merits is too great for humanity to bear. These habits may start as mere calf-paths of the social mind, and may later become ludicrously or dangerously wasteful. But we cannot discover that fact if we take the calf-path for granted, or study it merely as an example of the social value of a line of least resistance to each successive traveller. We must study it in the light of economy of effort for all the traffic of the city street which may, if the city be Boston and the legends be true, have been built on the track of the calf's meanderings.

Or, to use another figure, if we explain why it does not pay a locomotive engineer to run his engine off the rails in the search for a more economical route, that is good so far as it goes, but it is hardly more than the beginning of wisdom in railroad economics. While the engineer is running on the old route, the managers are studying whether the saving from a tunnel or a cut-off will apply to a large enough volume of traffic to be worth its cost to the road. There are few calf-paths on the route of a well managed railway. The greatest use of the data of social science should be in eliminating the calf-paths of social habits, by methods as like those used in calculating the best route for a railway as the more elusive nature of the problem will permit.

The outcome of this process will be laws: laws which, instead of embodying past customs seek to modify them and improve on them. Such laws are conscious means to calculated ends and their value lies wholly in their expected results. We have, then, considered two kinds of legal values, those which embody custom and those which do not, and we find that neither can be understood apart from the multitude of concrete cases on which they take effect.

When the study of economics brings us face to face with these broader values of institutions, one simple inquiry can always be made. We want to know, first and foremost, what society is giving in exchange for what it gets; what price is paid for the fulfilment of any one of its impulses, whether this be the impulse to personal display, the impulse to law and order, or any other.

This inquiry is in itself a mere question of fact with no doctrines of social ethics attached to it, but it cannot fail to have an effect on social policies and judgments. Teach a man the psychological facts of impulsive or ideo-motor action and he is never again quite so completely at the mercy of a chance stimulus. Teach a state that its citizens have a persistent myopia which warps them regularly in a given direction and brings disaster on many, as when workmen underestimate industrial risks—teach a state this, and it sets to work studying antidotes or remedies. And if the state itself, *via* its representative organs or its citizens acting collectively, have any such myopias, the first thing is to exhibit them for what they are.

Peoples do have such myopias, beyond a doubt. Their valuations are not wholly rational, are not always justified by their results, and show distinct leanings now in one direction and now in another.

The epithets "conservative," "radical" and "progressive" apply to whole states and whole areas as well as to individuals, and states change their mood somewhat in these respects from time to time. A state may be so hidebound that it seems to set almost infinite value on traditional institutions as such, although the phrase "setting a value" implies too much of rational choice to be fittingly applied to the mere social "moment of inertia" which is at work in such cases. When a society awakes to the fact that it is setting a value on customary behavior as such, over against the healing of abuses, it is already on the way out of the rut. Where the old has a semisacred value for its own sake, consciously or unconsciously, enormous evils may persist untouched.

Is there then no more rational standard than a conflict of forces between temperamental or professional radicals and temperamental or professional conservatives? It may be admitted that there is not, so long as men regard laws and institutions, oldness or newness, as ends in themselves, but as soon as men begin regarding anything as a means to an end, so soon they begin to weigh it more or less rationally against other means; and social institutions are no exception. Even the courts never actually reach the point of regarding the law and the constitution wholly as ends in themselves: indeed they are much freer than many people imagine to decide, for example, the constitutionality of labor laws, according to their judgment of what is demanded by the good of society or the settled conviction of the people. And even the politician who advocates the laws merely to solidify his party, must present them to the voters as tools of social welfare.

The modern tendency is increasingly to view institutions as means to definite ends, and nothing can further this tendency more than a study of the particular economic gains and costs to society for which such institutions are responsible. This study the economist would seem to be specially qualified to make.

The whole problem of value to society is of course more than economic, and yet it seems to be one problem and not many separate ones.[14] While its economic aspect is far from exhausted, the chief thing to be striven for is that this central problem shall have all the light that can be thrown on it from all angles, and that problems of exchange should be treated with this aim constantly in mind.

[14] Cf. Cooley, *Amer. Jour. of Sociology*, vol. 19, p. 192.

III

THE CHANGING BASIS OF
ECONOMIC RESPONSIBILITY*

I. FORECAST OF THE ARGUMENT

TWENTY years ago an economist writing under this title would have been expected to deal chiefly or solely with the responsibility of the individual for his own economic destiny: his responsibility for paying his debts and keeping out of the poor-house. Economic responsibility meant self-reliance and self-dependence.[1] Today any treatment of the subject from such a limited standpoint would be an anachronism. The ideas of obligation which embody the actual relations of man to man in the twentieth century, and answer the needs of the twentieth century, are radically different from the ideas which dominated the nineteenth.

Some have failed to realize what the change means and have resisted it uncomprehendingly. Interdependence means no more to them than it did in the days when free exchange seemed adequate to organize the world, and enlist the far islands of the seas to furnish London breakfast tables. That was one kind of interdependence, marvelously far-reaching

---

* Reprinted by permission from *The Journal of Political Economy*, vol. 24 (1916), pp. 209-29.

[1] Cf. Hadley, *Economics*, chap. ii. Cf. also Henry C. Adams, *The Relation of the State to Industrial Action*, pp. 80-85. Here the dominant note is reliance on free competition wherever free competition naturally prevails. Action by the state is urged, (1) to enable the majority in a trade to decide what the plane of their competition shall be, and (2) in the case of natural monopolies. The author announces the theory of responsibility as the keynote of this policy, using the term "responsibility" none too definitely, but in a strongly individualistic sense.

66

and marvelously effective—but not the interdependence that is putting its peculiar stamp on the life of the present generation.

Some have gone to the other extreme and have lost their old sense of personal accountability in an easy philosophy that lays the burdens on the impersonal state, and the blame on heredity and environment. But most of us have not gone so far as that. We do not want a state that shall prohibit all our vices, syndicate all our virtues, and render old-fashioned self-reliance obsolete, if indeed that were remotely possible! Instead, many men are honestly seeking to know what their obligations are in this new era, that they may meet them on their own initiative. More knowledge is wanted, that men may guide themselves. The modern prayer is not so much for strength as for wisdom.

In the economic world this issue is presented more clearly perhaps than anywhere else. We have inherited an economics of irresponsibility. We are in an economy of control with which our intellectual inheritance fits but awkwardly. To make control really tolerable we need something more; something which is still in its infancy. We need an economics of responsibility, developed and embodied in our working business ethics.

2. THE SWING OF THE PENDULUM

We have gone through a revolution of late in many realms of thought and policy. We have swung far away from narrow individualism toward a sense of solidarity and social-mindedness. In religion the dominant ideal is no longer a narrowly personal salvation granted from above as a reward of personal faith, but rather an attitude of love and service to one's fellows which are in themselves salvation. The old idea of free will is giving way to determinism, individualism to public control, personal responsibility to social responsibility.

This changed attitude shows itself in economic matters in a hundred ways. The common law treated industrial accidents as matters of personal responsibility and attempted to fix a personal blame. The results were intolerable. Something was wrong. Contrast the attitude of a system of compulsory compensation which blames nobody, and seems almost to take away all responsibility, distributing it between the state and the employer and treating the employer impersonally, as the representative of the industry. This policy expresses a new idea of responsibility.

Not long ago we were almost morbidly afraid to do anything to relieve distress, for fear of undermining people's independence and perpetuating the disease we aimed to cure. If these unfortunates could not quickly be put in a condition of doing for themselves there was danger in doing too much for them. Anything looking toward permanent assistance was a confession of failure in the present and an omen of evil to come. Meanwhile poverty continued to breed poverty. Now free meals for school children are becoming more and more common, the minimum wage in a mild form is being seriously tried out, and we seem to be on the threshold of similar experiments with old-age pensions, mother's pensions, and insurance against unemployment.

The old-time lumber-gang boss or division superintendent promoted men or discharged them at will. He was responsible to his superior officer for getting results, and to his conscience, if he had one, for the rights and wrongs of his actions. Often he adopted a policy of rewards or punishments that were sudden, unexpected, and intentionally arbitrary, his object being to keep the men in proper awe of what might happen, and to keep them on their good behavior in little things: things so small in themselves that only the momentary impulse of an arbitrary autocrat would take any notice of them. It was every man's own lookout that the blow did not fall on his head. This system could work tolerably well in a young country, so rich in opportunity that most men could "fall on their feet" whatever happened and whenever and wherever they might be cast adrift.

But today the consequences are too serious to be treated thus cavalierly. Compare the situation of the modern official dealing with a strong union. He cannot discharge men without the possibility of having to face a committee of their fellow-laborers who will make him give an account of his actions. A group has assumed responsibility for its members and a new responsibility of an individual toward the group is being enforced. How shall the group, the union, have brought home to it its own responsibility to the larger group of which it is a part? That is the next chapter of the story, and the end is not yet written.

Unemployment used to be considered largely a matter of personal fitness and willingness to work; now it is spoken of as a disease of our economic system. Criminals and prostitutes used to be regarded quite simply as wicked people. Now they are quite as often looked upon as victims of the social order. In fact this explanation is so much in the air that it has become a habit, an unthinking reaction to anything and everything that goes wrong, and anyone and everyone who goes to pieces. There is little room to question that our habit of overworking this conveniently impersonal scapegoat is closely connected with what Miss Repplier has called our national "loss of nerve." It is all a most disquieting phase of the spread of deterministic ideas among people ready to absorb them one-sidedly.

But it is all part of a movement we cannot escape, with its successes and its failures, its inspiration for the man big enough to catch it, and its enervating effect on those without the vision. It is the product of new situations and new knowledge, and we must use the knowledge to make the best of the situations. We must take what it gives and fight to keep whatever of good it threatens to take away.

It is the product of many things, from psychology to life insurance and from bacteriology to large-scale manufacturing. The bottom facts are, first, that we are becoming interdependent in new and unforeseen ways, and, second, that we are finding out more about the remote causes of things, which we used to take for granted.

Psychology shows us our minds as products of inherited tendencies and the environment to which they react. This makes the living conditions of the slum responsible for the gangster's criminal tendencies and many lesser personal faults and failures. Mortality tables show us occupational environments as killing so many men out of a thousand every year, and statisticians correlate hot weather and suicide, and attempt to correlate crime and heredity.

Indeed, statistics, together with the mass-phenomena they measure, have been the instrument of a surprising deal of altered thinking. When we are looking at John Smith alone, we cannot tell just what he will do in a given situation or what a change in environment will do to him. He is still an independent personality and a law unto himself. But we can tell in advance what such a change will do to a thousand John Smiths. It may kill so and so many, or save so and so many alive, and we become accustomed to the idea that enfeebling environments have made so and so many criminals, and so and so many good-for-nothing idlers, who would otherwise have remained on the safe side of respectability and self-support. The environment has become responsible for John Smith.

But at the same time John Smith has become responsible for the environment. A knowledge of bacteria makes criminal neglect out of what were once matters of purely private concern, and the outcome is to make medicine more and more a matter of maintaining a healthful environment and hence a matter of public prevention rather than of private cure.

Man is ever in the presence of powers too strong for him to cope with, and never knows when they may reach out and take his life. Where the environment that threatens and the powers that kill are the environment and the powers of nature, he worships and watches his priming, learns to sleep lightly, to read footprints, and to know the signs of water. Where the environment is man-made and the powers are those of machinery, he ceases to worship, and he may begin instead to resent, to protest, and ultimately to revolt. Large-scale industry puts the laborer in surroundings, no more dangerous perhaps than the forest or desert which faced the old-time frontiersman, but surroundings which, dangers and all, are the work of human hands and human brains. All these things have given us new ideas of causes and effects, and these have given us new ideas of responsibility. We are finding out that many things are not to be taken for granted as of old, because they are things over which someone can exercise control, and that means they are things for which someone is responsible.

3. CAUSATION

If we try to trace the causes of anything fully, we are overwhelmed. Everything is a joint result of so many contributing causes that the whole universe may seem to have conspired to make one commuter miss the four-thirty train. So that when we talk about the "reason why," we never mean more than a few out of an infinite series of reasons. How do we go to work to pick out those few?

We are likely to look first at the cause that is closest to the event and gives the most obvious push or offers the most obvious resistance. The teacup broke because the maid dropped it. The workman lost his fingers through a moment of carelessness at his machine plane. The panic was precipitated because of such and such failures.

Of course we shall never get anywhere on any such superficial principle. And yet we cannot go wandering through the mazes of infinity looking for the ultimate and the fundamental. We have a purpose: to shape the world— or our little bit of it—"nearer to the heart's desire." We want to know two things: "which are the causes that are really important in deciding the exact nature of the outcome?" These are the significant causes. Also, "Which are the causes over which we have some control and before which we do not stand entirely helpless?" These we may call the responsible causes.

The failure of such and such a bank may have precipitated the panic, but the panic would have arrived and run much the same course in any case. Sun-spots may cause crises, or they may be symptoms of something else which causes climatic changes and these may be a cause of crises, and statistics may support this with its most convincing proofs. But these climatic cycles are not the only things that disturb the smooth running of the machinery of production and consumption, and the essential thing seems to be that we have an industrial system in which misfits work cumulatively, regardless of the source from which the original disturbance arises. In a system of private production with enormous use of capital, involving the staking of industrial fortunes on a distant future, any irregularity is intensified in some quarters. An unexpected weakening of demand is felt more keenly by wholesalers than by retailers, since the retailer not only has sold fewer goods, but is allowing his stock to diminish. For the time being he buys even less than he sells. For the same reason the manufacturer feels the slackening of demand more keenly still, and the machine industries and construction industries most of all, since new construction is suspended and even maintenance is likely to be postponed. Those engaged in these industries can buy less, and this may lead to a slackening of demand for many products. Even in active times contractors may be squeezed by a rise in the price of their materials, and their profits turned to losses. Their failures, in turn, embarrass their creditors and may spread a feeling of panic to the whole financial community. The part played by banks in making both expansion and contraction cumulative is too well known to call for comment here.[2]

Compared to these qualities of our industrial organization the exact nature of the one most regular disturbance of production would seem to have little to say in determining the exact nature of the outcome. We should in all probability have panics without sun-spots or climatic cycles, but with a different industrial system sun-spots could come and go without producing anything like the present type of panic. Sun-spots may help us to predict the time of stress, but apart from this they are probably not the most significant cause for our purposes. Moreover, we cannot do anything about sun-spots, while we can change our credit system. Sun-spots are therefore not a responsible cause of panics.

[2] For a full treatment of these and other causes contributing to crises, the reader is referred to W. C. Mitchell's *Business Cycles.*

One of the greatest things that the progress of science and industry has done for us is to give us responsible causes of a social and environmental sort. We used to think we could change men more easily than their environment, and we preached thrift, industry, and all the economic virtues, and let the rest stand as "natural laws," unchangeable. Now we are finding that to change the individual we must change his environment, and that preaching is not usually a big enough environmental change to get the desired results. We are coming to take a certain amount of human carelessness for granted and demanding safeguarded machinery and shortened hours with a view to securing an environment in which the natural weakness will be guarded against and the limited endurance not overtaxed.

When a man is discharged because he is not worth a living wage and the employer seeks another in his place his personal shortcomings are certainly the cause of his trouble, whatever we may think about the ultimate causes of his inefficiency. But when a railroad or an industrial corporation turns off thousands of men at a time because a cut of a certain per cent is deemed necessary or advisable, how does the case stand? It is still the least competent who go and their incompetence is the cause of their being the ones selected. But it is not absolute incompetence in this case, but relative incompetence: merely the fact that they are at the bottom of the list.

If some are absolutely incompetent, that is an evil to be remedied. But something tells us that no amount of personal effort and no amount of education or hygiene can hope to prevent 10 per cent of the men from being less efficient than the other 90 per cent. In such a case the incompetence of the men may well cease to be the responsible cause in our minds, and instead the industrial situation, under which an industry wants now 10 per cent more men and now 10 per cent less, may come to stand as the thing we try to change, the thing we hold responsible for the evil of unemployment.

Not that personal efficiency does not make a difference, but opinion is unfortunately divided between those who think that the laborer ought to try to solve the problem by improving his efficiency and those who think that this would only make matters worse and that if the men increase their capacity 10 per cent there will be fewer men needed. In this disagreement the economist takes the side of those who emphasize individual self-dependence and would hold the laborers to the duty of making the utmost of whatever capacities they have and whatever situation they may find available.

In this case as in all other cases anyone who thinks that individual responsibility is becoming less because collective responsibility is becoming greater is making a mistake somewhat like that of the dog in the fable, who dropped his piece of meat to catch the other which he saw reflected in the water. For what is collective responsibility but personal responsibilities reflected in the social mirror? We need all the sense of responsibility we can arouse, of all kinds, organized and directed into the most intelligent and efficient channels, to make even moderately satisfactory headway with the increasingly complex problems that are piling up ahead of us.

The scope of personal responsibility is broader than ever before, not narrower. It is a false notion of the meaning of determinism which interprets it in such a way as to undermine the responsibility of the individual for his own choices. John Smith is still a law unto himself, whatever the statistics may tell us about the thousand. We cannot predict him, for the determining causes of his destiny lie partly in his own personality. The power over his environment of a man who does not know when he is beaten is the last thing we can afford to belittle or ignore. It is only too obvious what a difference it makes whether men who are free to act as they will, choose to act with courage, self-reliance, and generosity or not. The only way the environment can overcome man completely is by persuading him that it can do so.

And laying responsibility on the environment cannot take it off the shoulders of persons so long as the environment of each of us consists chiefly of the rest of us. The responsibility is harder to bring home to the subject, and the duties it imposes are harder to fulfil effectively, for "what is everybody's business is nobody's business." But that simply means that our first obligation is to organize machinery by which these most difficult of obligations can be first effectively brought home and, second, effectively performed. This means, again, that we are facing the difficult task of keeping the sense of obligation alive while delegating to specialists the bulk of the active work involved in meeting our obligations and fulfilling them.

But it is not alone by making us jointly responsible for the general social environment that our personal responsibilities are being broadened. We are coming to see that our everyday business dealings have more far-reaching effects than we have ever realized, and that the system of free contract is by itself quite inadequate to bring home the responsibility for these effects. We have begun to realize the many inappropriable values that are created and the many unpaid damages that are inflicted in the course of business exchanges. New possibilities at once of parasitism and of service are here revealed, and here at least is a field in which responsibility is being concentrated instead of diffused. Instead of unearned increments which come from a shadowy social environment, and wastes for which an impersonal "system" is responsible, we are making some beginnings at tracing these things home to the policies of particular enterprises and the doings of particular individuals. Unemployment is being traced partly to seasonal trades, as one of their unpaid costs of production.

4. RESPONSIBILITY AND THE LIBERAL ECONOMICS

By comparison with the scope of responsibility as it has been conceived and presented here the laissez-faire economics may well be characterized as the economics of irresponsibility, and the business system of free contract is also a system of irresponsibility when judged by the same standard. Of static theory we must simply say that while it does not deny social responsibilities it does to a large extent ignore them. Since its abstract premises leave out most of the facts on which such responsibilities are based, they are left to be taken account of in other departments of the science. Liberal economics or business economics in general accomplishes much the same result by separating business sharply off from the rest of life.

"Business is business," and while men are unselfish and recognize many kinds of obligations to their fellows beyond the letter of the law, their unselfishness is not carried into business relations, and the extra-legal responsibilities are not business responsibilities, except such as have become so firmly established in business morals as to have the binding force of laws. In business, men do not render services without being paid such price as they are willing to accept nor undergo sacrifices except for a consideration which they deem sufficient. From this it may be concluded that both parties are better off for every business transaction, at least in their own minds at the moment, than if the transaction had not been made.

With this dangerously inadequate idea of bargaining and contract, and with the equally inadequate idea of business competition as a sort of Darwinian struggle for survival, constantly tending toward the natural selection of the fit, it is small wonder if the business man is willingly convinced that in the struggle for financial success he is fulfilling the whole duty that society can reasonably impose upon his business hours. In other words, theory and practice combine to further an irresponsible attitude among leaders of industry and laborers alike.

Meanwhile the demand for control has grown with amazing speed, and in every direction experiments are being tried. This should properly be regarded as a recognition of special kinds of responsibility which the business economics leaves out of account and which the machinery of free contract furnishes no way of bringing home to the proper persons. But instead, this regulation is looked on by too many as a phase of the old irresponsible struggle, merely translated from the field of business into the field of politics. It is under suspicion as being mere irresponsible class legislation, and unfortunately the suspicion has some justification.

Hence employers often feel either contemptuous or deeply injured when laws begin to interfere with customary business practices, and when investigating committees ask prying questions which imply a demand for a righteousness that shall exceed the righteousness of the scribes and Pharisees. Business men with this point of view oppose the growth of public control with a resistance that is now adroit and now stubborn but nearly always powerful. The economics of control is at war with the economics of irresponsibility.

Beyond all the special issues of this struggle there stand

out certain general questions of attitude and interpretation that are most real and most vital. Are these new policies of regulation to be regarded as exceptions to our general economic philosophy or are they an integral part of it? Are they special and disconnected cases or are they phases of one consistent program whose central features can be formulated? And above all, are they mere matters of political struggle and political compromise; matters to be temporarily settled by a show of hands, or of teeth, and perpetually unsettled again with every real or fancied change in the strength of the contending parties? Or are they matters of economic law, with a solid foundation in real relationships of cause and effect which no party in the many-sided struggle can permanently ignore? Do our economic regulations mean merely the creation and attempted enforcement of arbitrary requirements or do they mean the recognition and bringing home of existing and very real responsibilities? And, if the answer to this last be in the affirmative, is there a twilight zone of obligations not yet enforced by law or custom but no less real for that? If there is such a twilight zone, how shall we act toward it?

It is good and necessary that new proposals should be first treated as exceptions to economic theory, for they need to be settled on their merits, but it is not good that they should remain permanently unassimilated. It is good and necessary that they be urged by men intensely devoted, each to his special cause, but it is also good ultimately to absorb them all into a broadly constructive plan. It is good when political force breaks down stereotyped codes and precepts masquerading as "natural rights" and natural law, but it is not good to imagine that there are no laws to which men and groups of men are responsible other than the law of getting all they can.

The task of economic theory in these matters is clear, and the importance of this task is often too little realized. There are principles underlying our multifarious social policies— principles as general and far-reaching as those underlying the "theory of value and distribution." In fact, they are all phases of one process, social housekeeping. And until "free exchange" and "social reform" are both interpreted as governed by one consistent set of laws, they are not interpreted correctly. The crucial task of such a theory is to reveal those causes and consequences of things men do which transcend the scope of free exchange. These create responsibilities which, in turn, the policy of regulation is attempting to enforce. In a broad sense the great task of the theorist of our tremendously dynamic age is to substitute an economics of responsibility for the economics of irresponsible conflict. That is his part in furthering the growth of willing co-operation in the endless process of adapting our organization and industrial ways to the unforeseen needs and relationships which machinery and science are continually thrusting upon us.

5. DIFFICULTIES OF PUBLIC CONTROL

Any system of regulation of private industry needs a well-developed basis of agreement as to what in general the mutual obligations of the parties are, or else the system will not work. For without it confidence is lacking and as a result co-operation is crippled. It is expensive when the people distrust the leaders of industry and are in turn distrusted by them: it is only less expensive than trust misplaced. It is hard enough for those familiar with trade practices to adopt rules for their own observance; it becomes well-nigh impossible when the rules are passed by outsiders, themselves unfamiliar with the details of the situation, who are forced to interpret all advice from the interested parties in the light of those parties' interests and to suspect it of subtly aiming to thwart the ends of public policy. This is not a complete picture of our present situation, fortunately, but it is a true picture of one most exasperating phase of it, showing itself particularly, perhaps, in legislation on banking and on unfair competition.

Another weakness of regulation of private enterprise is, that while it consists largely in forbidding things, it often is forced to describe these things in terms of form, not of spirit and essential effect. The result is the widespread feeling that useful ways of doing business are being outlawed because they are capable of abuse.

Attempts to limit speculation and capitalization, for example, are so regarded, with how much or how little justice we need not stop here to inquire. All of this leads to a hostile public opinion on the part of a large and solid class, and against such a solid and sincere opinion laws cannot be profitably enforced. Indeed, regulation would not now be able to show its present record of success unless this hostile opinion had been to some extent convinced and won over to a belief in the need and the justice of control.

This attitude is in itself a clear recognition that the business economics is inadequate and needs revising, at least at certain points. But many fail to see what a far-reaching change of attitude is involved in this simple admission, though they may feel uneasily that there is a camel's head inside the tent. The conservative expects things to continue on the principle that "business is business," meaning that it is a self-regarding business, and that his only business obligations are those enforced by law and settled custom. They have been added to somewhat, but that is all, and wherever the law has not yet spoken there is no reason for taking any but the old irresponsible attitude. Further responsibilities there may be of a social or charitable sort, but not further business responsibilities.

This view might be more convincing if only every business transaction were a wholly isolated fact, concerning only one buyer and one seller at one moment of time, and having no possible effect on other people or on other transactions. Only if that were true, most of our existing body of business regulations would be wholly unnecessary, so that the question at issue would not be likely to arise at all. But to argue about modern industrial dealings as if they could be so insulated in their effects from all other relationships would seem to imply a certain lack of insight.

After what has been said already, it is only necessary to point out that, thanks largely to modern machinery and the complex organization that goes with it, every act has numberless effects on others, furthering or thwarting their purposes in ways often unknown to them personally, but known to someone nevertheless. These by-products may often be far more important in the aggregate than the one service or the one sacrifice over which a voluntary bargain happens to be struck. And thanks to science, the specialist can find out about these matters on which the man in the street could never by any possibility inform himself. And not only could he not inform himself, but he cannot even understand if he is told. Science has made available for society's use an amount of knowledge of what is happening to its members vastly greater than they can ever absorb individually and use individually in the daily course of looking out for their interests. No one who appreciates this fact can hold that a system of free contract normally protects all interests, and that every free business transaction is automatically self-supporting and productive for society as a whole.

Now we can expect the employer—a specialist—to watch his own business and to know what it is doing, though we could not expect the same man in his rôle of unspecialized consumer to watch with the same effectiveness every producer whose policies affect his welfare. And if men are responsible for the known results of their actions, business responsibilities must include the known results of business dealings, whether these have been recognized by law or not. Indeed, when they have passed into the statute books they are no longer responsibilities at all in the highest sense: of obligations which the individual must himself decide how to meet. The decision is made for him by government and he has only to obey or take the consequences. But where the law has not spoken, every man must decide on his own initiative.

Now if men are to follow this out in the simplest way, if they are merely to make good as nearly as possible all actual damage they cause, they will find themselves going far indeed before the task is accomplished. The ideal is to pay one's way, not to hurt others without compensation, to get value only for value given, and to leave the world in other respects just as one found it, or at least not to leave it the worse for one's presence.

In other words, it is a static idea of business we are discussing. But it is simply impossible for anyone to leave the world just as he found it, especially if he is one whose decisions have any importance. As Professor Veblen says: "Invention is the mother of necessity" in the most unexpected ways. The necessity for writing these words (if there be any such necessity) is a by-product of the mechanical inventions that gave us the industrial revolution and the subsequent vast "advances" in scientific production and large-scale industry. Every lumberman in the Mississippi Basin is jointly with others a cause of the new flood conditions that are inflicting so much damage and calling for so much expenditure of money and thought to devise methods of prevention. Some few have managed their property so as to avoid increasing the danger of floods; others have contributed to relief funds and studies in flood prevention. But whether they have met the responsibility or not, it is there.

To the extent that each of us is a factor in economic evolution, be it only that his presence adds one member to the population, he shares in all the increasing difficulties which economic evolution brings with it. He cannot do anything so far-reaching as building a house without affecting other people's property interests for better or for worse. Unless he affects them for the better he is pretty sure to affect them for the worse. And unless he leaves society stronger in its power to master the manifold troubles of modern industry he will leave it relatively weaker by just so much as those troubles have grown in size and complexity. Modern industry gives a new meaning to the text, "He that is not with me is against me," and is constantly showing new ways in which, whether we like it or not, we are our brothers' keepers.

In many such matters, such as the policy of lumbermen toward the danger of floods that comes with deforestation, or the employer's attitude toward the unemployment that arises from the seasonal nature of his trade, the responsibility is one which we are not yet ready to crystallize into a legal obligation. Law and custom can at best never keep pace with the needs which they are made to meet, for the simple reason that the need must be there before it can be felt, and it must be felt in a substantial way to be worth making a law about, and felt for a long time and by a considerable number to give rise to a custom. These agencies which prescribe just how a man shall take upon himself the consequences of his acts can never cover more than a few of the more direct and the more obvious. By far the greater number must always remain in a sort of extra-legal borderland.

If they are neglected, the result may be evils which will ultimately call forth legislation of an experimental sort, ill-informed and inept perhaps, and usually not calculated to improve the morale of our attitude toward government. But if these matters are treated as public obligations by those most directly responsible, much of this friction and waste motion can be avoided. The interested parties may ultimately want a law to help control them, for the sake of controlling also the bolters in their own ranks. But it will be a law asked for by the governed, not imposed on them from outside.

We have become accustomed to the idea that nineteen men who want good conditions may be coerced by one competitor whose standard is more unscrupulous. They may actually be unable to do as they wish unless commanded by law. We have not always seen that this is a two-edged doctrine. It has been used to show how far regulation can go without transgressing the principle of industrial freedom and the natural right of the business man to run his enterprise as he sees fit. It has been used by the individualist to set limits on the sphere of government.

But surely the more significant thing about it is the fact that it takes for granted that competitive standards and standards of public good are not one and the same, whether the majority in the trade are awake to that fact or not. And it further takes for granted a widespread sense of responsibility on the part of a majority of business men, not limited to the letter of the law. If this sense of responsibility is to be a guide to legislation, it must go before the law and be independent of it.

This is one great reason why the state cannot afford to assume all responsibility for the outcome of the business system and leave individuals to look after their own interests with a single eye and a clear conscience. Some feel that the state has taken the responsibility, once for all, of a system in which individuals are supposed to look after their own interests and that while there may be abuses it does not fall on the individual to correct them. Moreover, they hold that the state is the only agency that can effectively bear the burdens and perform the tasks of correcting the miscarriages of free contract. Men who are under the compelling force of competition must seek their own interests foremost and all the time or go to the wall. If they try to correct abuses, to follow fairer tactics and leave off using competitive weapons that do damage, the general practice will not be changed, they will simply be forced out of business and their place will be taken by others less scrupulous.

We have seen that the state cannot well do all that this attitude would demand of it. Let us look at the idea further. It is possible that free contract would do more good than harm even in the hands of a wholly selfish and irresponsible population, though nowadays there is more and more evidence to the contrary. But there can be no doubt that enough harm would be done to offset much of the good, and it is quite possible that the strain of conflicting selfish interests might ultimately rack the system to pieces.

Indeed, this is just what the Socialists think is now happening before our unseeing eyes. What with the unmeasured wastes of competition where it remains active, the exploitation where competition has ceased to act, the parasitism which is so inextricably bound up with the guidance of sound production, and the disintegrating effects of the distrust and hostility that rule between large bodies of the population, roused by the sense that each is reckless of the interests of the others—with all these to combat it often seems that we need all the saving sense of public obligation we can possibly muster, merely to keep the machinery running at all.

It is often raised as a conclusive objection to Socialism that it relies on altruism, while the present system harnesses to our service the more reliable force of self-interest. The fact is that in this respect the contrast between the two systems is a matter of degree only. Socialistic industry would find many ways of enlisting and utilizing selfish motives, and we cannot say how great its demands on altruism would be without more extensive experiments than have yet been tried. But we do know that the present system also calls for a great deal of public spirit to make it run properly, and this fact is daily becoming more prominent, and is driven home afresh by every reading of the morning paper.

Suppose the state does take its chances of the harm which business selfishness can work, and with its eyes open sanctions a system which it knows to be capable of abuse. Does it thereby tacitly approve all abuses, or take for granted that men will commit as many (always inside the law) as they see fit? Does not its very act impliedly make every man responsible for the balance of good or harm that may come from his own efforts?

And as for the argument that private persons cannot do anything effective, there are three reasons why that is not conclusive: First, when we are speaking of human relationships, "impossible" is a relative term, and we may occasionally find ourselves forced to choose between two courses, both of which seemed impossible till one was forced upon

us. Secondly, we have seen enough to realize fully the well-
nigh fatal weakness of state action without a strong sense
of responsibility in the people at large to make the way
as easy as possible. Thirdly, private individuals can act collectively where one alone is helpless and get results which
would be impossible for the official machinery of government.

Is it not probable that more could be done to check
unfair competitive practices by trade organizations regulating their members and adjusting relations between each
other's members than by any number of special laws and
court decisions? If only we could trust such bodies to act
truly in the public interest, and not merely to eliminate
competition for their own benefit or to fortify a wastefully
numerous class of middlemen against the competition of
more direct and efficient methods!

6. RESPONSIBILITY AS AN ACTUAL FORCE

And this brings us to the final point, which is that business
responsibility beyond the law is not an ideal only but to a
considerable extent a fact. Business men's associations are
the very effective embodiment of it. The retailer and manufacturer take the responsibility for not short-circuiting the
wholesaler, and in return the wholesaler does not "poach"
on the retailer. This is responsibility to a group, enforced
by mutual interests. All that is needed is to make it cover
a larger group—to make it general.

The sense of general responsibility is a fact, also, though
it is weaker than the tie that binds a class, a trade, or a
profession. In proportion as it grows in strength we can
rely on it more and more to guide public policy. Perhaps in
some future century we may even venture to ask business
men's advice on proposed laws for the prevention of unfair

competition without the uneasy feeling that their only purpose in giving of their wisdom is to make the laws ineffective
and keep things as they are.

With the idea generally accepted that "wealth is a trust"
the next order of development is a gradually broadening
revelation of how far the trusteeship extends. It most surely
extends to the earning of the wealth as well as the spending
of it. It extends to a sincere effort to make labor conditions
as nearly right as possible in plants from which one draws
dividends, and conditions of competition as fair and free
from waste as they can be made.

In fact, one of the most serious objections to the present
degree of concentration of wealth is that the largest capitalists are interested in so many industries that they cannot
do by any of them what their position demands. They have
undertaken, or have had thrust upon them, responsibilities
utterly beyond their power to fulfil.

Still more effective in bringing about this result is the
corporation, which holds out a standing invitation to every
man of considerable means to split his investments with a
view to greater safety. Sometimes this is carried so far as
to defeat its own end. The eggs are in many baskets and the
baskets cannot all be watched. But long before this point is
reached the watching is reduced to the bare essentials necessary to knowing if the investment is profitable and safe.
And when a man's familiarity with his own money-making
enterprises—and every investment comes under this head—
when his familiarity dwindles to the irreducible money-
making minimum, something has evaporated, and that something is a social interest of incalculable importance. Private
fortunes may be safer, but not without cost to the nation.
Has the principle of limited liability been carried too far?
If a moderate curtailment of that privilege should result

in concentrating each man's investments in fewer enterprises, the commonwealth would be the gainer in a very real way.

From the same point of view one of the worst features of the internal organization of corporations is its wonderful aptitude for dividing responsibility, concealing it from outside observers and even from the members themselves, and making it thoroughly ineffective for other than "business" purposes. To an economics of irresponsibility this might appear as an incidental blemish; to an economics of responsibility it is one of the very roots of evil.

Many men would fulfil their responsibilities in a very different spirit if they were put before them in present and tangible shape: for example, if they had to bargain with their laborers directly. But it is an unusual stockholder who will so instruct his paid officials that they shall feel free to lessen dividends if necessary to make the industry truly a source of gain for the other participants, laborers, and others. And yet they usually have it in their power to make it either a source of gain or a source of net loss to those whom it affects by its operations.

7. CONCLUSION

In conclusion: the world is familiar enough with the conception of social responsibilities. These do not need to be rediscovered in the year of our Lord 1916. But the fact that a large part of them are business responsibilities has not yet penetrated, and this fact does need to be brought home to a community in which business men and theoretical economics alike are still shadowed by the fading penumbra of laissez-faire. This issue is deeper and more far-reaching than anyone can realize who has not tried earnestly to understand the sources of the deep sense of injustice that animates the discontented classes. The trouble is not that the unfortunate are not helped, but that they are helped in the name of charity, regardless of whether they are victims of their own weakness or of the misfit grindings of our none-too-perfectly-adjusted industrial machine. To many the very word "charity" is as a red rag to a bull, and this will never be otherwise as long as so much that passes for charity is merely repairing the damage or salvaging the wreckage for which industry is the chief responsible cause; the same industry which distributes the dividends out of which charity funds so freely come.

The cry for "justice, not charity" may cover a deal of hysteria and wrong-mindedness, but it also has a solid basis in scientific fact, and the way to quench the hysteria is to investigate sanely just what that solid basis is. Such studies are the task of experts and specialists. All that is here attempted is to show the important place which such work has to fill in our scheme of social management and social interpretation, and to do whatever may be done to hasten by ever so little the growth of a broadened attitude toward the responsibilities of business relationships.

IV

ECONOMICS AND MODERN PSYCHOLOGY*

THE PROBLEM

I. INTRODUCTION

ONE August day three years and a half ago, so the story went, the captain of a German lake-steamer on Lake Nyassa leaned out of the cabin window and cursed excitedly at a British improvised gunboat whose third shot had knocked a piece out of the pier alongside: "You — — fool, vot you think you do? Next time you shoot you hit de ship!" He had not learned that there was a war, and that he was being fought with. As the tale was told, the absurdity seemed all on the side of the attackers, and the victim appeared as one sane man in a world gone mad. But that is perhaps the same as one madman in a world of normals. The war has touched all of life, and nowadays thought that has no concern with the combat or with reconstruction has an air of coming from some planetary satellite inhabited by beings not quite human. And if the world is to tolerate the leisurely luxury of speculative theorizing in this time of action, and to have patience with the demands of logical analysis amid the pressure of expedients and expediencies, it may certainly demand in return of theory that it shall prove that it knows the world is at war.

War means sudden and huge mobilizations in industry

* Reprinted by permission from *The Journal of Political Economy*, Vol. 26 (1918), pp. 1-30, 136-66.

which overtax the "natural" mobility of free economic agents. It treats industry first and foremost as an instrument of national service, not of private profit, and finds the two in some respects incompatible. It installs a quasi-socialism in the direction of production, and discredits and supersedes the rule of supply and demand. It stops the production of luxuries which could be made at a profit and distributes necessities sometimes at a loss. It dethrones exchange value as the guide of economic life and enlists and educates the consumer to buy what is for the national good.

Reconstruction will present the problem of how much of all this we shall keep, and the answer will depend largely on whether the lessons learned have become a working part of our general economic philosophy. An economic philosophy which can assimilate these lessons must needs be dynamic and national. Or we may say "evolutionary and social," if the reader dislikes the mechanical implications of "dynamic" and hopes for a reconstruction on a basis broader than national boundaries. The "formal" or systematic theory which we inherit is largely conditioned by a search for levels of equilibrium rather than an unfettered study of economic processes.[1] Its study of processes hardly dares press beyond those processes that can be shown to tend toward equilibrium, or those aspects of broader processes which can be treated in terms of an equilibrium of the exchange-value sort. The processes thus studied are those of organizing human forces to achieve human ends, and their interpreter today cannot afford, any more than Mr. Hoover can, to limit his study to the organization of these forces by the one agency of price under free exchange, or to measure human ends solely by

[1] To be distinguished from broader currents of social-economic thinking, even in the case of those economists whose names are identified with systems of formal theory.

their expression through the one channel of a price-determining demand. Formal theory, however, has so far made but few and incomplete excursions beyond the realm of static and price-governed assumptions, and the need of an overhauling based on broader premises is more than ever a pressing one.

It is pressing because the kind of economic theory suited to the twentieth century and its place in the growing body of differentiated studies and activities are yet to be decided, and they will be different from what they have been in the past. The writer began some years ago a study of the extent to which economic theory was limited by its premises, and of the character and extent of readjustment necessary to carry on the work done by his father in formulating theory free of static limitations. The result has been to indicate that not merely the doctrines, but the very inquiries (except perhaps the most fundamental), the forms in which they are cast, and the quantitative and systematic character of the results demanded, are themselves dependent on those limiting assumptions from which a fulfilled economics must make itself free.[2] One thing to be thankful for is the evidence that there is more economic theory in the world than many theorists have realized, since many inquiries that seem foreign to formal theory are really just the sort of thing that must inevitably result from following theory's fundamental undertakings to the point of realism.[3]

For instance, the present series of papers starts with the attempt to square economic theory with modern psychology.

[2] Hence the feeling of many a theorist that modern criticism is not completed by any constructive offerings, and that until something positive is forthcoming to take the place of the theories which are under fire, he will not discard them. He is perhaps looking for something constructive *of the familiar general type*, and cast in the familiar mold. If so, he will never find it—for a reason.

[3] Such studies as those of Professor Hoxie and Professor W. C. Mitchell meet this requirement. Professor Mitchell's *Backward Art of Spending Money* is a

This leads direct to the thesis that when theory has studied the meaning of value in terms of utility [4] its very attitude and inquiry have presupposed an equilibrium between utilities and thus have been oriented by a static point of view and static assumptions. The emancipated counterpart of this equilibrium inquiry is a study of the entire process of economic guidance, in which the utility theory appears as an interpretation of one phase only of guidance by one agency only, viz., the static or the hedonistic phase of guidance by individual initiative. For this is the only phase of guidance which falls within the requirements of a theory of equilibrium. To the economic problems of a century ago this phase of guidance was supremely relevant, but for the problems of today it is the other phases of guidance that claim attention, if only because their principles are so little formulated and so completely unannexed. It needs no proof that such a study is vital to our needs today, when new and socialized forms of guidance hold the center of the stage. What may need proving is that it is but the logical continuation of the same study in which the marginal utility theory of value represents a way-station. It is the form into which the utility theory necessarily evolves in achieving verifiable meaning and a fuller measure of truth.

2. WHY ECONOMISTS SHOULD STUDY PSYCHOLOGY

The only way in which the economist can keep his studies from duplicating the psychologist's work is by taking his

perfect example of the type of study that theory must make, if it is to be more closely relevant to real life than past theory has been.

[4] Cf. Downey, *Journal of Political Economy*, XVIII, 267, "No generalization about price which is of much significance can be true." No generalization about anything in economics which is of any significance can be 100 per cent true, and Downey's statement is itself a generalization about price and hence, if true, is not of much significance. It does mean that thinking which has centered in price must find a new keynote if possible.

psychology from those who have specialized in that field. To rely on the mere fact of choice, regardless of the kind of motives behind it, might seem to take economics out of all dependence on psychology,[5] but it does not really do so, save at the cost of becoming utterly meaningless. The economist may attempt to ignore psychology, but it is a sheer impossibility for him to ignore human nature, for his science is a science of human behavior. Any conception of human nature that he may adopt is a matter of psychology, and any conception of human behavior that he may adopt involves psychological assumptions, whether these be explicit or no. If the economist borrows his conception of man from the psychologist, his constructive work may have some chance of remaining purely economic in character. But if he does not he will not thereby avoid psychology. Rather he will force himself to make his own, and it will be bad psychology.

In putting economic hypotheses to the test of psychology much waste motion may be avoided by adopting the principle that the real meaning of a hypothesis lies in the different way things must happen if it is true, as contrasted with the way they would happen if it were false. A hypothesis capable of fitting any state of facts is one on which no predictions can be based. It is as true and means as much as the statement that white is white. Of this sort is the assumption that men seek their interests in purchases for consumption. Lacking further information, one would be utterly at a loss to devise means of putting this statement to the test, especially when told that the consumer's purchase is itself the evidence from which to infer what his interest is, and that men's interests are continually chang-

---

[5] Cf. W. C. Mitchell, "The Rôle of Money in Economic Theory," *Amer. Econ. Rev., Supplement*, VI, 149-51. Here this tendency is discussed in connection with the money economy which it presupposes.

ing. For "interests" one may read "maximum pleasure" or any other form of words, and the statement is still fruitlessly non-committal.[6] The present argument pays attention only to statements that mean something definite in terms of human behavior.

Some phases of the study of human nature there may be which are of no direct use to the economist. For our present purpose we need not take up the detailed study of particular instincts and dispositions, nor the greater part of social psychology, being concerned first and foremost with the general theory of individual desires. Even the study of the social origin of wants does not seem to be universally recognized as belonging to the economists' study of value. "Quite true, but what of it?" may be the reaction. "We begin by taking wants as we find them, and our doctrines are drawn up on that basis: hence one want is as good as another in our eyes. Indeed it is only this impartial attitude that makes economics possible as distinct from ethics. Our doctrines trace prices back to their basis in finished wants, so to speak, but no farther, and hence they cannot be disturbed by new studies of the origins of desire, interesting as these may be."

This attitude is quite natural, but quite misleading. To put it briefly, the suggestions that mold men's wants and demand schedules may be a direct part of the business of earning a living, or they may be an incidental result of some economic process of production, or of consumption as conditioned by production, or they may arise out of those spontaneous contacts of man with man which would go on just the same under any economic system, at least so far as we can tell. Only in this last case, if at all, is the economist

---

[6] Cf. Downey, *Journal of Political Economy*, XVIII, 253, 259. He claims that to expurgate marginal utility of psychological error robs it of its whole content. Cf. also Carlile, "The Language of Economics," *Journal of Political Economy*, XVII, 434-47. He holds the language meaningless.

justified in ignoring the origin of wants to the same extent and for the same reason that he ignores "free goods."

3. GENERAL SIGNIFICANCE OF DEVELOPMENTS IN PSYCHOLOGY

When Marshall wrote his *Principles of Economics* the age seemed an age of self-reliant foresight beyond other ages,[7] and this is the force around which nineteenth-century economics centers. The twentieth century is an age which, beyond other ages, is aware how much man is molded by his environment, and is deliberately undertaking to control this molding process. This fact must be a dominant note in constructive contributions to theory in the immediate future, if the proper balance of emphasis is to be restored.

So far as terminology goes, little readjustment seems to be made necessary in economic theory by the developments of psychology since the days of Jevons and Menger or even of Bentham. The "pain" of the older systems is what the modern psychologists call "unpleasantness," since pain in the newer psychology is a mere localized sensation, co-ordinate with heat and cold and not always unpleasant in its feeling-tone.[8] However, such terms as "want," "satisfaction," and "gratification" can still be used, although "balked dispositions" and other similar terms involve a shift of emphasis.

Perhaps the chief effect of speaking in terms of balked dispositions rather than in terms of unsatisfied wants is to remind us that the human values and costs of industry take effect in a healthy or an unhealthy human organism, not merely in pleasant or unpleasant states of consciousness. The

---

[7] Marshall, *Principles of Economics* (5th ed.), Book I, chap. i, sec. 4.

[8] Cf. Herrick, *Introduction to Neurology*, pp. 256-57. Apparently there is some lack of unanimity on this point of terminology.

growth of scientific knowledge of mental and physical health and disease is working a revolution in this matter, undermining the idea that each individual is the best judge of his own desires. For ill health is not only the greatest source of defeated desires, but also one about which the doctor knows more than the patient, and the public health officer, by virtue of statistics, may know more than either. Thus the social costs of industry in disease and accident may be recorded and studied quite objectively in a way far more useful as a guide to public action than is the a priori doctrine of equality between marginal disutility and marginal reward.

In psychology proper the first importance of the newer knowledge seems to lie not so much in new ideas of welfare as in changed conceptions of the way wants are aroused, their relation to human actions, and the way they behave from moment to moment and from day to day. In these respects psychology does seem to call for some real changes of doctrine in economics, both as to marginal utility and as to the nature of production. In a word, it offers a dynamic interpretation of consciousness in place of the static conception which plays so large a part in theoretical economics. The interpretation is dynamic in two closely allied senses, one economic and the other psychological. It is dynamic in the sense that impressions which enter the mind from outside are motives urging to action of one sort or another and so have a dynamic force from the psychologist's point of view, thus constituting an explanation of those changes in desires which are dynamic facts in the economist's classification.

We used to think that we sought things because they gave us pleasure; now we are told that things give us pleasure because we seek them. We built economics on the idea of rational choosing, only to be told that rational choosing is but a small and very imperfectly developed part of our mental life. We thought of the self as a sovereign will, in some sense independent of the universe. Men had their wants, and the universe granted or denied their gratification. Production consisted in turning out goods and services to suit these pre-existing wants. Now, however, we find a self which is but a series of attitudes toward the universe; a set of tendencies to react and to seek, which are themselves the joint product of certain underlying tendencies, developed and given their shape and direction by the universe outside. Our wants (tendencies to action with a feeling-value attached) are molded by our environment just as surely as are the means of satisfaction.

Indeed, natural selection gives color to the statement that the means of fulfilment existing in the environment have molded the desires of the race by determining which desires equip men for survival. With the qualification that a desire may fulfil its racial function without being literally and fully gratified, it might seem that supply creates demand in a biological sense, which is more fundamental than that in which Austrian theory puts demand as the cause of supply. Those survive on the earth whose impulses equip them to utilize under terrestrial conditions the materials the earth has to offer, and others perish, regardless of their possible adaptability to some other planet offering a different set of materials and conditions. But be that as it may, the fact remains that what every man brings into the world of markets and trading is not wants, in the sense of the economist who says: "We take human wants for granted," but merely the raw material out of which wants are fashioned. The primitive instincts appear to be few in number, general in character, and attached to no one particular object. Economic wants for particular objects are manufactured out of this simple and elemental raw material just as truly as rubber heels, tennis balls, fountain pens, and automobile tires are manufactured out of the same crude rubber. The wheels of industry grind out both kinds of products. In a single business establishment one department furnishes the desires which the other departments are to satisfy.

4. THE THEORY OF PLEASURE

First, why do things please us? In answer we are told that "whatever furthers the conscious activity at the moment in progress will be felt as agreeable, whatever impedes such activity will be felt as disagreeable." [9] And again, "agreeable feeling is the accompaniment of such ideas as further our momentary interests; disagreeableness, on the other hand, is the mark of that which obstructs or thwarts our interests." [10]

But neither furnishes the ultimate reason why those interests are what they are. When the psychologist ventures into this field, he speaks in terms of the reaction of the organism to stimuli which come, directly or indirectly, from the world outside and in terms of natural selection of the most successful reactive tendencies. Selection must, apparently, have favored those in whom successful activities and certain valuable adaptive reactions carry with them the experience we have come to know as pleasure. This selection is presumably an extension of the more fundamental selection of

[9] Angell, *Psychology*, p. 264; cf. also Herrick, *op. cit.*, pp. 257-58.

[10] *Ibid.*, p. 269. These quotations refer to matter reaching us through the higher mental channels such as imagination, memory, and reasoning. Mere sensations are treated differently. The word "interest" is used, of course, in the psychological, not in the economic, sense.

those underlying reactive tendencies which have survival value. Our ultimate motives, however, are many and concrete, and not one abstract quality, whether pleasure or anything else. They are incommensurable.[11]

The problem of welfare nowadays appears largely as the problem of what to do with misplaced instincts. Natural selection is an extremely wasteful process. A trait survives because it fitted a past environment, and persists in inappropriate situations in which it is useless or worse. It probably never fitted every situation even in the environment to which it was best suited, and may conceivably have cost the lives of nearly as many individuals in situations where its characteristic reaction was harmful, as those whose lives it saved in situations where its characteristic reaction was useful. Pugnacity is a particularly blundering trait, but many others could be mentioned.

Now that man has developed powers of intellect capable of discriminating between the requirements of different crises more flexibly than animals can, he is confronted with the need of finding harmless outlets for his left-over impulses. It may be found that some may be simply repressed without injury, but not all, and it needs more knowledge than we have at present to tell us which ones may be so treated. Even in their proper surroundings, though we may be reasonably sure that our traits have survival-value, what guaranty is there that they go beyond this minimum and further the development of the higher qualities which can alone make sure that the life that survives shall be worth living? Unless indeed a sense of the worthwhileness of life

[11] They are sometimes spoken of as commensurable in the sense of being ranked in an order of preference. If these scales of values had stability there would be no quarrel with this usage, save that the establishing of the scale is not done by a process of measurement.

be itself the last supreme survival value in the make-up of the human personality.[12]

To sum up: the quest of welfare evidently involves far more difficulties than can ever be surmounted by the mere calculating faculty of the individual. In proportion as scientific research progresses, minimum standards of welfare will become more and more matters of social knowledge and less and less matters of individual taste—but only minimum standards relating to those necessities which are generally accepted as such. The calculating faculty which Bentham seemed to idealize is quite incompetent to give us any really progressive standards going beyond such a minimum.

Calculation may tell a man just what it is he must sacrifice if he does a certain thing, but it cannot tell him whether he wants the thing badly enough to accept the sacrifice. That is something he learns directly, and often he learns only when the choice is actually forced on him and he surprises himself by acting in a way he himself would never have expected. Indeed, it would seem that the calculating faculty of man has the same function and the same limitations in private as in collective studies, in household management as in social science. It can show us what we are getting, but cannot tell us whether we want it, or whether we want it enough to pay the price. Calculation is necessary, but not final. In fact the calculating man can hardly come to his own completely save in some machine-made utopia where we might expect the capacity for pleasure to become atrophied as being no longer needed to guide human conduct, its place being taken by a grotesquely color-less calculation of health-values or survival-values. For

---

[12] I leave it for those who are more competent in these matters to discuss the possible effect on this element in natural selection in case birth-control comes to be more evenly practiced by the different strata of society.

then the sole supreme end would furnish the necessary common measure for calculation.

5. DESIRE AS A REACTION TO STIMULUS

Of the many cruel shocks which the study of psychology has in store for the self-satisfaction of the naïve and innocent beginner, perhaps the most disconcerting comes when he is forced to conceive of his sovereign personality as reacting to the stimuli furnished by the outside universe rather than as generating its own stimuli and acting independently upon the universe from an inner self possessed to some extent of a quality called "originality." The youth who has been fondly imagining that he was somebody may well feel as if the somebody he thought he was had been ruthlessly annihilated at a blow. He can make nothing out of the world that the world does not first make out of him; he cannot even desire of the world save as it has taught him to desire. He is limited by the range of stimuli that have come within his experience. He is at the mercy of whatever system he happens to be born into for creating, transmitting, and directing stimuli. The slum tenement or the hill farm, the school, the church, the newspaper, the trade journal, the advertisement, the arrangement of the street one walks on, the laboratory, and the social contact of the saloon—everything, in fact, that discovers real or fancied truths, every act that may furnish an example, and every conceivable method of communication—all are parts of this system which determines men by determining the stimuli to which they are exposed.

Let us suppose for the moment that man is, within the range so set for him, a perfect economic being. He will buy goods in proportion to their marginal importance to him, will he not? Yes and no. According to the importance they are capable of having for him under the existing system, yes. In other words, he manages his income as economically as his environment equips and enables him to manage it. But what answer is this to one who is asking whether the present industrial environment tends to promote a more economical management of men's incomes, in general, than any other possible environment would promote? A marginal utility management of income may be a very efficient or a very inefficient one, according as the conditioning environment is favorable or unfavorable in a million and one particulars. The typical environment of today, developed under the system of competitive industry and commerce, is earmarked with many grave shortcomings and is capable of improvement in many directions.

In trying to pass judgment, then, on the competitive system as a whole or on any one nook or corner of it, what profits it to demonstrate that our productive powers are organized into a system of maximum efficiency, if price be taken as the measure of efficiency, and that prices are actually in proportion to the marginal importance of the various products to the consumer, this marginal importance being in turn determined for good or ill by the environment which the competitive system itself plays so large a part in molding? This appears strangely lacking in conclusiveness.

In a word, from the fact that the human mind is limited by the range of stimuli presented for it to react upon, we must conclude that "marginal utility" means nothing absolute and can furnish no ultimate measure of social efficiency with which to judge different industrial systems. Its meaning is relative: relative to the existing system of stimuli, some of which are largely independent of the industrial system, but some of which are an integral part of it.

6. THE DYNAMIC NATURE OF CONSCIOUSNESS [13]

We used to think that we gave attention to many things, but desired comparatively few and sought these few alone. Now we are told that anything the mind attends to, it also seeks. Every idea is in its nature dynamic—an impulse to its own realization, which, if let alone, will act as a motive force until some other idea takes its place. To make a man desire a thing, then, in the sense of seeking it, it is not necessary to convince him that it is good for him or to persuade him that it will give him pleasure. It may be necessary only to keep his attention focused on the idea of getting it.[14] If the idea be presented strongly and persistently, it will take a man strong-minded to the point of eccentricity to summon the positive effort required to resist. Thus the stream of consciousness is guided by outside forces.

"Modern psychology knows nothing of a permanent mind, or of faculties or activities or manifestations of such a mind." [15] And pleasure is not absolute but relative to the "conscious activity *at the moment* in progress," [16] and psychologists speak of "momentary interests" and of impulsive or "ideo-motor" action as occupying a large part of life. Even in making certain types of deliberative decisions "the whole scale of values of our motives and impulses undergoes a change" as we suddenly pass from one mood to another.[17] One type of advertising and salesmanship relies wholly on ideo-motor responses in the victim, insinuating or hammer-

[13] It has already been noted that consciousness is shown to be dynamic in two allied senses, one economic and the other psychological. See p. 99 above.

[14] See especially Wm. James, *Psychology* (1900), chaps. xxiii and xxvi. While the more rigorously experimental psychologists of today have little respect for the methods of James, they have not attacked these general principles (or theories) nor have they as yet carried their own work into this region of inquiry.

[15] Tichener, *Psychology*, p. 267.

[16] Angell, *op. cit.*, p. 264. The italics are my own.

[17] James, *op. cit.*, p. 432.

ing into his consciousness the idea which, once there, determines his choice and action often without any critical weighting in the light of all the possibilities and all the interests of a rationally unified self.

Perhaps one reason for our slowness to recognize the full consequences of the difference between advertising and other types of production lies in the fact that, while salesmanship is as old as exchange, and the deliberate production of information as old as markets, they have but recently differentiated themselves to the point at which independent entrepreneurs specialize their large establishments to some one of these types of service. Just as the problem of interest is not raised where the craftsman works with his own simple tools, and only comes into view with the rise of a class that receives interest without labor, so salesmanship was not differentiated when the owner of the shop ran it himself and did his own enticing of customers. But now that it has become the source of a class income, and now that we have the beginnings of an understanding of the laws by which it works upon its human raw material, it has become an economic category and is rapidly attaining the dignity of a problem. This is equally true of business experimentation, research, and information. How much net addition does advertising make to man's power over nature, to his ability to fulfil the motives that animate him, or to the supply of the material means of fulfilment? As a whole the use of ideomotor stimuli is no doubt highly productive, but what of the contribution made by a marginal unit as compared with a marginal unit of power spent in raising crops or carrying them to market?

In the light of the foregoing argument it seems strange that one can read orthodox texts in economics and find utility and production treated in a way which either ignores entirely the implications of the psychology of advertising or is absolutely inconsistent with it. This is the case wherever production is treated as nothing more than adapting matter to the satisfaction of existing wants, and wherever it is laid down that the prices a man is willing to offer for different things are in proportion to the marginal satisfaction he gets from their consumption, or even where it is assumed that the consumer's demand is determined by the goods offered and the price set, so that given the nature of the goods themselves it varies only with the price.[18] The principle of marginal utility and even the principle of diminishing utility in the strictest sense are inconsistent with this dynamic principle in human nature. The principle of diminishing utility holds true only apart from changes in the consumer himself; it is, in other words, a static principle. It does not go so far as to deny that the consumer may change, but it takes no active

[18] The following passages may be cited in illustration:

Seligman, *Principles of Economics* (1910), p. 275; also chap. xii.

Seager, *Principles of Economics* (1913), pp. 89-91, 97-100, 122-23. While Professor Seager treats of purchasers' mistakes, he regards them as errors in calculating prospective utilities. If the views embodied in the present study are correct, it is something very different from calculation which decides these choices.

Ely, *Outlines of Economics* (1909), pp. 16, 94-95, 121. The author admits other motives than mere calculation of prospective satisfaction, and mentions advertising in the same paragraph in which he states that "every person tends to keep the marginal utilities of the different kinds of commodities he consumes equal." His definition of production, however, leaves no room for salesmanship, though his discussion of the variability of wants invites a broader treatment of production.

Marshall, *Principles of Economics* (1907), pp. 63-67, also Book III, chaps. iii and iv. Professor Marshall considers the purchaser as coming to market with a demand schedule predetermined; one in which price is the only variable which can affect the outcome. This extremely reputable assumption cannot be squared with the facts of salesmanship save in a way which makes the conventional assumption as to competition untenable. Marshall discusses the education of producers by consumers, but not the reverse process.

Irving Fisher, *Elementary Principles of Economics* (1911). This work may be cited negatively. While not necessarily inconsistent with the principles here advocated, it makes no mention of them.

Taussig, *Principles of Economics* (1915), chap. ii.

notice of the fact. This is always legitimate as a temporary expedient, and it may be legitimate as a permanent attitude, but only if the things ignored are things that do not concern the economist.

The law of demand tells us that an increase in prices tends to diminish sales. It is commonly based on the law of diminishing utility and hence involves the same static abstraction, excluding changes in the consumer himself. If one were to attempt to verify this law by observation he would find the results sufficiently irregular to indicate the presence of some independent variables besides the ones that are accounted for in the formula.[19] One use commonly made of the law of demand price is to combine it with the law (or laws) of supply price into a formula under which all the forces governing value may be summed up. This virtually says that the demand schedule is an ultimate fact for the seller, as the supply schedule is for the purchaser; or that the buyer has one and the same demand schedule throughout his relations with the seller. Otherwise the forces of demand and supply could never be shown to lead to any determinate result, even temporarily, or to any level of equilibrium. The demand with which the buyer goes to market must be the same as that which settles the final price. Given the commodity that is for sale, the volume of sales is supposed to be uniquely determined by the price, and to vary inversely with the price. This independent demand schedule is akin to the static assumptions already mentioned. It assumes absence of all disturbance other than the one factor included in the formula. Are the disturbing factors things which the economist need not consider? If they are, the business man is not so care-free about them. A recent book on production from the business man's point of view devotes one major

19 Cf. Fetter, *Source Book in Economics*, pp. 58-60.

division of nine chapters, out of a total of nineteen in the entire volume, to the subject of "The Creation of Demand." [20] The producer does not take demand as he finds it, nor leave it in a "static state."

It may be objected that the hypothesis of a demand curve is not vitiated even though purchases are swayed by suggestion, because when that happens a new utility is introduced so that the resulting commodity is just as different, economically speaking, as an upholstered chair is different from a plain one. This is, of course, a perfectly permissible way of looking at the case, but if it is to be used consistently it carries with it the recognition that virtually all of the competition that counts is competition between different commodities, or what is more often called "substitution." For no commodities, no matter how nearly identical in themselves, are brought to the consumer's attention in exactly the same way. As stimuli to the act of purchase they are all different. Possibly this shift from "competition" to "substitution" is the most desirable outcome, since there is so wide a field in which a difference between the goods offered by the different makers is one of the essential features of the competitive struggle that this is really the typical case rather than the exception.

But, on the other hand, why shrink from the idea of identical goods selling at different prices in the same market? Now that markets are world-wide, differences in accessibility make possible differences in the prices charged different purchasers of identical goods, and we are faced with the alternative of giving up one or the other of two much-used assumptions. If a market is a place where there is but one price then there is but one conclusion: most producers sell their goods in many different markets, not in one. But the

[20] A. W. Shaw, *An Approach to Business Problems.*

law of competitive price regularly assumes, so calmly that one hardly realizes it as an assumption, that each producer sells all his goods in one market, the same in which his competitors sell them. It goes farther and assumes, explicitly or tacitly, that some, at least, of the producers are of negligibly small size compared with the total output disposed of in this market.[21] On the whole the fact of nation-wide and world-wide "markets" would seem to be the fact of general acceptance, and the part of wisdom would seem to be to adjust the idea of the nature of a market to this use of terms. This has been done, of course, to some extent, but more completely in the preliminary descriptions of markets than in the later theory of prices in which the conception of a market should be seen at work.

The theory of competitive price for identical goods in a one-price market, having served nobly as a point of departure, needs to be fulfilled, if possible, by the development of a theory which takes as its normal case the rivalry of slightly different commodities in a market where prices, even for the same commodity, may differ on account of distance, ignorance, or suggestion. Indeed it seems capable of proof that the doctrine of the tendency of competitive price to the level of cost, based as it is ostensibly on the assumption of the one-price market, really presupposes as a necessary condition that prices can and do remain different for a substantial period of time. For the first competitor to start a cut in prices can gain no advantage thereby, save in the time that elapses after the customers learn of his cutting of prices and before they learn that his competitors have fol-

[21] Cf. Marshall, *Principles of Economics* (5th ed.), Mathematical Appendix, p. 850; cf. also H. L. Moore, "Paradoxes of Competition," *Quarterly Journal of Economics*, XX, 214-24. Professor Moore works havoc with received theories on the assumption of the existence of two large competitors.

lowed suit. If the competitors always follow suit at once it is difficult to see how anyone gains by price-cutting.

Let us have, then, our theory of price differences within the market, including those due to ignorance or information, suggestion, salesmanship, and advertising. The result will be a clear recognition of these as essential phases of economic production at the same time that it forces to light the fact that they are radically different from the types of production which the traditional forms of theory are adapted to handle.

What of marginal utility? Its exponents assume, in the first place, as even their opponents [22] do, that choices behave in the fashion that the law of diminishing utility would lead one to expect. Further than this they assume that the motive to buy reflects the motive to consume, or the fulfilment that comes with consumption, thus implying that the customer knows what he is getting and what he is giving up—a requirement which calls for information, intelligence, and foresight. Man acts in anticipation of consequences. And in particular they assume that a buyer is consistent enough so that his different purchases record the same scale of choices. Or they may regard this consistency as an ideal of prudent or efficient expenditure, to be approximated if it is not perfectly attained [23]—an attitude which at once rouses the curiosity of any scientist as to the nature and behavior of the disturbing elements. In all these cases the least obvious, but not least fundamental, element is a something static about the behavior of the purchaser.

Böhm-Bawerk has stated quite explicitly that "every rea-

---

[22] Fetter, *op. cit.*, and B. M. Anderson, Jr., *Social Value*, pp. 108-9. Fetter, after renouncing marginal utility, retains this minimum, and Anderson, though an unsparing critic of utility theories of value, states that "power in motivation," though different from utility, behaves in the same diminishing fashion.

[23] Wicksteed, *The Common Sense of Political Economy*, pp. 19-20.

sonable man who acts economically" is strongly induced "to maintain a *fixed* order in the satisfaction of his wants." [24] Thus Böhm-Bawerk, though he does not deal with quantities of pleasure and pain as Jevons does, achieves a doctrine of marginal utility which is essentially the same, through his assumption of stability in men's choices. Jevons, on the other hand, is more obscure in bridging—or failing to bridge—the gap between the statement that "it is self-evident that the want which an individual feels most acutely *at the moment* will be that upon which he will expend the next increment of his income," and the conclusion which "obviously follows," that "in *expending a person's income to the greatest advantage,* the algebraic sum of the quantities of commodity received or parted with, each multiplied by its final degree of utility, will be zero." And at the top of the same page we find: "Thus the general result of the facility of exchange prevailing in a civilized country is that *a person procures such quantities of commodities that the final degrees of utility of any pair of commodities are inversely as the ratios of exchange of the commodities.*" [25] It is obvious to the careful reader that these two propositions do not follow directly from the "self evident" assumption on which they are based. The momentary decision organizes no budgets. It tells us nothing about the relation of a man's purchases to one another, or the relation of his expenditures in general to his wants in general. It tells absolutely nothing about the apportioning of one's purchasing power among the many yawning openings. It gives us no marginal ten cents out of a day's or a week's outlays. In fact, it would seem to be little more than an elaborate way of saying that one buys what he buys,

---

[24] Böhm-Bawerk, *Positive Theory of Capital*, p. 147. The italics are my own.
[25] Jevons, *Theory of Political Economy*, p. 151. The italics have been somewhat altered from the original.

and is more akin to Mill's treatment of demand than to that of many a more recent writer.

Now the point of most essential interest in the study of man and wealth, and the point to which Jevons at once turns, is not a disconnected series of decisions, but the relation between them—their place in the management of income and outgo over a period of time. And yet if the idea of a scale of choices is enlarged to cover a period of time, it clearly implies that a man's scale of choices is the same when he is buying shoes and when he is buying theatre-tickets. It asserts that the purchase of shoes and the purchase of theatre-tickets can both be explained by reference to the same scale of choices, else he might buy theatre-tickets and next day wish he had the money for shoes. Changes in desires may occur, but they must be foreseen and intelligently provided for, which means that they must be organized into one comprehensive scale of choices.

It may seem that in claiming stability as the sufficient quality of the economic man the ethical implications of the utility theory are being overlooked. However, the only ethical standard in question is of that professedly inferior grade concerned only with the individual's fairly obvious duty to himself and sometimes called "prudence." It is concerned only that stronger motives shall not be sacrificed to weaker, and even so it refers only to short periods. Now if at any given instant the prevailing motive is, *ipso facto*, the stronger (regardless of its moral character when judged by more exacting standards), it only remains to get a scale of choices that will last long enough to organize a budget [26] and the gratifications it includes will be, *ipso facto*, the strongest. One is tempted to append a "Q.E.D." In other

[26] Downey, *Journal of Political Economy*, XVIII, 260, mentions the importance of stability over an interval of time in organizing a budget.

words, the marginal utility doctrine is a bit of static theory, and is based on the premise of a static man who bears much the same relation to real men that the "static state" he lives in bears to the world about us.

How could such a proposition be verified? If people make purchases and then regret them, that is evidence that their scale of choices has changed.[27] If advertising pays, it can be only by altering or directing these scales of choices in some respect or other. In some cases there is no doubt what a man wants, and also no doubt that he cannot tell whether or not he is getting it, and that many do not succeed. All these are forms of tangible evidence, and they need only be mentioned to carry their case. If the consumer's scale of choices behaved in this rigid fashion, the guidance of consumption would be wholly in his own hands. In order to satisfy the conditions of this theory, demand should be independent of anything producers do, except the making of goods and the fixing of prices, and production for profit should consist of these activities and nothing else.

. If wants are stable they cannot be swayed by the seller for his own ends. This being so, there are only two ways to gain continuously through exchange. One is to raise the price of something and submit to a falling off in sales. This is monopolization. The other is to increase the supply of something adapted to gratify existing wants. This involves an increase in gratifications without any apparent offset

[27] Marshall represents marginal utility as achieved if one has no cause to regret choices in looking back on a past budget (*op. cit.* [5th ed.], p. 117). He takes demand prices as prima facie measures of gratification for the economist's purpose (*ibid.*, pp. 18-20), and appears to take the demand curve, habitual or deliberate, as an ultimate fact for economic study (*ibid.*, p. 342); but his fulfilment is better than his promise, for his treatment of the concentration of trading (*ibid.*, pp. 287-88), of cognizability in goods (*ibid.*, pp. 326-28), of industrial training (*ibid.*, pp. 216-17), and of similar topics contains germs of some of the broader principles of economic guidance.

(aside from the possible cost to the seller), and hence may be spoken of as "social production" in a sense that distinguishes it from parasitism. It appears to fulfil the maxim of Francis Bacon which Jevons quotes with such approval: "While philosophers are disputing whether virtue or pleasure be the proper aim of life, do you provide yourself with the instruments of either." [28]

If business takes the consumer's aims as it finds them and concerns itself solely with the instruments of their attainment, then production may be defined as the adapting of things to gratify existing wants, and it can still be contended that production and monopolization are the only two ways of getting a continuous income [29] in exchange. But if business is concerned with men's aims themselves, guiding general instincts into particular channels and focusing general wants into the desire for particular objects, then the study of business cannot limit its investigations to the furnishing of the means of gratification. If it does so it will be studying but one element in a joint process and will be wholly inadequate to explain either the whole process or the whole result. The guidance of wants by business enterprise may be something quite different from monopolization on the one hand and additions to humanity's supply of the means of life on the other. There is no a priori guaranty that it does not systematically stimulate certain kinds of wants at the expense of others, and there is no a priori way of telling whether the net result, good, bad, or indifferent, is in reasonably efficient proportion to the amount of human effort expended. An inefficient system of guiding wants may seriously impair the possible efficiency of our system of grati-

[28] Jevons, op. cit., p. 29.
[29] Aside, of course, from disposing of existing property, which is not a continuous source of income.

fying them. It is surely more than merely a significant coincidence that the economics which lays almost exclusive emphasis on production as an increase in the sum total of the *means* of gratification should be also the economics whose formulae of demand or utility leave no room for changes in wants save as exceptions to be passively admitted, but not actively interpreted or investigated. And if something more positive can be accomplished, the result should be important, not merely for the theory of value itself, but for the theory of the organization of social production in which exchange value is the most active and omnipresent force.

In brief, what economists have gained in "marginal utility" is in appearance a theory of equilibrium and something to gratify the treacherous yearning for a psychic entity which price can be said to measure. It also offers one view of the guidance of economic choices, and this aspect becomes inevitably the most important thing about it. Its picture of economic guidance takes various forms, but does not go beyond (1) men's somewhat imperfect tendency toward a prudent budget, or (2) the fact that men, whether acting on impulse or not, still act according to some demand schedule or supply schedule, in terms of which their bargains may be explained. By comparison with the older maxim that each individual can judge his own interests better than any one else can do it for him, these latter-day formulae are evidently safer from error to just about the extent that they are non-committal. Most cautious of all is the statement that the individual's mistakes are none of the economist's business, and that the economist must on no account assume either that there are mistakes or that there are none, but take whatever decisions he finds in the market as the ultimate evidence of human desire.

If the individual is, in fact, the best available judge, then no matter how imperfect he may be we shall save ourselves trouble by treating his judgments as final. If there are errors, they are the necessary costs of the best possible system of economic guidance, and a system that ignores them will not be far wrong in its practical conclusions. If the individual in the market is not the best judge, then an abstraction which ignores that fact is, just to that extent, a crippling abstraction, refusing a theory of economic guidance where it is needed because it would disturb the purity of the economic analysis—as if that were an end in itself! There is a third possibility, equally pertinent whether the individual is the best available judge or not. Provided the efficiency of his judgments varies with economic circumstances, then the questions arise: "How can these circumstances be made most favorable to efficiency?" and: "What circumstances are favorable to efficiency and what circumstances are unfavorable in the business world as we see it?" In this case the theory of guidance becomes an integral part of the theory of business itself.

If the individual is not the best judge of his interests, it may still be held that his mistakes have nothing to do with the industrial system, but arise out of a wholly separate compartment of life, the domain of the student of ethics, the inner shrine of the independent sovereign personality. In such a case economics may well make peace with psychology by defining utility as "desiredness," and go its way untouched in any substantial part. But since desires are roused and directed, as we have seen, in ways that are matters of business, it would seem that ethics cannot take command of this compartment of life to the exclusion of economics any more than an economic study precludes an ethical one. As a matter of economics, the guidance of our

choices is a form of valuable activity which cannot be regarded as itself guided by formed scales of choices. The
stimulation of demand is a variety of economic service whose
supply has hardly been adequately explained by saying that
it is stimulated by a (pre-existing) demand and is governed
by it as the ultimate fact in the case. The analysis must run
in wholly different terms.

7. EFFORT OF DECISION—AN IMPORTANT COST

Decision involves effort of attention,[30] and this effort
cannot be sustained beyond a few seconds at a time, nor repeated without limit [31]—a fact which suggests the using up
by fatigue of a limited capacity for this kind of mental act.
Cooley especially stresses the exhausting character of choice,
so exhausting that it becomes the part of wisdom to choose
to yield up our prerogative of choice, save in the things we
hold most important,

in other matters protecting ourselves by some sort of mechanical control—some accepted personal authority, some local custom, some
professional tradition, or the like. Indeed, to know where and how to
narrow the activity of the will in order to preserve its tone and vigor
for its most essential functions, is a great part of knowing how to live.
An incontinent exercise of choice wears people out, so that many
break down and yield even essentials to discipline and authority.[32]

James describes something similar on a smaller scale in a
certain type of choice when no clear decision comes, till we
weary and "feel that even a bad decision is better than no
decision at all." Then "some accidental circumstances . . .

[30] W. James, *op. cit.*, pp. 433-34, 450. J. R. Angell, *op. cit.*, p. 369. Angell
specifically mentions financial decisions as involving a sense of effort partaking
of the nature of fatigue. Wundt and McDougall also treat will as depending
on effort of attention.
[31] W. James, *op. cit.*, pp. 224-25.
[32] C. H. Cooley, *Human Nature and the Social Order*, pp. 33-34.

will upset the balance in the direction of one of the alternatives . . . although an opposite accident at the same time might have produced the opposite result."[33]

If one wished to be unfair to economists in general, he might select, for purposes of comparison with these psychological principles, a certain well-known though fictitious character whose idiosyncrasies furnish alternate joy and irritation to modern readers of economics. He is a somewhat inhuman individual who, inconsistently enough, carries the critical weighing of hedonistic values to the point of mania. So completely is he absorbed in his irrationally rational passion for impassionate calculation that he often remains a day laborer at pitifully low wages from sheer devotion to the fine art of making the most out of his scanty income and of getting the highest returns from his employers for such mediocre skill as he chooses to devote to their service. Yet he cannot fail to be aware that the actuarial talent he lavishes outside of working hours would suffice to earn him a relatively princely salary in the office of any life insurance company. So intricate are the calculations he delights in that even trained economists occasionally blunder into errors in recording them.[34]

[33] W. James, *op. cit.*, p. 431.

[34] This refers to the traits from which the actual doctrines of "economic theory" have been derived, not to the preliminary descriptions of human nature, quite unexceptionable for the most part, but sometimes quite disconnected from the theory that follows. To show that this fanatically economic man still lives, consider two instances in *Wealth and Welfare* (published in 1912), by A. C. Pigou, devoted to studying the fact-basis for progressive social-economic policies. On pp. 118-19 the author assumes that laborers err in estimating the relative gains open to them in different places, but that, having made this error, they then base their movements on a calculation sufficiently abstruse to cause Pigou himself to overlook one vital element—the cost of movement—in his own estimate of the social gain or loss resulting. Again, on p. 160, this footnote is found: "If k be the fraction of importance that I attach to a pound in the hands of my heirs as compared with myself and $\phi(t)$ the probability that I shall be alive t years from now, a certain pound *to me or my heirs* then attracts me now

His enemies consider him eccentric and quite incompetent to support the responsibilities which economists insist on thrusting upon him. They are right. He *is* eccentric. Indeed, he is not even a good hedonist, a fact which the reader may have suspected. And it needs no specialist in psychology to expose his folly. A good hedonist would stop calculating when it seemed likely to involve more trouble than it was worth, and, as he could not in the nature of the case tell just when this point has been reached, he would make no claim to exactness for his results. He would strike a balance between getting the most out of his expenditures and getting more money to spend; also between time spent in getting the best possible bargain when he had something to sell and time spent in getting more to bring to market.

In special cases, when there seems no likelihood that calculations will reveal any course that will bring more pleasure than the one immediately claiming his attention, may he not, after a brief moment spent in satisfying himself of this fact, permit himself the rare luxury of following an impulse without a single backward-looking, joy-killing thought of other things he might perhaps better be doing? And shall we consider a man a good hedonist who calculates that this

equally with a certain pound multiplied by $\{\phi(t)+k(1+\phi(t))\}$ *to me* then. This is obviously increased by anything that increases either $\phi(t)$ or k.

"If, through an anticipated change of fortune or temperament, one pound after t years is expected to be equivalent to $(1-a)$ times one pound now, a certain $\{\phi(t)+k(1-\phi(t))\}$ pound of the then prevailing sort to me then attracts me equally with $(1-a)\{\phi(t)+k(1-\phi(t))\}$ pounds, of the now prevailing sort, to me then. Therefore, a certain pound to my heirs will be as persuasive to call out investment now as the above sum would be if I were certain to live forever, and always to be equally well off and the same in temperament."

The reader will note that my principal thesis rests, not on such extreme cases as this of the actuarial economic man, but on the static view of human nature embodied in marginal utility, the independent demand schedule, and current definitions of production. See pp. 112-116 above.

weighing of alternatives robs experiences of their joy by robbing them of their spontaneity, and who therefore chooses to act on impulse? Or a man who joys in seeking the novel and the unexpected, which can hardly, in the nature of the case, be weighed beforehand? Man's vulnerability to suggestion is not wholly a loss.

Since it is rational to make "bad bargains," it would also be rational to pay someone to protect one against them, and some people find a partial remedy in this way. If one could tell just how much his bad bargains cost him, he could tell how much it was worth his while to pay for such help and judge its quality when he got it. But if he knew so much he would not need the help at all. Like other forms of guidance this one is not itself guided adequately by an independently determined demand. To preserve a healthy-willed citizenship at as little expense as possible such service should be furnished, under public or co-operative supervision as to quality, to just the necessary extent and by the cheapest route. Will private enterprise do this better or worse than other available agencies? The answer must be sought by other methods than those furnished by the general demand-and-supply or productivity analysis. It is certainly not to be assumed a priori that private enterprise will handle this service satisfactorily in the face of the fact that so far it has done next to nothing in this highly important field.

Mill upheld individualism on the ground that people learn by their mistakes. True, but they also degenerate, as Cooley says, through wearing out their power of decision. Self-education is not best promoted by giving the victim unlimited opportunities to make mistakes and profit by them if he can. This process would be safer in a slower moving and less crowded world than the present, but it has never been safe. The educative problem is one of adjusting the exposure to the individual's power to benefit by it, and this is one of the most delicate problems waiting to be attacked by a constructive program of social control.

8. QUASI-STATIC ELEMENTS—HABIT AND ARRESTED DEVELOPMENT

But if human nature is so largely dynamic there remains one static element, namely, habit. And indeed it is only by the aid of habit that the marginal utility principle is approximated in real life,[35] for only so is it possible to have choosing which is both effortless and intelligent, embodying the results of deliberation or of experience without the accompanying cost of decision which, as we have seen, must prevent the most rational hedonist from attaining hedonistic perfection. For habit is nature's machinery for handing over to the lower brain and nerve centers the carrying on of work done first by the higher apparatus of conscious deliberation.

To be sure, it is not always the deliberate decisions that are perpetuated nor the truths one has learned by experience. It may be one's past mistakes that grip him in spite of himself, or his unconsidered impulses that are thus hardened and set. There are habit-forming drugs on the market: illegal ones such as cocaine,[36] and legal ones such as golf.

The chief value problem here involved does not concern itself, however, with the healthful or vicious character of the habits formed. That side of the matter may appear indi-

[35] Since writing the foregoing, the writer finds in Professor Stuart's contribution to the joint volume *Creative Intelligence* a development of the thesis that the utilitarian economic treatment applies to routine choices and does not interpret the processes by which progress takes place. Cf. *Creative Intelligence*, by Dewey and others, pp. 312-13, footnote, and 350-51.

[36] In such a case it is obvious that the habit is not a static thing, but a progressive disease.

rectly in the recognition that the fewer vicious habits a man has the more he can produce, and that the employer therefore has an interest of a more or less diluted sort in doing things that may produce healthful habits of life among his employees. This seems to be becoming more important as a form of social production, but its relation to the value-problem is a distant one.

More direct is the effect which habit has in binding customers to a known brand of article, regardless of slight changes in the relative price and quality of this and competing goods. Thus the good-will of a business is partly a matter of habit on the part of the customers. This is an obstacle to the attainment of the marginal utility ideal; it slows down the movements of customers in response to the competitive bidding of producers and has a definite tendency to make price-cutting over limited periods less profitable than it would otherwise be.

The importance of habits and custom is best shown in their failures, when we see how much we have lost. Their value depends on a stable environment and vanishes if the environment refuses to hold still. The positive gain is the progress made through concentrating one's whole energy on successive problems, but this may turn to loss if the new problems come too fast to be handled one at a time, and one cannot hold the ground gained. A contract does not usually displace custom so much as it stipulates a few items in a relationship otherwise governed by custom and law. If courts never enforced anything not expressly stipulated, business could hardly be carried on at all.[37] When a radical technical change destroys the value of customary shop rules and practices or creates new trade dangers, the labor contract becomes fear-

[37] Cf. L. D. Clark, *The Law of the Employment of Labor*, especially pp. 50-212.

somely complex, and labor union and employers' association alike rely on highly expert specialists to protect their interests. When war compels us to eat unaccustomed foods, we must be not merely persuaded to do so, but educated at great expense, and it is urged that France, absorbed as she is in a war that taxes national energy to the last ounce, cannot make the additional effort or bear the additional cost of learning to use cornmeal in place of wheat. Such is the helplessness of the individual "economic man" when habit and custom fail him even in such an everyday household matter as diet.

When many problems demand concentrated attention at once—and this is always happening in modern industrial society—reliance on the expert specialist is the only resource. And the development of machinery for insuring that the full benefit accrues to the rank and file is yet in its infancy. Only in an extremely slow-moving society can habit and custom take care of enough of life to deceive people into thinking that conscious choice cares for the whole, and to make the deception harmless.

Almost equally needful of recognition is the case of the morons and those above and below them in the gradations of feeblemindedness. Static their minds may be in one sense, but wholly unstable and highly suggestible and uncalculating. Their presence in the community means, first, that various policies of exploitation, socially unproductive salesmanship, and quasi-fraud can gain just that much more profit and find just that many more victims before reaching the marginal one whose tough-mindedness is sufficient to enable him to resist. If there are enough of these subnormals, a parasitic policy may pay, even though the average or typical citizen is intelligent enough to be safe from its false attractions.

Secondly, the mistakes of these individuals are not compensated by any resulting growth in strength of mind or character, and so they lose the positive value they possess in the case of the normal man. The net result of both these considerations is to furnish a strong argument against allowing these classes to remain unprotected and bearing the brunt of the economic struggle in the world of free exchange; and also to impose serious qualifications on theories based on the normal man, so long as these deficients remain in the competitive field. For the rest of us the prevailing social ideal is dynamic, but for them no such ideal has meaning. The rest of us must make mistakes and suffer for them, because protecting us would protect us against growth and the self-dependence which our type of citizenship demands. For these unfortunates their own present happiness and the safety of others are the prime considerations.

9. CONCLUSION

If the foregoing analysis has justified itself it has been because it attempted something more than mere criticism or the exhibiting of exceptions to orthodox doctrines. In a purely negative direction little has been proved here that is not to be found in the works of leading writers. The consistent economic man has long been known to be a sheer abstraction, though not everyone has realized the importance of the elements left out. We are familiar with the idea of "irrational wealth." [38] Fetter, in his latest book, not merely mentions the fact of impulsive action, but abandons the doctrine of marginal utility.[39]

---

[38] J. B. Clark, *Philosophy of Wealth*, pp. 205-6.

[39] Fetter, *op. cit.* (1915), Preface and pp. 13, 19, 37. But cf. also pp. 27-29, 33, where traces of hedonism appear. Professor Whitaker, in reviewing this volume, approves of it on the ground that it has *not* departed from the essentials of Austrian theory. *Political Science Quarterly*, XXXI, 433-41, especially 438-39.

Again, most of the negative contentions here put forward are most admirably expressed by Wicksteed along with his more positive contributions. The fact that a personal budget governed by relative marginal utilities is an unattained economic ideal,[40] that there is a point at which it becomes poor economy to lavish attention on economies of this sort because the gains are not worth the outlay,[41] that scales of choices are not even self-consistent, but rather so illogically constructed that it is quite possible to prefer A to B, B to C, and C to A,[42] that the alternative sacrificed in making a purchase is but vaguely sensed [43]—all these and others are included in his most comprehensive treatment.

The question is: How can they be made positive use of? How assimilated and raised from the limbo of negative qualifications upon equilibrium theories of value into the dignity of an integral and working part of a broader theory? When economic disagreements have gone as deep as they can go, the decisive consideration is always the furthering of progress. Even habit is useful chiefly in so far as it contributes to growth. And progress is not to be had by eradicating error and returning man to a sort of hedonistic Garden of Eden, but by using trial and error as its chief tool.[44] Progress implies imperfection, and it also implies more or less imperfect guidance of every man by himself or by others as a costly and valuable form of human effort. This cannot be accomplished through the static conception of independent demand schedules or the static "ideal" of marginal utility. Everything in the foregoing study has pointed to this con-

[40] Wicksteed, *op. cit.*, pp. 19-20.

[41] *Ibid.*, p. 21.

[42] *Ibid.*, p. 32.

[43] *Ibid.*, p. 35.

[44] H. W. Stuart (*Creative Intelligence*, pp. 304-7) makes the point that departures from the utilitarian "ideal" are not so much evidences of ignorance as means of growth in knowledge through the process of "constructive comparison."

clusion. A subsequent paper will attempt to outline a method of studying the theory of economic guidance, and to indicate some tentative conclusions. In the nature of the case the result cannot be a deductive system, determining levels of equilibrium with quantitative exactness.

CONSTRUCTIVE STATEMENT

I. INTRODUCTION

The guidance, formation, and determination of economic choices is a process which, in large part at least, must needs be classed and treated as economic production. It is a source of money income under free competition; it adds exchange value to a given supply of goods by increasing the total desire for them rather than by limiting the supply; and it renders as a whole indispensable services to mankind—services secured at a heavy economic cost. These services cost labor, time, and strength even if they are not marketed (for example, household management), and where the service is professionalized it has a financial cost and takes its place in our national economy along with all the others. It is productive by all the recognized tests.

But it is a form of production to which the traditional analysis of economic theory does not apply. So far as the writer is aware it is a new division of production—new, that is, as a basis of classification in general economic theory. The material to be treated is of course not new. The literature of business is full of it, and even economic literature treats many scattered phases of it safely outside the confines of "formal theory." Formal theory has been repelled from this subject partly because it could not be analyzed into laws of equilibrium and partly because it leads to an eternal circle of cause and effect between production and consumption, and many theorists have wanted to end their inquiry in some ultimate fact from which the chain of cause and effect could be assumed to start. These demands of theory cannot be gratified by the facts as they are, for the facts do not behave in these preconceived fashions. What these demands lead to is a type of theory that stops short of a full study of all the significant facts. The drama of life as so presented is one in which the work of guiding economic decisions, which can never be in equilibrium nor reduced to a single ultimate cause, is carried on "off stage," so to speak, and only the results are shown to the audience. This work is really a complex drama in itself, with many actors, and the nominal hero —the person whose decision forms the outcome of the play —has often the most passive rôle of all, like the nominal hero of many a historical novel. A true description will put him in his proper place.

Again, theory is accustomed to speak of the "state of the arts" as if it were a form of all-pervasive free good. This reminds one of the claim that fishing is not an action but a state of being. The "state of the arts" is not a state of being but an active organizing process. The preservation, diffusion, and advancement of this unique class of productive assets involve an economic process governed by far more complex laws than the technical laws of material production, and the results are by no means "free goods," either to individuals or to humanity at large.

This work of guidance turns out a product whose selling value cannot be a measure of "marginal utility" because its very nature is to upset the stability of the personal budgets which is essential if prices and marginal utilities are to be in proportion. Its magnitude cannot even be explained in terms of existing demand schedules, nor can it be truly described as adapting materials to existing demands, since it works on desires rather than on means of gratification, and determines what the demand schedules are to be. Hence this new division of production must be studied on its own merits if the study is to throw light on the machinery by which producers' gains are connected with consumers' gratifications, or to show how social production really works in this neglected field.

Such a study of production must needs start with a declaration of independence from the old-time supremacy of the theory of value (which was a theory of equilibrium). It will, of course, lay as much emphasis as ever on price as an instrument of productive organization, but will tend to discredit it as the aim, end, and final measure of all things economic.

In spite of disturbing shifts in the point of view adopted such a study will be at once constructive and in a proper sense conservative, for it will act to limit the much-assailed theories of free private enterprise to a field within which they may be so framed as to be significantly true; at the same time it attempts to establish a working relationship between this field and the others within which very different forces are acting. It is just as unscientific to assume offhand that private enterprise is all wrong as to assume that it is all perfect, and it would be just as expensive in practice. The forces of service in private enterprise give us something invaluable to tie to while experimenting with other forces, and the same is true of the study of these forces in economic theory.

2. A RECLASSIFICATION OF PRODUCTION

There are three general ways of giving things increased power to satisfy wants. You can adapt the things to satisfy existing wants, you can adapt or direct the wants to be satisfied by existing things, and you can settle disputes between rival claimants whose wants are mutually exclusive and deny the claims of some in order that the claims of others may be satisfied. The first way is the only way covered by the customary treatment of production, yet there are really three co-ordinate fields of social production [45] corresponding to these three ways of giving things value, and one cannot name a finished product in organized society to which all three have not contributed. The first is the production of objective gratifications: "utilities" of form, time, and accessibility. The second is the shaping, informing, and guidance of human impulses which are responsible for their taking the form of definite desires and attaching themselves to definite concrete objects. The third is the maintenance of order to protect the enjoyment of these gratifications from destructive interference. Manufacturing may serve as an example of the first field of production, salesmanship of the second, and jurisprudence of the third.

The logical order would seem to be, first, the rousing of wants; secondly, preparing means of satisfaction; and thirdly, settling disputes over possession of the products. However, the last is necessary before either of the others can be worth while. Historically—or prehistorically—the settling of disputes was probably the first to command the concentrated attention of the ancestors of the monkey tribes, who presumably fought over the preglacial equivalent of cocoanuts before they thought of collecting them in some place of storage. And the guidance of demand is the last to

[45] This is, of course, not the one and only correct classification, but it appears to be the significant one for certain purposes of some importance hitherto unattained. Certain writers have regarded the protective work of government as a co-ordinate form of production without analyzing it in detail on this basis. Cf. especially Senior, *Political Economy*, pp. 74-76, 87, 183; and J. B. Clark, *Essentials of Economic Theory*, pp. 10-11.

command productive efforts on a basis of self-interest, for it waits on the organization of exchange; and indeed exchange must be quite highly organized before producers become aware of this kind of production as a distinct object of effort.

So far as economic theory has dealt with the connection between value and production for exchange on the one hand and desires and gratifications on the other, it has been almost exclusively confined to the field of gratifying *existing* wants. Here its generalizations are largely true, "other things being equal," and "other things being equal" covers both the other major fields. Some of the generalizations are true, that is, so long as there is no change in the social efficiency embodied in the fundamental laws and customs or in the methods of directing people's wants; other statements are true on condition that no such change is possible; while some are strictly true only on the assumption that the two outside fields of production are carried out in absolute perfection. A few illustrations may serve to give more definite meaning to this statement and to the idea of mutual restraint and the settling of disputes as co-ordinate branches of production and joint contributors to every product.

It is essential, if one is to get out of an object all the gratification there is in it, to exclude anyone else who may undertake to use it without his consent, and to prevent anyone from invading it with evil sounds, sights, odors, germs, or more tangible nuisances. This means more than the "possession utility" which the retailer is sometimes said to create. The dealer does not create title of ownership in the goods any more than he creates the matter they are made of; he merely transfers the title. Ownership is created by the state, though it is administered by the joint efforts of private persons guarding their own rights and of the state which defines and enforces them. It is a preventive value [46] produced in large part publicly and for the rest under minute public regulation. Private production of preventive values is quite possible without public aid or control, but it is little more than a clumsy name for a state of brigandage and anarchy. For in this particular matter private interests are in direct and inevitable conflict.

There are two grades of conflicting interests to be arbitrated. I may want the same house my neighbor does to live in, or the same food to eat: the court decides the dispute in his favor and the police dispossess me, thus producing value for him and by the same token the opposite for me. The net result is to grant my neighbor a more valuable kind of possession than either of us could have established if we had been left to fight it out. The exclusion value which the courts and police have produced is one of the most highly valued of all utilities.

On the other hand I may make myself obnoxious to my neighbor in the course of following my own devices with my own possessions. Such things range all the way from serious dangers, such as the manufacture of dynamite, careless storage of gasoline, or unsanitary conditions, through such things as the introduction of manufacturing in a residence section or the admission of undesirable tenants or the building of unsightly fences, down to mere personal cruelty, such as practicing on the cornet. In every case I am lessening the value of other people's property to them, and if police ordinances and real-estate restrictions prevent me they are productive of something which we may call protective utility

[46] "Value" is here used to mean human value, implying a "utility" sufficiently scarce or expensive to have economic importance. The values immediately in question have no adequate measure in price, though all values take some effect on prices.

or value. Exclusion and protection, then, are the chief forms of preventive values.

With direct invasion prohibited and the worst indirect nuisances under the ban, there are still many conflicts of interest remaining unsettled, and under modern conditions this must always be so. The attempt to make protection complete would probably prevent the production of any other kind of value. But the present condition leaves much room for improvement, especially in a system based on free contract, which can at best insure true social productiveness only to the extent that preventive services have already been cared for by some other agency. If the universe were so constituted that all damage could be either forbidden or permitted only with the consent of the parties affected, then the more obvious forms of parasitism would be at once impossible, and the sphere of free contract would properly include almost the whole of economic life.

One form of value which will never be protected against trespass is that which consists of superiority over one's fellows: invidious value. The ever-changing styles furnish a constant cycle of invidious and emulative values, continually being established at each other's expense and continually destroying each other. This mutual destruction is a fact, apart from any judgment of approval or condemnation, that may be passed upon it. It does not, probably, represent total loss, since the human mind is so made that it is quite possible for every man to be not only as good as every other man but considerably better. And these are the same men who show by their actions that their natures need someone whose superiority they can acknowledge by the sincerest form of flattery. They cannot be happy without models to imitate.

Thus we may, if we like, classify utilities or values once more according as they are invidious or not, but it would be an optimistic scientist who could expect to establish an absolute test and measure of the extent of invidious utility in a family budget. And he would need to be still more optimistic to hope to determine just what part of the invidious values is a social waste, and how this waste can be scientifically prevented. "Pitiless publicity" such as Professor Veblen delights in is probably the most hopeful prescription.

But to return to the formulated laws of economics and to show how they hinge on certain implications as to the unrecognized fields of production. For example, consider the statement that an increment of labor increases the total product, though by a smaller proportion than the increase of labor bears to the total supply. This would seem to follow, granted the law of diminishing returns, if there were no change in the proportion of our productive power that is lost through misinformation, or predatory actions unprevented, or damages uncompensated. Again, take the general doctrine that competition tends to direct productive power into those channels in which the demand is greatest. This is true (demand being defined as "effective demand" and measured by its effects in the market) as long as those demands which can only be satisfied through changes in institutions are doomed to be completely ineffective. But demands that are ineffective today may gain a legal status that will make them effective tomorrow. A demand for freedom from infectious disease cannot be satisfied by letting the individuals offer a price for protection. No matter how strong the individual demands are and how much they would be willing to pay, they remain largely ineffective until a public-health service is established. The demand for an assurance of desirable conditions for a residence district may be never so strong, but a Philistine minority or a business enterprise can defeat it without redress unless there is a zoning system or some form of real-estate restriction. Much of social legislation is the making effective of personal demands for protection that were not effective before. If economics is to have anything to say in these matters it must begin before the struggle is all over; it must study demands before they become effective. These demands are like others in that people would be willing to pay a price for their gratification if it could be bought in that way. As things are the gratification commands no price, and the demand for it falls within the blind spot of formal economic theory.

If one says that the static-competitive distribution of productive factors is the best, he may mean either one of two things. He may mean that it is a conditional best: the best possible, so long as it is impossible to eliminate any of the existing maladjustments resulting from the gaps, blind spots, and general shortcomings of the institution of private property as it now exists, and from the imperfect ways in which demand is guided. If it is to be an absolute best the static conditions must include two very far-reaching ones not commonly mentioned: First, a property system that permits no uncompensated damages and in other respects fulfils the static condition of a changelessness based on the fact that, though change is freely possible, there is no adequate motive. Secondly, there is required a perfect system of education and information. But the best system in practice is one in which a balance is struck between the marginal efficiencies of productive power spent in increasing the supplies of goods, in improving the conditions of demand, in increasing the effectiveness with which established principles of law and equity are enforced, and in devising improvements in the institutions themselves. Each must in the very nature of the case fall short of absolute perfection, and each must fall still farther short of its humanly possible maximum, because much energy must needs be diverted to caring for the others. And the static-competitive standard of distribution cannot tell how much each should absorb, or on what principle the balance should be struck.

Possibly a simpler case of a doctrine which hinges on perfection in the production of order and of demand is the statement that an increment of competitive income to any enterprise involves an increment of social gratification. Clearly this has no reference to income springing from the mere summation-of-stimuli type of advertising, nor to the top story of a tall building which, while it barely succeeds in showing a doubtful margin of gain to the owner, means a clear loss of light and air to surrounding buildings and an increase in the congestion of the streets, causing delay to individuals and expense to the city. These are some of the ways in which theories of the production of gratifications are conditioned by the systems for guiding demand and for establishing and maintaining a restraining order.

The shaping and maintenance of a system of order as a form of production has been recognized by economics,[47] but the field has not been actively occupied. Even the recognition of it is marred by some misconceptions as to its nature (for which the jurists themselves were originally responsible). The prestige of Blackstone still rests upon the law and perpetuates the idea that rights are something with an independent existence somewhere in the universe, which courts have merely to discover with more or less accuracy. Leading thinkers have but lately broken away from this idea, and it may still be regarded as orthodox. The newer conception, not yet supreme among jurists themselves, has certainly not had time as yet to permeate economic doctrines in all those subtle

[47] Cf. especially Senior, J. B. Clark, in passages noted above (p. 131).

implications whose dependence on the theory of legal rights is not obvious to any but a searching scrutiny. Hence we still lack correct and adequate analysis of the true nature of the dependence of objective production on this half-realized system of order (legal, customary, or ethical) within which it does its work. Even Professor Ely's recent and most welcome work on the subject hardly fulfils this last condition, while certain passages in the works of Mill [48] and others leave a sense of promise unfulfilled. The field offers an unrivaled and almost untouched opportunity for analysis of the bearing of its general principles on those of the other types of production and on the central theme of economic study.

Possibly one reason why this field is so little worked may be found in the prestige attaching to the traditional classification of utilities into those of form, time, place, and possession. This classification gives the content to the definition of production, where production is defined as the creation of (exchangeable) utilities. But this classification of utilities has failed to keep pace with the facts of production, and so long as the conception of production is cramped to fit these terms it must needs be inadequate to the work it has to do.

This classification had its origin in an obsolete controversy. The classical writers treated as unproductive many occupations which did not create material commodities. As compared with this attitude the fourfold classification of utilities marks an important step in advance and serves admirably to show that no occupation is to be stigmatized as unproductive merely because it deals in services and does not produce material things.[49] But it offers no alternative

---

[48] J. S. Mill, *Principles of Political Economy*, Book V, chap. viii, secs. 1 and 3; chap. xi, secs. 8-16. Sidgwick also has suggestive passages.

[49] This issue of productive v. unproductive occupations clearly determines the analysis of utility in the following cases: Marshall, *Principles of Economics* (1907,

principle on which we may carry the inquiry farther, now that the old heresy is dead, and try to distinguish between different varieties of productiveness and unproductiveness on some more scientific principle.

The old distinction between labor that was productive and other labor that was unproductive though necessary and useful is pale and academic beside the insistent and almost frenzied overhauling of the economic order that is now going on in search of the sources of waste and the springs of disorder and conflict. Neither the logical correctness of the categories of "form, time, and place," nor their fitness for combating past error, is any guaranty that they are relevant and adequate to the special needs of this present inquiry into the wastes and maladjustments of free private enterprise.

3. THE PRINCIPLE OF ALTERNATIVES

So much for the reclassification of utilities and services. If it results in discrediting price as the final measure of economic performance, economic values, costs, and efficiency become complex things to deal with, and it will be worth while to note here a few fundamental principles. If one is to estimate the value or cost or efficiency of any course of action in terms of its realized effects rather than in terms of anticipations or of its momentary force as a stimulus to action, one must not merely know the course of action one is studying but the alternatives as well. Such judgments are ambiguous unless the alternative is clearly understood, for the cost or value of anything is a difference between what happens if the thing in question is chosen and what would

5th ed.), pp. 63-67; Ely, *Outlines of Economics* (1909), p. 121; Seager, *Principles of Economics* (1913), pp. 122-23; Taussig, *Principles of Economics* (1915), chap. ii.

have happened if it had been rejected. The ambiguity of the idea of cost is largely due to neglect of this principle of alternatives. The second principle is one of standardization. Efficiency may be of two kinds, which we may call, for lack of a better name, standardized and unstandardized. Their achievement calls for different sorts of policy, and some of our shortcomings in theory and practice are due to treating one sort of efficiency with the tools that are proper to the other. Let us see what these principles mean.

We have seen, for example, that the principle of marginal utility has not necessarily been shown to produce the best organization of personal consumption, even if it can be shown that everyone organizes his own consumption in the best way he personally can organize it under the existing system for information and under the desire-molding forces of the present social-economic environment.[50] It remains to be seen that we cannot prove that our social organization of consumption is the best available, even if we could prove that it is the best possible *under a system of inherited inequality in purchasing* power, so long as that inequality may conceivably prove to be in itself fatal to the attainment of the really best distribution. Without some inequality less goods would be produced, and we must strike a balance between maximum production and maximum gratification per unit of goods produced. But it may be that one reason why the best balance has not yet been found is that it has been taken for granted that inequality in reward must carry unequal purchasing power in all departments of consumption. This is by no means necessary, and the advantage possessed by the rich may some day be strictly confined to a limited amount of those pleasures and luxuries of life which can be

[50] See above, pp. 104-5.

had without unduly limiting the output of the fundamental necessities. That is about what a war-time system of rationing and priority amounts to if it really limits the output of non-essential industries. Many varieties of policy may conceivably be tried.

In such a case no judgment of efficiency can be regarded as absolute which arbitrarily closes any door of choice which is in fact open to the will of humanity. To the individual many doors are closed which open to the collective power of society, and this is the fundamental reason why "social efficiency" means something radically different from the sum of individual efficiencies. The range of possible attainment is vastly broader; the standard is for that reason vastly more exacting, and the ranking of things as they are, vastly lower, when judged by that standard. In a state without adequate public employment agencies a million citizens might each one reach the maximum efficiency possible to him *under those conditions*, which no one alone is able to change. But it hardly follows that the million are working at the maximum efficiency possible to them collectively if they could collectively establish agencies which would substantially reduce the amount of unemployment.

Thus economics must be on its guard in reasoning from the sum of individual efficiencies to social efficiency that individual efficiencies of this limited and almost irrelevant sort are not added up uncritically into a false social sum. Rather than this the thing which economics needs to contribute to the search for social efficiency is a study of the effect on individual economic efficiency of the various outside influences which society is capable of exerting or modifying.

So much for the first principle of efficiency, which has been characterized as a principle of relativity.

4. THE PRINCIPLE OF STANDARDIZATION

Wherever we can define attainment that is 100 per cent complete, so that success has the characteristic of accuracy, we have thereby standardized efficiency in that particular pursuit. We can speak of it in terms of a tendency toward the standard or of deviation from the standard. If measureable, it is by a percentage figure less than one hundred. The amount of possible gain is finite; the standard itself is static.

Where this standardization has not been accomplished or cannot be accomplished the idea of efficiency remains essentially dynamic. The possibilities are unknown and indefinite, and progress can be known only as exceeding what has gone before. Studies of this type of efficiency must needs lack absoluteness and finality. They are relative, not absolute, and are limited in scope to the range of alternatives that are suggested for consideration.

In general, any work of conveying information is one in which efficiency is standardized so far as accuracy is the end in view. If newspaper writing is less standardized, calls for more of initiative, and depends more on the "personal equation" than the composition of an engineer's report, that fact may be taken as evidence of its place in the realm of creative art rather than of mere information. In the work of judging the quality of goods the determination of chemical composition and other objective facts are standardizable, while matters of taste are not. A pure-fabrics law may accomplish much, but it cannot measure the superiority of a Poiret gown. Science is continually increasing the amount of standardization, and "scientific management" is an attempt to introduce it in place of the more elusive craftsmanship and rule of thumb. The known capacity of a machine sets a standard for the efficiency of the operative. The task of equaling one's competitor's performance or one's own past performances has a set goal, and the search for industrial efficiency is standardizable so far as it can be reduced to these terms. All work whose purpose is the prevention of accident or physical damage is standardized in that its end can be definitely stated, though the methods may offer such scope for innovation as to give the task a mixed character. The protection of recognized property rights by the police is almost wholly standardized, but the delimitation of property rights in doubtful cases by the higher courts is one of the most fundamentally unstandardized forms of economic production, second only, if at all, to the revolutionary changes of technique which have made them necessary. For our changed ways of doing things have brought about new conflicts of old interests as well as other interests newly created or newly revealed, and thus have forced the courts to trench upon old rights and recognize new ones.

In general, economics must be on its guard against applying to one type of efficiency the conceptions that belong to another. The doctrine of natural rights and its surviving aftermath, the idea of property rights as a pre-existent something which courts discover and protect, but whose nature they do not mold—these are the conceptions of standardized efficiency applied in an unstandardized field. In this field 100 per cent efficiency is a contradiction in terms, since one man's restraint is necessary to another's freedom. But since private property is the residuum of freedom left over and above the restraints, a restraint imposed is in its essential effect a taking of property.[51] These restraining rules of government are aimed to prevent individuals from unduly restraining each other, but as for determining the exact divid-

[51] Not technically, of course, if the property right was already qualified by the power of the state to impose this restraint whenever it chose to do so.

ing line between a rule that protects more important use values than it destroys, and one that destroys more important values than it protects, who shall define this line or standardize or predict it for the future?

The idea of efficiency embodied in "marginal utility" is also one of the standardized sort to be achieved or approximated by the individual consumer. But the work to which this idea is applied is largely unstandardized work, and the most definitely standardizable part of it (the work of finding out what one is really buying) is often beyond the consumer's power and possible only to a well-equipped laboratory, and is becoming more and more a specialized department of public production. It is, then, not because the consumer gets a well-standardized result that consumers' freedom is to be defended, but because a large part of his work is essentially unstandardized. For where no standard exists personal liberty is paramount, but where standards do exist the most efficient agency will generally be called on to do the work. In general, rival means to a common end may be measured by their effectiveness in promoting that end, but for the ultimate ends of life there is no established common measure. Consumption as an end in itself is unstandardized; as a means to recognized personal and social ends it is in some sense standardizable.

War, for example, changes all things in this respect, for at one and the same time it forces nations to recognize that society's interest in the individual is paramount to the individual's interest in himself, and it strips this social interest bare of all the unstandardized superfluities, down to the sheer necessities of life and health. The result is national control of consumption on a huge scale.[52] This may conceivably take permanent effect after the present world-

[52] It is not intended to imply that this is the only reason for bread tickets.

conflict, and as a result states may refuse to be as lax as formerly in allowing those standardized health-values of which the consumer is not the best protector to be sacrificed to ignorance, quackery, and vice in the name either of freedom itself or of the harmless social stimuli of alcohol or the fantastic and dearly bought artistic inspirations or other values which may be found in various kinds of vice.

Again, at the time when political economy was forming its traditions, efficiency in business management was hardly standardized at all. Since that time science and machinery have been busy introducing standards and standardizable operations and problems to an extent which makes it pertinent to inquire if there has not resulted a change in the requirements of industrial progress. In a general way the existence of standards of efficiency, especially if there is no danger of their being quickly attained, has the effect of lessening the need for individualism as a means of attaining efficiency. There is less need of relying on the spur of private profit in carrying the mails than in making automobiles, and less need of letting laborers suit themselves as to the technique of their work after time-studies have found a better way than any of them had learned from their fellows or worked out for themselves. Incidentally it may be worth reminding ourselves from time to time that social efficiency in a democracy is unstandardized and calls for just those qualities in all the people of which standardized industrial work has less and less need in the ranks of labor. Needing them less, it has less and less tendency to develop them and offers more and more chance for them to atrophy. This issue transcends economics, but any remedies that may be suggested will have economic costs, whether they involve regulation of private industry or attempt to utilize the hours of leisure.

In summary, an attempt has been made to show what is meant by the mutual relativity of doctrines in the three great productive fields of supplying objects of desire, of molding desires and guiding choices, and of the creation and maintenance of order and mutual restraint. We have discounted in advance any claim of conclusiveness for deductive theories or for judgments of efficiency as commonly drawn from them, and we have noted two kinds of efficiency, standardized and unstandardized, and have seen that the distinction is important enough to justify further study. In trying to indicate what this study may include, and how important a field it will cover, the writer has found it almost necessary to compress the presentation into outline form. Only in this way can an adequate idea be given of the scope and content of this department of economics. At the same time the attempt is made to show how certain common principles are carried through the study, and to indicate at certain points the conclusions toward which the results of the foregoing study strongly point. In general, the study reveals many shortcomings in economic guidance under private initiative, and points toward the need of co-operative or public agencies to make good these defects. Where guidance is left too much to private business enterprises, large-scale production has an unnecessary advantage due to the fact that guidance is in a sense a "natural monopoly." On the other hand, co-operative guidance may bring producers so close together as to make far-reaching changes in the character of business competition.

v. outline of study of guidance of "free" economic choices

A. GENERAL PROCESSES
    I. Self-guidance

1. Deliberative action in deciding whether or not to act on a stimulus presented from outside

  a) Where no common measure exists, deliberation depends on

    (1) Power to call to mind alternative courses of action as "centrally excited stimuli." This depends on

      (*a*) The individual's habit of deliberation, which is affected by education and industrial environment

      (*b*) These "centrally excited stimuli" must at some time have have been presented from outside. Need of a system that furnishes these stimuli in quantity and form suited to men's capacity to make use of them

    (2) Power to judge the extent to which these courses of action are mutually exclusive (intelligence and information)

    (3) Power to give centrally excited stimuli approximately the weight they would have if presented externally (the essential condition necessary to "marginal utility"). This is "will-power," and is affected by education and environment, including the success achieved in past attempts to exercise it. Need of presenting men with problems suited to their powers. Failure tends to deaden endeavor and to fatalistic attitude. Need of economic-psychologic studies in this field

  b) Where common measure exists, deliberation takes the form of calculation and depends on

    (1) Information

    (2) Ability to calculate

    (3) Time, effort, and expense involved (compare different situations in these respects)

    (4) Availability of resources to make calculations on a large scale, with division of labor

2. Habit, custom, imitation
   a) Result of past deliberative choices
      (1) Where conditions remain the same
      (2) Where conditions change
   b) Results of other kinds of choices
   c) Bias toward one type of reaction likely to be applied to situations calling for a different type

3. Ideo-motor action and suggestibility. Results depend on outside agencies (see detailed analysis below)

4. Variant human types
   a) Differences in foresight, responsibility, loyalty (quality and group to which it attaches), intelligence. Include pathological types. Innate differences v. differences due to environment
   b) Stimulation of qualities by different industrial rôles
   c) Selection of existing types by different industrial rôles
   d) Type problem: can an increase in the number of higher human types lead to a corresponding increase in the supply of positions offering superior rewards to these types, or is the proportion of such positions largely predetermined by our technical-capitalistic methods of production?

5. Many social interests not represented in individual calculations. Unpaid costs and inappropriable services. E.g., employer with little fixed capital may feel little financial interest in regularizing employment: gain would accrue chiefly to labor in the first instance and not be discounted in this employer's rate of wages. See B IV, d), e), f), below

II. Guidance by commercial agencies; circumstances favorable and unfavorable to efficiency, chiefly
   1. The imperfectly appropriable character of the product
   2. The fact that it needs to be free to all in order to achieve maximum efficiency, a condition that would destroy private incentive to carry on the work

3. Mutually destructive character of competitive guidance (See detailed study below)
4. Where work is standardized, public enterprise is favored by that fact

III. Guidance by co-operative and public agencies. Needed to supply deficiencies in commercial incentive noted above, particularly where the work is standardizable

IV. Conscious informal guidance, codes of conduct. Effect varies with inclusiveness of the group. One trade or one class v. all trades and classes

V. Unconscious guidance
   1. Codes
   2. Unpremeditated and unrealized effects of industrial environment on men's habits of self-reliance, loyalty, or suspicion, etc.

B. Detailed Analysis

I. Guidance of entrepreneur's choices
   1. By the entrepreneur himself
      a) General considerations
         (1) Effect of entrepreneur's guidance best seen by comparison of personal entrepreneur, corporate entrepreneur, public manager, co-operative manager and independent civic associations, throughout following treatment
         (2) How affected by range of alternatives open to him: alternatives set base line from which effective costs are calculated (i.e., those costs, which govern present decisions)
            (*a*) In general, alternatives open to entrepreneur represent a surplus over minimum needs, in contrast to those open to labor, which may represent a shortage
            (*b*) After committing one's self to an enterprise, range of alternatives less favorable. May involve bankruptcy. Lessening of

prospective losses is equivalent to a business gain if losses are already irrevocably incurred

(*c*) Most efficient policy for business as a whole may not be open to single entrepreneur, e.g., best location for any one produce jobbing house is near the others, even if they are not in the best place for the trade as a whole. Intelligent individual decisions will not prevent perpetuation of location that has become uneconomical. Community could avoid a cost which the individual cannot

(*d*) Individual may avoid costs which the community still has to bear (e.g., discharging a misfit workman v. finding a place where he will fit. Society must do the latter in any case, or suffer the greater loss of the workman's degeneration—a loss not confined to the workman himself. For workman's range of choice and responsibility in this matter, see IV, 1, below). System of competitive bidding to acquire efficient productive factors and discard inefficient ones not necessarily best way to develop efficiency or cure inefficiency

(3) Motives: entrepreneur not below the average in sympathy, group loyalty, morality. Above the average in emotional enthusiasm for work as such and readiness to assume positions of responsibility

(4) Justification for regarding him as primarily governed by calculating self-interest chiefly due to situation

(*a*) Money furnishes common measure for calculation in most matters (*b*) Entire net income may hinge on narrow margin between gross income and expenses

(*c*) Resources available (in proportion to size of business) for bearing the costs of calculation

(*d*) Compelling force of competition

(*e*) Wide range of stimuli to varying courses of action (varies with large-scale v. small-scale business, city v. country, etc.)

(*f*) Extreme caution, which leans toward custom and habit, put at a discount by limited liability and easy bankruptcy laws

(*g*) The foregoing circumstances tend where strongest to develop a habit or bias of innovation, even where considerable chances are taken (contrast different industries and public employments). This bias possibly overstimulated in view of risks not borne by entrepreneur but imposed on others by his innovations

(*h*) Compare, in this respect, large-scale manufactures, small-scale manufactures, scientific agriculture, agriculture on poor lands in backward sections, etc. The poor soils are left to the least progressive farmers. Such regions may come to furnish the best opening for "new blood" to make money, because of the very backwardness of prevailing methods

b) Standardizable work: calculation of prices, qualities, performances, costs, etc.

(1) Entrepreneur has greater interest in accuracy than consumers and others, because his entire income may hinge on a narrow margin between expense and income of business, especially if competition is active

(2) He has resources, if his business is a large one, to make expensive studies

(3) Disadvantage of small producer may be made good by co-operative action. If not, small-scale production gets no chance to show how efficient it can be, e.g., farmers and book-keeping

(4) Limitations of cost-accounting: expense, impossibility of adapting one formula for apportionment of overhead items to varied requirements of shop policy, marketing policy, large v. small increments of business, short-time v. long-time increments, labor policy, etc. Need of business statistics, rather than mere accounting formulae for apportioning general items of expense. Such work most economically done by an agency covering many plants and many industries. Peculiarly inadequate is knowledge of costs and values of employment departments, labor turnover, and labor policies in general. Cf. proposal of federal government to standardize labor policies during the war

c) Finding the "best proportion of factors" (subject to limitations mentioned above)

(1) Process largely one of imitation and custom modified by trial and error, with competition weeding out the worst mistakes

(2) Imitation and custom strongest in small-scale industries, competition weakest with small local producers and very large-scale industries

(3) No hard-and-fast line between quantitative changes in proportion of factors and qualitative changes in methods, since unfamiliar proportions demand unfamiliar forms of capital and uses of labor

d) Innovations (see (1) and (2) above)

(1) Technical innovations

(a) Results largely determinable by experiment

(b) A "business of increasing returns," since a given technical discovery involves a constant outlay no matter how much product is turned out by its aid. A harmonious increase of all the other productive factors used with this fixed factor is not subject to "diminishing returns"

(c) Hence, if the process is used by all, correct imputation will cause the marginal shares of the other factors to absorb the entire product [53]

(d) If the process cannot be used by all, its productive efficiency is limited

(e) If it is used by all subject to royalties, these payments are a subtraction from the marginal products of the other factors when working with the new process, hence they limits its use to a point short of maximum efficiency

(f) If the process must be granted freely to all, the originator has no reward and other possible originators no incentive

(g) Since this form of productive wealth is necessarily unique, property and monopoly are inseparable in this case, and sum of differential products attributable to all the factors, including past contributions to knowledge, vastly greater than entire product. Hence, if each prospective innovator expects to appropriate a large share of the differential worth of his invention, this incentive, together with "instinct of workmanship" on the part of the inventor proper (as distinct from the entrepreneur-promotor of inventions),

---

[53] Space does not permit proof of this proposition. One example of it is the tendency of unlimited competition to bring price to the level of the sum of the variable costs and leave nothing for constant outlays.

makes it possible that more may be spent on inventions than the results are worth

(*h*) Commercial failures contribute to the knowledge on which ultimate commercial successes are built. No test of value of contribution

(*i*) Patent system: Term of patent not proportional to life of commercial value of invention. High cost of protection against infringement may lead to unduly small reward. Ownership of many patents may deprive public of advantage of power to substitute second-best processes and so lead to unduly large reward. Collective research on salary basis as substitute. Difficulty of determining value of contribution (see above)

(*j*) The foregoing facts furnish a strong case for public or co-operative research. If not combined with public operation of industry, the unprogressiveness of public ownership would be avoided

(2) Innovations in commercial and business organization. Same principles as (1) above, without patent system.

(*a*) Private possession of resulting gains partly secured through business reticence, and time and effort necessary to adapt one man's methods to another man's business. Secrecy seems on the decrease (commermercial associations promote frankness and realization of joint interest)

(*b*) Experimenting more costly since not confined to laboratory or testing department. Hence collective research a peculiarly valuable method in this field

(3) General principles

    (*a*) So long as innovation is on an individualistic basis, increasing returns in this field favor large-scale production more than would result from the economies in routine management of the other factors of production alone

    (*b*) Balance of social gain and loss includes cost of revising institutions made obsolete by technical revolutions: of delegating experts to care for terms of increasingly complex labor contracts; of being forced to trust these experts; of making consumers' judgment of commodities more difficult and reducing the value of habits and customs of consumption, or cost of expert services to make good this loss; of unforeseeable damages to physical and mental health resulting from unfamiliar working environment. In general, the work of adaptive specialists needed to protect us from the results of the innovative specialists' work

    (*c*) Possible further deductions for amount of increased productive power devoted to invidious or other mutually defeating pursuits, and further amount not permanently embodied in standard of living and hence taking effect only in increasing population. Estimate of the latter depends on national-militaristic v. cosmopolitan-pacifist points of view

e) Judgment of efficiency of subordinates

    (1) Value and limitations of formal tests

    (2) Methods of informal judgment

f) The corporation as an economic man. If corporation is to act with calculating selfishness *as a corporation* directors and officers must act with perfect loyalty in the rôles assigned by their positions. In proportion as corporations dominate business, economics becomes the science, not of self-interest within the law, but of loyalty beyond what the penalties of law can enforce

(1) Development of codes of intra-corporate honesty

(2) Competition as a force in this direction weeding out the badly managed enterprises

(3) Types of business affording opportunities for profits through disloyalty

2. By other agencies under commercial incentives

   a) Internal (see cost-accounting and innovation above): Routine records v. creative work. Information of value only to one entrepreneur v. information of value to trade as a whole—e.g., routine accounting. Though a form of guidance, its primary value is inalienably private, and private enterprise secures this service with reasonable adequacy. Contrast the devising of the best accounting system for small-scale industry; essentially a joint or public interest

   b) Specialists in news services, business barometrics, technical and commercial periodicals. Value limited by reticence of business men from whom information must be obtained

   c) Advertising and selling services: Since the entrepreneur is able to take care of his own interests as purchaser, sellers are compelled to rely chiefly on verifiable information, hence less wasteful than selling to consumers. This less true of selling to small-scale producers

   d) Other ways of attracting customers

      (1) Railroads' industrial departments

      (2) Inducements offered by local bodies to attract industries to their town

3. Informal co-operation of entrepreneurs

   a) Contact in trade and technical associations

   b) Codes of fair dealing

4. Formal co-operation of entrepreneurs
   a) Exchanges with rules of trading, etc.
   b) Grading of goods (also done under public control)
   c) Information services of co-operative associations, agricultural especially
   d) Co-operative buying, chiefly agricultural
5. Outside non-commercial agencies chiefly acting from civic motives
   a) Economic and industrial research
   b) Mediation in labor disputes
   c) Educative effect of political propaganda in attracting attention to unprotected social interests
   d) Education in general: its best service in this matter is to develop in business men and others a lively sense of the remote effects of business policies, and a bias toward treating these effects as they would if the people affected were acquaintances and the effects were visible and immediate
   e) Public agencies
      (1) Fundamental legal institutions (forms of restraint rather than guidance of free choices)
      (2) Services of value to employers as a group and not adequately cared for by limited resources of single employers
         (*a*) Experimental and publicity work in agriculture
         (*b*) Testing done by Bureau of Standards
         (*c*) Consular service and possible enlargements of such functions
         (*d*) Improving conditions in which buyer and seller meet, e.g., public wholesale markets (see 1, *a*), (2), (*c*) above)
      (3) Research in means of furthering interests which single employers do not have adequate financial incentive to protect (see sections on laborer and consumer as economic men)
         (*a*) Safety studies, e.g., Bureau of Mines
         (*b*) Unemployment studies
         (*c*) Studies in effects of adulterations

(4) Work combining features of (2) and (3). Standardization of methods of dealing with labor, studies of causes and costs of labor turnover, etc.

(5) Control of conditions of bargaining, of location of industries (e.g., city zoning and city planning), etc. Forms of restraint rather than guidance of free choices but made necessary by blind spots in entrepreneur guidance. See A, I, 5, above

II. The professional classes (whose work is itself largely guidance)

1. Self-guidance
    a) Calculating self-interest highly influenced by professional and social standards
    b) Technical ability in a sense an "overhead cost." Study to what extent discriminations are on commercial principle of charging what the traffic will bear and to what extent work is done at a positive sacrifice

2. Intercommunication: highly developed (study of reasons for this; compare relative reticence of doctors toward patients, of business men toward all others)

3. Codes
    a) Limit the bargaining interest; no strikes
    b) Public-service obligation stronger in some professions than in others
    c) Study of extent to which codes embody
        (1) Professional class interest
        (2) Reflection of standards of other classes with whom associated
        (3) Public interest at large

III. Investors

1. Self-guidance
    a) Twofold character of work: calculation of financial income and of desirability of methods by which income is gained

b) Difficulty of calculating financial prospects on part of small investors

(1) Imperfect information in published reports

(2) This itself caused partly by small investor's incapacity to analyze such reports and resulting failure to demand effectively that such reports be adequate; partly by opportunities for "inside profit" through concealment; partly by desire of entrepreneurs to conceal commercial facts from competitors (such concealment a doubtful gain to business as a whole)

c) Result: stimulates tendency to divide investments for purposes of safety. This already stimulated by limited liability

d) Result of this

(1) Still further reduces power to judge safety of single investments and effective demand for adequate information

(2) Hence tends to reduce general safety. Single investor escapes, community does not

(3) Reduces to vanishing-point the knowledge of the human characteristics of the business on which depends the check investors would otherwise exercise on undesirable methods of production, leaving managers under pressure for earnings without adequate regard to methods

e) Field for investment of what is virtually "social capital" in developing personal knowledge and skill; limited by fact that the results are inappropriable unless one is investing in himself. Study of extent to which employers have interest in training employees

2. Inadequacies of present system furnish large field for co-operative action by investors, and public action for better information. Associated action might develop codes of investors' responsibility among a group at present too unorganized to develop strong codes

3. Effects of occupation and other economic circumstances on thrift

IV. Laborers

  1. Self-guidance
      a) Twofold character of choice as in case of investor
      b) Incentive to close financial calculation
          (1) Weaker than entrepreneur's, since a failure to get the best bargain does not shrink wages to zero (as it may shrink net earnings in business)
          (2) Stronger than consumer's, since one contract governs his entire income
      c) Many labor contracts too complex for laborer to grasp
          Note difficulties of language, also cumulative effects of getting the worst of the bargain at the start
      d) Knowledge of advantages of different trades too expensive if obtained at the cost of drifting from one to the other
          (1) Sacrifices chance to develop specialized skill
          (2) Danger of degenerating into a chronic "casual"
          (3) Hence alternative to acceptance of a bargain may be a condition of virtual human deficit. This the base-line from which "effective disutility of labor" in a given plant may be measured
      e) Working conditions are a complex "bundle of utilities." Such things get adequately valued in a free market only if purchaser (workman in this case) has option of all conceivable combinations. In view of limitations on his range of choice shown in *d*) above, it follows that free contract is not an adequate method of registering the worker's real demand for good working conditions
      f) Effects of working conditions not traceable save by specialized research. Especially true if conditions are rapidly changing. Fatigue not adequately measured by worker's sensations at the time it is incurred

g) Bias of class hostility; causes and effects. Include costs of racial and linguistic cleavages. Causes of hostile feeling may be different from the objects it selects to attack or to strive for. Need of economic-psychological study on this point

h) Ambition and foresight governed by opportunity which the industrial system affords to use these qualities successfully. Family solidarity a strong favoring influence, and employments that weaken it weaken foresight, ambition, and thrift. Pathology of casual labor

2. Unions as forms of labor guidance
   a) Specialists in bargaining employed
   b) Difficulties of integrity (cf. corporations)
   c) Subject to the bias and possible pathological state of their members
   d) Do not secure far-reaching scientific research

3. Commercial agencies
   a) Employment bureaus
       (1) Inability of laborer to judge quality of what he is getting leaves room for abuses
       (2) Waste of unco-ordinated service
       (3) Disinterestedness and reliability, not energy and originality, the paramount qualities needed—hence suited to public management
   b) The employer: weakness of incentive; service to labor not appropriable by employer rendering it, but employer has at least temporary possession of the results and is improving this branch of service (employment departments; reduction of labor turnover, etc.)

4. Other agencies needed for intensive study of economic, social, psychological, and legal problems

V. The consumer
   1. Self-guidance
      a) Grades of consumers' interests
          (1) Interest in one commodity as compared to another

(*a*) Unstandardized

(*b*) Choice commonly made outside the market environment

(*c*) Commonly fortified by habit and less subject to sway of salesmanship than choice of rival brands

(2) Interest in one brand as compared to another

(*a*) Frequently reducible to standardized terms: price and objective tests of quality

(*b*) Less fortified by habit and more subject to sway of salesmanship than choice between different commodities

(3) Choice between buying a service and performing it one's self

(*a*) Unstandardized

(*b*) The chief case in which consumer has sufficient control over working time and output to bring "marginal disutility of labor" into play as an active factor in choosing whether to make a given purchase or not

(*c*) Such work is a change from one's main vocation, and more healthy than attempts to speed up in one's "gainful employployment." This tends to balance low efficiency of unspecialized work

(*d*) Collective guidance may increase efficiency of such avocational work

b) Standardized work; comparison of prices and of quality so far as that can be tested by objective standards

(1) Incentive relatively weak

(*a*) Not much money generally involved in any one purchase. Some have distaste for price-searching and avoid it as far as possible in ordinary purchases, though not in contracts where getting a living is at stake (*b*) Exceptions: housewife's pride in buying as a profession. Not universal. Success limited by lack of all division of labor.[54] Sportsman's or connoisseur's judgment of qualities. Limited in scope and itself an expensive pursuit

(2) Means available

    (*a*) Investigation previous to purchase. More effective as to prices than qualities, and chiefly for large purchases of goods not often renewed. For other purchases preliminary investigation is limited by trouble of carrying it out. This affected by location of shops and affects it in turn (see below)

    (*b*) Trial and error through repeated purchases; only obvious errors eliminated. Especially if new article may call for slightly new method of using (e.g., cooking food), consumer has no assurance of being adequately forewarned or instructed. Habit tends to continued use of anything not actively unsatisfactory (use of branded package foods giving less food value than other forms, but more assurance of getting the same thing one has had before)

    (*c*) Habit (necessary reliance of single consumers): fails to keep pace with changes in production and commercial conditions. Is fortified by distrust of commercial channels of information as not being disinterested

(3) Particular quality-values. Health-value of food; accuracy of information; durability of a house, etc.

[54] Mitchell, "The Backward Art of Spending Money," *Amer. Ec. Rev.*, II, 269-81.

c) Unstandardized work; choosing between services of different kinds. More dominant in consumer's work than in any other field of guidance

  (1) Range of choice limited by standardization of production under influence of economy of large output. Effect of this?

  (2) Range of possible standardization of consumers' wants increasing with

    (*a*) Growth of scientific knowledge (e.g., food-values, health-values, industrial effects of alcoholism)

    (*b*) Increasing dominance of social purposes resulting in regarding personal consumption as a means to definite social ends rather than solely as an individualistic end in itself; cf. democratic-individualist and autocratic-militarist economies (see discussion in text, p. 144, above)

  (3) Fundamental method: trial and error acting around a core of habit and custom and often changing the personality itself, including the unforeseen crowding out of present interests and pursuits

  (4) Limitations

    (*a*) See A, I, 2, and B, V, 1, *b*), (2), (*b*) and (*c*) above

    (*b*) Leaves room for control by suggestion in determining what things shall be tried first

    (*c*) Nature of alternative courses not definitely known, hence bias toward frugality or extravagance not necessarily corrected and may itself be affected by outside stimuli

  (5) Buying registers not average judgment, but may record moment of maximum susceptibility

  (6) Effect on others' interest

(*a*) Dependent relatives, friends, government, have interest in individual's health

(*b*) Invidious values

(*c*) Conformity-values

(*d*) Destructive consumption of common property and (so-called) "free goods," e.g., solitude-value of the wilderness

(*e*) Contagion of example. Fortified by active propaganda. Extreme case the morbid desire of a vice victim to make others converts to his vice

2. Commercial agencies

   a) Location of stores as a form of guidance of consumers

     (1) Businesses that concentrate v. those that scatter (see B, I, 1, *a*)

     2, (*c*) above). Where each purchase is important enough to consumer to make him investigate brands and prices, dealers tend to concentrate; where the opposite is true they tend to scatter in search of quasi-monopolies of location

     (2) Consumers' interest in access to all the various competitive brands. E.g., factor's agreement viewed in this aspect is undesirable chiefly in the trades where dealers scatter so that consumer needs to find all brands in one shop

     (3) Attention-value v. "place utility" in store sites, e.g., taking store sites for public uses may result in transfer rather than destruction of a large part of their attention-value, and may even increase the total

   b) Advertising and salesmanship

     (1) Service of information

       (*a*) Identification of goods, value limited by uncertainty whether quality is maintained or not (*b*) An unnecessarily expensive method of getting this work done

      (*c*) Information has an important incidental attention-value in directing customers' attention and inhibiting inconvenient inquiries

      (*d*) For this very reason its value *as information* is discounted by customers

  (2) Stimulus or attention-value

      (*a*) A necessary and valuable economic service as a whole

      (*b*) Effects to some extent mutually inhibitory

      (*c*) Competitive gain in increasing it beyond the point of maximum social gain? Measured by

        i) Gain to the trade as a whole

        ii) Gain to all trades (maximum industrial activity)

        iii) Maximum effective stimulation of consumers' desires

        iv) Stimulation suited to consumers' power to organize his wants harmoniously

        v) Harmonious stimulation of commercial (or expensive) and non-commercial (or inexpensive) desires. Quantitative consumption v. qualitative living

      (*d*) Statistical study of costs of this form of guidance

      (*e*) Consumers' susceptibility varies with margin above absolute necessities; possible decrease in salesmanship outlays as result of war, and increased focusing of competition on price

      (*f*) Example: manufacturers' fixing of resale prices as subsidy to services of salesmanship

(g) Example: trading stamps. Gain largely
due to consumers' inability to estimate
worth of competitive inducements in the
less conspicuous form of concessions in
price or quality. Unnecessarily compli-
cates the consumer's decision. Is the Supreme Court right in saying it appeals to
less rational faculties than does advertising, or will the proof that advertising is
largely suggestion rather than information
lead to upholding possible further limitations in this general field?
c) Determination of styles
(1) Are producers responsible for frequency of
changes? (See 5.)
(2) If not, their control of channels in which
change is to run makes chiefly for regularizing
of production by determining demand in advance
d) Printed matter as aid to consumer
e) Professional sellers of guidance: doctors, etc.
f) Industrialized housekeeping (hotels, apartment-
houses, etc.) as substitutes for personal household
management. Effect on consumers' desires

3. Co-operative agencies
a) Co-operative retailing as eliminating many expensive features of competitive guidance
b) Informal co-operative buying
c) Co-operative housekeeping

4. Public agencies: functions viewed in light of foregoing
study of other agencies
a) Pure-commodities laws
(1) Information
(2) Prohibition of harmful goods
b) Standardization of consumption, especially in time
of war when economy and changes of habits of consumption become necessary, and if unguided might
endanger health. More standardization possible in

temporary emergency than would be endured as permanent policy, since the standardized health-values become temporarily paramount, and are in unusual danger

c) Education

d) Playgrounds, public recreation centers, social settlements, churches, etc., as agencies in formation of desires and offsets to guidance by pure commercial principles embodying social ideals

5. Social standards

a) Of prestige; display. Why do styles change so fast?

b) Of moderation, good taste, and reasonable economy

c) Of generosity and public spirit and other standards

C. Basis for Judgment of Existing System

Existing aims and ideals for the most part not attainable save by general social action, hence not sure to be adequately secured under "individualism." This applies even to "freedom" in a broad sense.

I. Maximum gratification of existing wants. Meaningless as standard to judge system of guidance of wants

II. Maximum fulfilment of innate tendencies of man. Needs fuller knowledge of what these are and effects of industrialism on them [55]

III. Individual freedom as an end in itself

IV. Individual health. If mental health included, it is not an individual matter, but one of social relationships. Society has stronger effective interest in health than individuals have. Its protection involves limitations on freedom

V. Growth in individual self-reliance. Conditions are

1. Chance to make mistakes in a wide range of important decisions, but not necessarily in all matters

2. Exposure to unpleasant results of mistakes with protection against demoralizing results so far as possible (not entirely possible nor entirely impossible; cf. modern

[55] Cf. paper by Carleton H. Parker, read at American Economic Association meeting at Philadelphia, December 28, 1917.

prison policy in attempt to make prison unpleasant but not demoralizing)
VI. Development of desirable types of citizenship
VII. In wholly standardized work, the most efficient system as judged by objective standards

6. CONCLUSION

The task of self-guidance which modern industry imposes is largely beyond the powers of the unaided individual, and the social need of large-scale co-operative guidance is largely beyond the reach of individualistic commercial incentives. Even so, the value of individual initiative in this field is so great that a change in any case may well be called on to bear its own burden of proof, a process in which the principles contained in the foregoing outline will play a decisive part. This outline is suggestive rather than complete. No attempt has been made to give full references to existing studies of the topics presented. The chief aim is to present an orienting method of approach and a framework of study. Needless to say, the carrying out of such studies is not to be accomplished by the methods of old-time "general theory." The burden of freedom from static assumptions and inquiries is not a light one.

V

ADAM SMITH AND THE CURRENTS OF HISTORY*

I. INTRODUCTION

THERE has recently been a revival of interest in that type of economics which interprets things in the light of their origins, the influences which have made them what they are, and the processes by which they have reached their present state. It is from this standpoint that I am asked to speak of Adam Smith. It is frequently said that the germs of all subsequent theories are to be found in his many-sided work, and accordingly one might fairly expect to find germs of this "genetic" type of thinking also. But in view of the fact that his system is in the main an exposition of the "natural laws" and of the "natural order" of liberty, we should naturally expect that such elements of the genetic method as we might find would be of a secondary and subordinate character. And this is, in fact, what we shall find.

But this is not the end of the story. Even more interesting and significant than the search for elements of the genetic method in Adam Smith is the application of this method to his work in its entirety, seeking to interpret his non-genetic theories and principles in the light of the influences which molded them and the forces and conditions to which they were a response. Such a study, if pursued in a captious mood

---

* Acknowledgments are due not only to the University of Chicago Press for permission to reprint this essay, but also to the Brookings Institution, which permitted the University of Chicago Press to use an essay incorporating portions of an earlier lecture delivered at the Brookings Institution and published by them in a volume entitled *The Spirit of '76*.

or without a sympathetic sense of values, may have a belittling effect, making social theories seem the playthings of historical accident and robbing their makers of the credit of orginality and independence. But if the research be animated by a more open-minded and appreciative spirit, great thought will emerge from the test with renewed vitality. Elements which otherwise seem merely quaint or perverse are revealed as natural adaptations to conditions of time and place, and often acquire a degree of pragmatic validity in relation to a given situation. Such a study does not invite us to accept such doctrines literally, or to reject them *in toto* if we cannot accept them, but rather to give our own thought a relation to the conditions and needs of our time similar to that which we find in the great constructive thought of the past. To understand such thought we must take into account the conditions of the time and what went before; to select from it the elements of value for our own use we must see it in relation to what has come after and to the changed conditions which now prevail. For the first purpose we must view Adam Smith in relation to an age in which factories were tiny, the machine was still hardly more than a machine tool, the competitive system was young and struggling against eighteenth-century mercantilism and survivals of medieval restrictions which had outlived their function. For present purposes we must view Smith's individualism in the light of such facts as railroads, holding-companies, centralized banking, business barometrics and giant power. The teleology of his "unseen hand" must be appraised in terms of Darwinism; its optimism in the light of modern psychiatry. Specific doctrines will be discredited, yet something, perhaps of more value, will remain.

The type of environmental interpretation of economic thought which is here attempted is far from a complete one.

It deals with the relation of that thought to the larger conditions of its time rather than with the more intimately personal factors and those of particular intellectual contacts which account for so many details of doctrine. On these matters you have already heard a distinguished and original contribution.

2. AN ENVIRONMENTAL INTERPRETATION OF ECONOMICS

The balance of forces in social life is continually shifting—between the few and the many; king, nobles and common people; between authority, science, and popular opinion or free personal choice; between the need of common action and the power of individual initiative; between capital and labor, etc. Existing institutions set the mold in which forces act, and govern their relative opportunities. And, with the familiar fact of institutional lag, they are likely to be adapted to the relative position of the forces as they were when the institutions took shape, a generation or a century or more in the past. They give weight to certain forces, usually not in proportion to their present strength or capacities.

Social thought may follow this emphasis, giving weight to those forces which are dominant in the institutions of the time—then it is "conservative." Or it may emphasize those forces which may become dominant in the millennium —then it is "utopian." Or it may emphasize those forces which are now in existence but to which prevailing institutions give inadequate outlet and recognition in proportion to their present importance and force—then it is "radical" or "progressive" and becomes the keynote of forward movements. Of this general sort was the social philosophy of Adam Smith.

This emphasis may be expressed in various forms, with

different degrees of dogmatism on the one side or careful qualification on the other. The practical partisan tends to one kind of statement, and the scientist or philosopher to others. But in either case, the same emphasis may be conveyed, whether in a fighting slogan which ignores all but one side of the case or in a scientific abstraction which focuses attention in certain directions and accomplishes its results by means more unobtrusive and more likely to be unsuspected. Furthermore, writers whose glimpse of truth is derived from conditions of time and place show a tendency—shall we follow Adam Smith and call it a "natural propensity"—to universalize their particular glimpse of truth. In so doing they often give it a far stronger appeal to the men of their own time; but by the same token they make it less adaptable and less likely to survive changing conditions and issues. Even the issues of one time are seldom so unified and simple that all of them can be correctly approached via any one principle of this universalized sort. An economics made up of such principles must either be inconsistent or be wrong part of the time; but if the economics of the past had refused to employ such principles, it would have refused its most effective weapons. Whatever way it takes out of this dilemma, later students can make the necessary allowances, with the help of historical hindsight. They must strip dogmas of their universality and interpret them in relation to time and place, because only thus can they give themselves a fair chance to sift out the elements of truth which the dogmas usually contain and to re-apply it to their own problems, so far as it may be applicable.

And what happens if the theory succeeds and new institutional adjustments are made which give the new forces the recognition for which they have striven? Then the theory passes into another stage in which it becomes the gospel of things as they are: a conservative rather than a radical force. Its continuing growth is likely to be self-perpetuating; new developments building on the theory itself and carrying it through to its logical conclusions. As to the disturbing forces of the new era, theory is likely to adapt itself to these with as little change as possible rather than make them the key-note of the system. And ultimately the process may have to be repeated.

In all this it is worth while emphasizing that the new theory, while it may be in accord with the manifest destiny of the time, does not therefore necessarily weigh things exactly according to their present force and importance. It must emphasize the things the age does not yet see, not those on which its institutions are consciously founded. Thus when Alfred Marshall speaks of self-reliant, deliberate, foresightful judgment as a fundamental characteristic of modern industrial life, he presumably has in mind the characteristics which are fundamental to an understanding of our more recent and conscious social adjustments; and he justifies this interpretation by seeking chiefly the characteristics which distinguish this age in contrast to previous ages.[1] What makes a thing fundamental for theory may be the fact that it is recent enough to raise problems of conscious readjustment.

This method of interpretation of economic doctrines leads, among other things, to the following maxim: To understand any forceful writer and to make the necessary allowances, find out what it was against which he was reacting. You may then expect to find the value of his message in the direction in which he is swaying the thought of his time, not in the exact distance to which he may carry it. As Smith himself

[1] See *Principles of Economics* (5th ed.), pp. 5-10.

said: "If the rod be bent too much one way, in order to make it straight you must bend it too much the other." He made this remark of the Physiocrats' emphasis on agriculture, but it applies quite as well to the emphasis on liberty which Smith and the Physiocrats had in common.

Furthermore, the errors and excesses of the prevailing system may be diagnosed by observation; but the corresponding errors and excesses of a system which is advocated and is not now in full force, must be largely matters of conjecture. Thus theories are likely to have greater scientific validity as reactions away from previous error than as embodiments of ultimate truth: they serve better to indicate a direction of motion than a final goal.

In the light of this approach, what was Adam Smith? He was the interpreter of the forces of economic liberty against certain types of restraints prevalent in the mid-eighteenth century, and of the interest of the country as a whole, viewed from a standpoint in which the common man had a large part, as against the exploitive interests of the particular classes then in power. And he had the rare fortune to stand at a changing-point of historical eras when the world stood ready to accept and use his ideas as part of a great economic transformation. Liberty was about to be supremely justified in the riches brought by the industrial revolution, especially to England, which took the lead in this movement. And the masses were about to gain political power, so far as voting equality could give it; a great increase in economic power; and the embodiment of their interests in the accepted ideal of economic policy: the good of the greatest number.

This theory of liberty has persisted into a new era when new issues are arising in bewildering variety; not so much taking the place of the older issues as added to them. So far as the older issues persist, the truths embodied in Smith's message persist also, but they cannot be expressed with the old degree of generality and emphasis. Fortunately, Smith has set the example, not of dogmatic and universal absolutes, but of a sane and balanced treatment of conflicting interests, consciously adjusted to the conditions and needs of his own time.

Let us now look in more detail, first at his environment, and then at his doctrines.

3. ADAM SMITH'S ENVIRONMENT

The close of the eighteenth century, which witnessed the publication of the *Wealth of Nations*, saw also the American Revolution, the French Revolution, and the Industrial Revolution. These marked the end of the first era of modern Nationalism and the beginning of the second, which appears already to have worked out its destiny in bringing us well into a third.

The epoch which was coming to its close in 1776 was that of dynastic-aristocratic Nationalism: the dark ages of modern times. It had passed through the heroic days of idealized buccaneering typified in Francis Drake, and had subsided into the more commercialized, calculating, and materialistic attitude which characterized the first half of the eighteenth century. One of the dominant forces was war, and the mutual rivalries of the various nations, viewed from the standpoint of dynastic aggrandizement, and with war never far in the background. Such nations naturally did not think in terms of mutual advancement in their dealings with one another; rather, a nation felt that it gained from the losses of its rivals, apart from its own absolute advancement in wealth or welfare. A large population, national self-sufficiency, and industries subserving the army and navy—all were ends in themselves; while a high level of wealth for the masses was not a goal of national policy but—strange as it may seem—rather the opposite, as expressed by numerous candid spokesmen of the dominant undemocratic materialism. Aggregate rather than per capita wealth was the economic goal.

Socially, education was still the privilege of the few, and the common people were rather frankly regarded as instruments of production, food for powder, and means of sustaining the elegance of the gentry. The state of humanitarian feeling may be exemplified by the death penalty for theft, replaced in practice by transportation, but remaining on the statute books. Liberty could have little meaning for the great majority. The chief practical exponents of increased freedom were the mercantile classes; and the liberty for which they spoke was not general liberty but particular liberties in which they had an interest. The increasing liberty of the masses, largely expressed in the substitution of the wage system for the feudal status, was hardly an articulate movement, or a part of the dominant philosophy of the time. Liberty of thought, however, already existed to a large extent in England, though in France the Mercantilist Abbé Galiani defined eloquence as the art of saying everything without going to the Bastille.

Politically, Englishmen had won rights and representation of which they were justly proud, but the system was far from democratic in theory or ideal in operation. The government was largely in the hands of the landed aristocracy, though seats in Parliament were marketable commodities which members of other classes were able to purchase. The methods of filling positions of public trust were marked by a certain genial inappropriateness which was saved from worse results chiefly by the fact that the landed gentry in their blundering and amateurish way still showed a well-meaning conscientiousness about fulfilling the responsibilities which their station placed upon them. (In France, the lack of this saving quality paved the way for the Revolution.) Commissions in the army were bought and sold; prisons were farmed out; and of government as a tool adapted to the enlightened discernment of social needs and the efficient prosecution of them, there was little trace. For such tasks the government of the time was not fitted; even less so than the government of today.

On the economic side, the early system of Nationalism was marked by a great increase in the scope of free contract and free exchange as compared to the medieval economy of local units, largely self-sufficing and governed to a great extent by status. In this local economy, rural tenants paid their customary dues in kind, and town craftsmen received their customary "just price" and controlled entry into their "mysteries." This idea of a "just price" was not applicable to distant trade, or indeed to any but dealings within a small and closely knit community; and it weakened with the increase of distant trade and disappeared with the transition from the gild craftsman to the capitalist employer. Free exchange in determining the prices of goods was paralleled by the wage system and contractual rents payable in money. The king built up his paid standing army in place of the feudal levies, and his strength began to be measured by his treasure rather than by lands, vassals, and retainers. The vast supply of precious metals from the New World reinforced the emphasis on specie, which was natural in this situation, and drew the nations into a conscious struggle for their share.

In this situation arose the well-known system of Mercantilism, which we think of as a system of restrictive control, but which was, from an historical standpoint, based on a transfer to the nation of controls previously exercised locally, in which process most of them were considerably relaxed. Within the boundaries of the nation, the principle and practice of free trade and exchange made great headway, as already indicated, despite the retarding effect of many survivals of earlier restrictions, including apprentice laws, the law of parish settlements in England, and local customs duties in France.

Early Nationalism strove to keep money in the country by the direct and crude method of prohibitions on the export of specie. These not only proved unworkable but they unduly restricted trade and were opposed by the growing interests of the mercantile classes. These interests found in the theory of the balance of trade a defense for their desire for a greater degree of freedom, harmonizing it with the accepted notion of the importance of conserving the specie supply and showing how the traders could be permitted certain kinds of profitable trade while the country's interest in its money supply would be promoted more effectually than before.

This theory represented a rudimentary form of scientific economics, examining the effects of transactions and policies in order to show how desired results could be better obtained by indirect than by direct means, taking advantage of the natural laws of exchange and utilizing them. Thus the balance-of-trade theory was not solely the result of a desire for increased specie, but rather a combination of this with the merchants' direct interest in greater freedom of trade. But it served the interests of freedom only to a limited extent, and it was not to be expected that this material interest would remain permanently content with the precise degree of freedom which this theory justified.[2] It was a compromise, representing a temporary and unstable equilibrium between the various interests concerned. It did not represent the interests of consumers, for whom Adam Smith spoke, nor did it regard trade fundamentally as an instrument for the acquisition of more goods for all to enjoy.

In the meantime, the same forces which built the national economy were developing the basis for a more democratic view and a more inclusive treatment of interests. The disruption of feudal status ushered in a struggle for a new adjustment of the powers of different classes, from which the people at large could not be permanently excluded. As they gained political representation, their economic interests could not longer be ignored, though at first they were spoken for largely by members of other classes, animated by the humanitarian sentiments which began to be respectable as the democratic movement proceeded. From this time on, Mercantilist economics, or any economics expressing solely or primarily the interests of the mercantile classes, could not hold an uncontested supremacy.

The new economy was also laying the basis for the development of scientific economics as we know it: a more or less quantitative study of the natural results of a system based on free exchange. In medieval times, free exchange was most evident in distant trade, and distant trade was adventurous and speculative to an extent which almost precluded the observation of quantitative regularities. Interest on loans for sea commerce, besides being concealed to avoid the laws against usury, contained such a large element of premium for risk that the interest-component was indis-

---

[2] The main features of this interpretation are similar to that of Alfred Marshall. See his *Principles of Economics* (5th ed.), Appendix B, "The Growth of Economic Science," esp. p. 755.

tinguishable. Manufacturing capital consisted of the simple tools of the craftsman; and domestic loans were largely for non-productive purposes. It is not safe to assume that the laws of supply and demand were wholly atrophied in domestic trade, but the restraints on mobility prevented them, under ordinary conditions, from getting far out of line with the customary standards which the medieval system enforced as just.

But with the broadening of the economic unit to national size, and the development of domestic free exchange and competition, profits and interest became more distinguishable and more nearly standardized; and wages also reached something like a system of levels under the visible operation of the laws of supply and demand. The loan for productive purposes began to take the place of the loan for consumption, as the typical form of transaction; and interest became a more regular thing, with an observable relation to business earnings. In short, more and more regularities were appearing in the unregulated behavior of economic phenomena, governed by the principle of self-interest and checked by competition and the forces of demand and supply. Thus the subject matter of economics took on a shape susceptible of analysis into laws of a scientific character, as they are generally understood.

Meanwhile the concept of laws in social life had been set up as a goal by the Encyclopedists; and the Physiocrats identified the natural order with the order of liberty; and both with the most efficient development of society. With this weapon they attacked not only the restrictions of Mercantilism but also the hideously unjust, corrupt, and inefficient tax system—or rather tax chaos—then prevailing in France. The system laid crippling burdens on trade and enterprise, and especially on the labor of the peasants; and

exempted the church and the landowning aristocracy. Thus
Physiocracy was an attack on the greatest vested interests
of the time, though it was sugar-coated by the argument that
these interests already bore the ultimate burdens of taxation
and that if they should bear them directly they would
actually have more left than before, on account of the
increased productivity which would result from removing
the burdens on work and enterprise. Whatever may have
been the intellectual roots of this idea, it seems clear that
without such a sugar-coating no doctrinal attack on the
exemptions of the privileged classes could have failed to
bring its advocates to the Bastille.

The Physiocrats were still monarchists, believing in the
enlightened sovereign who should follow the laws of the
natural order as the conductor of an orchestra follows the
laws of musical harmony. This again was the only safe form
of liberalism in France at that time. Thus the very features
of Physiocracy which we cannot accept, were, consciously or
unconsciously, adaptations to environment, marking this as
the only liberal doctrine which could be openly advocated
at that time and place. Even so, the beginnings of a practical
application of Physiocratic principles, by Turgot, was more
than the privileged interests would tolerate; and his reforms
were promptly extinguished. France was not ready for freedom through reason, but had to wait for a political revolution, after which the peculiar conditions no longer existed
which had given appropriateness to the peculiar features of
Physiocratic doctrine, and the principle of liberty naturally
found its expression in a different form.

The vogue of the Physiocratic doctrine bears witness to
the readiness of the world to listen to ideas of liberty despite
obscurities and extravagances which taxed human credulity.
Elsewhere, other general advocates of liberty were being

heard, and the way was paved for Adam Smith's synthesis of liberty and economic science. This, then, was the situation, and these were the issues at which his thinking was directed. And his mind grasped them largely, constructively, and on the side of human progress. He was great in the sense of being the child of his time, but the child of its unsatisfied urges rather than of its established complacencies.

While the issues of the time furnished the material and governed the trend of his thinking, the thought of the time gave him tools with which he worked and preconceptions with which he approached his task. One of these was the idea of an order of nature, to be found by searching nature itself for the universal or the original. He was in the current of a notable revival of liberal thought in the Scotch universities; and from Hutcheson he had the opportunity to absorb, among other things, the idea of the good of the greatest number. His personal bent led him to amass a great array of facts, so that he has been called the best-informed man since Aristotle. In either case, it is only fair to judge the accuracy of the information in the light of available sources and prevailing standards in the matter of verification. Aristotle's equipment of "facts" included many an astounding fable.

Smith also had a considerable historical perspective, seeking for the roots things have in the past. He was a realist; hence he never forgot such facts as the existence of classes; but his standards of welfare looked beyond the mere *fait accompli* of present power and took in the welfare of the undistinguished masses, giving them in an unspectacular way more fundamental importance than the ambitions of the rich. And this, needless to say, marks a great advance on the Mercantilist attitude.

4. ADAM SMITH'S DOCTRINES

Not all of Adam Smith's specific doctrines, of course, are direct attempts to puncture Mercantilist fallacies or to set up antitheses to them. But most of them have some relation, direct or indirect, to this great controversy. And one fancies, in reading the *Wealth of Nations,* that where the relation is most direct the style acquires an added zest which is very revealing. Smith reveled in exposing the false standards of economic policy which served to mask the interests of particular producing classes and in setting up instead the basic standard of producing more goods for people at large to consume.

Money, instead of being a great desideratum, was with him a tool, of which it was as wasteful to use more than was needed as it would be to use two wagons to haul one load. This dethroning of money as an end of all things probably carried with it a certain underestimate of its importance as a tool: an error which we are now attempting to rectify. Exports were not good in themselves, nor were imports in themselves forms of economic calamity; rather imports were goods to be consumed, and exports were the means of securing imports and paying for them. To secure general acceptance of this view was no small contribution. By defining Mercantilism in terms of its monetary notions, Smith put its most vulnerable aspect foremost and not only strengthened his case against it but enabled himself, without evident inconsistency, to adopt some of the sounder standards of national policy on which the mercantile system in a larger sense was built.

His own ideas, then, of the ends of economic policy were a mixture, in which anti-Mercantilist elements held the central place, while other special purposes were allowed as justifying particular departures from the general rule of laissez faire. In setting up consumable goods as the prime desideratum, he also adopted the criterion of per capita rather than aggregate wealth, but this standard finds little reflection in his later discussions of those methods of production which set a maximum amount of productive labor in motion. He also urges that it is only just that those who feed, clothe, and lodge the whole society (it is labor which does this) should themselves be tolerably well fed, clothed, and lodged. And he nowhere expresses similar solicitousness for the consumption of the rich! He does not claim that all men are equal, though he does consider the difference between a philosopher and a street porter mostly a matter of environment.

A characteristic example of his point of view is found in his treatment of the struggle with the American colonies. He minimized the burdens laid on the colonists, but condemned the restrictions as violations of "natural rights." And he gave decisive weight to the inevitable pressure of the minority of "natural leaders" in the colonies toward a chance to make the most of their talents and position. This affords an almost ironic contrast to the language of a certain great Declaration which these same "natural leaders" were then on the point of signing. Though Smith shared the belief that men were *born* (approximately) equal, his practical mind solved problems in terms of the inequalities they acquired after birth. In these terms he not only argued for giving the colonies (or their "natural leaders") representation in Parliament, but calmly contemplated the time when they would outweigh the British Isles and when the capital might be moved across the Atlantic!

On the other hand, he not only reacts against Mercantilism and attacks its premises and standards; he also borrows some of its less controversial features. He recognizes national ends as vital. "Defense is more important than opulence," and economic measures looking to this end are justifiable. They must, however, appear in their true colors and not pose as means of economic gain when they are really economic burdens undergone for the sake of a more important end. He is a Nationalist, though his Nationalism is not primarily invidious, being colored by his philosophy of mutual gain in international exchange. But when he justifies the Navigation Acts, invidious Nationalism certainly enters in, and the rivalry between England and Holland is continually before his eyes. While he does at times suggest viewing the world as one economic society, he thinks prevailingly of the societies we actually have. He is a Nationalist because he is a realist.

But perhaps the strongest feature of his work—unless it be his mass of descriptive evidence—is the strengthening of its claims to scientific standing by the theory of value and distribution which forms, in one sense, the backbone of his book. This theory seems not to be related to specific points in the Mercantilist controversy, though it has an indirect relation. Smith's labor measure of value helps to bring into relief changes in the value of specie, and this in turn helps to weaken the claims of money to the homage formerly paid it. And the theory of the tendency of values to natural levels is part of a system of natural equilibrium whose naturalness carries some weight of approval. The tendency toward equalization of the real attractiveness of different occupations is part of this system and helps it to appear good as well as natural. The mere fact that Smith's individualism is part of the argument which centers around the science of value lends it a certain force.

But logically there are conspicuously weak points in the

chain of connection between these two ideas, and the individualism is logically far more independent of the value theory than is usually supposed. And Smith's theory of value was not sufficiently coherent or complete to afford a permanently adequate basis for the science of economics. From our present standpoint his individualism would be weakened rather than strengthened by being made to rest on this as its sole foundation.

The annual revenue of the society consists of the "exchangeable value" of the commodities produced; and a large revenue of this sort is desirable, though admittedly it does not measure the utilities received. This end is to be promoted by putting in motion as much productive labor as possible and allotting this labor between the different branches of production in accord with the strength of the respective demands. But demand, as a criterion of what is socially desirable, remains unsupported, hanging in the air. Thus under critical examination, Smith's rule of laissez faire finds but weak support in his theory of value.

It is more directly supported by a number of more practical observations. Smith noted that scarcities of foodstuffs seldom degenerated into famine if supplies were free to distribute themselves in response to demand; or rather, he noted that where famines occurred, there was always some obstacle to the free movement of supplies from less afflicted regions. As to standards of workmanship, he stated that the customer is the best source of trade discipline—better, that is, than the rules of gilds or of national officers. Would he have maintained this faith in the modern era of synthetic substitutes and jerry-building? He argued that freedom of international trade brought the consumers more goods: a proposition not fundamentally dependent on any one theory of value.

Another aspect of the extra-logical character of his individualism is seen in his theory of human nature. He did not believe in the competence of man's reason to guide and control his destiny. In the "Theory of Moral Sentiments" we learn that nature implants impulses in man's breast which are wiser than his reason, since nature intends always the good of the species and endows man with social sentiments. And this despite the fact that the "Theory of Moral Sentiments" is as full of vices as of virtues. The pursuit of happiness through wealth is delusive, but justified by its results through this same wisdom of nature. Yet its results include the stultifying effects of the subdivision of labor on the mass of routine laborers, of which Smith in one passage draws a truly appalling picture. Why select the good effects as those which nature intends? If one replies that the benevolent order of nature was an idea which Smith absorbed from his contemporaries, this merely forces us back to the question why this idea was growing in force at this time. Was it not perhaps fundamentally because this aspect of economic liberty was precisely the one which at this time most needed to be interpreted to a world whose established order was built on its negation? If so, an interesting conclusion follows. We of today have no such justification for giving this idea the same place in our economics that Smith gave it in his.

The "invisible hand" did not prevent Smith from making many departures from laissez faire. He followed it only so far as the facts appeared to him to warrant. And the warrant of facts was found chiefly in the errors of Mercantilism, of the apprentice laws, of the law of parish settlements, and other outworn restrictions on the general liberty to choose one's trade and to produce what the market might demand. The superiority of natural liberty is really a relative superiority: relative to the forms of control then in vogue and to the existing capabilities of private enterprise. And Smith continually falls back on such comparisons to support it.

5. WAS SMITH A GENETIC ECONOMIST?

To what extent did Smith himself appreciate the relation between economic doctrine and the forces of history which lie back of it? And to what extent was he a "genetic economist"? As to the first question, it seems clear that if he had regarded his doctrines as no more than the reflection of a particular and passing historical situation, they would have been robbed of their greatest effect. And as to the question of Smith's claims to rank as a genetic economist, the answer may hinge on the choice of a definition. And a fair definition for the purpose in hand is not easy, since to the modern mind the term "genetic" has a content which it could not possibly have had to anyone who lived and died in the eighteenth century. It implies explaining things in terms of the conditions out of which they arose. And a genetic economist would naturally be one in whom this element is so fundamental as to give him a sense of the relativity of all institutions to the circumstances of their origin. To this the modern mind adds the idea of endless evolution, not directed by rational purpose toward any previsioned end nor explainable by a tendency toward any ultimate "natural" system. Purposes are among the impelling forces, but are not supreme; and none of them explains the ultimate outcome. Indeed there is no outcome that can be called ultimate. It is clear at the start that no economics can be fully "genetic" in which the purposes of nature and the "natural order" of liberty play so basic a part as they do in the system of Adam Smith.

Smith's treatment of origins falls partly in the class of

"hypothetical history," serving mostly to explain how the forces of "natural liberty" might have operated under primitive conditions. His "propensity to truck and barter" must probably be placed in this class, on account of its slight basis in actual historical evidence. Here also belongs his rationalized picture of exchange leading to the division of labor in a hunting society and to a labor basis of value under primitive conditions. Here also belongs his idea that rent arises when all the land is owned and his discussion of the origins of money. It is noticeable that he takes legal tender as an institution for granted, the only question being what materials had this quality in different stages of development.

But Smith deals far more with actual than with hypothetical history. He traces the policy of Europe from the fall of Rome, showing how it has consistently favored town as against country industry. He holds that this has been the result of the prejudices of different classes, but has given rise to different systems of political economy. This is a truly genetic point of view, but he stops short of applying it to his own system. Even Mercantilism he interprets, as we have seen, too much in terms of a single dogma about money and too little in terms of its whole institutional setting and purport.

He discusses at length the development of water trade, how ancient civilizations centered around the Mediterranean, and how commerce led to a taste for the finer manufactures. But all this appears to be in support of his general doctrine that the division of labor is limited by the extent of the market. He also traces the different progress of opulence in the different nations; but he finds therein a natural order of development, the reflection of his static "natural order," often thwarted and distorted by human institutions. Indeed, this is the light in which institutions are typically mentioned.

He thinks of productivty as relative to the development of institutions, for he speaks of countries as having developed the full degree of productiveness which their institutions permit; but here again the stage of development of institutions is regarded in the light of a greater or less approximation to the system of natural liberty. More promising is his discussion of the manner in which commerce leads the rich to buy goods rather than keep retainers, leading to a surrender of their power and permanence of position; but even here one seems to see the change as a setting free of the forces of natural liberty from the trammels of customary status.

To sum up: Smith used genetic evidence, and it lent his system much of its strength. It gave him a sense of the relativity of institutions—some institutions—those which thwarted the laws of natural liberty, but not those which followed these laws. And it gave him a sense of the relativity of systems of political economy—some systems, but not his own. It gave him a sense of probable future change, but only toward a predetermined goal. The germs of a genetic treatment are there, but they are tributary and subordinate to the system of natural liberty.

6. THE SPIRIT OF SMITH IN THE LIGHT OF LATER CONDITIONS

The immediate success of Adam Smith's views in England, especially in the practical work of freeing her from the restraints he attacked, undoubtedly had much to do with the fact that class interests had shifted and no longer required these restraints. But this topic belongs to a later lecture in this series. Let us pass, then, to the question: What can we learn from Smith today? Viewing the heritage he has left us in the light of its origins, how much can we keep? The most fundamental thing to preserve is the thing which gave his thought its power and vitality; namely, its grasp on the interests of his time to which the institutions of the time gave inadequate opportunity and expression. And since these interests and institutions have changed greatly in a century and a half, our answer must change correspondingly; otherwise we shall not be imitating Smith in the most significant sense.

The theory which traces its lineage most directly to Adam Smith has now reached that second stage of development in which it expresses the forces on which the prevailing order is consciously built. It takes care of certain interests, as the theory of the balance of trade did; but it is not sufficiently comprehensive for modern conditions. In the first place, Mercantilism is still with us, complicated by the abnormal state of international indebtedness. This affords ample opportunity for pouring new facts into the mold of Smith's analysis and for renewing his outspoken exposures of false standards, inconsistency, and unworkability. But these matters are less paramount; other issues have grown to an even more insistent importance, especially those of industrial relations and the control of large-scale industry.

There have been immense developments of control in the interests of labor, which Smith said were always just. But we must remember that the reason he gave was that these regulations must run the gauntlet of a government which represented the employing interests, and that this reason no longer holds good to anything like the same extent. Universal suffrage has given an opposite bias, against which the employing interests wage a struggle, with varying fortunes.

Our intellectual tools and preconceptions have also developed. In Smith's time the world was just awakening to a scrutiny of institutions and retained a bias toward justifying them by finding that they were in accord with original nature. Since then we have passed through the age of Bentham, who would test them by their results, but who viewed them too much as bits of machinery to be tinkered with at the will of the tinkerer. We are now realizing that while they are not eternally natural in any one form, they are the results of natural forces, both of change and of stability. And while we still submit them to Bentham's test, we cannot hope to mend their shortcomings by a light-hearted shifting of gears or substitution of rolls. We must study them as living things and influence their growth by indirect as well as by direct means, expecting many failures and disappointments.

The modern economist, like Smith, is forced to use the yardstick of price for what it may be worth; but he is developing statistical data and techniques which enable him to study the physical quantities that lie behind the money measure and to supplement it in other ways. Like Smith, we may recognize standards of welfare and of public policy independent of price: and at present we are returning to an attitude more like his in that we do not trust the all-sufficiency of reason, but lay increasing emphasis on the impulses. One school builds its chief criterion of welfare out of the "impulses implanted by nature." But, needless to say, the eighteenth-century concept of nature has been revolutionized by Darwinism. Darwinism justifies the idea that nature intends the good of the species only so far as the environment remains substantially the same as that in which the present human characters were developed. Our fitness to the new environment which we ourselves have made remains an open question and a serious one.

One thing we must, of course, reject is Smith's idea that corporations cannot operate industry efficiently. But if we wish to develop the best capabilities of these organizations, we have not yet done with the sources of weakness he pointed out. We can no longer be content to take corporations for granted as artificial economic men and build on them a pseudo-individualism which Smith himself would have instantly rejected. On this point perhaps the best model for a would-be follower of today is found in his discussion of an established church. He approves of small-scale competitive enterprise in religion on the basis of its effects on the actual individuals engaged—both clergy and parishioners.

The modern economist who would follow the lead of Smith must be alert to new alignments of classes, to their conflicting interests and to the habits of mind and limitations of intelligence which they exhibit. He will not be a doctrinaire democrat or a socialist. He will neither despise government nor idealize it as the all-sufficient social agency. He must strike for himself some balance between the new departmentalized representative government and the new integrated industry; between the liberties of individuals, increased industrial output, and the pressure of various brands of "natural leaders" toward scope for their talents.

Above all, he must search for interests which have outgrown the customary avenues of expression. And in the light of this search he may modify Smith's attitude toward trade associations and other co-operative agencies; indeed, Smith's purely negative attitude is now clearly untenable. We must recognize the dangers of group power and selfishness, but we must also see the part such agencies are playing and are destined to play in preventing evils and injuries which unregulated free exchange does not prevent and in protecting interests which it leaves unprotected.

Indeed, the modern follower of the spirit of Smith might be justified in concentrating his emphasis on such controlling, moralizing, and associative agencies, not because the principle of free exchange has lost its validity, but because these moralizing agencies are the things which are new and undeveloped, relative to the place they seem destined to fill. On the other hand, so long as mercantilism persists and revolutionary communism remains an active possibility, the basic serviceability of free exchange cannot safely be left wholly out of sight. The range of alternatives to which our economics must be relevant has increased. Between the "thesis" of free exchange and the "antithesis" of communism we are challenged to build up a working synthesis which may have a relation to the needs of our time similar in kind, if not in genius, to that achieved by Adam Smith. One may even conjecture what the keynote of the synthesis will be: the building of moralized economic communities, expressing and protecting by appropriate agencies all the essential interests concerned.

But whatever one's conclusion may be on that point, it seems clear that we also stand at a changing-point of historical eras. The raw materials for a new synthesis lie temptingly about us; and the place it can fill, if successful, can hardly be over estimated. We face a need no less insistent and an opportunity no less commanding than that which was so greatly met by a certain absent-minded Scotch professor in the year 1776.

VI

THE RELATION BETWEEN STATICS AND DYNAMICS*

I. FORECAST OF THE ARGUMENT

THE task which forms the subject of this essay is essentially that of one who wishes to carry forward the work of his greatest teacher from the point at which that teacher left it. From this standpoint the main problem is how to proceed from static to dynamic economics. This problem will be viewed in the light of the fact that we possess a substantially complete static economics, while dynamics is in its infancy; of the further fact that statics is essentially provisional, a stepping-stone to dynamics, simplifying the problem by attacking first those features which do not involve change; and of the final fact that dynamics must restore realism by putting in everything that statics leaves out, so far as possible within the limits of human understanding.

In this view of the purpose of statics and the scope of dynamics, the writer is directly following his father's teachings on these matters. Naturally, in attempting to do justice to such an all-inclusive view of dynamics, it becomes necessary to utilize material derived from a multitude of sources, often widely divergent in character.

As to method of procedure, the question arises whether we should start with static conclusions, add dynamic elements one at a time and make allowances for the resulting "disturbances" of static equilibrium, or whether we should

* Reprinted from *Economic Essays in Honor of John Bates Clark,* edited by Jacob Hollander, by permission of The Macmillan Company.

follow a more fundamental method, going back to the premises and replacing static by dynamic assumptions and then building upon them. This will, of course, require inductive methods in establishing the premises of a dynamic study; after which the problem remains whether, having got such premises, we shall be in a position to proceed deductively, or whether more induction will be necessary in reaching the conclusions of the dynamic study. The further question arises, to what extent it will be found that dynamics differs from statics not merely in its conclusions but also in its problems.

In pursuing this question we shall first look at the origin of statics, finding it in one out of a considerable number of problems with which classical economics dealt. The development, however, of a complete static society, causes statics to reach out into the realms of the other problems, where this static method of approach is not so clearly indicated. It also appears that the conclusion of the more developed statics—the level of static equilibrium—is, in the earlier forms of the study, essentially an assumption based on observation; and the assumptions of the later form of the theory are, in a real sense, deduced from it, being the conditions necessary to bring it about. Thus the relations of premise to conclusion may with propriety be reversed, or the entire structure be regarded as an assumption, to be justified by its usefulness in interpreting facts of experience.

So far as dynamic conditions differ from static in mechanical ways only, static conclusions may be converted into dynamic by quantitative allowances; but so far as the differences are qualitative or "chemical" in character—to use the figure employed by John Stuart Mill,[1] the more far-reaching

[1] John Stuart Mill: *A System of Logic*, Book III, Chap. VI; Book VI, Chap. VII. J. B. Clark also uses this figure. See *The Philosophy of Wealth*, p. 33.

methods are indicated, and new inductions are likely to be necessary.

In examining the assumptions proper to dynamics, these are found in many cases to differ from static premises in qualitative or "chemical" ways; including the dynamic character of human nature and the evolution of institutions. The result is to broaden the scope and modify the character of the study. The work of J. B. Clark includes examples of both the narrower deductive and the broader qualitative modifications of statics. The former are found in his *Essentials of Economic Theory*, while the most challenging fragments of the broader type of study are contained in his earlier work: *The Philosophy of Wealth*.

If dynamics must be built largely by new inductions, what will be left of statics? In the first place, dynamics will never answer all its problems, and the static answers, provisional as they are, will to that extent continue to fill their former place. In the second place, in relation to the original static problem of levels of prices, much can be done by quantitative modifications of static formulas. And in the third place, throughout dynamics there will arise situations which will be clarified by a reference to a set of static assumptions—not necessarily a complete static economy— for purposes of comparison. This will probably, more often than not, take the form of that kind of inverse deduction already mentioned; the reasoning running thus: to bring about such-and-such results, such-and-such conditions are necessary. Actual conditions differ in such-and-such respects. Hence we should expect actual results to differ in such-and-such general ways. Or, if actual results differ in given fashion from the static, a probability arises that the difference is due to the discrepancy of conditions from the static ones.

This is a use of static reasoning eminently suited to dynamic studies.

2. ORIGIN OF STATICS

The contrast which we are considering is between realistic economics and economics simplified by the method of static abstraction, which studies levels of equilibrium under abstract conditions. These make equilibrium possible (1) by eliminating elements of disturbance and (2) by confining the adaptive forces and processes to those which are self-limiting and not cumulative in character. Static economics, of one sort at least, is complete in its main outlines. It is not wholly past the stage of controversy, nor of further developments, but the controversies are largely matters of proper formulation rather than of the essential logic of the main structure; and the further developments, aside from reformulations, are matters of detailed refinement whose accuracy is hardly justified in view of the wide gap between the assumed conditions on which the whole structure rests and the reality in the interpretation of which its ultimate service must lie. The significant field for present work lies in the development of more realistic economics, which may be defined, in contradistinction to statics, as dynamics. Unlike statics, dynamics is in its infancy, and very possibly is destined always to remain in that stage, on account of the fact that conditions change so fast and so endlessly that analysis and interpretation cannot overtake them.

But the difference between statics and dynamics is not merely a matter of simplification of the data of the problem. This simplification has its roots in something deeper; a delimitation of the problem itself. Hence we should be prepared, in stepping outside the limitations of statics, for an enlargement of the scope of our problems as well as of our data. The relation of statics to the scope of economic problems can be seen by a consideration of its origin.

The most highly developed form of static economics, that of J. B. Clark, arose out of the attempt to make explicit the real assumptions underlying the search of the classical economists for "natural" levels of prices, and of their "component parts," wages, rent and profits.[2] But this is not the one all-embracing problem in the classical economics. We may distinguish six major problems or groups of problems, arranging them roughly in the order of the emphasis they receive in *The Wealth of Nations*. First is the theory of national efficiency from which the book derives its title: the search for the most efficient system of organization of the production of wealth on a national scale, and for the policies appropriate to put this system into effect. Second is the search for the "natural" levels of prices, wages, rent and profits. (With Ricardo, this takes first place in emphasis.) Third comes a study of the variations of economic behavior from the type indicated by the "natural" levels of things. Fourth comes the relation of economic quantities to utility or to human well-being. Fifth is the question how things came to be as they are—here belongs Smith's "propensity to truck and barter," and his discussion of the order of development of town and country industry. With this should probably be grouped speculations as to the future. And sixth comes the question of the justification of the underlying institutions, such as property. This is, of course, inseparable from the first question, but the nature of the connection appears to have been seen but dimly. Smith's theory of national efficiency is at once a conditional justification of private property and free contract, and dependent for its validity upon the proper operation of these institutions. But with Smith

[2] J. B. Clark, *Distribution of Wealth*, Preface, p. vi.

they are taken for granted as natural rights, and the full nature of this problem was not realized, at least in this country, until it was forced on our attention by the evolution of these institutions, bringing visible changes in the content of legal rights, to meet economic needs and protect economic interests. In other words, this problem has little meaning until it takes a dynamic, rather than a static, form.

Of these six groups of questions, one is in its very nature static—the search for "natural" levels of prices, etc. Two are in their very nature dynamic—the study of "whence" and "whither," and that of departures from the "natural" levels of things. These three between them constitute the more impartially descriptive section of the inquiry. The other three groups of questions are evaluative—the relation of economic quantities to utility and to human welfare, the theory of national efficiency and the justification of the underlying institutions. The more one considers these questions, the more is one convinced that in this realm dynamic considerations are paramount; until one may even doubt whether the questions have workable meaning apart from dynamic change. But the question of utility and welfare has received a static answer in the marginal utility theory; and the static economics colors the view of the other two questions, as we shall see.

With Smith and Ricardo there was a loose and uncertain connection between the law of the natural level of price, on the one hand, and the three evaluative problems, on the other. Price did not measure utility; and while wages-cost was thought to be an approximate measure of labor's sacrifices of production, even this idea did not stand the scrutiny which led to Mill's statement that the hardest work is often the poorest paid, and to Cairnes' theory of non-competing groups. Ricardo specifically separated "value" from "riches," or the abundance of goods. So long as the search for "natural levels" of price and of the shares of distribution is in a rudimentary stage, and its premises not fully realised or expressed, it remains simply one out of a number of major problems, each of which is dealt with in such terms as appear appropriate. The static character of the one problem does not necessarily govern the treatment of the others. The comparative independence of the theory of value and the theories of welfare and of efficiency is a striking feature of the early classical economics.

The early theory of institutions was static in a slightly different sense. They were taken for granted as natural, and even after Bentham dethroned this view, private property and contract were looked at as "unit characters," so to speak: things with fixed characteristics, which might be wholly kept or wholly discarded in favor of public ownership or communism, and which were to be justified or condemned *in toto*. An evolutionary view, on the other hand, raises an endless number of problems which the static view leaves out of sight, and calls for justification of one form of an institution as compared to other possible forms, and for a weighing of the interests protected by one definition of rights as against the interests protected by another.

Returning to the questions of welfare and efficiency, their early independent character has been vitally affected by two great developments. One is the Benthamite utilitarianism and its natural sequel, the marginal utility theory of value. The other is the development of the search for "natural levels" into a substantially complete static picture of society: one in which "natural levels" would exist, would be stable, would be attained. This hypothetical society has its characteristics and laws of efficiency, and of the relation of price to welfare, and thus statics enlarges its scope and annexes new ranges of problems. The means used to approach the problem of levels of price becomes, as a by-product of its own fuller working out, a source of provisional answers to these other questions which were not originally cast in a static mold. Is the static method as appropriate to these other questions as to the original one? Without prejudging this question, for or against, we should preserve an open-minded attitude on it, and be prepared for the possibility of finding that dynamic economics may need to re-establish the autonomous position of these various problems. Not a complete isolation, it goes without saying. We should also be prepared to find old problems taking new forms, and new problems arising, suggested by the new ranges of data which dynamics forces us to consider.

3. THE PROBLEMS OF DYNAMIC ECONOMICS

The key to statics, as we have seen, is a problem: that of levels of equilibrium. This is an abstraction based on observation of the relative stability of economic values, and of oscillations whose behavior suggests a normal level toward which the economic forces of gravity exert their pull. The key to dynamics is a different problem: that of processes which do not visibly tend to any complete and definable static equilibrium. The importance of this shift from the search for levels to the study of processes can hardly be overemphasised; it is not less significant than the change from static to dynamic conditions. It might be interesting to try the experiment of assuming static conditions, except that prices, shares in distribution and the allotment of productive factors are not at their static levels, and then to focus attention on the processes by which the ensuing adjustments will be made as economic forces seek their levels. Carried out with vision and imagination, such a study would go a long way toward the development of dynamics.

Dynamics, then, is not limited to the examination of the discrepancies between actual values and their static levels. Nor is its study of processes to be confined within the sub-ject-matter of value and distribution as such; since these processes reach out into all aspects of life. To illustrate this, we might start with the narrowest possible problem that can be called dynamic: that of discrepancies between actual values and their static levels, and see how far this problem will carry us in the search for a solution.

Why do prices seldom reach their supposed static level and never remain there? The answer involves the whole baffling problem of the business cycle. Among the causes of this phenomenon are, apparently, original disturbances from outside the economic system proper; such as wars or climatic cycles affecting agriculture; but the character of the cycle is more directly determined by the processes through which the business system adjusts itself to these disturbing forces. Here it appears that there are not merely forces of the kind which may be described as self-limiting, but others of the cumulative sort, and that the self-limiting factors do not operate effectually until after the cumulative forces have driven things so far that a reaction is produced, which in turn goes so far as to produce another revulsion. The study of this process leads into the realms of the credit mechanism— or organism—markets and contracts, the interrelations of debtor and creditor interests, and of buyer and seller inter-ests, technical factors governing the behavior of costs of production under conditions of varying output, forms of contracts governing the financial incidence of these varia-tions, the relative responsiveness of labor costs to such changes and, underlying this, all the elements of bargaining position, customary standards and other psychological elements influencing the behavior of wages, and many other factors. In short, the problem reaches out into the fields of technical production, of human nature and of social institutions. We are carried, for instance, into a treatment of wage levels (and of limitation of output) in terms of the ever-present fact of unemployment rather than in terms of the theoretical tendency of supply and demand to become equal.

Or, if we search for the causes of discrepancies of utility and disutility from their static standards, we are not merely led into the whole question of human nature, but into the processes by which, and the conditions under which, decisions are made: into the nature and adequacy of available alternatives and their relation to the reality of competition, into the elements of compulsion in "free" exchange, into the changing character of the human costs of industry, as affecting body, nerves, morale and social relations, into advertising and the whole system of economic guidance, into standardized contracts and the force of law and custom in determining the incidental terms of contracts; the whole culminating in a picture of the biased and imperfect character of the market as a means for the expression, furthering and protection of different kinds of interests, and the need of other forms of protection than those afforded by "free" contract.

From another angle, if we study "dynamic friction" we are led into the whole question of the processes of bargaining and negotiation, with their weapons of maneuvring and obstruction, of information and concealment, of offering and withholding, and of the effect of it all on the underlying processes of production—something which can probably never be reduced to measurement. This opens up the area explored, for instance, by Veblen in his *Theory of Business Enterprise*. In short, we are led into all the aspects of economic life and its essential conditioning human facts and institutions; and if not into evaluative judgments, at least into those facts and relationships on which such judgments must, if they are intelligent, be based.

4. DYNAMICS OF HUMAN NATURE

The static view of man is embodied in the marginal utility theory. This is an advance on the classical view in two respects. (1) Instead of focusing on self-interest and the reproductive instinct, it allows for all the motives of man, while remaining simple enough for deductive treatment. (2) It is an answer to the classical conclusion that price could not be a measure of utility, because coal, for example, has more utility than diamonds, but less value. As a rebuttal of this blank negative, establishing an approximate relation between price and utility, the theory is true. While it is, as has been said, a natural derivative from the Bentham psychology, it does not depend on the "calculus of pleasure and pain," but can be presented in terms of any other description of human motives; so long as the motives behave in a certain way. The essential assumption is that the individual has a scale of values or preferences: good or bad, wise or foolish, conscious or unconscious; and that his various economic acts are the expressions of this one scale of values.[3] They are consistent; the scale holds while he is making the various decisions which are involved in the budgeting of his time, energy and resources.[4] Thus the values in his personal economy reach an equilibrium which is the parallel of the

[3] No consideration is here given to that form of the utility theory which attempts to be completely agnostic as to how human choices behave and to deal only with momentary preferences. But the writer believes that this type of theory acquires meaning just so far as there is attached to it some premise as to how choices actually do behave.

[4] The writer has elsewhere gone into this point in more detail. See "Economics and Modern Psychology," *Jour. of Pol. Econ.*, 26; 1-30, 136-66; Jan.-

static equilibrium of prices in a market. This fact is expressed either as an actual tendency, or as an ideal of good personal management. As indicated, it has sufficient truth to justify its place in a static economics, being itself a static assumption.

In contrast, in the attempt to put together the most realistic picture of human nature for which the materials are readily available, one is struck by its prevailing dynamic character. It contains static elements, but they differ essentially from the static character of the marginal-utility assumption.

Man is a mechanism of stimulus and response, conditioned not only by the present stimuli to which he may be exposed, but by past stimuli which have played their part in shaping the personality with which he now responds. Desires and ideas are not separate, but ideas are themselves impulses to action. Deliberative choice—the nearest approach to the rational action of theory—is a check on this tendency to act on the immediate stimulus, and a very imperfect check. Even the static elements of instinct or inborn tendency, habit and custom, change their quality when placed in a changing environment. Adapted to a past environment, they may be unadapted to the present, and the maladjustments which result are a part of the dynamic theory of human nature.

And human nature is paradoxical. The pleasure we take in many activities is not the reason why we want to do these things: the reason goes back to our inborn equipment of impulses and the particular forms which our environment has caused them to take; and pleasure is apparently a secondary and reinforcing factor, strengthening certain types of activity which have survival-value, and hence having survival-value itself. Biologically, it is presumably a means to survival, and

Feb., 1918. These articles contain the material on which this entire section is based. They appear in the present volume, pp. 92-169, above.

justified on that ground and to that extent only. Our impulses are sprung from primitive nature; and primitive nature is lavish of life, of death, of motives and of suffering. This fact of nature is constantly at war with our recently-developed ideal of economy. In particular, the strength of those desires which have their roots in the primitive, is adapted to conditions of struggle for existence in which wants could not be satiated, or else the world was saved from the results which would follow satiation under civilized conditions. Hunger could not be permanently satisfied; the fighting impulse could not render itself obsolete in a *pax Romana;* and the particularly lavish reproductive instinct could afford to run riot because nature employed, for the ends of biological progress, a method of keeping down the increase which, from the standpoint of civilized man, is wholly intolerable.[5] Now we save the weak, outlaw the fighting impulse (until a war occurs) and are free to overeat habitually. Thus the power to gratify wants brings with it new conditions, some of which are even dangerous, unless we can find substitutes for the checks imposed by primitive nature.

Reason itself is paradoxical when it takes the form of "rationalizing" or evolving ostensible motives for actions, where the real motive is one which civilized standards deem less respectable, or one which might even have to be suppressed unless it could be successfully disguised. Here means and ends become confused, and mere introspection cannot extricate them with any certainty. "Rational" weighing of values is also paradoxical in that it is irrational to pursue it to the point of perfection. To do so under modern conditions would leave no time or energy for earning a good living or

---

[5] Even primitive men, however, exhibit numerous institutions the natural effect of which would be to keep down the birth rate.

enjoying the fruits of one's labors. It is rational not to look after one's interests perfectly in every respect and every relation of life; and this fact has real significance in judging the effects of an economic system which is built on the supposition that every individual does look out for his own interests in all his relations with his fellowman. Rational decision can attain perfection only in dealing with things familiar and customary, but it is only needed in dealing with things new and not yet reduced to custom or routine. And those strategic decisions called "marginal" include many and significant departures from the static norm of rationality.

The so-called "instinct of workmanship" is another paradoxical trait, for it is essentially one whereby any means may become an end in itself: a worker gains interest in the technique of any process which the attaining of his ends make necessary, and having done so, he may lavish his efforts, rather than economize them, or even sacrifice the end to the technique. Yet this waste and possible perversion is the price of that direct interest in the work as such, without which the most effective work is not possible. Here again, perfect efficiency, conceived after rational models, is an ideal which is not in accord with human nature as it is actually constituted. Waste of some sort is inevitable.

Since intelligent choosing is so largely a matter of "trial and error," it is important to ask how the errors operate, how they correct themselves (if they do so) and what happens if they do not. For our purposes "error" is probably an unfortunate term, suggesting as it does a mathematical calculation or the determination of an objective fact, in which there is one accurate result and departures from it can be definitely determined. This is true in many cases, especially in the field of business decisions, where it is a question of cheapening production or increasing profits. This also applies to consumption, so far as it is a matter of economical use of particular means to attain a definitely given end. But where it is a case of choosing between different ends, the case is altered. Here there are two great classes of choices: those in which it is possible to sample alternatives and then follow for the future the one which experience leads one to prefer, and those in which such sampling is difficult or impossible and the individual may be disappointed in his choice without knowing that another course would have produced greater satisfaction, or may be reasonably satisfied without knowing that a different policy would not have worked still better. Even successful business policies are commonly of this latter sort. They are not the best that could have been done; but so long as the errors are not greater than those of one's competitors, one may never be forced to those further experiments by which alone it can be determined that anything better is possible. Even where sampling is relatively easy, as with consumption goods which are bought repeatedly, it involves some trouble, and is not likely to be carried to anything like completeness. And thus many errors persist, and it is possible to fool some of the people all of the time.

Some errors are cumulative in their effects rather than self-correcting. They have permanent effects on the individual's character or opportunities for revising his course for the future. This is particularly true of the choice of an occupation. By accepting a poverty wage and a low standard of living one may be accepting also a low level of efficiency which will tend to make the poverty permanent; [6] or by entering the field of casual labor, one may be accepting also the mentality and social ideas and ideals which go with it, and which may be inconsistent with those qualities we think of as the "economic virtues," and with the ability to strive

[6] Cf. Marshall, *Principles of Economics* (5th ed.), pp. 560-63, 569.

effectively for something better. This does not mean that free choice is not still the best system, but it does give added meaning to the well-known principle that freedom needs to be limited and safeguarded to prevent it from being so used as to destroy or limit effective freedom for the future: and it emphasizes the point made by Cooley, that freedom and degeneration are definitely linked together. Moreover the ideal to be sought is not a static one of perfect use of freedom, but a dynamic one of an educational character. It involves tasks proportioned to one's ability to perform them with sufficient success so that one may grow in the process, and safeguards against the most disastrous results of errors.

This raises the question of levels of intelligence and capacity, and here we are faced with the fact of great differences within the population. Dynamic economics cannot work successfully with the idea of one "economic man." Even if the non-existent average individual could be found, still departures from this average would be important enough to demand consideration. This is true also of differences in temperament producing biases of judgment and susceptibility to different types of biased appeal. Wherever such susceptibilities exist in considerable numbers, people will find a profit in catering to them or exploiting them, and this is one of the essential facts of a dynamic economy.

Then there are more external differences, not of temperament and capacity but of available knowledge and information; and this raises the further question of methods of putting the available knowledge and information at the service of the unspecialized citizen, that he may be able more successfully to cope with the interested parties with whom he has to deal, who have specialists at their service. In these respects the actual economic system works far better than it would if it were really one of pure and unmitigated individualism—which would be clearly intolerable—and this means that to understand the system we must interpret it as containing a large admixture of non-individualistic action, both public and private, and action governed by incentives and motives other than material self-interest. These cannot now be dismissed as non-economic, for they are necessary parts of the explanation of how the business system actually works, as well as of plans to make it work better.

It is obvious that the varied and complex human nature which has been roughly sketched does not lend itself to much definite and simple deduction. A realistic view of man is sufficient in itself to make dynamics largely an inductive inquiry. Further significances of this will appear as we glance at certain of the other premises of dynamics, dealing with a few of the institutions and conditions under which human nature works out its economic destiny.

5. THE DYNAMIC CONCEPT OF A TRANSACTION

The basic element of economic life—a transaction of exchange—is so complex and varied as to be inadequately represented by any simple stereotype of "free exchange." Freedom implies that neither party is dependent on relations with the other, and that a refusal to accept a given offer will leave tolerable alternatives open.[7] But as such relations become habitual people become in a real sense dependent on their continuance, and the refusal of an employer to continue dealing with an employee, in certain states of the labor market, may leave him an alternative which is anything but tolerable. There is real compulsion in such a situation. Under competition, the compulsion is not the arbitrary doing of

[7] The writer has developed this point elsewhere. See *Social Control of Business*, pp. 37-8.

any one employer, but employers as a group may benefit by it; and competition is not perfect enough to prevent all compulsion of a more personal sort.

Further, a transaction is supposed to be agreed to by both parties, but actual transactions often include many matters in which one or both of the parties exercise no choice or have no effective option. The terms and conditions of employment have never been very largely determined by free individual bargain, but rather by the custom of the trade, by the changing techniques of production at the command of the employer, by social legislation and, of late, by collective bargaining, which is not an individual affair, and involves all the problems and difficulties of representative government. In some respects, what we have is not so much a system of free contract as one of standardized relations, into which one is free to enter or not, (subject to the general compulsion of entering into some relations in order to get a living), but many of the terms of which one is not free to change. And the methods of settling these standard terms, and the interests which control them, are evolving continually.

The power to withhold, which is the key to the meaning of liberty, itself varies with changing economic conditions and legal institutions. Also the freedom of third parties—their immunity from having their interests infringed—is not absolute, and is itself evolving with the development of new kinds of injuries and new kinds of protections. The Federal Reserve System, a collective and not an individualistic institution, is one way of protecting business men from being caught in a panic as the result of the things other business men have done; and this protection could not be afforded by any more individualistic method.

6. COLLECTIVE ECONOMIC PERSONALITIES

Modern business is carried on, not by individuals, but by vast collective organizations, to which the classical economists did not apply their individualistic principles. Free contract with such organizations is only a pseudo-individualism. In their operations the interests of many groups are involved: stockholders, bondholders, managing employees, laborers, those who sell to them, those who buy from them, those whose property values are affected by their operations, their competitors, and other fellow-members of the general business community. Some of these interests are expressed through the machinery of free contract, some by that of representative government, industrial or political, and some by no recognised machinery. Moreover, the real character of the machinery is different from its nominal character, and is visibly changing, as a result of the fact that it is not uniformly appropriate to its task, and leaves some interests without adequate means of expression and protection. This evolution is one of the very vital things which is now going on in industry. The trade association is only one expression of it.

In this economy of organizations, the motives of individuals shift from a simple and exclusive attention to personal self-interest, and come to involve a considerable measure of loyalty to collective interests. This loyalty may be made the best policy, up to a certain point, but not sufficiently so to prevent a director from being able at times to make more money at the expense of his company than by loyally serving its interests. And there are conflicting loyalties, as every schoolboy or union worker knows—the psychology of these two groups is in some respects quite similar. The contrast between public and private conduct of business is not the simple thing it once was, but is a contrast between two systems of exerting pressure on a large force of hired employees, the difference hinging on the incentives of those in ultimate control, but often taking very similar forms as it reaches the actual worker.

7. LEGAL INSTITUTIONS

Passing on to the legal institutions which underlie all this, we may note that where the earlier economics was content to ask: what is the justification of private property or occasionally: what was its origin, the realistic economics asks the more inconvenient question: what is private property and what is it doing? And just as a commodity has been analyzed into a "bundle of utilities," so property is analyzed into a bundle of rights and privileges, its content defined by law, varying significantly in different legal systems and changing from time to time as the systems develop. When wealth is defined as that which is useful, limited in supply, appropriable and exchangeable, one does not at once realize that the last two characteristics are determined by the law, which therefore decides what shall be wealth, and what shall be the scope of economic study.

A static economics may, perhaps, consider that it applies to whatever is appropriable and exchangeable under existing law. And if changes in the law result in broadening or narrowing the range of utilities which may be appropriated and bought or sold, the subject-matter to which the laws of static economics applies may be said to be enlarged or reduced; while the nature of the laws themselves remains unchanged. Thus these laws would be unaffected by such changes. But a realistic or dynamic economics will want to know all about such interesting changes, and will find therein most pregnant implications as to potential changes of the same sort which have not actually been made. Its picture of interests, utilities and disutilities will do its best to be comprehensive, and not leave out any merely because the existing law declines to afford them specific protection. Indeed, interests which the law does not protect will be even more interesting than those which it does, for they will create problems and be the probable focusing points of future changes.

The function of economic life is to serve the interests of human beings, so far as they may be served by business processes. Price is one agency for furthering that purpose, and those interests which command a price are the ones served by the system of private enterprise. Some interests are of such a character that they might command a price but do not under existing laws. If we are to judge the effectiveness with which the function is being performed, and the success of the system of private enterprise in performing it, we shall stultify the inquiry if we do not contemplate the whole function, and include all the interests, whether they command a price or not. Otherwise we prejudge our inquiry by defining the function itself so as to include only that part of it which the particular agency covers. If we see no interests except those which command a price, we are hardly in a position to make a searching scrutiny of the adequacy of price as an agency for the furthering of interests. Thus the theory of inappropriable weath [8] and its twin-concept, uncompensated costs, become an important part of economic dynamics.

8. ETHICAL FORCES

A legal system which should protect all interests is unthinkable, no matter how much it might be developed. And

[8] See *The Philosophy of Wealth*, pp. 12-15.

where the law ends, the peculiar realm of ethical obligation begins. One of the striking developments of the present generation is the recognition of common interests and collective obligations of a moral nature, and the formulation of codes of fair practice by great numbers of trades. And many of the unwritten codes are more powerful than the written. Some of the articles of some of these codes have tremendous force; such as the unwritten article which, if violated, brings down on the violator the epithet: "scab." Others are probably little more than words on paper. The question what these codes really are and how they operate, as well as how they need to operate to perform their social function satisfactorily—this is a fascinating inquiry with which very little has as yet been done. And it is an essential part of any survey of representative economic forces.

Another question is how much the sense of right and wrong alters the bargaining force with which persons and groups strive to further their interests. To what extent will a sense of the inequity of the terms offered to labor lead the worker to submit to unemployment rather than accept? To what extent may a similar sense of a fair wage in the mind of the employer himself lead him to refrain from taking advantage of the opportunities for depressing wages which would be afforded by the unmitigated law of supply and demand, in time of business depression and unemployment? To what extent is a sense of inequity one of the forces back of certain varieties of restriction of output by labor? To what extent is a strike a moral phenomenon, and to what extent are the outcomes of strikes governed by moral forces?

9. COMPETITION: ITS VARIOUS DEGREES

Considering the central part which competition plays in economic theory, singularly little effort has been spent defining it. For static purposes, it can perhaps best be defined as whatever behavior among independent producers is necessary to bring about one price for one good in one market, at the level of "normal" expenses of production. Under actual conditions, price does not tend to an exact level on a typical market, normal expense of production is an inference rather than an observable fact, and actual expenses differ widely, so that their relation to price offers material for much inductive study.[9]

Among the special situations of actual competition are those preferences and habits which give rise to "good-will," and the ownership of brands which have some real or supposed uniqueness and thus have some of the quality of monopoly about them, but of which only the most successful can earn a consistent quasi-monopoly profit. Another situation is the state of mind among entrepreneurs which leads to sustaining the price in the face of the fact that the demand is falling off and will not take the full "supply" (a term which itself needs redefining for dynamic purposes). Those mores of business which resist cutthroat competition and the "spoiling of the market" are phases of actual competition, yet they have no place at all in the competition of abstract theory. Another situation is that of a trade in which there are one or more concerns so large that their price policy is said to "dominate" the trade, in spite of the existence of many smaller rivals. Such a situation cannot be fully and quantitatively explained by deduction from the assumption of independent and self-interested action, though a shrewd observer of human nature in business may make surmises which will afford useful first approximations and material to be tested by further inductive study. To mention only one

[9] This topic is given more extended treatment in *Social Control of Business*, Chap. IX.

specific instance, the degree and kind of competition among American railroads—which are clearly far from being complete monopolies—is probably not exactly the same as that found in any other business, and can best be handled by direct induction.

10. THE BUSINESS CYCLE

Assuming without argument the great importance of the business cycle and the need for inductive study in handling it, let us ask further what its effects are on some of the general assumptions which economic theory is accustomed to make and the tools it is accustomed to use. For one thing, in place of a universal tendency of supply and demand to equality, it exhibits a definite tendency toward persistent inequalities. And in place of supply of goods it forces us to look at the productive capacity or potential supply, if we are to get at the forces actively at work on the supply side of the balance, though the more important forces appear to be psychological. Along with this goes a transformation of the static idea of a margin of employment. It becomes clear that the rewards of labor and capital bear no close relation to their marginal productivities at any given moment; and if there is a long-run marginal productivity which has a close relation to the rewards of labor and capital, it requires careful redefining.

11. OVERHEAD COSTS

In all this a large part is played by the existence of overhead costs, or costs not specifically traceable to particular units of output, and costs which frequently do not vary with the variations of output, or not in anything like the same degree. At its most difficult levels, the problem of overhead costs is identical with the problem of surplus capacity. It gives rise to the danger of cutthroat competition, to the practice of discrimination with its uses and abuses, to the wastes of irregular production and to the chief financial incentive to their removal, and to some of the most definite of those ties of common interest which nowadays bind producers together into a genuine business community.

A concern which expands its orders is bestowing intensified gains upon those with whom it deals, for their expenses will not increase as fast as their output—within limits. And a concern which reduces its purchases is imposing an uncompensated burden on the rest of the business community, because their costs cannot be made to shrink as fast as their output. The concern which reduces its purchases does so in order to retrench, but the entire business community cannot retrench to anything like the same extent, and it is a doubtful question to what extent it can really retrench at all at a time of general depression. But even aside from this question of shifted burdens, it is clear that overhead costs introduce doubt and ambiguity into the most essential economic service of costs: the service they render when we compare values and costs to decide whether a given thing is economically worth doing. Thus the economist is deprived of one of his ready-made yardsticks of economic soundness, and must repair the loss somehow, not trusting the results of private enterprise and private accountancy to be necessarily correct from the standpoint of community economy.

12. THE CONCEPT OF CAPITAL

The shift from the static to the dynamic point of view has quite far-reaching effects on many of the fundamental concepts, of which we may take, as examples, the concepts of capital and of production. The term capital really applies to a rather large family of ideas, as can be easily seen. Some writers have attached the term to one of these ideas and some to another, and dynamics must solve their controversies by including all these ideas as parts of the process, or institution, to which its studies are directed. And certain things which no one has included in the *definition* of capital are still such vital *prerequisites* that they become essential parts of the picture which the term must convey to anyone studying it from the dynamic standpoint, as a process or institution.

One of the essential starting-points is a productive idea. Ideas, knowledge, habits and customs of the shop and markket-place, constitute a vitally important form of social capital: possibly the most vital form. Without it, nothing else can have value. It is in the main a common heritage, but differential advantages are elements of private wealth, and the whole is far from being a "free good."

Of joint importance with this is the "waiting" or abstinence of the original saver. And some writers make "waiting," rather than physical or financial capital, the third great factor of production, using it for the purpose usually assigned to capital in the general theory of distribution.

As the result of waiting, there is a fund of purchasing power destined to investment. Related to this is a fund of lending and investing power in the hands of financial institutions. Being invested, this becomes a quantity of purchasing power in the hands of an entrepreneur who is looking to spend it on productive assets. All these are forms which capital takes, and while only a part of capital is in any of these forms at any one time, it is that peculiarly mobile part by which marginal adjustments are typically made, and which thus holds a particularly strategic position.

Another obviously essential part of the process is the existence of supplies of "capital goods" or productive assets which the entrepreneur wishes to buy and use. These are, of course, capital in the enterprises that make them; but their availability conditions the dynamic behavior of capital in the industries which buy and use them. If they are not forthcoming, an increased flow of money into the coffers of entrepreneurs may not increase the physical amount of capital, but only raise the prices of the constituent "capital goods." [10] Thus for certain purposes, to find if capital can be increased, we must look to the supply of facilities for the production of the capital goods on which the funds in question are destined to be spent. America's war-effort to make guns, airplanes and ships is an illustration of the kind of limitation we are considering. There was no lack of funds, but the mobilization of funds far outstripped the fastest possible mobilization of the machines-to-make-the-machines to make the guns and other specialized equipment. The limiting factor was not capital in a financial sense, but physical capacity to make capital goods.

If the capital goods are available, certain kinds and amounts are selected and fitted together into what is really a new organism: the productive equipment of a going concern. This maintains its existence by the process of replacement. It may be viewed as investment, at original or reproduction cost; or it may, finally, be viewed as capitalized earning power or as rights therein; these being the last but not the least important members of this family of concepts.

Where the problem is static, most of these different phases of the process involved in capital may be ignored, and attention focussed on original savings and on the resulting fund of productive equipment. No error is involved in

[10] An extreme assertion of this fact is found in Veblen, *Absentee Ownership*, pp. 86-8. His view here is like that variant of the wages-fund theory in which the wages-fund consists of goods destined to be consumed by labor. Veblen implies a capital-goods-fund of similar character.

assuming that the loan fund of purchasing power goes hand in hand with original savings and automatically calls into being a corresponding amount of capital goods, while there would be no discrepancies between original cost of equipment, reproduction cost, and capitalized value of earning power. Earning power would depend on technical productivity and not on other factors. An interesting test of this proposition is found in the fact that Böhm-Bawerk's concept of a time-period of production and J. B. Clark's concept of a fund of technical equipment are for static purposes so close together that there is a *prima facie* case for the position that they are in effect identical and interchangeable, in the realm of statics. But where the problem and conditions are dynamic, discrepancies between the behavior of these various elements are of the essence of the inquiry. Investment funds are spent on other things than technical productive equipment, and capitalized earning power rests partly on these other things, and partly on things for which no investment funds may have been spent at all. These elements must be carefully distinguished and their relations to each other inductively studied. No one of these aspects of capital can be made paramount or all-sufficient at the expense of the others. All must be recognized, and some sense of their dynamic interplay must be a part of that concept of capital which is to be an appropriate tool of dynamic study.

13. THE CONCEPT OF PRODUCTION

The static problem and static assumptions make it possible to treat production as a quantitative addition to human gratifications, or at least to the means of gratification. Human wants are taken for granted, and the molding of wants is therefore not a part of static production. The protection of legal rights prevents the wants of some from being gratified at the expense of others, and competition prevents business incomes from being increased by withholding gratifications rather than by creating and bestowing them. The perfect static market prevents any gains being made by sheer "higgling and bargaining." Thus the so-called technological concept of production is applicable, and is an adequate description of the process by which income is to be secured, in the static state. The process of bargaining, and the characteristic work of the enterpreneur, have, before the static equilibrium can be fully reached, worked themselves out to the point of zero return and have no further functions to perform, either from the standpoint of private gain or social production. Thus the concept of production is much simplified.

But from the dynamic or realistic standpoint, the concept of production undergoes a transformation similar in general character to that which we have already seen in the case of capital. Discrepancies arise between its various aspects: especially the aspect of private gain, that of technical production, and that of social creation of utilities. Private gains are to be secured by the adjustment of prices in bargains, by the modification of desires and the guidance of choice through salesmanship and other methods, by the limitation of output to maintain price, and by the adjustment of rights through litigation and through the more fundamental process of modifying the rights themselves by statutes or court decisions which make new law.

Thus all these things are productive from the purely private standpoint, though the gains of some individuals must usually be weighed against the losses of others. These activities are also essential contributing factors in the process of technical production and of social creation of utilities; performing certain essential functions; though they are not the only possible agencies by which these functions can possibly be performed: merely the agencies to which these functions are entrusted under the present economic system. They are thus productive as a whole, in all the main senses of the term; but particular acts may still be purely parasitic, increasing the gains of one person wholly at the expense of others. They involve conflicts of interest, in which the gain or loss of any one party cannot be taken as a gauge of the resultant gain or loss to the community.

These conflicts of interests are unavoidable, and any system of settling them inevitably involves "wastes" of some sort, and the defeating of certain interests that others may prevail. Thus the mere existence of "wastes" in the present system does not necessarily carry condemnation, any more than the fact that the present system of handling these conflicts performs a necessary productive function carries necessarily a verdict of approval. A discriminating study of the facts should furnish the scientific basis on which efforts at improvement may be based, but parasitic activities can at best be minimized, and never totally eliminated. These are some of the difficulties necessarily faced by the dynamic concept of production.

14. CONCLUSION

From the foregoing it appears that there are many factors in dynamics which involve qualitative or "chemical" changes in the static assumptions, and require new inductions to establish their effects. Does the change to dynamics, then, mean the disappearance of statics as such in the pursuit of a study of a wholly different type? This is a question which will ultimately be answered by the test of experience. Dynamic study must not be cast in static molds: so much is clear at the start. In dealing with questions of utility, sacrifice and efficiency, it will necessarily view society as an

organic whole, rather than a mechanical summation of the
results of theoretical acts of independent "free exchange."
It will leave room for moral forces and its ideals of value
and efficiency will be dynamic and not static. In all this its
general point of view will be essentially similar to that
exhibited in the *Philosophy of Wealth*: a study which contains many elements of a true economic dynamics, and stakes
out territory which dynamic theory has not yet been able
effectively to occupy. But to say in advance that such a study
can have no use for the static method of approach or for
static pictures as partial representations of reality: this would
be premature. In fact, it seems possible to predict that certain
elements of statics will find a place, and probably a permanent one, in the actual pursuit of the dynamic analysis.

In the first place, the dynamic picture will never, in the
nature of the case, be complete. The facts change so rapidly
that induction can never hope to catch up, and they are so
multitudinous that a complete picture would not only be
unattainable, but would hardly help the human mind to
grasp the facts, since it would be as complex as the facts
themselves. Interpretation means simplification, and economics must always simplify in order to be of any use as a
mediating agent between the human mind and the facts with
which it deals. One effect of the dynamic approach will be
to limit statics again largely to its original problem: that of
the forces governing the levels of prices and the shares in
distribution. And in this field, the static picture will for a
long time, if not permanently, afford an indispensable point
of departure, and inductive studies will reveal the effect of
the static forces, combined with others suggested by the
dynamic point of view.

In the realm of price theory, quantitative modifications of
the static hypotheses will produce quantitative allowances

from the static results, and these will probably always be of use. An interesting example is found in the recent work of Professor H. L. Moore; in which he develops the concepts of partial elasticity of demand, and of a moving equilibrium of economic forces, putting the theories of demand and supply, and the marginal productivity theory of distribution into forms permitting of inductive verification.[11] Such verification will, of course, always reveal the presence of other forces than the purely static ones, modifying the results in any given case. Inductive studies will deal, not only with the trend-values around which actual values fluctuate, but also with the forces setting limits on their oscillations. Here the static forces, corresponding to the force of gravity in mechanics, are at work, but under conditions which differ from the complete static picture, and require correspondingly different methods of study.

And finally, in the inductive study of actual conditions, there will always arise the difficulty that a mere description of facts does not afford an explanation or interpretation of them. The question will still remain why they behave as they do. And here again the static approach will prove useful and effective, chiefly in the form of inverse deduction, which has already been mentioned. The reasoning takes the following form. If the facts were found to behave in certain simple ways, we should infer the presence of static forces only, acting under static conditions only. Since the facts behave differently, we infer the joint action of static and dynamic forces, and attribute the departures from the static model to the dynamic elements in the situation. And the nature of these departures are, if properly understood, such as we should expect from the nature of the dynamic

[11] See "Partial Elasticity of Demand," *Quar. Jour. Econ.*, XL, 393-401, May, 1926; "A Theory of Economic Oscillations," XLI, 1-29, Nov., 1926.

forces. Thus brief reversions to the static method of isolation will help us to separate out the forces acting under actual conditions, and to make of dynamics an explanation, rather than a mere description of economic behavior.

VII

LONG-RANGE PLANNING FOR THE REGULARIZATION OF INDUSTRY *†

I. SUMMARY

I. INTRODUCTION

I T IS generally agreed that there is something seriously wrong with private enterprise as at present operating. It has succeeded in organizing the technique of machine production with marvelous efficiency, but it has failed miserably to utilize this technique to anything like its full capacity.

* Report of a Subcommittee of the Committee on Unemployment and Industrial Stabilizational of the National Progressive Conference: the subcommittee consisting of: J. M. Clark, Chairman; J. Russell Smith, Edwin S. Smith, George Soule. Reprinted by permission from *The New Republic*, Jan. 13, 1932, Part 2.

† This report is genuinely a joint product of the four members of the subcommittee. While the Chairman assumed the task of putting on paper the purport of our discussions, it seems certain that the substance of the report is different from what any one member would have drafted if working by himself; and each member drafted in his own words sections of varying length which have been incorporated in the final report. By way of example, Mr. Soule is in large part responsible for the general scheme of organization recommended in Part V and for the wording of a considerable portion of Part I, Section I; also significant passages in Part IV, including paragraph (1), p. 245. Mr. E. S. Smith similarly drafted a substantial portion of Part VI, while Mr. J. Russell Smith contributed various specific recommendations as to policy. The report also benefited by helpful and searching criticisms, especially from Mr. Lewis L. Lorwin of the Brookings Institution and Mr. Harlow S. Person of the Taylor Society.

A word may be in order as to the sense in which my own advocacy of this report is to be taken. It both is and is not a recommendation for immediate action. It presents the action which, to the best of our vision at the time, would be desirable to take if both government and industry could be brought to sufficiently genuine comprehension and support of the principles and policies recommended. But that seemed to me too much to hope for at the time; and my real hope was that this report might play a part in a long process of education

The income from production is inequitably distributed; and this reacts on the amount and character of consuming power and thus sets limits on our power to produce.

Unemployment and poverty still exist, even in the most prosperous periods; while, despite large aggregate profits, a large proportion of business enterprises (by number) do not make earnings adequate for safety and stability.

Periodic depressions cause untold misery and suffering. At times we enjoy prosperity ever rising to new high levels, and at other times, with the same needs to meet and the same powers to meet them, in natural resources, labor energy, productive equipment and technical skill, we are unable to use these powers to meet these needs. Modern society can no longer acquiesce in this misuse of the powers which nature and science have bestowed upon it.

It is frequently asserted that a collective economy would be a remedy for this grave evil; and if nothing is done to remedy it under private enterprise, a few more major depressions may make this issue acute. The more pertinent course seems to be to see what can be done to introduce collective planning into our existing system. This must be done experimentally, with the expectation that measures will change and develop with experience. It does not appear to us important either to safeguard private enterprise for its own sake, or to seek a collective economy for its own sake. What is important is to organize for the purpose of making the best possible use of our resources, and to take whatever measures such organization requires. We hold that this task of organization is not beyond human powers, and that a beginning at it must immediately be made. We cannot foresee the end, but we can outline first steps.

and experiment, in the course of which the specific recommendations here made would in all probability be superseded.

We are therefore advocating an elastic system of organizations for planning, relying on voluntary action to the fullest extent consistent with ensuring that whatever action is taken is guided by the interests of the whole community, and that these interests are adequately protected.

Private individuals and groups are now advocating systems of planning within single industries. Such proposals lay chief emphasis on limiting production to prevent it from exceeding demand. In fact, this is the one thing single-industry organizations could most surely be counted upon to do, since their interests lie in that direction. Yet it is obvious that a policy of restriction, generally followed out, is no remedy for a condition whose chief evil is failure to use our existing powers of production. General limitation of output will not produce general prosperity.

The danger of such a program is all the greater because there are particular branches of production in which, in the present emergency, measures of limitation are quite proper. What is needed is that power to control production should not be granted except to organizations so broadly constituted as to represent adequately those groups whose interests lie in maintaining production rather than in restricting it.

A program of maintaining production is vastly more difficult than one of limiting output, and will take more time to show results. But it is the only general program that deserves the name "national planning" or planning in the interests of the whole nation, as distinct from industrial planning or planning in the interests of single industries.

II. OBJECTIVES OF NATIONAL PLANNING

Desirable objectives of national planning include the following:

(1) *Not general limitation of output, but increase of total*

production. The true objective of planning is not less production, but more. It is not stabilization at any given fixed level, but regularized growth. It is the full utilization of our powers of production, which are continuously growing, in order that our consumption may grow correspondingly. Contributory to this basic end are various more specific objectives.

(2) Increasing the proportion of income going to the majority in the lower income ranges, who will spend more of it for the products of mass production.

(3) Especially raising the lowest wage rates, which are inadequate to sustain a demand for the requisites of comfortable and hygienic existence. This will incidentally be favorable to successful planning, since these demands are easier to anticipate than demands for luxuries.

(4) Improving or eliminating the highest cost concerns, which are often responsible for these lowest wage rates, being unable to pay more.

(5) Making purchasing power more stable than the business activity from which it is derived, by the use of reserves or insurance against unemployment.

(6) Discovering and bringing about a desirable balance between productive equipment and demand, with adequate anticipation of growth.

(7) Discovering and stimulating other ways of using capital than wasteful duplication of existing facilities.

(8) Maintaining a balance between savings and the expenditure of capital funds for plant, equipment and materials; and bringing about conditions conducive to a fairly steady flow of both.

(9) Regularization of capital expenditures and of the flow of raw materials, intermediate products and finished goods through the various stages of production and distribution. The object is to prevent concentrations of capital

construction and inventory growth from causing basic production to fluctuate markedly more than sales of ultimate products to consumers, as it now does.

(10) Stabilization of price levels so far as practicable, but not a price system pegged at certain points only.

(11) Systematic canvassing of the possibilities of latent as well as actual demand; including demand which might be made actual by fuller and more stable employment and higher wages.

III. PROPOSED ORGANIZATION

We propose a National Economic Board, appointed by the President with the advice and consent of the Senate, and with preliminary advice from various national organizations. The members of the Board should represent special types of expert knowledge rather than special economic interests. They should include men expert in finance, scientific management, labor relations, economics and agriculture or agricultural economics; but should be chosen for their ability to represent the interests of the public at large. The Board should have a corps of statisticians, economists and technical experts. The duties of the Board should be:

(1) To assemble a nationwide statistical survey of all information essential to a national plan for production and, so far as possible, for consumption, bringing together for the first time all the elements whose movements must be fitted into each other if the whole national economic machine is to work smoothly. Such a survey is a necessary basis of effective planning.

(2) To initiate organizing councils in the various major branches of production and distribution (including finance), for the purpose of setting up such permanent organizations as might be adapted to the special needs and conditions of

the different industries, with due regard to conserving the results of any planning that may already have been done. These organizing councils and permanent organizations might be built upon existing organizations, but the organizing councils should be representative of all the essential interests involved. This calls for representation of organized labor, consumers, large and small producers, and possibly producers of raw materials. In the permanent organizations these interests should be so far as practicable represented, or if this is not practicable, they should be safeguarded by governmental participation or regulation, or both.

(3) To co-operate in the whole process of organization, suggest changes in plans, approve or disapprove them, or propose substitutes. The Board should not have compulsory power to require the adoption of any plan or organization, but if within a reasonable time an organization is not adopted in any industry where in the judgment of the Board an organization is required in the interest of the success of the whole program, the Board should have power to propose legislation for the setting up of such an organization. Ultimately, a national federation of these organizations might be found desirable; also local federations into regional-planning councils, co-operating with existing regional-planning organizations.

(4) To recommend any new legislation which may be required: (a) to carry out such organization and permit it to function and (b) to safeguard the public interest. The Board should also have a general power to recommend any national policy which may contribute to the general end of improving our economic system. In proposing legislation the Board should consult with any governmental body or bodies now active in the field or fields affected; for example, the Federal Trade Commission.

The duties of the permanent organizations should be the general promotion of the fullest and most effective operation of industry in the service of all concerned, with the cooperation and guidance of the Board and with the help of its organized economic survey.

The forms of these permanent organizations will obviously have to be different in agriculture, coal mining, steel, merchandising, credit, etc., and large reliance must be placed upon the interests themselves to work out appropriate forms. Possibilities run all the way from extension of present trade-association organizations and functions to consolidations with the status of public utilities or even public corporations to operate particular industries.

IV. POLICIES

The National planning organization should be guided by the following policies, so far as they are within its field of operation. So far as they are national in character, they are essential conditions of successful regulation.

1. *Limitation of Output*

If regularization of capital expenditures is brought about, and excess producing capacity kept within reasonable bounds, it seems probable that limitation of output itself will not be needed except in special cases and as a temporary emergency measure. In such cases, where monopoly profits are clearly out of the question, it seems probable that limitation of output could be permitted without formal machinery for the regulation of prices and profits. Any permanent limitation of output should be accompanied by effective control, including power to control prices where necessary.

2. *Prices and Price Control*

While approximate stabilization of price levels would be of the utmost importance, pegging of a limited number of particular prices should be avoided. It is more important to maintain harmony between different prices, and between prices, incomes and production, than to adhere rigidly either to certain particular prices or to an abstract price level. If prices of basic materials change, prices of products should change in harmony with a minimum of resistance.

3. *Credit, Investment and Speculation*

One of the most important councils would be that charged with developing a more unified and effective control of credit and finance. The discount rate is not in itself a sufficient means of control. Careful studies should define the different uses which credit serves, and devise methods of controlling them to meet the ends of regularization.

Uniform corporate reports and more conservative control of securities issues are essential, under federal incorporation if the end can be gained in no other way.

4. *Labor Policy*

We advocate a nationally organized labor market with a nationwide employment service, vocational guidance and vocational re-education for workers displaced from their trades.

We believe that a general system of unemployment reserves or unemployment insurance in some form is not only necessary, but can be made to act as a stabilizing rather than an unstabilizing force in industry, by making purchasing power more stable than business operations.

More general organization of labor is desirable both to

raise the lowest wage rates and to co-operate in stabilization policies.

During a period of unemployment, available work may be distributed by working less than a standard working week. Under normal conditions, a gradual and progressive shortening of the standard week itself should go hand in hand with a gradual increase of weekly earnings. The goal is to use the increased productiveness of industry partly to increase the incomes of workers and partly to increase their leisure; not, as at present, to be compelled to reduce the working hours and earnings of some in order to be able to give employment to others.

5. *Public Works*

We advocate an elastic system of public works, which can be greatly enlarged in dull times. This will require many measures of preparation and advance authorization. The available volume of such work is not sufficient to stem a depression, but it can be a useful part of a comprehensive policy which also includes regularization of private construction.

6. *Public Finance*

In order that governmental employment may operate to counteract rather than to reinforce business depression, it is necessary that expenditures be expanded at just those times when revenues fall off. If taxes are sufficient for the average needs of good and bad times, there should be no fear of using credit freely to increase expenditures during depression. The effect of such expenditures on economic stability is more important than accurate balancing of the budget in a single year.

Taxes should at all times avoid forms which directly

burden productive activity (*e. g.,* a sales tax) and especially so in a depression.

7. *War Debts*

It is not in our interest to insist on international debt payments which will seriously handicap Europe's recovery or threaten her continued economic stability. Our international economic policy must be consistent with the needs of domestic and world stabilization.

Further details, and reasons for the various positions taken, will be found in the fuller report which follows.

II. DEVELOPMENT OF THE IDEA OF PLANNING

The idea of economic planning on an industry-wide scale appears to be gaining wide acceptance among responsible persons and groups. Notable examples are the Swope Plan and the plan proposed by a committee of the National Chamber of Commerce. The present report attempts to include the desirable features of such programs and to go farther in the direction of safeguarding the public interest and especially in the direction of planning that shall be nationwide and not merely industry-wide and shall represent all the interests of the nation. One vital reason for this is that while the interests of single industries lie in limiting output, the combined interests of the nation as a whole lie in increasing it.

It is probable, in fact, that some industries would be centrally controlled today if there were no legal obstacles. The law has not permitted this because of the justifiable conviction that such power should not be entrusted to business units alone. There must be assurance that planning will not mean stabilizing profits by limitation of output at the expense of full employment. Even sincere statements of intention to stabilize employment also, welcome as they are, need to be given the backing of an organization representing the groups whose interests lie solidly and obviously in that direction.

Back of this present movement are certain facts of recent history and experience, each of which has probably played a part in the development of the idea, and each of which affords useful suggestions, but none of which affords a perfect parallel to the present situation or a perfect model for present action.

One is the experience of the World War, when centralized control was needed in the interest of efficient mobilization of the nation's resources. In the main, private enterprise was retained even in that emergency in the work of actual production within single enterprises, that being the realm in which the greatest efficiency of private enterprise lies.

Another is the Russian Five Year Plan, which applies the methods of centralized control to ordinary peace-time production, but under a system of compulsory socialization which we are not ready to imitate. This development has given considerable impetus to the search for methods of applying the principle of planning within our own economic system; but it clearly does not furnish a usable model, to a nation which does not wish a communistic dictatorship.

Less obvious but perhaps even more enlightening is the development of planning which has taken place in private industry itself within the present generation, beginning with the work of F. W. Taylor. This has amounted to a revolution in intra-industrial organization, and is responsible for the greatest increases in efficiency made in this period. Business men have gone to school and relearned their businesses. Formerly they relied heavily on the skill of their employees, their own part being largely the application of the spur of self-interest under the wage system. The result was haphazard and rule-of-thumb methods, and faulty correlation of the whole scheme of processes. Now they set up planning departments consisting of experts, independent of the organization of administrative officers in charge of the actual work of production, to apply methods of scientific precision to the search for the best processes and the best correlation of processes within the plant. Using a military analogy, they speak of the separation of the "staff" function of investigation and planning from the "line" function of direct administration of the work. The result has been enormous increases in efficiency.

It is not surprising that those trained in these methods should begin to feel sufficient competence to improve on the haphazard methods still operating in the broader field of relations between independent business enterprises, and of the correlation of our economic system in the large. In the past, most observers felt that central control could not do better than unplanned competition; and they focused their attention on the marvelous fact that free exchange without central planning does produce some sort of order. This may have been a proper attitude at the time, in view of the prevailing ignorance of the principles of large-scale organization, and of the nature of the problem of business depressions. But it is not a proper attitude now.

If the principles which have revolutionized plant organization should do something similar in the larger economic field, the results would be even more important. This is perhaps too much to expect, in view of the greater difficulties, but a hopeless attitude is clearly unjustified.

None of these models is completely suited to our needs, and we cannot solve our problem by following an analogy borrowed from any of them. The United States at war had no problem of over-production, nor has Soviet Russia now. Neither the Soviets nor scientific management face the problem of influencing the actions of independent enterprises whom they cannot order to produce. Communistic planning and planning within a single industry have the relatively easy tasks of scheduling production directly. National planning in a system of private enterprise faces the more difficult task of changing the conditions that govern industrial production-schedules, by attacking the causes which produce instability under the present system.

Nevertheless, we can borrow elements from these precedents. From the war experience and the Five Year Plan we can borrow the basic survey of resources and needs. And from scientific management we can borrow the separation between planning and administration, neither being supreme over the other, and each having its appropriate type of personnel. But we must set these elements in a new framework.

III. EVILS TO BE MET

The outstanding evils which challenge us to nationwide planning may be summed up under the headings of sick industries, technological unemployment, and business cycles and depressions. Since intelligent planning must deal with causes, a study of the causes of these conditions is vital. Among the causes to be dealt with will probably be found the following:

I. SICK INDUSTRIES

Sick industries suffer from a variety of ills; most general of which are a condition of chronic excess capacity and occasional actual overproduction. This in itself has causes, historical and current. It is not merely excess capacity beyond

what the market will keep fully occupied at profitable prices
—some excess in that sense is normal—but in some cases
there seems to exist an excess above actual need or reasonable use at any thinkable price. Another trouble is the undue
persistence of inefficient, high-cost concerns.

2. TECHNOLOGICAL UNEMPLOYMENT

Technological unemployment is traceable to a lagging in
the processes of reabsorption of labor displaced by improvements. The less labor is needed to satisfy existing wants,
the more is available to satisfy new wants. But so long as
the workers are unemployed, their wants are not market
demands, because they lack purchasing power; and it is
market demands for which business produces. Hence business may have difficulty in finding profitable uses for the
displaced labor. Given time, it will overcome this difficulty,
largely because it is so ready to produce for demands which
are not yet actual but are merely anticipated; or wants
which are waiting for business itself to stimulate them. And
as unemployed workers are absorbed, and set to work, the
purchasing power resulting from this employment furnishes sufficient demand to absorb the enlarged total of
production (though particular goods may fail to find favor).

But business cannot do this at an unlimited rate. And it
is quite natural that absorption chronically lags behind
displacement. The indicated need is a speeding-up of the
processes of absorption, centering in the searching out of
new demands, producing for them, and furnishing the necessary purchasing power by the process of production. If the
attempt to avoid overproduction resulted in a refusal to
produce in advance of established demand, that would be
the worst possible outcome from the standpoint of techno-

logical unemployment, since that would do away with the chief natural cure.

3. BUSINESS CYCLES AND DEPRESSIONS

Business cycles and depressions are due to a combination of non-cyclical disturbing forces, together with the responses of a business system which cause disturbances to spread and intensify cumulatively. This quality is due to causes, partly mechanical, partly financial and partly psychological.

Prices rise and fall with the swing of the cycle, wholesale prices changing far more than costs of living, credit expands and contracts, and these movements have cumulative results. In addition there are larger movements of prices such as the world decline since the War, which helped to make the present depression unusually severe.

One far-reaching cumulative force arises from the fact that, when demand weakens or costs encroach on earnings, business enterprises, each acting separately, may escape losses by contracting operations, largely because they can throw the losses due to contraction upon others. The loss is passed on to those who supply them with goods and materials, to their own workers, and ultimately to all those industries and workers the demand for whose services is curtailed by the resulting shrinkage in purchasing power. An organization representing a broader range of interests might act differently; one representing all the interests concerned would certainly do so.

Such a process of contraction is obviously cumulative, starting the vicious circle in which demand is curtailed because curtailed production has curtailed earnings and the resultant purchasing power; and production is curtailed because of this curtailed demand.

Moreover, demand for machinery and plant structures may shrink without any shrinkage in ultimate demand for the products they turn out. Producers of plant equipment are working to a large extent to provide for expansion; and if consumers' demand merely slackens its growth, demand for plant equipment to satisfy it may suffer an absolute decline. The resulting unemployment may cause such a shrinkage in consumers' demand as to cut off almost entirely the demand for expansion or even, temporarily, replacement of productive facilities.

Thus arises another vicious circle, due to concentrating the work of producing capital equipment into active periods, when it could better be spread out more evenly. Production of capital equipment fluctuates far more than production of goods for consumers. And it is a paradox of private enterprise that we never reach our maximum rate of production for consumers except at just those times when we are wasting possibly 5 per cent of our productive power in a needlessly concentrated production of capital equipment, crowding into one year more than one year's quota of expansion in buildings and machinery, and something more in a similar concentration of residential construction.

IV. OBJECTIVES OF NATIONAL PLANNING

These problems furnish the setting which dictates the objectives of economic planning. But it would be easy to make a wrong choice. With certain industries suffering from genuine overproduction, and with a widespread feeling that this is the basic trouble with industry in general, planning could too easily mean merely general limitation of production. But the foregoing survey shows clearly that this is the wrong remedy. And it is obvious that we cannot all prosper by such a method.

Stabilization of production comes nearer the true objective, but is not in itself sufficient. Stable operation would require less labor and capital. Thus it would release more productive forces than we have ever fully utilized, but it would not automatically provide for their utilization. It would probably stimulate it, since surplus workers in a regularized industry must obviously look for other employment, while in an irregular one they may hang on, hoping for partial employment in the more active times. But this does not create employers; and our experience with technological unemployment since the War does not strengthen the belief that private enterprise would automatically absorb the surplus of labor as rapidly as it was created. If the loss were distributed through enforced curtailment of hours of work, the resulting suffering would be lessened, but the loss would remain; purchasing power and output would both be limited by our failure to co-ordinate them.

(1) *The true objective of planning is not stabilization at any static level, but regularized growth. It is the full utilization of our powers of production, which are continually growing, in order that our consumption may grow correspondingly. To this end the purchasing power of the masses must be maintained and must expand. Viewed from the other side, then, the objective is the progressive raising of the purchasing power and the standard of living of the people to the full extent which our powers of production make possible. Increased production and a raised standard of living must go hand in hand; neither end can be gained without the other.*

(2) Granted this objective, the means of breaking out of the vicious circle are still not obvious. One thing which

might help would be to *ensure that income destined to expenditure for goods should fluctuate less than the financial volume of production.* If incomes were reasonably stabilized, the resulting sense of security would probably further stabilize the spending of them, and so by stabilizing industrial activity, tend further to stabilize incomes themselves. The results of movements toward stability would be cumulative, as those of instability now are. This calls for unemployment reserves or unemployment insurance.

(3) Another major objective is greater equality in the distribution of incomes, increasing the proportion going to wages and the lowest salaries, to farmers and to the lower-income groups in general. The result will naturally be that more incomes will be spent for consumable products, thus striking at the problem of restricted demand for the things mass production is waiting to produce. This seems more useful than increasing the savings of the well-to-do, especially as those "savings" are so likely to be dissipated in sustaining stock-market booms or in wasteful duplication of productive facilities.

It is especially vital to raise the lowest wage rates, which are inadequate to sustain a demand for the requisites of comfortable and hygienic existence. This would incidentally contribute to successful planning, since these demands are easier to anticipate and to plan for than demands for luxuries.

More specific objectives include the following:

(4) Improving or eliminating the high-cost concerns which are often responsible for the lowest wage rates, being unable to pay more.

(5) Discovering and bringing about a desirable balance between productive equipment and demand, with provision for adequate anticipation of growth.

(6) Discovering and stimulating ways of utilizing capital not needed to finance mere quantitative expansion in existing industries—*e.g.*, new products and more intensive use of labor-saving devices, in proper balance so as to avoid technological unemployment.

(7) Maintaining a balance between savings and expenditures of capital funds for productive equipment, and bringing about conditions conducive to a fairly steady rate of both.

(8) The control of conditions leading to fluctuations in the various parts of industry more intense than the fluctuations of sales to ultimate consumers. This requires regularization of capital expenditures and of the flow of raw materials, intermediate products and finished goods through the various stages of production and distribution. Fluctuations of stocks of goods are a disturbing element, at least in parts of the industrial system.

(9) The bringing about of stabilization of prices and price levels to the fullest extent possible, but not a price system pegged at certain points only.

(10) The canvassing of possibilities of latent as well as actual demand. (This will be more fully developed in the section on the basic factual survey.)

V. ORGANIZATION

I. GENERAL SCHEME OF ORGANIZATION

The proposed scheme of organization consists of two permanent parts and one temporary one. The permanent parts consist of (1) a national board of experts to have charge of fact-finding and planning on a national scale, and (2) organizations of various sorts in the various branches of production to have charge of formulating and carrying out policies for the several industries to further the ends of national planning. Since no such organization should be imposed on industries from outside, there is necessary a series of temporary organizing councils within the several branches of production, to set up the more permanent organizations.

2. THE NATIONAL ECONOMIC BOARD

General character.—We propose as the central national body a board of experts with functions of investigation, suggestion and correlation rather than with administrative duties and authority. It is thus of the general character described in the language of scientific management by the term "staff," as distinct from "line" or administrative officials.

But as no central administrative authority exists—and none is here proposed—the duties of the central board will naturally be different from those of the "staff" of a single business enterprise under scientific management. They will be in some respects larger and in others more limited. There will be need of taking measures in the direction of seeing that the policies followed by the various organizations charged with putting plans into action fit into a harmonious whole. But it will not be necessary for the central board to prepare plans for action down to the last detail. The most detailed planning functions would naturally fall to further bodies of the planning or staff type within the working organizations set up in separate industries or industrial groups.

We propose an act of Congress creating a Board of seven (or nine) members who should be men of the highest caliber acting in the interest of the whole country and not representing any particular economic interests. Among them should be persons expert in or expertly informed on:

finance, scientific management, labor relations, economics. But a primary qualification should be character and background tending to impartial thinking, and the ability to act independently of any incidental economic interests the members may have acquired.

The Board should have a corps of statisticians, economists and such other technical assistants as might be needed.

Method of appointment.—The Board should be appointed by the President with the advice and consent of the Senate for terms of seven years, one term expiring each year. (If the Board consists of nine members, terms of five years might be used, with two terms expiring in each of four years and one in the fifth.) Preliminary to making appointments, the President should invite such bodies as the National Chamber of Commerce, the American Federation of Labor, the Taylor Society, the Federated Engineering Societies, the American Economic Association and possibly others, each to suggest names for the full membership of the Board (when the Board is first constituted), or for vacancies as they occur.

Duties.—The duties of the Board should be:

(1) To assemble a nationwide statistical survey of all information essential to a national plan for production and, so far as possible, for consumption; thus bringing together for the first time all the elements whose movements must be fitted into each other if the whole national economic machine is to work smoothly.

(2) To institute organizing councils within the various major branches of production and distribution (including finance) for the purpose of setting up such permanent organizations as may be adapted to the special needs and conditions of the different industries.

(3) To co-operate in the organizing process at all stages,

and to collaborate in the subsequent process of administration, with a view to seeing to it that the plans proposed and carried out are in the public interest.

(4) To propose any legislation which may be necessary or useful in furthering the ends of the whole process.

The Board should have access to all statistical material in the possession of the government which may be necessary and proper for the making of a comprehensive national economic survey. And it should be granted adequate power to require the furnishing of further data.

Other features of its powers will appear in the discussion immediately following, of its relations to the other parts of the system.

3. INDUSTRIAL ORGANIZING COUNCILS

The Board should see to it that the organizing councils contain genuine and adequate representation of all the interests essentially concerned, including large and small producers, organized labor, consumers and in some cases producers of essential raw materials and distributors of the goods produced. In any case they should have effective *liaison* along the lines of vertical integration which run from producers of raw materials to retailers of finished products.

The Board should be empowered to require each of these organizing councils to prepare a plan within two years' time, or less if possible, for organizing a permanent council or other organization of whatever sort might be best suited to the needs and conditions of the industry, subject to the basic condition that all the interests essentially concerned shall be represented, either directly or *via* the protection afforded by public regulatory bodies. Consideration should be given to conserving the useful results of any planning which may already have been done by either public or private bodies.

The Board should collaborate in the organizing process at all stages and should have power to suggest changes or to propose substitute plans. It should have no power to compel the adoption of any plan. But if at the end of two years any industry has not adopted a plan of organization which in the judgment of the Board meets the requirements of the public interest, and if in its judgment an organization in that industry is necessary to the general national program, the Board should in its discretion have power to propose a plan of organization for that industry and to recommend to Congress legislation for carrying it into effect.

4. PERMANENT ORGANIZATIONS IN PARTICULAR INDUSTRIES

The duties of the permanent industrial organizations should be the general promotion and carrying into effect, in their several fields, of the purposes of the national economic program as herein set forth.

These organizations should, as noted above, afford all the interests essentially concerned either direct representation or protection through public regulatory bodies.

It will frequently be found that regularization in one industry hinges on what is done in others; hence the permanent organizations should probably have *liaison* along lines of vertical integration, like the organizing bodies. Ultimately, a national federation of these organizations might be found desirable; also local federations into regional-planning councils, co-operating with existing or future regional-planning organizations.

As already noted, the forms of these organizations must vary with the special character and needs of the industries. Among the possible forms are the following:

(1) In some cases, trade associations might serve as a nucleus, with additional representation of all essential interests, including those of producers not members of the association. Provision should also be made for uniform accounting and the gathering and circulation of essential statistics and of material from the national survey. Such organizations might accomplish much without having sufficient power to bring about positive limitation of production and control of prices. Regularization of capital expenditures, with incidental reduction of excess producing capacity, and with the facts always available to the National Board, would be in harmony with the purposes of national planning and might do much to stabilize an industry without giving rise to the need of public control of prices.

(2) In other cases, organizations with power to control production might be permitted, but subject to public power to control prices and some jurisdiction over capital expenditures for expansion; also power to investigate efficiency of operation and point out possibilities for improvement. Such regulation might be voluntarily accepted in exchange for partial exemption from the anti-trust laws.

(3) Organizations with production allotted by quotas might be used temporarily as an emergency measure if nothing better seemed possible at the moment, but this expedient is not suited to permanent use, largely because it tends to perpetuate a condition of excess producing capacity and to permit relatively inefficient producers to continue to hold a share of the market which they do not deserve, at the expense of the consumers. In such cases the facts as to capacity, output, costs and prices should be placed at the disposal of the National Board and the Federal Trade Commission; and they may show clearly that in a given emergency there is no possibility of monopoly profits. In such

cases no control of prices may be needed. But any permanent system of limitation of output should carry with it the scrutinizing of prices and profits by some public body with power to control them if necessary. Such control might be voluntarily accepted in return for the necessary relaxation of the anti-trust laws.

(4) In other cases private consolidations with public-utility status might be set up.

(5) In some cases of sick industries in which private enterprise in any form offers little chance of a cure, a public corporation might be set up to operate the industry.

5. POWERS OF THE NATIONAL BOARD TO RECOMMEND LEGISLATION

The Board should have broad powers to recommend to Congress legislation for the furthering of the purposes of national planning.

(1) As already indicated, it should have power to recommend legislation for the setting up of a permanent organization in cases where this is necessary and where voluntary effort fails to bring it about.

(2) In some cases new legislation may be needed to permit a proposed organization to be set up and to function: for instance, a relaxation of the anti-trust laws. The Board should have power to recommend such changes, together with measures to provide whatever protection to the public interests may be needed in its judgment; whether by control of prices or by any other means.

(3) In addition, the Board should have general power to recommend any legislation or any national policy which may contribute to the general end of improving our eco-nomic system.

In proposing legislation the Board should consult with

any governmental body or bodies now active in the field or fields affected.

VI. THE BASIC FACTUAL SURVEY

A comprehensive survey of economic conditions should be made and kept up to date. For this purpose data will be needed beyond what are now available, notably in the fields of consumption, savings, investment and plant capacity, while new types of data on profits may be needed.

Such a survey should aim ultimately to include a summary of past experience and trends of the following factors:

(1) Increase of production, sales, etc., in the various branches of production and distribution. The main figures should also be analyzed on a per capita basis.

(2) Increase of productive power and history of surplus capacity. This last is a difficult and ambiguous item, and the present types of figures are insufficient, largely because they do not distinguish between equipment of standard and of sub-standard efficiency. There is much equipment worth keeping for stand-by service, economical to use for short periods of unusually active demand because it represents little or no capital overhead, though its relative inefficiency would make it wasteful to use regularly. Present attempts to take account of differences in efficiency take the form of engineers' percentages which reveal nothing as to total cost (operating expenses plus overhead) in relation to different degrees of regularity of operation.

(3) Consumption and standards of living by groups, income, total and per capita, and how divided between:

(a) Expansion of existing industries,

(b) Development of new industries, such as radios and household electrical appliances at the present time,

(c) Professional and personal services, not of an industrial character, such as education and medical and dental services, (d) Savings and how they were used—how much were wasted in duplication of existing productive facilities; effects of developments such as social insurance, with forecast of proposed development.

(4) Cyclical movements of income, consumers' expenditures, consumers' credit and savings. The timing of movements in these items should be noted as closely as possible. Note of the special movements of perishable, durable and semi-durable goods, staples and style goods, etc.

Employment and unemployment.

Record of failures with causes.

Record of net earnings; total and in relation to sales and to investment, and also to wages and salaries. Figures should be available by industries and plants.

(5) A more difficult but hardly less essential undertaking is a study of potential demand, such as must be uncovered if industry is to operate more fully and the standard of living raised. This would be a very hazardous field of investigation because of changing fashions even in such supposedly staple items as foodstuffs, to say nothing of types of clothing. In the category of luxury goods the problem is even more difficult. It would be impossible to estimate, for instance, the future demand for radios versus household electric refrigerators. However, there are certain minimum comforts of life universally desired and not now possessed by great groups of our people. Such commodities are: a sufficient number of rooms in which to live, central heating, running water, etc.

An investigation to determine the potential demand for such goods might, for example, proceed to determine:

(a) Number of families by geographical location and size of town.

(b) Number of rooms per family, also by geographical location and size of town.

(c) Number of families having less than a comfort minimum in terms of number of rooms.

(d) Number of families lacking inside toilets, bath tubs, central heating, electricity, gas, telephone.

In order to put these facts to work, it would be necessary to consider:

(a) How far the present industrial plant could take care of these needs.

(b) The volume of employment and realized income which the work of gratifying those needs would provide in the raw-materials industries, manufacturing industries, building trades, public utilities, wholesale and retail distribution.

(c) The probable resulting increase of consumers' expenditures.

(d) The natural consumers' goods markets for this purchasing power (in terms of budget studies of workers and other groups) and the further increase in employment its expenditure would call forth and the further increase in purchasing power to which this employment would give rise. (This is in theory an endless chain, but it tapers off and stops somewhere.)

(e) The extent to which the groups benefited by the new spending power of industry would be those in which the needs for more dwelling space, plumbing, etc., are great; indicating the extent to which increased output would be likely to be matched by increased demand.

Another approach might be as follows:

(a) Start with a budget of possible spending power representing what would be afforded by reasonably full operation of industry, with a desirable distribution.

(b) Estimate the types of goods in which it would naturally be spent.

(c) Plan for the production of at least those items on the list where the element of uncertainty as to the particular thing that will be wanted is not too great.

(d) Scrutinize plans in the more doubtful fields to see whether their total amount at least fits in with the estimate of total spending power; in other words, whether we are producing for a total demand which cannot only be reached under temporary stimulus of expanding credit sales or what not, but one which can be sustained.

In all these calculations the element of normal growth should be an essential part.

(a) The result might be something in the nature of a standard to test overexpansion even in the newer and more rapidly growing industries, at least as a total group.

(b) It might also have some influence on the direction of consumers' demand, calling attention to those goods for which needs are greatest and most calculable.

(c) It would also call attention of business, banking and investing interests to sources of new business in the most useful fashion; as parts of a rational national budget of production and consumption.

This project of an economic survey calls for a considerable amount of statistical material which does not exist, and much of which would be very hard to collect. In some cases, especially in times of crisis, certain statistics might injure the standing of an industry if made public. In such cases statistics might be collected in confidence, to be used only in devising policies to help meet the emergency, and published only after lapse of time has removed all fear of dangerous consequences, and only as totals. It goes without saying that the survey should at all times be kept as closely up to date as possible.

Those who have dealt with statistics know how much easier it is to call for complete figures than to bring them into being. Hence the reality of such a survey is sure to fall short of ideal goals. Nevertheless, if the attempt is made, it can hardly fail to produce results of great value. It has been suggested that new corporations should receive that part of the current survey bearing on their own field of operations along with their papers of incorporation. Thus the inevitable risks of pioneering might be materially reduced, and the capitalization of hopes based on conditions which are certain not to continue, be eliminated.

VII. POLICIES

1. LIMITATION OF OUTPUT

If regularization of capital expenditures is brought about, and excess producing capacity kept within reasonable bounds, it seems probable that limitation of output itself will not be needed except in special cases and as a temporary emergency measure. In such cases, where monopoly profits are clearly out of the question, it seems probable that limitation of output could safely be permitted without formal machinery for the regulation of prices and profits. Any permanent limitation of output should be accompanied by effective regulation, including power to control prices where necessary.

2. PRICES AND PRICE CONTROL

The approximate stabilization of general price levels would be of the utmost importance to the regularization of production and employment. The subcommittee expresses no judgment as to the practicability of general stabilization, though it seems probable that it would have to be international. Lacking this, attempts at pegging particular prices are to be avoided. The measures of regularization already proposed should help to reduce the more extravagant fluctuations of particular prices. But where the prices of raw materials change, prices of finished products should change in harmony more promptly, rather than less promptly than at present.

In addition, if increases in productiveness lower production costs, and the average level of money incomes cannot be easily raised as fast as productiveness is increased, it is desirable that prices should come down in the industries where costs are lowered, regardless of the precise effect on the average of all prices as expressed in a general price index. This may be the easiest method of adjustment. It is more important to achieve and maintain an equilibrium among prices, incomes and production than to prevent all changes in this abstract price average. Such movements in prices as might result from this process would be too slow to disturb general business conditions, and thus would not be open to the criticism that falling prices are bad for business.

The regulation of prices, suggested above as a possibility, is a serious undertaking and one not to be entered into lightly. Under favorable conditions it might aid stabilization of production; but it might produce the opposite effect at times by causing producers to hold up programs of production and expansion while waiting for the outcome of rate cases, which might drag on for months. Public utilities dealing with services can hold up their programs of capital expansion under such conditions; but manufacturers might go even farther and hold up current production and allow inventories to run low.

The character of regulation would be different from that with which we are familiar. There would be more emphasis on the differences in cost of production in different establishments and less on the rate of return to investment, which would necessarily vary from producer to producer. It might well be wise to fix, not the price, but the margin above cost of basic raw materials. In some cases return on sales might be emphasized rather than return on investment, though the latter would always need to be considered. Regulating bodies would need a deal of backbone to resist the pressure of the high-cost producers who could not earn a living return at such prices as the public should pay. These high-cost producers would naturally be backed by the interest of the more efficient producers, for obvious reasons. Yet prices should be set at levels which should force the marginal producers in most cases to improve or retire; then after a due interval the process might be repeated, as often as the advance in the arts seemed to justify. If this method were successful, it should narrow the differentials between the best and the poorest producers and thus reduce the average rate of competitive profit. At the same time greater stability would reduce risk and make it possible to attract capital for a smaller return. Thus there might be more to divide between wage-earners and consumers—if the policy were successful. But success will not be easy.

In view of the difficulties, reliance might be placed provisionally on publicity of profits, with power to regulate prices held in reserve.

3. LABOR POLICY

We advocate a nationally organized labor market with a nationwide employment service, vocational guidance and vocational re-education for workers displaced from their trades. These measures do not hinge in any way on the program of economic planning. They would fit in with it, but are necessary whether it is adopted or not.

We believe that unemployment reserves or unemployment insurance in some form is not only necessary, but can be made to act as a stabilizing rather than an unstabilizing factor in industry. They should be so organized as to give employers the maximum incentive to regularization of work. But even without this they can have a good effect by making purchasing power more regular than the productive activity from which it is derived. If stabilization succeeds, the burden of unemployment insurance will become moderate, but the need will still exist; because there will still be ups and downs in particular trades, even if seasonal unemployment is partly or wholly taken out of the scope of insured risks, as would be quite possible.

We agree that the best remedy for unemployment is work and not "doles." But properly organized insurance is not a dole, and we must face the fact that there is little likelihood for a long time of our being able to find work for all who should have it. This would be especially true if stabilization should, at first, succeed better in the relatively easy tasks of preventing overproduction than in the more difficult task of expanding demand and output together.

Increasing uniformity between the states in labor legislation should be an object of policy.

More general organization of labor is desirable, both as a force tending to raise the low wage rates now prevailing in unorganized fields and as a means to the more effective co-operation of labor in policies of industrial stabilization. Where labor is already well organized, these organizations can be relied on to protect standards of wages and conditions. And if the policy of the stabilization organization in the

industry were genuinely directed toward as high wages as
possible, the result should be a co-operative attitude on the
part of organized labor which would make it possible to
enlist their efforts in aid of stabilization policies. In industries where labor is not effectively organized, this result will
be more difficult to secure. All legal obstacles to the organization of labor should be removed.

During a period of unemployment, available work may
be distributed by working less than the standard working
week. Under normal conditions, a gradual and progressive
shortening of the standard week itself should go hand in
hand with a gradual increase of weekly earnings. These two
kinds of shortening should not be confused. One is normal
and desirable, the other an emergency makeshift which
should be temporary. The goal is to use increased productiveness partly to increase the incomes of workers and partly
to increase their leisure; not, as at present, to be compelled
to reduce the working hours and incomes of some in order
to give employment to others.

4. SEASONAL IRREGULARITIES

In the reduction of seasonal fluctuations in industry and
employment, the interest of the business concerned is so
strongly on the side of regularization, and there is so little
question of injuring other interests, that this matter can
probably best be left on a basis of voluntary action, with the
staff acting as a promotive agency and a clearing-house for
information as to what results have been accomplished and
by what kinds of methods.

5. PUBLIC WORKS

*We advocate a system whereby public works shall be con-
ducted on an elastic schedule* with postponable projects

prepared ahead of actual construction; with sites provided for, plans and contracts drawn up, and financial authorizations ready at all times for the quick raising of the funds necessary to enlarging the volume of work. However, as large new projects take sometimes years to reach their full possibilities of affording demand for labor, emphasis must be upon varying the rate at which work regularly in process is carried on, wherever this can be done without serious inefficiency. The volume of work which can be so controlled is far from sufficient to stem a depression in the absence of a corresponding regularization of private construction. It can merely be a useful part of a general program; but as such it should certainly be used to the utmost. And its effects can be larger than the numbers directly employed. Every man set to work on highway construction employs not only makers of concrete and highway-construction machinery, but makers of all the consumption goods on which he spends his wages, thus in turn employing others. This chain of cumulative effects is not endless, but it goes a long distance.

6. PUBLIC FINANCE

In order that governmental employment may operate to counteract rather than to reinforce business depression, it is necessary that expenditures be expanded at just these times when revenues fall off and budgets are straitened. A government in the strong financial situation of ours, backed by our generally strong national economy, need not and should not be afraid of using public credit freely or of incurring deficits at such times, relying on balancing the budget from surpluses secured in more prosperous years. *The effect of government expenditures on economic stability is more important than accurate balancing of the budget in each single year.* There need be no fear that borrowing will depress business by removing funds from the general capital market, at a time when business expansion is not calling for such funds in anything like normal volume, provided measures are taken to mobilize the lending power which actually exists, *e.g.*, by thawing out frozen credits. Even increased taxes, whose yield and burden are likely to be deferred a year or more, with short-term borrowing in anticipation of their yield, cannot depress business as much as prompt expenditures can stimulate it. By the time the taxes come to be paid, business may be in a stronger position to pay them.

Of course, it is not always possible to tell exactly where we are on the curve of prosperity and depression, or where the next swing will take us. And hence the borrowing policy should be used with caution to avoid the temptation to general inflationism in normal times. Such borrowing should be for a short term of years, and stringent measures should be taken to see that they are retired on the return of prosperity. The point is that if taxes are sufficient to support the government in the general run of good times and bad, a deficit in an admittedly very bad year need not be thought to necessitate desperate efforts at retrenchment to balance the budget.

Taxes should at all times avoid forms which directly burden productive activity (e.g., a sales tax) and especially so in a depression. The fiscal need of balancing a budget should not lead to the imposing of this type of tax at such a time.

7. CREDIT, INVESTMENT AND SPECULATION

The Board should initiate organization in the fields of credit, investment and speculation as in others. There is peculiar need for unitary control, or at least unified policy, in all the various branches of this field, including the use of corporate surpluses; and one great task of organization would be to determine whether this should be done under an enlargement of the scope of the Federal Reserve System or by setting up somewhat similar systems in other fields, with close affiliations. Among the groups to be drawn into the general organization are: state banks and insurance companies and the state departments regulating them, trust companies, investment bankers, stock exchanges, finance companies and organizations dealing with consumers' credit in general.

One of the most promising controls might result from the use of the Board's statistical survey. This should serve as a basis for a more effective qualitative control of the uses to which credit is put. This is vitally needed as a supplement to mere quantitative control of discount rates or amounts of credit issues.

Speculation in securities is inherently difficult to regulate; and in devising specific means of enforcement it will be necessary to enlist the co-operation of the authorities governing the exchanges. This should be done under the guidance of the most appropriate nationwide planning body or bodies concerned with the general structure of credit and investments. Such body should have the power to recommend legislation setting up more formal means of control, if more informal measures fail to produce adequate results, and if appropriate tests of unsound practices can be devised.

Here again use could be made of the Board's statistical survey. This could serve as a means both of diagnosing dangerous trends and of checking them, *e.g.*, showing when security values are out of line with any conceivable future trends of production and earnings, or when particular industries are overbuilt. In such cases estimated normal values might be substituted for momentary market prices as a basis for the use of securities as collateral for loans. The regularization of capital expenditures, already set up as a major objective, would react on speculation and be reacted on by it. The general effect of planning for stabilization in production should help reduce speculative fluctuations.

As a basis for the information necessary to a comprehensive plan, as well as for sound conditions in the security markets, corporate statements and reports on an adequate and uniform basis are necessary, as well as more conservative regulation governing incorporation. If these ends can only be secured by federal incorporation, that is recommended. The federal corporate-income tax may also be made a vehicle for the gathering of highly valuable statistics, especially if combined with more uniform accounting.

8. INTERNATIONAL TRADE, CREDIT AND THE WAR DEBTS

Planning by one country is insufficient without taking into the reckoning the whole range of international economic factors. Our policy in these fields must be rationally consistent with our whole attempt at a regularized economy. Our new status as a creditor nation calls for internal and external adjustments which we have not yet made. Where our business activity hinges on international movements of an essentially temporary character—such as our post-war export of capital—the least we can do is to avoid building on such transient foundations a more or less permanent productive structure and a whole superstructure of impossible expectations for the future. It is not in our interest to insist on international debt payments which will seriously handicap Europe's recovery or threaten her continued economic stability.

VIII. WHAT CAN PLANNING ACCOMPLISH?

We have chosen to advocate planning of the voluntary sort without giving any public body power to draw up schedules of production and compel adherence to them. The natural question with reference to this type of planning is whether it has power to make any real difference to forces so powerful as those which topple business against its will from prosperity into depression.

If we test proposals for planning by asking what they could do to save the situation if once a major depression got under way, the answer will be discouraging. But that is not a fair test, since the most important work of planning is preventive in character. To take a single instance, if the stock-market mania of 1929 had been checked, the depression that followed would not have been so severe. Not only would domestic conditions have been sounder, but Europe's finances would not have suffered the disastrous strains that resulted from her loss of funds, attracted by our speculative boom. And the worldwide decline of prices, probably due in any case, would probably not have been so sharp and heavy.

Planning cannot prevent all disturbances that shake the economic system. What it can hope to do, is to mitigate or curb those features of the system which cause disturbances to spread and intensify cumulatively; and to prevent business from getting into such a top-heavy condition that outside disturbances will start it on a long downward slide. Even this will be sufficiently difficult.

There can be no absolute certainty in advance that the type of machinery here proposed will develop power enough to overcome these difficulties; but there seems a very fair prospect of at least partial success. If the attempt fails, it will have formed a transition system affording us an opportunity to gain a working acquaintance with the nature of the problem and make the basic surveys which are necessary in any case before a more compulsory system of planning could work successfully.

Another reason for hope is the fact that business appears to realize that it is facing a serious situation, not merely this year but for future years, and to be in earnest about the need of rescuing itself. The proposed plan gives it a chance to do so, with a reasonably free choice of means and methods. We cannot afford to give business the right to say unchallenged that it is only the "obsolete" anti-trust laws which prevent it from regularizing itself. Neither can we merely abolish these laws and leave business free to regularize as it will. The project outlined above would, in effect, give business its chance under reasonable safeguards. *Some such attempt must be made;* and a great deal hinges on whether it succeeds or not. Private business has not failed, but the laissez-faire method of keeping people at work, and machines at work, has failed to accomplish endurable results. It is both logical and urgently necessary to give business the chance to try a different method.

The main hope of results lies in the combination of scientific fact-finding directed to uncovering the causes of instability, a standing organization devoted to the problem, and representation of all the interests involved, which between them have a far larger stake in stabilization policies than single business enterprises feel. No one of these alone would be sufficient, but from the combination of all of them some results may fairly be expected.

More specifically, the use of statistical reports and surveys should help toward forming the habit of referring to this kind of guidance instead of relying on the indications of the immediate market, with their "illusions of competitive bidding," whereby the effect of a given demand in the market is often multiplied like a mirage. It may expose demands which rest on mere temporary concentrations, for example, of two years' construction in one year, or six months' purchasing power in five months, through increase in the volume of consumers' credit. Such concentrations cannot in the nature of the case continue, but must almost surely be followed by a reaction; at least when the cumulative force of their impetus has spent itself. The tendency to present such things as the beginnings of a "new era" might possibly be deflated and replaced by a rational skepticism of all such predictions.

Another possibility is to enable business men to distinguish profits due to excess of demand over supply from those due merely to disproportionate changes in money values of raw materials, finished products, wages, interest, etc. The former justify expansion, while the latter do not; but private business is not ordinarily in a position to distinguish.

One saving possibility is that the same cumulative forces which now intensify fluctuations may equally intensify the effects of any measures of stabilization that may be adopted. Another is the possibility that the most crucial unstabilizing forces are located in a particular section of industry—construction and the creation of capital equipment. Here special efforts may be concentrated. Like all new things, the technique will require learning.

PART II

Dynamics of the Economic Mechanism

VIII

A CONTRIBUTION TO THE THEORY OF COMPETITIVE PRICE *

I N formulating economic laws, the student has the choice of two policies. He may make the statement in the simplest terms, leaving out most of the disturbing elements, which must then appear as forces causing variations from the standard. Or he may so state his law as to include as many of these disturbing elements as possible, thus sacrificing simplicity, but gaining in completeness, and cutting down the number of necessary exceptions. Such a formula includes automatically the simpler cases covered by the other type of statement. Thus the physicist's parallelogram of forces needs no readjustment in the limiting case of two forces acting in the same line, and our mathematical friends frame an equation for the ellipse which simplifies itself automatically when the two foci coincide and the ellipse becomes a circle. This type of law is characteristic of the more exact sciences, while students of economics still seem to prefer treating the ellipse as an exception to the circle rather than the circle as a simple form of ellipse. We are too easily content with treating inconvenient facts as exceptions to static law, rather than earnestly undertaking to unearth the laws that govern these facts—laws which must contain the static law as the ellipse contains the circle.

It is hardly necessary to say that this implies no criticism of the abstract method of static theory within its proper field. None will deny that it is "necessary for man with his

* Reprinted by permission from the *Quarterly Journal of Economics*, vol. XXVIII (Aug., 1914), pp. 747-71.

limited powers to go step by step, breaking up a complex question, studying one bit at a time, and at last combining his partial solutions into a more or less complete solution of the whole riddle." [1] But it is the last step that costs. It takes resolution to go forth from the ease and beautiful simplicity of a well-formed hypothesis and struggle with amorphous facts. It takes more than resolution to win through to some degree of order and of truth. The question at issue is how to attack the problems of dynamic theory: what method to use in trying to bring order out of those phases of the actual world which the static hypothesis was not framed to cover. If one were to say that the same abstractions used in static theory would never do as a basis for dynamic studies he would rouse about as much interest as by stating that black is not white. And yet to many people "theory" seems still to mean "static theory" and dynamic studies seem sometimes in danger of degenerating into mere exceptions to static law.

Even Marshall, who has said that "every plain and simple doctrine as to the relations between cost of production, demand and value is necessarily false," [2] still keeps touch not only with the static method but with static conclusions. Shreds of discarded hypotheses still cling to his argument and he still gives us deviations from static law at points where we had reason to expect something more radical.

Is it possible that the loss of prestige from which economic theory has suffered comes partly from the vast number and importance of these exceptions? Where exceptions rule, the theorist is no better off than his opponent: he is reduced, if not to the level of the man in the street, at least to that of

---

[1] Marshall, *Principles of Economics*, Book V, chap. v, § 12.

[2] *Ibid*. The writer's own indebtedness to Marshall is so great and so obvious as hardly to call for acknowledgment in detail.

any educated and informed man of no special theoretical training. And if the exceptions grow, as they seem to be growing with the increasing complexity of business relations, what wonder if many economists turn aside from theoretical study? All the more reason, then, for a determined effort to make room within the theories for as many as possible of the obstinate special cases and exceptions. The tendency of progress in our theoretical study is all in this direction. Thus the statement of the quantity theory of money with its blanket phrase "other things being equal," gives way to the detailed statement and quantitative study of the chief of these "other things" in the "equation of exchange." Could not the method of stating the law, or laws, of competitive price be developed in the same direction with advantage?

Men have a way of ignoring things until an extreme case forces them into the field of attention, then recognizing the one extreme case as an exceptional one, and finally discovering that all other cases are like it, to some extent. The economic peculiarities of specialized capitals and "general expenses" furnish a case in point. We learned first that a railroad is not like a soap factory; the next step was to learn that a soap factory is more or less like a railroad, and that the things we thought peculiar to railroads are, in fact, well-nigh universal. The discovery of "potential competition" as a check on trusts may lead to the further discovery that most competition is potential, active competition being limited in many fields by understandings and informal agreements.

I. ECONOMICS AS A THEORY OF LIMITS

The study of these facts is dynamic theory, and in approaching it, it may be well to "stop, look and listen"; and even to ask what economic theory really is before asking how dynamic theory is different from static. Economic theory is essentially a theory of limits. Strictly speaking and with a view to practical applications, it is not so safe to say that competitive price tends to equal the expense of production as to say that the difference between competitive price and expense of production tends to become smaller than any assigned quality. Of course this depends on the assumption that the supply can be adjusted with infinite delicacy. If capital and labor can come and go in infinitely small instalments, it makes no practical difference whether we say "price equals cost" or "price approaches cost as a limit"; and the static hypothesis furnishes these conditions by assuming perfect mobility of labor and capital.

But when we cut loose from this assumption and begin to study "dynamic disturbances and friction," we enter a world to which the theory of limits can no longer be applied in the same simple way. Capital and labor are mobile, but not ideally so; they come and go under difficulties and in instalments of some size. Suppose a man trying to put just five pounds of water into a pail. He cannot do it exactly, perhaps, but he can come so near that he cannot measure the difference. But five pounds of potatoes? If he must put in at least five pounds, all he can be reasonably sure of is that he will not go over the limit by more than the weight of the smallest available potato. So it is with capitalistic production. Infinitesimals are clearly out of the question when the marginal increment of capital consists in double-tracking a railroad or building a modern steel plant. Even a new grocery store or barber shop in a small town may make just as big an impression on the local market as the steel plant on the output of the nation.

Aside from these facts, the chief peculiarity of dynamic theory is its dependence on time, in contrast to static theory, which is virtually timeless. Let us consider some of the simpler consequences of this fact before going on to the more complex problems of fixed capital and joint-cost production. And always let us keep in mind the attitude of the mathematician seeking an equation that will include under a single statement the ellipse as well as the circle.

2. THE FACTOR OF TIME

We have, apparently, several "laws of normal competitive price." In the case in which different units of output involve different expenses of production due to causes that are permanent and inevitable, we have one statement of the normal level of prices, and in the case in which different producers have, from avoidable causes, different expenses of production, we have two other statements. There is a short-time tendency of price toward the level of the expense of producing the article in question in the establishment of a rather inefficient producer who is, for the time being, the marginal one. And there is a long-time tendency of price toward the expense of the most efficient methods of production, which we consider the less efficient must imitate or be displaced by the enlargement of the superior establishment.

These three laws can, if desirable, be included under the one statement that within any given period of time, the normal price for that period is equal to the highest unit expense that must needs be incurred in order to complete, at the end of that period, a rate of output large enough to bring the price down to the level of the aforesaid highest expense.[3] This form of statement may not be suited to the

---

[3] The objection might be raised that the above method of formulating the law of price exposes itself unnecessarily to the charge of circular reasoning which arises (mistakenly) out of the undeniable facts that both selling price and marginal expense of production are variable functions of the same third variable, supply; while the direction and rapidity of changes in supply are a function

popular lecture platform, but it includes all three of the cases above mentioned, in a way that shows conclusively (if there were any doubt in the learner's mind) that the laws governing these cases are not inconsistent nor even disconnected from each other, but phases of one principle.

By "normal price" is meant a price such that if the actual price goes lower than the normal, some one can "make money" (or avoid loss) by doing something that will tend to raise it, and if the actual price is higher, a similar "economic force" will be set to work whose effect must be to lower it. Therefore we must specify a period of time. Suppose that within a year's time it will be impossible, without

of the difference between the marginal expense of production and the selling price.

To put it mathematically, let P = price, S = rate of supply.
$$E = \text{expense and } T = \text{time.}$$
Then $P = f_1(S)$ and $E = f_2(S)$ and also $\Delta S = f_3(P - E)\Delta T$, an expression which we know goes to zero if S increases indefinitely.

Or, if we put $S_1 + \Delta S_1 = S_2$, and $T_1 + \Delta T_1 = T_2$ and substitute for ΔS_1, P and E their functional equivalents, we have $S_2 = S_1 + f_3\{f_1(S_1) - f_2(S_1)\}\{T_2 - T_1\}$.

If that be inviting the charge of circular reasoning, the difficulty is inherent in the facts, and we can gain nothing by shirking the issue under any form of statement. Indeed, if we do evade the issue, we are fleeing from a dragon which may devour other victims. We lose an opportunity to impale a fallacy which may be strong enough to discredit much perfectly valid reasoning.

Here is no more circular reasoning than would be involved in the mechanical explanation of the exact volume of air in the closed end of a curved tube (see diagram) after a given quantity of water has been poured in the open end.

The volume of air depends on the pressure exerted, measured by the height of the column of water A B, which depends in turn on the law governing the manner in which the pressure of the air increases in response to a reduction of its volume. But the apparent circularity of this reasoning does not prevent the water in the tube from finding a level, quite definitely determined by forces beyond its own control, a level which a physicist would calculate in advance with perfect accuracy. Nor is the writer aware that the physicists are cutting each other's throats over the rival claims of the column-of-water theory and the elasticity-of-air theory as explanations of the problem.

producing some cloth that costs ten cents per yard to weave, to satisfy the demand of those willing to pay that much for the service of weaving. What matter if the best plants can do the work for seven cents, and what matter if in ten years' time these plants will have been enlarged and others will have copied their methods until the whole demand can be satisfied at the lower price? What matter if there be a further tendency for the expense to fall still lower as the best methods are improved upon? It remains true that if, for any reason, the price be lowered below ten cents within the year, the forces of economic equilibrium will act at once to raise it again to ten cents, not to lower it still farther. This price appears to satisfy the requirements of "normal price" so long as the calculations are limited to one year's time. It would seem that in this case the force of competition, tending to bring price down to seven cents per yard, is not nullified by obstructions, but rather reversed in its effect by the conditions which govern it. With reference to the ten-year period seven cents per yard is the marginal expense of weaving, while with reference to a period of one year, ten cents per yard is the marginal expense.

The static state knows no limits of time, and hence differences in costs do not exist for it, so far as they spring from innovations, or can be eliminated by imitation, or by the absorbing of weak enterprises and the extension of strong ones. The only differences to be recognized by static theory are permanent ones.[4] The student of actual conditions, however, is dealing with disturbances where time, and the speed with which actions and reactions occur, is of the utmost importance. The rate at which demand can grow, the

[4] Hence the application of the above law to a static state is much simplified and quite obvious. This is equally true, whether we do or do not choose to count rents and royalties among the expenses of production. Cf. Marshall, *Principles of Economics*, Book V, chap. v.

periods over which it fluctuates, the time needed to enlarge, reduce or improve the facilities of production, and even the speed with which a reduction of price reacts on the amount sold—all these facts are grist for his mill. He must study everything in terms of time.

3. FIXED CAPITAL AND JOINT COST

The most obstinate cases remaining outside the law of price as thus formulated are those of joint-cost production, either of different articles or of different units of a homogeneous output,[5] especially where the joint outlay represents an investment of highly specialized capital. Are these facts to be treated as mere disturbances and their effects measured as variations from a static norm, or can a law be framed broad enough to include them?

In the first place, the writer doubts if even a stationary state would be free from the effects of such phenomena, if we were to imagine such a state developed out of the present condition by stopping the processes of change and giving the factors of production unlimited time to find their level.[6] Some forms of capital cannot be shifted without loss, no matter how much time is allowed for the piecemeal transfer of the depreciation fund; a railroad embankment, for instance, or a tunnel.

Moreover in any large industrial plant, as well as in a railroad, the depreciation account is managed with reference to keeping the value of the plant undiminished in its original

[5] The writer does not insist on this extension of the term "joint cost." The reader may, if he chooses, think in terms of prime cost and supplementary costs or of fixed and variable outlays, and the argument will be unaffected. At present (1936) the writer prefers this latter usage, though at the time of writing the above, he preferred one term to cover both cases. Cf. *Studies in the Economics of Overhead Costs*, p. 58.

[6] This is not just the assumption of the perfect "static state," though it has been used sometimes for illustrative purposes as a working approximation.

use and in continuous operation—not with reference to scrapping the entire outfit at some time and building new. There is no moment in the normal career of a large manufacturing plant when it goes to pieces like the one-hoss shay, and the depreciation accounts are not accumulated with any such catastrophe in view. As a result, they would not be large enough at any time to rebuild the establishment entire, scrapping the original equipment and getting out without loss. Therefore in such cases producers would find it better to endure even permanently a loss of some part of the usual rate of income on their capital, rather than undergo the loss of a larger part of the value of the capital itself in shifting it to some other enterprise.[7]

4. PRICE IS INDETERMINATE

Thus even in the longest of long runs we should be compelled to admit that, in some cases, price would be indeterminate between two levels, one high enough to attract new capital and labor into the business, and another lower level, at which some of what is already in would be forced out. For we must admit that a certain amount of excess

[7] Exception may be taken to this form of statement by those who hold that capital is nothing other than earning power capitalized. Obviously, if this terminology be adopted the foregoing argument becomes impossible *in its present form*. But if the relation of expense to price is to have any meaning at all, the term "expense" must have some reference to the actual outlay involved in investment, and the result of changing the definition of capital would only be to shift the real issue over to the question of the normal relation between the earnings of capital and the expenses of reproducing it. And under this terminology, the entire argument of this paper could, if necessary, be restated without losing any of its validity. The question at issue is in part the same that is treated on pp. 285-288 of Professor J. B. Clark's *Essentials of Economic Theory*.

For the purposes of the present study, which is primarily from the individualistic standpoint, we may assume a rate of interest, and not undertake here the solution of the objection that the cost of reproducing capital includes interest on other capital. This paper is not a study of the theory of interest.

producing capacity might continue indefinitely. It is only
by virtue of assuming a demand that grows, but never
shrinks, that the economist can say that "price tends to equal
the expenses of production, including interest on investment."

Even Marshall's argument proves no more than this,
though it appears to carry much farther. If we look for
an exact definition of the expenses of production which
govern normal price, we become involved in a confusion
quite foreign to Marshall's usual reasoning. At one point we
read "the marginal supply price is that, the expectation of
which in the long run just suffices to induce capitalists to
invest their material capital." [8] Obviously, it is growing investments to which this statement applies. But two pages
farther on we read: "Price must be sufficient to cover the
expenses of production of those producers who have no
special and exceptional facilities; for if not they will withhold or diminish their productions and the scarcity of the
amount supplied, relatively to the demand, will raise the
"price." Again: [9] "Supplementary costs are taken to include
standing charges on account of the durable plant . . . they
must be completely covered by it (selling price) in the
long run; for if they are not, production will be checked."
Apparently these costs are taken as identical with the
"marginal supply price" of new investments, cited in the
preceding paragraph. But farther on we read: [10] "For the
capital already invested in improving land and erecting
buildings, and in making railways and machinery, has its
value determined by the net income (or quasi-rent) which
it will produce; and if its prospective income-yielding power

[8] *Principles of Economics*, 5th ed., p. 497, cf. p. 359.
[9] *Ibid.*, pp. 359-360.
[10] *Ibid.*, p. 593.

should diminish, its value would fall accordingly and would be the capitalized value of that smaller income after allowing for depreciation." Accepting this last, supplementary costs become equal to whatever the business can earn over prime costs, and the minimum limit on price turns into a vanishing quantity.

If the value of invested capital is derived from its earning power, obviously there is no meaning in the statement that the price of the product is governed by the necessity of earning the current rate of interest on the value of the capital. And if the "interest" which governs the selling price is the interest necessary to attract new investments of capital, obviously it will only be effective in a condition of growing demand.[11] Marshall sees that if price is governed by expense the governing expense must include no land rent, else there is circular reasoning.[12] Apparently he does not appreciate the consequences of the fact that he has himself placed standing investments of capital on the same footing as land and thus ruled their earnings out of the category of marginal expenses of production.

So much for the question whether price may remain permanently too low to pay interest on the full amount of the investment, if some of that investment is irrevocably fixed.

But in actual business the important question is not whether capital can move without loss if an indefinite time is allowed, but whether it can move fast enough to keep pace with the fluctuations of business. And a very great part of business capital is fixed with sufficient permanence so that all it can do in a period of depression is to wait for the turn of the wheel. With respect to the periods covered by

[11] This statement does not of course allow for the fact already mentioned that renewals have "supply prices" like new investments, so that the "depreciation fund" may be shifted from an unprofitable enterprise.

[12] *Op. cit.*, p. 499, cf. p. 593.

the fluctuations of prosperity in individual businesses, or by our more or less regular cycles of general activity and stagnation, such capital is fixed. The result is that the most pessimistic investor cannot withdraw such capital from a business, once it is in, while the most optimistic can always put in more. The level of such investments is like the maximum indicator of a self-recording thermometer. During considerable intervals it stands as a monument to the warmth of past enthusiasms, the summit of past hope. Thus periods of excess producing capacity are normal to modern business even tho the capacity is not too great for the demand of active seasons. This is true of so many businesses that it begins to appear virtually a universal condition varying only in degree. The structure of an ordinary retail store is fixed capital, while the fact that joint outlays affect the price problem even in retail trade is evidenced by the discrimination and higgling that are the vexation of the tourist in Europe and the chief business in life of the bazaar trader of the Orient.[18]

The typical example of capital which must be held partly idle through regularly recurring periods of slack demand is the plant of an electric light and power company, which must be in "readiness to serve" a "peak load" far greater than the average consumption, and which cannot store its service, even for a day. Of course the times and seasons of the daily and yearly changes in demand can be pretty well calculated, making the problem much simpler than that of business cycles and other fluctuations of an irregular sort. And of course the problem of charges for electricity is not the problem of competitive price. But the bottom

---

[18] As a further instance of the effects of joint cost, the writer recently found that a firm was selling the same grade of candy for 35 cents per pound, in bulk, or 55 cents per pound in boxes. Rather an expensive box!

facts of the situation are the same. Public service companies make low rates for current taken at times of the day when demand is slack, to encourage a more steady and therefore more efficient use of the plant. The United States Steel Corporation has attempted the opposite policy of "steadying" prices. Competition, again, tends to lower them sharply in slack seasons. Which is the wisest plan? It is a suggestive comparison.

To what level, in these circumstances, does active competition tend to bring prices? If prices are above the total expense of production in marginal establishments [14] there is an obvious force set in motion to lower them. To be sure, if business men were perfectly rational and ideally well-informed, they would not tie up capital in new fixed plants [15] unless the returns more than covered the outlay over the whole period of one of our business cycles. But then, if business men were all thus prescient, the great cycles would not happen. If we assume the cycles, we must also assume their causes, so far as we know them, including as one of these the behavior of the business man who invests as long as prices more than cover outlays, even tho it be at the high tide of prosperity. Under active competition, price tends to be not higher than the expenses of production, in the sense that if it does go higher, a force is set in motion to lower it.

When we come to the forces tending to raise prices when they have gone unduly low and to study the level at which these forces begin to act, the problem is more complicated. Assuming active competition and no collusion of any sort, we may say that even when unused capacity sends prices

[14] Defined with reference to the period of time in question, as stated on pp. 278-9 above.

[15] Fixed, in the sense that they cannot be shifted without serious loss within the period of a single swing of the pendulum of business activity.

below the cost level, competitive policy shows no force acting definitely to reduce the excess supply, until they go below the level that affords no return on the specialized plant but merely covers the variable expenses, including interest on such capital as can be shifted without loss within the time limits of the problem. This capital would be, roughly, the same that is commonly classed as "working capital" by business men. At this point some plants must needs be partially or wholly closed, and the fall in prices checked, tho it might not be stopped until some establishments well above the margin had temporarily closed down, the price going below their variable expenses.[16] Indeed, if the fall in demand be only sharp enough, there is no assignable minimum for the temporary fall in prices, short of the variable expenses of the most efficient producers.

5. CAPITAL WITH LIMITED MOBILITY

Some further refinements might well be added to this statement. In the first place, it fails to take into account the fact that some capital is strictly fixed, while some could be moved with a certain loss to the owner. For capital of this latter sort, earnings could never quite reach the zero point without an exodus that would be somewhat less disastrous than a shutdown. To include all varieties of capital under a general statement, we might say that the minimum would

[16] Strictly speaking, even the permanent downward tendency of prices would not be entirely stopped if there were so much difference between the efficiency of the poorest producer and the most efficient ones that the latter could earn profits well above the general rate on their investment while the former was earning nothing at all above maintenance on his. A producer as inefficient as this, however, could not be even a marginal producer by the definition here adopted, but would be already below the margin, defining the latter with reference to a period of, say, five years or more. In such a case the "tendency to minimum cost" would operate unmodified. But a more typical condition in periods of depression is that in which even the best producers are not making profits enough to tempt them into extending their operations on a large scale.

be set at the point where the loss of earnings of the whole enterprise (measured from the general rate as a standard) for the period covered by the calculations of the more fore-seeing of the entrepreneurs in question, should be equivalent to the loss in the value of the capital resulting from a hasty transfer, plus the unavoidable loss of earnings in the inter-val before the transfer could be made complete. As the accuracy of this statement is no greater than the estimates of the future on which it all depends, it would be more curious than profitable to reduce it to a mathematical formula.

Moreover, the statement only applies in case the level of price as thus determined is high enough to afford some return to the more or less fixed capital. In practice, if the business men in question carried their calculations no farther ahead than, say, six years, assuming that by that time there would be a recovery from the depression in which they found themselves, and if the capital in question would lose 12 per cent of its value if transferred in four years' time or 24 per cent if transferred in two years, and if the rate of return be taken as 6 per cent, such capital might as well stay where it is and endure a total loss of earnings for the full six-year period. And if entrepreneurs were more opti-mistic as to the prospects of recovery, they might keep their capital in the business even tho it were much more mobile than these figures represent. Thus we find that in practice the first rough statement of the law is near enough to accuracy, for an equation one side of which depends on business men's power of prophecy.

Another complication arises from the fact that the waves of prosperity and depression have their effect on the cost of production itself. Running at part capacity raises unit costs. But this is chiefly because the burden of joint outlays becomes heavier, and the greatest part of these have already been taken into calculation. Part of the loss may be borrowed from past or future through temporary economies in maintenance. What is left may be offset against the other kinds of losses in efficiency that arise from over-activity,[17] and the resultant may fairly be ignored. If it could be calculated in any given case, the result would be merely to increase or to minimize somewhat the quantitative variation in prices from one period to another, without affecting the qualitative statement of the forces that determine prices at either time.

6. FACTORS AFFECTING EXTENT OF PRICE CUTTING

But is there no way of judging how far toward this minimum limit the price is likely to fall in any given case? One statement would be that the price must fall in response to a falling-off of demand until all the productive capacity is at work which can earn anything above variable expenses at the new price-level. But common experience testifies that mills begin running at part capacity long before prices reach this level.

The statement is hypothetical, based on the implied assumption (among others) that a cut in prices, no matter how small, will at once enable the producer who makes it to take custom away from his competitors and so must necessarily enlarge his net earnings if he had any at all to start with. The corresponding assumption of the static law of price has no need to specify any rate at which business can be captured, for static theory is timeless. But to make valid a parallel conclusion in dynamic theory, the premise must be specific as to time. If new business is slow in coming

[17] Discussed in Mitchell, *Business Cycles.*

in, after a cut in prices, the immediate result will be a falling off of revenue, not an increase.

Obviously, it is not possible to transfer the allegiance of customers in an instant by any cut, no matter how small, in prices. Some approach to this would be possible in articles of standardized quality easily tested, where competition centers in price. But wherever the buyer's opinion of quality is important, and cannot be verified before every purchase, it must depend on past experience and on advertising, and furnish an inertia too great to be quickly overcome by minor changes in the price of one or the other brand of commodity. The only customers who would be attracted would be those who were hesitating already; not those who had fairly strong opinions as to the relative merits of their favorite make of article. For such articles, any serious attempt to take business way from competitors involves the time and expense of an advertising campaign. But a period of depression is not the time when expensive tactics of this sort are much indulged in. Therefore producers of this kind of goods will probably rely merely on the customary channels of advertising and can expect only a relatively slow response to any cut in prices. And in proportion as the gains are slow in coming in, the prospect of retaliation must loom larger and the motive to price-cutting be weakened.

Another element affecting the extent of price-cutting is the fact, so far disregarded, that bankruptcy awaits those who fail to cover not merely the variable outlays but interest on bonds and notes as well. It is true that a receivership does not necessarily end the competition of a corporation, even tho it can never earn the full interest contracted for. And for purposes of static theory we may be justified in regarding interest on all capital as included in the expenses of production and ignoring the different forms of ownership or credit obligation under which it is held. But the prospect of a receivership may have a very decisive effect on the immediate policy of any business manager, tho it works in devious ways that are hard to fit into any formula. Under one set of circumstances it might operate to check price-cutting and under other conditions it might precipitate a war. A producer whose solvency is in no immediate danger will be loath to begin a struggle which may end by sending prices no one knows how low. He will rather bear the evils that he has than fly to others that he knows not of, and will allow his plant to run at part capacity. But the dangerous man is the one who cannot adopt the Fabian policy without defaulting payment of his obligations. Perhaps his running expenses are high or he has mortgaged his property too heavily, or, worse still, he is called on to repay short-time loans which he has counted on being able to renew. In such a situation he cannot weigh the chances of retaliation; the prospect of renewed prosperity in a few years has no meaning for his present need. He will not even be deterred by the uncertainty whether he can enlarge his sales fast enough to save himself, any more than the uncertainty whether he can swim ashore or not will deter a man from jumping into the water if his boat is sinking.

If we can generalize at all as to this situation, it must be in the most indefinite terms. We may say that if the most efficient producers have borrowed conservatively, and the least efficient have been more reckless, the latter may go into receivers' hands without involving the leading establishments in anything that would amount to cut-throat warfare. But if there are among the efficient some who have used credit incautiously, the liability to heavy price-cutting is much increased, especially if the plants of less technical efficiency have avoided the financial drag of heavy fixed interest charges.

It is thus not possible to say definitely that the behavior of prices is governed solely by the extent to which the demand has fallen off. But it is none the less obvious that this fact is the prime cause at work, and that those industries will suffer the greatest losses in which, beside the fact of highly specialized equipment, there are great fluctuations of demand. Probably the greatest fluctuations occur in the demand for durable capital goods, while luxuries take second place.

A further disturbance confronts us when we realize that the rock-bottom prices may not be made on all of the output, but higher ones may be charged in such sheltered nooks of the market as are not open to the full fury of the competitive struggle. Discrimination is one normal result of these conditions, wherever the nature of the product, the situation of markets, and the legal and ethical standards of business conduct are such as to permit it. However, as it depends on some parts of the market being sheltered, and so not fully competitive,[18] we are justified in excluding it from our type-case and giving it separate treatment.

We may note in passing, however, that the smaller the proportion of his business that is exposed to cut-throat competition, the more free a producer is to cut prices without fear of bankruptcy. If his necessary interest charges are assured by customers for whose business he need not fight,

[18] This does not imply anything worthy the name of monopoly; merely local differential advantages of one sort or another, chiefly due to freight rates. These might be brought under the general theory of competitive price on the principle that active competition at Kokomo means potential competition at Pittsburgh, with the handicap of transportation costs weakening its effect. If the Kokomo price is a cut-throat price, the Pittsburgh price may yield more or less than a fair average return to the Pittsburgh producer, depending on the amount of protection the costs of carriage afford him.

he may cut prices freely to get other business, down to the level of variable expenses. But if his competitor is less fortunate, and is forced to compete actively for all or most of his trade, he cannot cut prices as low as this without going bankrupt, unless he happens to be entirely out of debt. Thus size is an advantage, apart from productive efficiency, and a big concern may drive to the wall a smaller one which is equally efficient, without ever cutting prices so low that they yield no return over the variable expenses of the business; for the smaller producer, whose costs may be just as low, cannot afford to cut prices all the way down to them. In view of these facts, the statement that the "trust loses money in one place and makes it up in another" is hardly an accurate description, as the trust may not be really losing money anywhere, merely charging what the traffic will bear at every point.

To sum up, then: the extent of price-cutting depends, among other things, on the variability of the demand, the situation of both weak and strong producers with regard to credit obligations, and the nature of the product— whether such that competition centers chiefly in price, or in advertising, salesmanship and the building up of "good will." In fact, it depends on so many things that it appears hardly worth while attempting to generalize further than to indicate the determining factors, leaving any special cases to be studied with whatever aid these general guide-posts may furnish.

So far as active competition goes, then, prices would seem to be indeterminate between the two levels suggested. It will be noted that this indefiniteness vanishes if the element of specialized capital invested for the business as a whole be eliminated. As this disturbing element gets smaller, the two levels approach each other, meeting in those rare

cases usually taken as points of departure in considering the
law of price, viz: those in which unit costs are calculable,
and either uniform or else governed by the law of diminishing returns.

But if normal competitive price is indeterminate over a
zone which lies entirely below the level of expense of production, how can business continue? In the first place all
that is claimed is that if price does go above this level, that
fact starts in motion a force acting to lower it; a force that
necessarily takes time to work and might be prevented from
ever attaining its result if progress went on without a check.
Progress—growth of demand and improvements lowering
expenses—is one saving grace in the situation. And it must
also be remembered that so far we have only considered
a state of ideally (or fiendishly) active competition, which
is far from representing accurately the real state of business
in these days of cosmopolitan friendships and long-distance
telephones.

7. AGREEMENTS AND POTENTIAL COMPETITION

In practice, we observe that mills begin running on part
capacity long before prices reach the low level suggested
as a minimum limit. And we also hear of secret agreements,
while tacit understandings are matters of common knowledge. In the steel industry there were the "Gary dinners,"
intended to meet the danger of cut-throat competition in a
business whose producing capacity cannot help being in excess
of the demand (at reasonable prices) for a considerable part
of the time. And before that there were "unwritten laws"
against using idle capacity to invade the field of competitors.
The indefinite nature of such practices defies deductive analysis, while the many disturbing elements preclude accurate
inductive tests. But the observer gains—shall we call it an

impression?—that these things are becoming more definite, regular and recognized, resulting in a condition that is hardly active competition, a condition in which the real check on prices is that force to which the name "potential competition" has been given. This not merely in the case of trusts, but as a normal thing in the field of general industry.

Is the effect of potential competition any more definite than that of the active variety? Provisionally, we may say that so far as it operates at all, it tends to eliminate profits save to producers whose methods are at least reasonably efficient. The expense of establishing a new enterprise as a "going concern" is a handicap, which will always serve to weaken the force of potential competition and so protect the profits of the most efficient producers already in the business. There are reasons for believing, also, that a system of agreements checked by potential competition may not always prove the most effective guarantee of increasing what efficiency we possess. Together with an obvious stimulus to improvements, it may also involve quite serious wastes.

Latent competition must lose most of its force unless it sometimes become actual. No proverb says that the child who is told that his older brother was burnt, dreads the fire. But what if these bursts of active competition end in merely initiating one new member into the circle and again agreeing on prices that will prevent any new intrusions for the time being? If the old price was higher than active competition would have brought about, there must have been some spare capacity already in the business—a condition which the new arrival would aggravate without suffering from the painful corrective of a disastrous fall in prices.

If periodical over-investment is normal to a state of active competition, may not over-investment in such a case as this be, not periodical, but chronic? In this new state there is little room for elimination of the unfit save in the most extreme cases. But there is no surer guarantee of inefficiency than a considerable number of producers, all working at part capacity and all earning at least interest on their investment. And this is a kind of inefficiency of which the prospective competitor could take no advantage for it does not spring from poor facilities for production, but from a wastefully large amount of them. Tho the existing plants, *as run*, are inefficient, no new enterprise could hope to be less so. In such circumstances is it not more nearly correct to say that the expense of production is raised to meet the price, rather than the price lowered to the level of the expense of production?

This form of waste probably has its best chance to operate subtly in mercantile business. Any one can tell if a factory is running on part time or running only part of its machines, and such a condition warns off possible invaders, but it is not equally obvious whether or not the middleman's rooms and office force, and his facilities for handling and storing his stock, are being worked up to their full capacity. The retailer's capacity is perhaps even more elastic, and the entrepreneur's own time represents a general outlay which is usually important and is equally necessary for a small or a large volume of business.

Moreover, understandings as to prices are supposed to be particularly prevalent among middlemen, while the relatively small capital needed to enter such business makes it especially easy for new competitors to enter. Wherever the manufacturer succeeds in fixing the final selling price and the dealer's margins, we have a situation admirably calculated to multiply the number of dealers competing for sales at these fixed margins until earnings are reduced to a normal level by reducing the dealers' average turnover. The American middleman is just now the target of the most serious accusations of inefficiency, beside which railroad rates and even crude farming methods sink into insignificance. Can these facts have any connection with each other, and if so, is this a case in which agreements have resulted in over-crowding the business with competitors and so reducing efficiency all around?

8. CONCLUSION

Summarizing now the main points in the foregoing argument, we may say that under dynamic (or actual) conditions, competitive price need not normally tend to equal expense of production, but may differ from it by some fairly definite amount. And we have seen that there may be different marginal expenses of production and different marginal producers corresponding to different lengths of time covered by the study in question. Taking fluctuations of demand as part of the "normal" data of dynamic economics, and inter-preting "marginal expense" and "normal price" in terms of a length of time no greater than the usual run of these business cycles, certain conclusions as to "normal price" were reached. Price tends to equal the expenses of produc-tion only if demand grows continuously or if the expenses are none of them "fixed." In general, normal price under active competition is anything from the amount needed to cover total expenses in marginal establishments down to the level of "prime" or variable costs to the more efficient producers.

However, the typical condition in businesses of large fixed investment is not one of "active competition" in the strict sense, but is coming to be more and more a condition of tacit understandings if not agreements, in which the true force governing prices is that of "potential competition."

The latter does tend to bring the level of prices to the level of the total outlay involved in production, but the combination seems likely to produce a certain amount of waste. With either kind of competition there is normally a temptation to discrimination to be dealt with in times of slack demand, so long as there is a fixed capital investment to be remunerated.

Admitting that discrimination may still best be treated as a variation from type in competitive business, especially as the law seems to be taking a more and more decided stand against it, may not the other disturbances here treated be absorbed into the general statement of the law of competitive price? One incidental result would be to throw new emphasis on the study of potential competition and the need of better and more systematized knowledge of its operation and effect—a need which at present is becoming increasingly evident.

IX

INDUCTIVE EVIDENCE ON
MARGINAL PRODUCTIVITY*

I. INTRODUCTION

A STATISTICAL analysis of production from the standpoint of marginal productivity is a notable event; and the recent pioneer effort in this field by Professor Paul H. Douglas and Charles W. Cobb[1] is deserving of the serious attention of economists, even if they consider (as the authors of the study would probably agree) that the quantitative results are not conclusive at the stage of development which the study has at present reached. Briefly, the authors have correlated an index of physical product of manufactures with indices of laborers employed and of fixed equipment (including buildings), the last being deflated to eliminate the effect of changing prices. The indices cover the period from 1899 to 1922 inclusive. The obvious features of the trends are: a more-than-fourfold growth of capital; an increase of 61 per cent in labor; and a growth of product intermediate between the two, but much nearer the lower figure representing labor. This is in harmony with the principle of diminishing productivity, and also suggests that capital has a smaller effect than labor in determining the amount of product.

The attempt to isolate and measure the marginal efficiencies of labor and capital depends naturally on the provisional assumption that the effect of the change in the

---

* Reprinted by permission from the *American Economic Review*, Vol. XVIII (Sept., 1928), pp. 449-67.
[1] See *Am. Econ. Rev.*, Supp., Mar., 1928, pp. 139-65.

proportions of the factors is not confused by any other fundamental change taking place at the same time, and that the failure of product to keep pace with capital is due to the relative shortage of labor, just as the increase in product per laborer is due to the relative plenty of capital and not, for instance, wholly or in large part due to technical progress.[2] Viewed the other way round, this implies that if capital and labor had increased at the same rate, product would have kept exact pace with either or both of them. On this assumption, one set of figures will show the marginal efficiencies of both labor and capital, the one by its relative increase and the other by its relative decrease, these being two aspects of the same movement. Under these conditions, the amount imputed to labor plus the amount imputed to capital will always equal the whole product.[3]

For instance, if product were consistently a mean proportional between labor and capital (the base year being 100 in each case), we should conclude—on this provisional assumption—that the influence of the two factors on product was equal. This would be expressed by the formula $P = L^{1/2}C^{1/2}$. Here the marginal effect on P of adding or subtracting an indefinitely small unit of either L or C, multiplied by the total number of such units employed, would always equal half the total P. In the present case, Professor Cobb finds the best fit given by the formula $P = L^{3/4}C^{1/4}$ (modified by

---

[2] As we shall see later, one kind of progress acts jointly with increased capital in such a way as not to violate the conditions necessary to this type of statistical measurement of marginal productivity. Other kinds of progress do violate these conditions, and make necessary other methods if marginal productivity is to be accurately measured.

[3] This proposition has been developed in different forms by Wicksteed, Flux, Professor Cobb and the present writer. Professor F. H. Knight has raised objections to an arithmetical illustration used by the present writer, though apparently agreeing with the algebraical form of the proposition. See *Jour. Pol. Econ.*, XXXIII, 550-62, Oct., 1925.

an almost negligible constant), making labor's imputed share at all points three-quarters of the whole, and capital's one-quarter. Of course, as he notes, there is always the possibility that the exponents might themselves be variables, in which case the shares of labor and capital would vary correspondingly. So long as there is no evidence of such variation, the figures lend provisional support to the claims of those who have argued that total wages should increase proportionately with increases of total product.[4]

While this function is mainly governed by the long-run trend of the figures, it also shows a remarkably high co-efficient of correlation with the short-time fluctuations—higher than is afforded by simple indexes such as labor alone, pig iron production alone, etc. However, in interpreting this finding we must keep in mind the fact that the Pearsonian coefficient may show perfect correlation between

[4] It may be of interest to note the relation between the present study and the form of analysis suggested by Professor H. L. Moore ("A Theory of Economic Oscillation," *Quart. Jour. Econ.*, XLI, 1-29, Nov., 1926). Moore assumes constant exponents to represent the partial efficiencies of the different factors of production (p. 19, equations 28), and in this respect the methods are alike. They differ in that Moore does not specifically assume that the sum of these exponents is equal to unity. While this may be implied at the point where he assumes that production has reached conditions of minimum cost (p. 21), his treatment up to that point contains no such assumption. Furthermore, his proposed method of study is based on departures from trends, not on the movements of the trends themselves. While this avoids the difficulties of segregating the effects of progress, the movements it would reveal are chiefly the fluctuations of the business cycle. These clearly involve departures from the condition of minimum costs and do not, according to the contention of the present paper, follow the long-run laws of marginal productivity, which are the only ones that could be expected to govern the rewards of the factors of production. Professor Moore's method also involves separate measurement of the partial efficiencies of the different factors rather than simultaneous determination, as does Professor Cobb's formula. Professor Moore's method assumes a single industry, and he might consider it inapplicable to manufacturing as a whole; though the difference seems chiefly one of degree, as single industries contain many heterogeneous processes. It would be interesting to see what results Moore's method would give if applied to the present figures.

a series of large fluctuations and another of much smaller ones, provided this unequal relation is uniformly preserved.[5] In the present case the cyclical fluctuations of actual product are consistently much larger than those calculated from the formula, showing that they have a behavior of their own, markedly different from the general trend. On this fact hinges one of the three main points of the present paper: namely, an attempt to assimilate both kinds of movement into one more comprehensive formula.

Two other major matters are: the nature of the necessary allowance for those factors of production not included in the original study, and the effect of technical progress. But before proceeding to these main topics, some attention must be paid to a number of other matters which can be more briefly disposed of. No general criticism of the indexes themselves will be here attempted; but it will be assumed that they will be improved and refined as the authors continue their researches. The many-faceted issue of "social productivity versus private acquisition" will also be passed over. Suffice it for the present that technical productivity exists, and is conditioned by the shifting proportions of the "factors."

2. THE AVERAGING OF DIVERSE CASES

We must keep in mind that no single industry, except by coincidence, will show exactly the curve of productivity expressed in the national total. The aggregate is the resultant of certain industries in which capital per laborer has increased little if at all, and others in which the increase is far more than the average; also of the relative growth of certain industries in which capital per worker is naturally

[5] Perfect correlation requires equal deviations when each is measured in terms of the standard deviation of its own series.

or necessarily large.[6] Neither of these facts has any vitiating effect on the type of study before us, but their effects are worth noting for the better understanding of the movements which this study records.

Let us express initial labor, capital and product by indexes of 100 each. Suppose 5 per cent of the product, by value, to come from an industry in which the proportion of capital to labor is four times the average, or four units of capital to one of labor. Suppose the value-products of all industries to be proportional to the costs of these factors, the costs to be proportional to the marginal productivities, and the marginal productivities to be in accord with the Cobb formula. Then the value product of one unit of labor and four units of capital should be ¾ plus ¼ or 1¾ units of value. Five value units of this same product would then require 2⁶⁄₇ units of labor and 11³⁄₇ units of capital. Let this industry double in size and an increase of 2⁶⁄₇ per cent in labor and of 11³⁄₇ per cent in capital will yield an increase of 5 per cent in value product (or in physical product as measured by the index). The percentage increase in product is equal to ¾ the percentage increase in labor plus ¼ the percentage increase in capital. For infinitesimal increments this would agree exactly with the formula $P = L^{¾}C^{¼}$, and for ordinary finite increments the discrepancy would be of no account. The change, then, has no material effect on marginal productivities; its chief significance is that it permits an increase in capital, relative to labor, without reducing its marginal productivity as would otherwise naturally be the case. It increases the field for employment of capital without loss of marginal efficiency.

The increase in capital has raised the marginal produc-

---

[6] Since writing the above, I note that this last point is emphasized by Woodlief Thomas, *Am. Econ. Rev.*, Supp., Mar., 1928, p. 132.

tivity of workers in general, but not equally throughout industry, if measured in physical goods. Yet workers of a given grade must get substantially equal wages whether working in an industry where increased capital has raised physical productivity greatly, or in one where it has had little or no effect. Hence we should expect a relative increase in the money cost of products, or of single processes, where capital has shown little growth; and a relative decline where its growth has been great. This, of course, tends to increase the incentive to combat these high costs by extending the reign of the machine to the yet unconquered provinces.[7] But this does not entirely overcome the inherent difficulties in the handicraft type of occupations. Incidentally, among the products whose relative costs and prices tend to decrease, are the machines (but not buildings) which form so large a part of capital itself.

3. EFFECT OF DEPRECIATION AND REPLACEMENTS

If, from figures of physical product, we are to draw inferences as to the net rewards payable to the owners of the factors of production, the necessary allowance for depreciation and replacements must be taken account of. It also has a vital bearing on the distinction between the gross product of industry as a whole and the net yield available for consumption.

---

[7] This point has a bearing on the recent controversy as to whether high wages stimulate the use of capital. The point was made that high wages resting on high productivity do not mean high costs; also that universal high wages affect the cost of machines, and hence of machine processes, equally with hand work. The fact is that a fairly universal increase in wages rests on an increase in physical productivity which is far from universal. The increased productivity, being mainly conditioned by increased capital, is unevenly distributed, and labor costs in relatively non-mechanized processes do rise, for the reason just indicated. And machines, the production of which is highly mechanized, become relatively cheaper.

To the manager weighing the economy of enlarging capital equipment, the physical results must be sufficient to compensate not only for interest on the investment, but for the further expenses for maintenance, depreciation and also taxes, where taxes are levied on tangible property. And where technical progress is rapid, there is correspondingly rapid obsolescence, with the result that managers frequently feel that a new type of equipment is not worth installing unless it promises to pay for itself in two years—some say one year. A rapid growth of capital per laborer calls for such frequent changes in its form as to cause rapid obsolescence of particular devices in many departments. This is not universal, but in general it is no more than safe to conclude that, of the technical "marginal product" of physical capital, not more than half is converted into net income available for interest and dividends.

Furthermore, in interpreting increased per capita product as an evidence of increased consuming power we must remember that an appreciable part of the increase consists of capital goods destined to replacements and enlargements of capital. Enlargements, of course, represent income which might, theoretically, have been consumed; but not if advances in productiveness are to be continued. So far as these elements absorb an increasing proportion of output as compared to the base year, they call for some deduction from the index of physical product in order to find the rate of increase in income really available for consumption.

4. THE NATURE OF THE FACTORS USED: LABOR

The index of labor is an index of man-years, although, as Professor Douglas points out, the number of hours' work represented is subject to two changes; a downward trend in the length of the working week, and fluctuations of part-time and overtime in prosperity and depression. Granting that these movements should be taken account of when they can be accurately measured, how can this best be done? Should the labor index be deflated and made into an index of hours worked? There are conclusive reasons why this change, by itself, would be an incorrect allowance for the purpose in hand.

The fundamental cause whose effect we are studying is change in the proportion of labor to capital, manifesting itself in its "normal" or long-run fashion: namely, in equipment more adequate in character, superior in quality, more automatic. Because the worker, *when he is working*, has better equipment, his productivity, *when he is working*, is greater. If we have a plant adapted to 100 workers and double its size without changing its character, so that it now calls for 200 workers, and if we then operate it with the original 100, there has been no effective increase in the proportion of capital to labor, and we should certainly not expect the increase in product which the Cobb formula calls for. To produce this effect the equipment must be adapted to the new proportion so that the additional amount will be effectively employed and not standing idle. Or if the original plant is worked half-time, here again is no doubling of the proportion of capital to labor, *when working*. A shorter work-day may increase productiveness per hour; but this is due to a different cause from increased equipment per worker, and presumably follows a different law.

It appears, then, that the "proportion of factors" is best measured by the ratio of capital to the number of workers to which it is adapted; or to number of workers employed when working at normal percentage of capacity. Since this last percentage does not change much in the long run, the ratio of capital to laborers actually employed is a satisfactory index for long-run purposes, with one qualification. Two or three laborers working in successive shifts should, in strictness, be counted as one worker for this purpose. Otherwise a plant working three shifts would appear to give each worker only one-third as much capital to work with as an identical plant working one shift. The substitution of three shifts for two in the steel mills created a slight fictitious decrease in the proportion of capital to labor, and any general tendency toward substituting continuous operation with shifts for ordinary daytime operation would have the same effect. In the present state of the development of this research, these errors are probably not important, though with greater refinement of the indexes they might have to be taken into account.

What, then, should be done about the trend to a shorter working week? Is it fair to gauge the effect of our vast increases in capital by a 30 per cent increase in product per worker without allowing for the handicap of a 16 per cent decrease in hours per week? [8] A perfect answer calls for more knowledge than we have of the causes, nature and results of this shortened work-week in itself. Is it mainly a way, as productive power increases, of taking only part of the gain in the form of more goods, and the rest in leisure? Then we should certainly use product per hour instead of per year to measure the increased productiveness due to capital. Or is the shorter week in itself as productive, other things equal, as the longer? Then product per year is the proper measure. Or—as is more plausible—has the shorter week been made necessary (and not unprofitable) by the use of intensive speeding methods, or by the added strain

[8] The figure of 30 per cent is taken, not from actual product, but from the "calculated product" of the Cobb formula, representing the trend of product in relation to labor and capital. The figure of 16 per cent is based on a provisional estimate by Professor Douglas, subject to correction.

resulting from the use of more elaborate machinery? Then again we should gauge the productiveness of these methods under the shorter week which their use makes necessary, comparing it on equal terms with the longer week which was possible under former conditions: that is, using annual or weekly product with no allowance for shortened hours.

The facts are undoubtedly a mixture of all these conditions, and the proper assumption lies somewhere between these two extremes—but where? Lacking data for a quantitative answer to this question, or even as yet for constructing a reliable index of production per hour, Professor Douglas has followed the only practicable course; but we should recognize clearly that the result minimizes the effect of increased capital in increasing output. By making no allowance for the handicap of the shortened week, it gives capital too little credit for increased output. If, for example, the standard working week was shortened by 16 per cent from 1899 to 1922, and this had the effect of making product per standard week 9 per cent less than it would otherwise have been, then an index of increased product *due to increased labor and capital as separate causes*, should lie, for 1922, $\frac{9}{91}$ or virtually 10 per cent above the index of yearly production.

Part-time and overtime raise a different question. Lacking data to the contrary, we may provisionally assume that they show no general upward or downward trend throughout the period, but merely fluctuate with the business cycle. They involve no change in the character of equipment, or in the effective proportion of capital to labor as defined above. They affect output, and are meant to do so, but for a different reason and presumably according to a different quantitative law. They reinforce the cyclical fluctuations in numbers employed, and the two effects are merged in the aggregate statistics.

We should naturally expect a 1 per cent increase in numbers employed in a given fixed plant to increase output by more than 1 per cent (indirect labor being relatively "constant"), while a 1 per cent increase in hours worked, relative to the standard week, would naturally increase output somewhat less than 1 per cent. Changes in numbers are greater,[9] and their effect is predominant. The indexes in the present study, showing only changes in numbers employed, serve to exaggerate slightly their effect on output by adding the effect of the unrecorded changes in part-time and overtime.

5. THE NATURE OF THE FACTORS USED: CAPITAL

With reference to capital a more serious objection is likely to arise: namely, that the various elements of equipment can only be added together in terms of their prices, which depend on their productivities and hence cannot be used to explain productivity without circular reasoning. One possible answer is simply that we have here certain observed uniformities of behavior, and there can be no circular reasoning in the mere inductive process of analyzing the behavior as observed. Indeed, circular reasoning in the sense used above appears to be a concept alien to the realm of the inductive student. He must translate it into other terms. "Is a phenomenon self-determining or indeterminate so far as concerns the causes under investigation?" If so, its behavior should afford evidence of that fact. In the present case, the evidence points strongly to a causal connection

---

[9] The study of W. I. King, *Employment, Hours and Earnings in Prosperity and Depression,* pp. 47-53, 83, indicates that part-time in the depression of 1921 was slight; but this finding cannot be regarded as conclusive for all cases.

between supply of capital as measured in the index and output of commodities. A theoretical interpretation of this relation presents difficulties, but these do not vitiate the inductive portion of the study.

6. SENSITIVENESS OF RESULTS TO ERRORS OR ADJUSTMENTS IN THE INDICES

In any such study as this, an important question is: How sensitive are the results to possible error or bias in the data used? In this case they are decidedly sensitive. The relative shares attributed to labor and capital are materially affected by including or excluding the decidedly abnormal years of war and post-war adjustment. As we shall see later, if the production index were converted to a basis of product per hour, this, together with the exclusion of the war years, would bring the imputed product of capital up to approximately half the total. Evidently the indices must reach a high degree of accuracy before the marginal shares of the factors can be regarded as closely measured.

One bias in the figures is worth noting, though it affects only the cyclical fluctuations and not the long-run trend. The method of computing changes in capital in the inter-census years seems to be such as to minimize fluctuations. These interpolations are made on the basis of output of certain commodities entering into capital equipment. But these commodities enter also into consumption goods, and into maintenance and replacements, none of which fluctuates as much as additions chargeable to new capital. Indeed, for the purpose in hand we should be justified in disregarding fluctuations in maintenance and replacements, or deducting skimped maintenance and postponed replacements from the nominal increase of capital. The index shows a surprisingly steady growth, even in years of deepest depression; but this must be taken as subject to a heavy discount.

7. THE SHARES OF LAND AND WORKING CAPITAL

So far as we have not questioned the limitation of capital to buildings and equipment. But any final interpretation, even of the purely technical phases of production, must take account also of land and of working capital, the relevant portion of which consists mainly of goods in process. Land is frequently thought of as different from the other factors in that they vary in amount and have a marginal productivity, while land remains fixed in quantity and has no marginal productivity of its own, but receives the remainder of product above the marginal productivities of the other factors. This difference, however, is only apparent. The fact that more intensive production on a fixed area of land is subject to diminishing returns carries with it the corollary that any producer who can secure more land to utilize with a given amount of the other factors will thereby be partially freed from the diminishing returns to which he has been subject, and his yield will hence be increased. This increase is the marginal product of land, and is mathematically identical with the residual share figured in the traditional way.

It becomes larger as a result of growth of the other factors, and land thus receives an "unearned increment"; but this increment takes the form of an increase in its marginal efficiency. So also does labor receive an unearned increment, in the same form, as capital per worker increases. Indeed, with reference to manufacturers, land presents quantitative characteristics similar to those of labor, but more marked. It increases, though presumably less than labor, and at a unit price which increases faster than wages.

The chief difficulty in dealing with land is probably the

lack of adequate statistics. Such figures as are gathered show neither acreage nor current value, but book values which range from original cost at some uncertain past date to something approaching current market value. Even if better figures were available, they would be complicated by the fact that excess land is often held to provide for future growth, in which case present physical output would show no visible effects from limited land supply; and land would be an "overhead cost" like any form of fixed equipment which has perpetual excess capacity and no marginal productivity. So far as land exerts any limiting effect on physical output, the result is to make the increase of product slightly less than it would be if labor and fixed capital were the only limiting factors. Fortunately this effect, in manufactures, is very small. Perhaps the simplest device is merely to reckon that, in order to use more labor and capital effectively, certain amounts of added land are necessary, and total capital must be enough for both purposes.

Goods in process would naturally be expected to behave differently from either labor or equipment. One fairly plausible assumption could be made without disturbing the form of function already used for these two factors by Professor Cobb. Assume that, in order to increase product, goods in process must be increased in the same ratio as product, no more and no less. They would then have no marginal productivity in the ordinary sense, since an excess of 1 per cent would be totally useless, while a deficiency of 1 per cent would decrease product 1 per cent and render some of the other factors totally useless. But this would affect the form of the productivity curve for capital as a whole by adding, to the element that must increase as the fourth power of product, another that need only increase as the first power; so that capital as a whole need not increase by as large a percentage in order to produce a given increase in output. Or, putting it the other way round, a given percentage increase in total capital would give rise to a larger percentage increase in fixed capital, and so would have a larger marginal productivity than the Cobb formula shows for fixed capital alone. This excess would be greatest when capital was scarce; since then the largest proportion would be absorbed by goods in process and the scarcity of fixed capital would be intensified. Throughout, however, this modified function would still fulfill the condition that N times *all* the factors would yield N times the product.

On this basis the present writer has made a rough calculation, assuming that the Cobb formula is correct for fixed capital, and also that goods in process are equal to product, which seems not too far from the facts.[10] The imputed share of fixed capital plus goods in process is then found to vary from about 46 per cent to about 38 per cent of the whole, as capital grows from the proportions of 1899 to those of 1922. This indicates the direction of the modifications required to adapt the Cobb formula to take account of goods in process, but exaggerates the amount of the correction, in all probability, since the assumption on which it is based exaggerates the peculiarity of the behavior of goods in process. The calculation is of some theoretical interest, since it illustrates how the marginal productivity of a composite "factor production" may be quite elastic in character, even though some of the elements of which it is composed must work in absolutely rigid proportions, and in themselves have no "marginal productivity" in the ordinary sense. If goods in process necessarily increase more

---

[10] The method used was to treat product arbitrarily as the independent variable, calculating the total capital necessary to various values of P, graphing the results and measuring the slope of the curve. This gives, of course, only an approximation.

than product, they could be analyzed into one component varying with product and another varying as fixed capital does.

8. CYCLICAL FLUCTUATIONS

As already noted, the short-run fluctuations of the figures follow a different law from that governing the long-run trend. Analyzing the years 1903 to 1922 into six cycles of recession and recovery, we find that in six recoveries an average increase of 13.2 per cent in labor, with an average increase of 12.8 per cent in capital, was accompanied by an average increase of 23.4 per cent in product. In six recessions, an average decrease of 8.43 per cent in labor, with an average *increase* of 7.22 per cent in capital, was accompanied by an average decrease of 10.2 per cent in product. This seemingly strange behavior accords fairly well with the equation: $P = L^{3/4}C^{1/4}$, though of course this expression would depart widely from the long-run trend. Before attempting to find an expression which will harmonize these two types of movement, we should study the theory of the situation, asking ourselves what kind of behavior it is rational to expect.

During depressions, increased capital in staple lines of production is useless so far as it merely increases productive capacity, and has a "marginal productivity" only to the extent that it takes improved forms and gives the remaining labor better instruments to work with, thus reducing labor costs. It is impossible to measure the amount of capital going into such improved forms every year, and the best that can be done is to assume that it follows the general trend of increase in capital relative to labor, and not the cyclical fluctuations. In recoveries, excess capacity installed during the previous depression comes into use; also some inefficient instruments and ultimately some that are obsolete except for emergency purposes.

The peculiar behavior of product during cyclical fluctuations is due to changes in the percentage utilization of plant capacity; or, what is roughly equivalent, in the ratio of labor employed to the labor the plants are adapted to work with. Since part of the labor is "indirect" and relatively constant with reference to such short-time fluctuations, we should naturally expect that fluctuations of product would be greater than those of labor, an inference which is borne out by the figures.

The problem is, then, to find an index of "normal" labor relative to the capacity of the equipment in existence in each year; as a base from which to gauge the effect of the business cycle. This the present writer has attempted by constructing seven-year moving averages (arithmetic) of labor and capital, and taking the ratios between these trend-lines for each year. These ratios are taken to represent (very imperfectly) the changing "normal" ratio of labor to capital in terms of the changing technique of the times. Applying these ratios to the figures of actual capital for each year, we have a figure representing approximately the labor employed when existing plants are working at "normal" per cent of capacity. This variable appears in the subsequent formula as L_n.

We should naturally expect that, when labor was above this normal figure, product would be above the Cobb formula, and *vice versa*. Inspecting the figures with this as a key, it was at once evident that the years 1917–1919 were peculiar in that, while labor was above normal, product fell below the Cobb formula instead of rising above it; while the rest of the period behaved substantially according to expectations.[11] During the war the violent shifts of production caused wasteful utilization of capital and dilution of labor with green workers, and other unfavorable conditions tending to prevent full employment from having its

Year	L	Ln	$L^{\frac{3}{4}}C^{\frac{1}{4}}\left(\dfrac{L}{Ln}\right)^{.65}$	$1.01\,L^{\frac{3}{4}}C^{\frac{1}{4}}$	P
1899	100			101	100
1900	105			107	101
1901	110			112	112
1902	118	113	122.7	121	122
1903	123	118	129	127	124
1904	116	120	120.6	124	122
1905	125	122	134.3	134	143
1906	133	128	145.9	144	152
1907	138	133	153.6	151	151
1908	121	135	130	141	126
1909	140	140	157.2	159	153
1910	144	143	163.3	164	159
1911	145	144	166.7	167	153
1912	152	147	177.4	175	177
1913	154	150	180.5	179	184
1914	149	151	174	177	169
1915	154	160	180.1	187	189
1916	182	171	225.6	219	225
1917	196	184	243.9	237	227
1918	200	187	255.3	247	223
1919	193	187	248.6	246	218
1920	193			250	231
1921	147			210	179
1922	161			226	240

usual effect. It is evident that any treatment of this variable which accurately expresses its effect in pre-war years will have precisely the opposite effect for 1917–1920. Under the circumstances it is clearly justifiable to consider the war

[11] Using $L^{\frac{3}{4}}C^{\frac{1}{4}}$ to represent P′ (for reasons given below), the coefficient of correlation between P/P′ and L/Ln is plus .57. This is not very high, but the nature of the test is so severe as virtually to preclude very high correlation. Using a "normal" P′ in which Ln is substituted for L, a much higher correlation would result.

years abnormal and construct a formula with reference to pre-war years only. And as Professor Cobb finds that $P = 101\ L^{\frac{2}{3}}C^{\frac{1}{3}}$ fits the pre-war years better than $P = 101\ L^{\frac{3}{4}}C^{\frac{1}{4}}$, the exponents $\frac{1}{3}$ and $\frac{2}{3}$ may be used to express the general trend of the figures.

Thus a formula was constructed as follows: $P = L^{\frac{2}{3}}C^{\frac{1}{3}}$ $(L/L_n{}^m)$. Analysis of the figures indicated .65 as the most probable value for m.[12] This formula may be converted into the equivalent form: $P = L_n{}^{\frac{2}{3}}C^{\frac{1}{3}}\ (L/L_n)^{(\frac{2}{3}+.65)}$ as expressing better the fact of a "normal" trend multiplied by a factor which intensifies its cyclical fluctuations. The first form happens to save some labor of computation. The results appear in the accompanying table.

For the years on which it is based—1902–1916, inclusive —the modified formula (column 4) affords a materially better fit to observed product (column 6) than does the Cobb formula (column 5), substantially reducing the sum of the squared errors. It fits better because of the increased amplitude of its cyclical fluctuations, approximating the amplitude of these fluctuations in the observed product, instead of having a consistently smaller amplitude as does the Cobb formula. This fact entitles the modified formula to serious consideration despite the fact that for certain

---

[12] This figure was secured from a trial-and-error search for the value which would meet the test of "least squares." It is sufficiently accurate for the purpose in hand, as any variation between .6 and .7 has no material effect on the results. In the second form of the equation this exponent becomes $\frac{2}{3}+.65$ or 1.31666— This may be written as 1.3 for all present purposes. The disappearance of the constant 1.01 from the Cobb formula is due to the fact that the method of computing L_n introduced an upward trend averaging very nearly 1 per cent. Others methods, such as geometric moving averages, would alter this.

Obviously, increased employment could not increase output indefinitely without regard to the limits of the capacity of the plants; and as the limit is approached it is natural to expect a certain tapering off of productivity per laborer. The formula used does not provide for this, but for the data studied the omission does not seem serious except for the war period; and here its effect is lost in that of other and greater disturbances.

years its fit is poorer. For 1917–1919 the original formula is too high and the modified one even more so. This may be taken as bringing into sharper relief the fact that production during these disturbed years was abnormally costly; labor and capital yielding less than they would ordinarily have done. Further evidence is afforded by events subsequent to 1922 when, with virtually stationary employment of labor, product rose so much that it seems certain to have risen above the level of 1.01 $L^{3/4}C^{1/4}$. All the more reason for not allowing these few abnormal years to pull the formula downward.

The compound formula tested above has very interesting properties. Under it, product is the resultant of two types of movement, on two scales. One is governed by capital and "normal" labor for that amount of capital. Movements of actual labor register on this scale if the ratio of actual labor to "normal" remains unchanged. The other scale is the ratio of actual labor to "normal." With reference to movements on the first scale, the imputed share of labor is 2/3 of total product, and that of capital 1/3. With reference to movements on the second scale, the imputed share of labor is more than the total product and that of capital less than zero. In other words, if part of the unused capacity were wiped out and the indirect outlays on its account saved, or if some plants were closed and their quota of labor concentrated in the remaining plants, product would be increased and not diminished (so long as the capacity of the remaining plants is not overtaxed). This result agrees with the common sense of the business man, and is precisely what the theory of overhead costs would lead one to expect.

This is true, be it noted, only of changes in the amount of capital without changes in the form it takes. An increase of capital which takes the shape of giving existing labor better equipment still has a marginal productivity, represented by $C^{1/3}$ in the formula which also assumes, for lack of better indication, that this kind of change takes place at the rate measured by the seven-year moving averages of capital and labor.

In showing how the formula leads to these results, it will be permissible, for simplicity in handling the fractional exponents, to express the basic equation as $P = L^{.67}C^{.33}$ $(L/L_n)^{.63}$ or its equivalent $P = L_n^{.67}C^{.33}$ $(L/L_n)^{1.3}$. These both reduce to $P = L^{1.3}C^{.33}/L_n^{.63}$. If now we let L_t and C_t represent the seven-year moving averages, or trends, of L and C; from which L_n was computed, we may substitute for L_n its actual value $(L_tC_t)C$. This gives us

$$P = \frac{L^{1.3}C^{.33}}{\left(\dfrac{L_t}{C_t}\,C\right)^{.63}} \quad or \quad P = \frac{L^{1.3}C_t^{.63}}{L_t^{.63}C^{.3}}$$

Before accepting these quantitative results or giving them final interpretation, we must consider some of the more obvious limitations of the data. There are two corrections to be made, both of uncertain amount but, unfortunately, in opposite directions. First we must remember that the growth of actual capital fluctuates somewhat more than the index shows. Correction for this would increase the fluctuations of L_n, and reduce the deviations of L/L_n from unity. As a result, a larger exponent would need to be applied to this factor. Secondly, as we have seen, part of the cyclical variation of product is due to the unrecorded variations in hours worked per worker; variations of numbers alone would not have such large effects on product. A more adequate formula would be $P = L_n^{.67}C^{.33}$ $(L/L_n)^p(H/H_n)^q$, where H represents actual hours worked per worker and H_n represents either standard hours or a normal departure from standard (a constant might need to be introduced into this factor). The exponent p might be somewhat less than 1.3 but would assuredly be greater than 1; while the exponent q would naturally be somewhat less than 1. In the present state of the available data, these refinements need not concern us.

One further possibility may be of interest. If it should happen—as is unlikely—that the whole expression were found to vary approximately as total hours worked relative to normal hours worked, then this latter ratio might be taken as an index of the degree of employment of capital. In this case the whole formula could be put in the form: $P = L_h^{2/3} C_e^{1/3}$, where L_h measures labor in terms of hours, and C_e represents capital multiplied by its degree of employment, or employed capital as distinct from total capital. This latter conception is, however, of doubtful or arbitrary meaning. And while the resulting expression might serve as an interpretative commentary, it would be of no help in the actual work of computation or prediction.

What is the ultimate result of this analysis of cyclical fluctuations? So far as concerns the marginal productivity theory of distribution, it has very little bearing. The less-than-zero marginal productivity of capital refers to fixed capital only, to fixed capital put to certain uses only, and only during a depression. And even so it may be good business to put fixed capital in these temporarily useless forms, by way of preparing for future growth at a time when construction is cheap. And the fact that the imputed share of labor (with reference to changes in the "capacity factor" only) may be greater than the whole, can obviously not be made the basis of any permanent system of paying wages, even when qualified by the need of sharing income with the working capital which is jointly necessary. There are times when wages and the payments for working capital may absorb virtually the entire income of a business, but this results from a fall in gross income rather than from a rise in the distributive shares. These latter appear to be governed by longer-run forces, including those represented by the original Cobb formula. As to the accuracy of the measure which this formula affords, judgment must be reserved until we have looked at the effect of one more major disturbing element: namely, technical progress.

9. TECHNICAL PROGRESS

One of the striking things in this study as presented is the fact that it seems to allow no room for the natural effect of advances in the "state of the arts." To one accustomed to crediting our increase in per capita output to the triumphs of inventive genius, it must be a rude shock to see the whole increase calmly attributed to increased capital; while even on this basis the share of capital is only one-fourth of the whole, which seems too modest to leave room for any deductions. What, then, has become of our boasted progress? Has it totally evaporated? This question places the student in an interesting dilemma. For purposes of isolating the marginal yields of the factors of production, progress is a disturbing force, and we should like to get rid of it, or at least to isolate it, in the interest of accurate imputation. But this scientific interest is hardly enough to make us glad to see progress eliminated from real life.

The answer to the problem is twofold. In the first place, adjustments in the data will alter the story they tell, and in the second place, the formula employed to measure marginal productivity in itself conceals the effects of a vast deal of technical advance. Let us take up the second matter first.

It has already been pointed out that, to find productive uses for such a vast increase in capital, it must be put in new forms. Were all these forms, and their productive possibilities, known in 1899? Of course not. There was then, and is now, a frontier zone of known devices just below the margin of economical use and capable of absorbing a considerable amount of capital if relative costs should become more favorable. But to find uses for a fourfold increase in equipment, or 2⅔ times the original amount per worker, this frontier zone has had to be pushed forward rapidly and continuously. At no time do definitely known and developed devices include more than a small part of those which would be found profitable if a shift in relative costs should give manufacturers a substantial incentive for further search. The increasing labor-cost of any process not thoroughly mechanized has afforded such an incentive; and it is typical of present-day methods of management to set a research department to work definitely on the problem created by changing cost conditions. The result is that any such change will call forth a crop of new devices or cause others to be quickly developed which would otherwise have been very slow in getting past the experimental stage.

These facts may be summed up by saying that the product attributable to added capital is also attributable to progress. Both are necessary to it. In a sense, the technical improvements may be said to have brought a deal of the new capital into being. They have enlarged the field of profitable investment. The prospective gains have caused manufacturers to go into the investment market to raise added capital, while the realized gains have furnished a painless source whence much of the necessary savings could come. With the modern credit system, making new equipment "pay for itself" is far more than a figure of speech.

Industry has had to evolve not merely increasingly automatic machinery, but also new commodities into which to put the increasing productive power without wasting it in a mere redundancy of familiar goods. What difference, for example, would it have made if the pleasure automobile had never been invented?

Among the new devices some may be close to the margin of economical use, but others are extremely profitable, creating uses for capital well above the existing margin. To the extent that this happens, the historical increase in aggregate product is not an accurate index of the marginal product of capital either before or after the introduction of the improvement. The change makes the marginal product higher than it would otherwise have been, and also adds to the supra-marginal product; and the mass statistics we are studying cannot segregate these two components. There are, of course, some inventions which require no added capital, or which save capital as well as labor; and there are improvements in method which take effect on labor directly. All these, including new supra-marginal uses of capital, may perhaps be called "pure progress" to distinguish them from those whose effects are merged in the marginal yield of added capital.

"Pure progress" is not the creation of labor or capital, but its result is to increase the marginal product of labor or capital or both, in the enterprises where the improvements have been made. For the time being, the gain goes as differential profits to the entrepreneurs, while the marginal product which governs distribution is marginal product under the less advanced standard practice of "representative concerns." But as soon as new processes become standard practice, labor and capital absorb the benefits, or most of them, either through increased wages, increased payments for capital goods or capital funds, or reduced prices which make the incomes of workers and capitalists buy more goods.

Capital and labor are both dependent on the "state of the arts," but the observed facts do not indicate that capital alone "corners" the results of current progress, still less the "wisdom of the ancients" as Veblen has suggested. Capital absorbs part of the effects, but labor absorbs still more, and this is definitely borne out by the figures before us.

In inquiring whether these figures afford any evidence of the existence of "pure progress," the only available method seems to be to make all reasonable adjustments in the direction which would tend to indicate such progress, and then see if the resulting trend of product is higher, relative to those of labor and capital, than can be plausibly explained by the action of labor and capital alone.

In the first place, we have seen that a formula assigning one-third, instead of one-fourth, to capital is more representative if the years 1917-1919 are disregarded as an abnormal interlude. But the most substantial need of adjustment arises from the fact that from 1899 to 1922 the length of the standard working week was quite steadily decreasing, so much so that the same product per worker would represent approximately 16 per cent more product per standard hour at the end of the period than at the beginning.

Two questions arise: first, is not this a true increase in productiveness or productive efficiency of the whole manufacturing process, over and above that recorded in aggregate product? And second, should not this extra increase in productiveness be taken account of in gauging the relative contributions of labor and capital? To the first question the answer is clearly "yes." To answer the second, we must first know whether, or to what extent, this increased productiveness per hour is due to the shortened hours themselves; in which case it is not relevant evidence of the marginal contributions of either capital or labor.

If the shorter week is, in itself, as productive as the longer, then the increased product per hour should properly be ignored in searching for the differentials due to labor and capital as such. On the other hand, if dropping eight hours from the standard week involves a clear sacrifice of just so much power to produce, then merely to counteract this loss requires added efficiency, to be credited presumably either to added capital or to "pure progress." In this case, the production index should be converted into an index of production per standard hour, and would rise to about 278 in 1922 instead of 240. The trend of product would be close to a mean proportional between that of labor and that of capital, indicating an imputed share of 50 per cent for each. Or if we "split the difference" and consider that the shortened work-week is one-half made up for by its own effects in increasing speed of output, then the adjusted index would result in attributing approximately 60 per cent to labor and 40 per cent to capital. This is perhaps the most plausible compromise.

This is a suspiciously large share to attribute to capital, suggesting strongly that capital is getting credit properly due to some other agency. Remembering that we are dealing with less than half of total capital, its owners can hardly receive as much as 14 per cent of total net income. Its cost to the enterprise, including depreciation and taxes, is presumably less than 25 per cent of the total "value added to materials." If it "produces" slightly more than it costs, its product would be about one-fourth of the whole. The discrepancy, as of 1922, between $L^{.3/4}C^{1/4}$, and $L^{.6}C^{.4}$, amounts to about 15 per cent; and this may be taken as one out of many possible estimates of the amount of "pure progress" during these twenty-three years.

In coming to this conclusion we have, it will be noted,

shifted from the statistical gauge of marginal productivity, in order to have some basis from which to judge the plausibility of its results; and have fallen back on the tautological device of judging the marginal contributions of the factors by what they receive, or by what they cost. In other words, to just the extent that we attempt to take account of the disturbing factor of progress, the index of marginal product derived from the historical trends of mass statistics inevitably fails us. Other statistical approaches may be found which will partially overcome this difficulty, such as comparative studies of the simultaneous costs of different methods of production in representative industries. Fifteen per cent is not a large allowance for progress; but it becomes sufficiently liberal when we remember that presumably the major part of our technical advance is already accounted for as merged in the marginal product of increased capital per worker. At any rate, the figures do not force us to conclude that technical progress is wholly an illusion!

10. CONCLUSION

To sum up, the study before us is a bold and significant piece of pioneer work in a hitherto neglected field. While it leaves out parts of capital, there seems to be a statistical possibility of enlarging it so as to take account of them. Some account can be taken of the fluctuations of the business cycle; and so far as this analysis has been carried in the present paper, it agrees with what the theory of overhead costs would lead one to expect. Even the disturbing effects of progress do not make the task absolutely hopeless. The difficulties are great, and it appears that the whole story cannot be told by the historical trends of mass statistics. These need to be supplemented by other types of evidence, which may help to segregate the yields of capital and labor as such from the effects of technical progress. One vital service of such a study is to force the theorist to formulate his theory in wholly concrete terms.

X

BUSINESS ACCELERATION AND THE LAW OF DEMAND: A TECHNICAL FACTOR IN ECONOMIC CYCLES*

I. INTRODUCTION

THE publication of W. C. Mitchell's book, *Business Cycles,* has rendered obsolete all attempts to explain crises in terms of any one fact or any one narrow chain of causes and effects. The central problem, however, is as clearly defined throughout his remarkably comprehensive study of the details of the actual process as in more abstract treatments of single phases of it. It is the question why business adjustments do not stop at a point of equilibrium, but go on to a point from which a more or less violent reaction is inevitable, and so on without apparent end. And it seems probable that of all the many circumstances which at every stage of the cycle lead to the next stage, the greater part can hardly be held primarily responsible for this primary fact; certainly not all are responsible in equal measure.

Disturbances originating outside the business world, so to speak, such as wars and crop fluctuations, can scarcely be held primarily responsible. Some such disturbances there are bound to be, and our system seems capable of manufacturing its crises out of any raw material that comes to hand, when the crisis is due, and of rising superior to serious provocation at other times. Some forces act to spread the effect of prosperity or adversity from one industry to another, thus in-

*Reprinted by permission from *The Journal of Political Economy,* Vol. 25 (Mar., 1917), pp. 217-35.

suring that a boom or sharp crisis will affect industry in general, but they cannot be held responsible for the condition which they merely transmit. Nor can the familiar "forces of equilibrium" be held responsible, though they are acting at all stages of the process.

There is one circumstance whose natural effect is different from all of these in that (1) it acts as an intensifier of the disturbances it transmits and (2) without any diminution of demand to start with it can produce a diminution. It can convert a slackening of the rate of growth in one industry into an absolute decline in another. This circumstance is not psychological, nor does it depend upon the nature of our credit system, nor upon the distribution of income, but rather upon the elementary technical necessities of the case. It is concerned with the way in which the demand for finished products is handed on in the form of a demand for machines, tools, construction materials, and unfinished goods in general. This circumstance is not to be erected into a "theory of crises," but it is put forward as indicating that the purely technical side of this phenomenon is of prime importance, though it has been somewhat overshadowed by the more spectacular features of credit inflation, speculation, capitalization, and mob psychology, while its details have been blurred in the more general theories of "overproduction" or "maladjusted production."

2. CHIEF DATA TO BE INTERPRETED

There are certain outstanding facts in the behavior of crises which point in one direction and can be linked together by one explanation. It appears, first, that raw materials and producers' goods in general vary more sharply both in price and in the physical volume of business done than do consumers' goods, while wholesale prices fluctuate more than retail.[1]

The work of constructing industrial equipment appears to fluctuate more intensely than other types of production.[2] Its revival coincides, naturally, with a sudden and very great increase of investments. The failures which precipitate a panic are likely to be among producers of industrial equipment, although as to this "there is no general rule." [3] Another fact closely connected with those already mentioned is the shrinkage of merchants' stocks of goods in hard times [4] and their expansion in times of prosperity. Raw materials for manufacture are also carried in larger quantities at times when production is more active.[5] In point of time, also, it appears that raw materials take the lead, beginning to fall in price before the finished products, while "technical journals usually report that the factories and wholesale houses are restricting their orders some weeks, if not months, before they report that retail sales are flagging." [6] Mr. Babson notes in one of his reports [7] that "the production of pig iron forecasts the condition of the whole building industry and construction of all kinds," and that "the turning point of the statistics on new building has been from two years to six months earlier than the general crisis." [8] In 1907 a comparison of prices indicates that certain goods bought by producers reached their highest point and began their de-

[1] Mitchell, *Business Cycles*, pp. 502-503, and charts and tables, pp. 97, 100-103.

[2] *Ibid.*, pp. 471-72, 483-84, 557.

[3] *Ibid.*, p. 512.

[4] *Ibid.*, p. 452.

[5] *Ibid.*, p. 482.

[6] *Ibid.*, pp. 502-503 and charts and tables, pp. 97, 100-103. (Quotation is from p. 502.)

[7] Babson, *Reports*, 1914, Charts Nos. 612 and 598, cited by Warren M. Persons, *Amer. Econ. Rev.*, IV, 741.

[8] *Ibid.*

cline earlier than the goods sold by the same producers.[9] These latter were in some cases goods for consumption and in some cases tools, etc., to be used in further production. Manufactured producers' goods are not shown to be especially quick in feeling the upward trend of prices, though they rise farther than other types of goods.[10] The demand for consumers' goods fluctuates quite decidedly, but the greater part of its fluctuations appears to be the result of the changes in the amount of unemployment which result from the business cycle itself. Some changes in consumption are independent of this cause, and these may well be among the independent causes of business cycles, but it would seem that only a comparatively minor part of the total fluctuations in consumption can be of this character.

3. INDUSTRIAL EXPANSION AND DERIVED DEMANDS

These data suggest a unified explanation, and group themselves about one industrial fact: the production of capital goods. Its importance has long been recognized, and several theories of crises have turned upon it. The aim of the present study is to present the underlying technical facts in a definite quantitative formulation.

Every producer of things to be sold to producers has two demands to meet. He must maintain the industrial equipment already in use and the stocks of materials and goods on their way to the final consumer, and he must also furnish any new equipment that is wanted for new construction, enlargements, or betterments, and any increase in the stocks of materials and unsold goods. Both these demands come ultimately from the consumer, but they follow different

9 Mitchell, *Business Cycles*, p. 501 and table, p. 98. Professor Mitchell's classification into "producers' and consumers' goods" does not quite accurately describe the commodities included in the table.
10 *Ibid.*, p. 461.

laws. The demand for maintenance and replacement of existing capital varies with the amount of the demand for finished products, while the demand for new construction or enlargement of stocks depends upon whether or not the sales of the finished product are growing.[11] Normally, over a long period of years, there is a certain demand for new construction on which producers can rely, and hence the demand for new construction is a normal part of any demand schedule for this kind of goods. But it does not come regularly.

The nature of the mechanical law at work can be emphasized by imagining the industry reduced to a mere machine. Price, for the time being, is to be disregarded. Finished goods are turned out as fast as wanted, and materials and means of production are instantly supplied as fast as the process of finishing requires them. On this simplified basis we can predict accurately how the speed of the different parts of the machine must needs vary, and the results will furnish an index of the varying strains that are put on the much less mechanical system that does these things in real life.

The demand for a certain product, let us say, begins to increase steadily, each year seeing an increment equal to 10 per cent of the original demand. At the end of five years the increase stops and the demand remains stationary. If the productive equipment has kept pace with the need, it is now enlarged by 50 per cent and calls for 50 per cent more expenditure for maintenance and replacements. Meanwhile there has been an added demand for new constructions equal in five years to half the entire original equipment. If re-

[11] If demand be treated as a rate of speed at which goods are taken off the market, maintenance varies roughly with the speed, but new construction depends upon the acceleration.

newals are at the rate of 5 per cent a year, the first effect of
an increase in demand at the rate of 10 per cent in a year is
to treble the demand for the means of production, since a
demand for new construction has arisen twice as large as the
previous demand for maintenance. At the end of a year the
demand for maintenance has been increased because of the
fact that there is now 10 per cent more capital to be main-

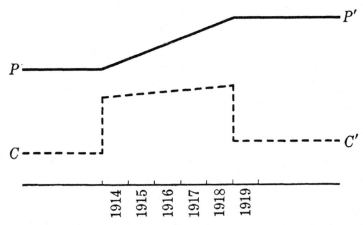

Fig. 1.—The figure represents the course of demand (measured vertically)
over a period of years (measured horizontally). *PP'* represents the demand for
the finished product and *CC'* the derived demand in an industry engaged in
construction and maintenance.

tained (see Fig. 1). Under practical conditions the increase
in maintenance would probably be considerably less than 10
per cent, as it takes some time for the new machinery to be
installed, and after that it is some time before it reaches its
average condition of wear and tear. Until then the repair
bills are comparatively light. However, this consideration
does not affect the main feature of our problem, which is
the suddenness of the increased demand for the means of
production and the fact that it is far greater as a percentage
change than the disturbance of demand that causes it.

What happens at the end of the five years when the demand stops growing? By this time the requirements for maintenance are 50 per cent greater than they were, while new construction has been going on at a rate equal to twice the original maintenance account. The total output has grown to three and one-half times its former volume. But the demand for new construction now ceases abruptly. This means that if the producers engaged in construction work had enough capacity to meet the demand of the fifth year, the sixth year would see them running with four-sevenths of their capacity idle.

This is a serious condition for any industry in the real world. It might well be serious enough to produce a panic if any considerable number of industries were in the same condition at the same time. And yet something like it is a normal effect, an inevitable effect, of changes in consumers' demands in a highly capitalistic industrial system.

Thus the law of demand for intermediate products states that the demand depends, not only on the demand for the final product, but on the manner in which that demand is fluctuating. A change from one year to the next in the rate of consumption has a temporary effect on the demand for the intermediate product which is greater than its permanent effect, in just about the proportion by which the total amount of investment in the intermediate product exceeds the amount annually spent for maintenance.[12] In order to bring about an absolute shrinkage in the demand for the intermediate product, all that may be needed is that the final

[12] The assumption has been made that the new construction actually keeps pace with the demand for it, simply in order to have some figures that would not be too complicated. In fact, the supply is almost certain to fall behind the demand, thus lessening the amount of the overrun and of the ultimate revulsion without altering the principle at work. The law may be expressed algebraically, if the reader will remember that it represents only a purely mechanical view

demand should slacken its rate of growth. Making all due allowances for mitigating factors in translating the illustration back into real life, it is still difficult to see how the building and machine-making industries can possibly avoid the disagreeable experience of outgrowing themselves in time of prosperity. For demand can never be expected to grow at an absolutely steady rate, and the slightest fluctuation seems destined to put the producer of capital goods in a situation comparable to that of a passenger forcibly carried by his station.

of the situation, and will supply for himself an allowance for the elements that are not included in the formula.

Let $t =$ years elapsed between two dates, t_1 and t_2.

Let $C =$ rate of consumption at time t_1.

Let $C + \Delta C =$ rate of consumption at time of t_2, the increase being distributed evenly through time t.

Let $I =$ investment necessary to produce output at rate C.

Let $L =$ average life of instruments included in I, in years. Then maintenance is required at the rate $\dfrac{I}{L}$. The demand for new construction during time $t = I\dfrac{\Delta C}{C}$, an annual amount equal to $I\dfrac{\Delta C}{Ct}$. Demand for new construction is to previous demand for maintenance as $I\dfrac{\Delta C}{Ct} : \dfrac{I}{L}$ or as $\dfrac{\Delta C}{Ct} : \dfrac{1}{L}$ or as $L\Delta C : Ct$.

If L be large, as in the case of long-lived instruments, the disturbing effect is great. If it be small, as in the case of merchants' stocks of goods of sorts that are turned over rapidly, the disturbing effect is far less, though still appreciable.

The total demand for replacements and for new construction may be taken to have increased from $\dfrac{I}{L}$ annually, at time t_1 to an annual amount equal to

$$\frac{I}{L}\left(1 + \frac{L\Delta C}{Ct}\right) + I\frac{\frac{\Delta C}{C}}{L} \text{ or } \frac{I}{L}\left(1 + \frac{L\Delta C}{Ct} + \frac{\Delta C}{C}\right)$$ at time t_2 after which it would

drop to $\dfrac{I}{L}\left(1 + \dfrac{\Delta C}{C}\right)$.

The last term of this expression is exaggerated, as has been mentioned, by ignoring the fact that it takes some time for new equipment to reach its average condition of depreciation and renewal. Any attempt to avoid this would only complicate matters without any substantial increase in accuracy. If we are thinking of dealers' stocks of goods which change hands quite rapidly, the third term of the formula would hold substantially true.

This principle may be illustrated by a town which grows rapidly up to the size at which its industrial advantages are fully utilized and beyond which its normal production can expand but slowly. When the point of transition is reached from rapid to slow expansion, the town may find that it has outgrown itself by the number of people engaged in the extra construction work involved in the process of growing. Houses to take them in, stores to feed and clothe them, trucks to haul the materials they work with, offices, etc., all will be demanded, and thus a boom may be created which is none the less temporary for being based on tangible economic needs. The experience of the boom town has been common enough in the growth of our western country, and the blame need not be laid entirely upon the vagaries of mob psychology. In a similar way the great work of rebuilding which must follow the present war will give rise to a huge temporary addition to the demand made upon the industries engaged in reconstruction, and as this special work is accomplished and a state of slower and more natural growth takes its place, these industries will have to count on a corresponding shrinkage, not merely relative, but absolute. This will almost inevitably lead to a depression, and, if unforeseen, it may lead to a crisis.

4. DERIVED DEMAND FLUCTUATES FIRST

This principle has another very interesting consequence. So far as the demand for new construction follows this law it not merely fluctuates more than the demand for the finished product; it also fluctuates in a way which gives it all the appearance of leading instead of following in point of time. This can be clearly seen if the course of business activity is represented by a curve as in Fig. 2 instead of by the straight lines used in the previous diagram.

In this figure the curve which represents the rate at which the wholesalers take the finished product from the manufacturer is drawn on the assumption that the normal stock of goods in the hands of all the dealers is equivalent to four months' consumption. The curve which represents the course of demand for a durable instrument of production is drawn

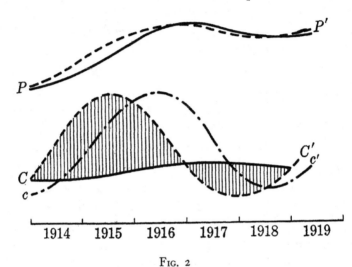

FIG. 2

———————— Demand for finished product.
- - - - - - - - Wholesalers' demand for finished product.
— — — — — Hypothetical demand for durable means of production. Shaded area shows excess or deficiency as compared to needs of maintenance.
—.—.—.— Hypothetical demand for durable means of production with allowance for lagging.

on the assumption that the life of the instrument is approximately eight years. Had a longer life been assumed, the disturbance shown would have been much more marked. No necessary relation is assumed between the absolute heights of the upper and lower pairs of curves, the significant thing in each pair being the percentage fluctuation.

The need for new construction, indicated by the shaded

area, reaches its maximum when the demand for the final product is at its point of fastest growth. As soon as this rate of growth slackens and long before it has reached its highest point the need for new construction has started downward. The curve CC' represents the same impossibly fluid condition of industry that was previously assumed, in which the need for new construction is satisfied as soon as it arises. The curve cc' is closer to the facts, for it represents the work of supplying the derived demand as lagging somewhat. It shows that, even allowing for this natural lagging, one might well expect to find some, at least, of the businesses that furnish capital goods starting their revival before the demand for the finished products has reached its bottom point, and starting their reaction before the demand for the finished products has reached the crest of its wave. This lagging would naturally be more marked in the case of machinery and construction generally than in the case of raw materials, partly because the disturbance in the case of long-lived goods is more intense, and because it takes more time to increase production by a large amount than by a small amount. Another reason is that the long-lived goods are of a sort that takes more time to turn out, and a third reason is that the first increase in demand for finished products can be taken care of by utilizing the excess producing capacity which an industry using much machinery habitually carries over a period of depression. Thus they do not need to buy more equipment the instant the demand begins to increase.

The investment in long-lived instruments cannot be reduced as readily as it can be increased. It is reduced, if at all, by the slow process of starving the maintenance account in dull seasons, and this policy is conditioned by such complex technical relationships that it is impossible to reduce it accurately to any set formula. The deciding factor is economic rather than technical, it is the force with which the financial pinch is felt rather than the fact that the reduction in output has made some of the equipment technically superfluous. On the opposite side stand the optimism of the employer or his industrial pride, or other elements of the "personal equation." Thus the formula would be correct in representing replacements as diminished or postponed, but when it comes to estimating how much this postponement amounts to it is impossible to make any assumption that would not be quite arbitrary.

5. THE HYPOTHESIS COMPARED WITH STATISTICAL EVIDENCE

This hypothetical case agrees remarkably closely with the observed behavior of the demand for raw materials, manufactured producers' goods, and manufactured consumers' goods. It accounts for both the greater intensity and the greater promptness of the price movements of goods at the earlier stages of the productive process as compared to the final sale to the consumer, as well as for the fact that raw materials rise probably more promptly, if anything, though not more sharply, than finished instruments of production. The bigger the stock of goods as compared to the annual wastage and replacement, the greater this element of intensification becomes. Anything tending to reduce the size of stocks and to speed up the turnover would seem to be advantageous as tending to lessen this intensification, so long as the stocks do not become so slight as to create the danger of an absolute shortage in case of strikes, or poor harvests, or other unpredictable interference with the normal course of supply.

In attempting a more detailed test of this hypothesis, the railroads furnish the most favorable case, both because of the full statistics available and because the railroad is under obligation to carry whatever traffic offers at the time it offers, and so must needs adjust its facilities as best it can to the fluctuations of demand. It cannot "make to stock" in slack periods like the manufacturer. Thus the technical needs of the business are unusually free from disturbing financial influences. In the accompanying chart (Fig. 3) a comparison is made of railway traffic and purchases of cars over a period of fifteen years.[18] The results of this comparison may be briefly summarized.

1. The percentage fluctuations in car manufacturing are vastly greater than in railroad traffic, though the line *BB* indicates that they are still not nearly great enough to cause the equipment to keep pace with the needs of the traffic in its up and downs, even if averaged over yearly periods.

2. The orders for cars have the appearance of fluctuating ahead of the movements of traffic. On the basis of this fact, Mr. E. B. Leigh, of Chicago, has urged in several addresses and pamphlets that railroad purchases are the cause of business prosperity. It seems undeniable that car orders reach their maxima and minima ahead of the index of general business activity, and even reach their maxima ahead of the maxima of railway traffic itself. As here analyzed, however,

[18] The data were taken from the Interstate Commerce Commission's *Statistics of Railroads in the United States*, with the exception of the line representing "cars ordered," which was taken from a chart made by the Brookmire service for Mr. E. B. Leigh, of Chicago, and published by him in various pamphlets urging the importance of railroad purchases as a cause of general prosperity. The 1915-16 figures for traffic and the 1916 figures for total car equipment and net change in car equipment were taken from the preliminary report of the Bureau of Railway Economics, based upon the same figures published by the Interstate Commerce Commission. Since these reports cover fewer roads than the Commission's final figures, the totals would be misleading, and hence the net change between the 1915 and 1916 reports of the Bureau itself is used in placing the final points in lines *AA'*, *BB'*, and *DD'*. The resulting inaccuracy is so small as to be virtually imperceptible save in a chart drawn to a much larger scale than the one used here.

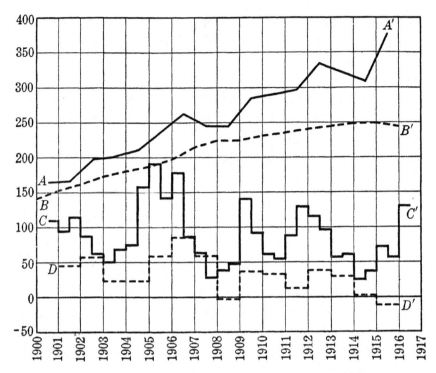

Fig. 3—Line *AA'* represents traffic (ton-miles plus passenger-miles 000,000,000 omitted) the total from July 1 to June 30 being plotted as one point at January 1.

Line *BB'* represents total cars in service June 30 (0,000 omitted).

Line *CC'* represents half-yearly orders for cars (000 omitted); taken from chart published by Mr. E. B. Leigh substituting horizontal lines covering an entire half-year for points located in the middle of each half-year.

Line *DD'* represents the yearly net increase in cars (000 omitted) divided by two in order to correspond with half-yearly figures for car orders.[14]

The vertical ordinates are drawn at June 30 of each year.

---

[14] By making the lower lines rectangular, a comparison is afforded of volume of demand for cars with rate of increase of traffic, and one that is fairer for judging how the significant data compare in point of time than if two lines of the same sort, rectangular or otherwise, had been plotted against each other.

If both lines were made rectangular, the growth of traffic would appear as taking place at one instant. Car orders would have the appearance of growing a half-year ahead of traffic, merely because the first half of the period of growing traffic would not appear in the graph. If both lines were plotted as the upper one is, on the single-point system, a fairer result would be obtained with regard orders for cars do not move in any different manner from that which would naturally result if they were wholly guided by the need of moving the traffic—a result and not a cause.[15]

3. The direction in which the slope of the traffic curve deviates from the average slope agrees with the direction in which the yearly volume of car orders deviates from the average volume in twelve out of fifteen years. The disagreement is comparatively slight in one case (1904), and the failure of car orders to rise above the average in that year may be explained by the fact that car equipment had been catching up on traffic in the year preceding.

4. A change in the rate of growth of traffic is accompanied by a similar change in yearly volume of car orders ten times, by an opposite change once (1908), and in three cases one change or the other is so slight that the result may be regarded as neutral (1902, 1911, 1914). These four years of

to the high and low points of car orders. In this case, however, another significant set of facts is wrongly dated; namely, the beginning of an upward or downward bend in the slope of the traffic curve as compared to the beginning of the rise or fall in the absolute volume of car orders, with which it is to be compared. The beginning of a bend in the traffic curve is postponed, while the beginning of an absolute rise or fall in car orders is dated ahead, if both are plotted in this way.

The method adopted makes the bends of the traffic curve and the rises and falls of car orders both appear as happening all at once, and shows them at their (probable) mid-point, ignoring the beginning of each movement. Thus a comparison between the two is not vitiated. With regard to the other sets of data, the attainment of a given rate of growth of traffic, and the attainment of a given volume of orders for cars, both phenomena appear too soon, in all probability, since the average for a period is shown as a uniform rate from beginning to end of the period. Thus the method adopted is one by which the data we are seeking to compare suffer similar distortions. By following other methods of presentation the writer has been able to give either set of data the appearance of lagging behind the other; a fact which serves to emphasize the conclusion that no proof of lag is contained in the figures.

[15] No one would deny that activity in the production of railroad equipment has an effect upon other branches of business. The effects of any disturbance are widespread. The present contention is that the fluctuations are themselves natural results of the technical situation. Their effect is, of course, self-re-enforcing.

negative or neutral results are in each case years in which car orders are lower with reference to the previous year than the state of traffic growth calls for, and in each case the preceding year was one in which car supply caught up with traffic noticeably. These cases, then, involve a retarded adjustment for which the contemporary slope of the traffic curve makes no allowance.

5. The noticeable peaks of car orders fall within the years of maximum growth of traffic. The year 1916 is an exception, the growth of car orders being much delayed. Of the twelve half-years of fastest growth of traffic, eight correspond to the eight half-years of highest car orders, while two (1915–16) are periods of wholly abnormal conditions. Of the eighteen half-years of slowest growth of traffic (including those of absolute decline) thirteen correspond to the thirteen half-years of lowest car orders. Of the four half-years of lowest car orders, one comes at the end of a two-year decline in traffic, another follows this one, and the other two follow immediately on the heels of the only other period when traffic absolutely declined.

6. In these minimum points the orders for cars appear to lag behind the shrinkage of traffic to which they correspond, thus supporting the contention that they behave as they would if they were governed by the needs of the traffic. The beginning of the recovery shows a similar lag. Apart from this there is no clear evidence of a tendency for either curve to lag behind the other when the level of car orders is compared with the *rate of growth* of the traffic, and the points of rise or fall in car orders are compared with the points of *increase or decrease in the rate of growth* of the traffic.

7. The general trend of car orders is slightly downward,

in spite of a great increase in traffic.[16] The net yearly additions to the equipment of cars trend quite strongly downward.

In short, the figures, so far as they go, bear out the statement that the demand for cars varies with the rate at which traffic is increasing or diminishing rather than with the absolute volume of the traffic.

6. WHAT GOVERNS THE SIZE OF STOCKS

So far the assumption has been made that the need for productive instruments and materials varies with the output. It may be that this assumption will be challenged in some cases, however well it tallies with common experience in most situations. Where the rate of turnover can be easily increased, it may seem natural that producers should take their gains partly in this way rather than bear the burden of an increased investment. However, this could only happen if the producers had previously been either careless enough to let the turnover become unduly slow, or else had been unable to speed up the turnover in slack times by carrying a decreased stock. In production of a technical sort such as that of factories, machine-shops, railroads, etc., the length of the process cannot be reduced at will. It is the business of the staff, from president to foremen, to keep the work moving at all times as fast as is reasonably possible, for waste time is waste time always. It is only in mercantile production that the rate of turnover can be increased more or less at will, and even here it is natural to increase the investment when the output increases.

The size of merchants' stocks is governed by many considerations, some psychological, some commercial, and some speculative. If a dealer knew beforehand just what goods

[16] This may be accounted for by an increase in the capacity of cars.

would be demanded and just when, what kind and brand and quality and quantity, he would really have no need of keeping any stocks at all, save to serve as samples. If the static state means absolute steadiness in the demand for everything—if there were absolutely no change and hence no uncertainty in the matter of consumers' wants—dealers would be able to predict demand exactly. Even stock for sample purposes would hardly be needed, and the necessity for the investment of capital in large reserve stores of goods would virtually disappear. This need is the child of uncertainty, and uncertainty is a dynamic fact. Goods held against future demand are the playthings of chance and change.

The chief reasons for keeping a stock are, first, to give the customer a wide selection of goods which he can actually inspect and, secondly, to give assurance of being able to fill large orders without delay. What is the effect of expanding demand on the amount of stock needed to fulfil these functions? Obviously, the larger the orders, the greater the danger of being sold out, unless the stock is increased in a corresponding proportion, or something not too far short of it. The increase in demand would not seem to make it necessary to keep any wider range of goods in stock. But if we are thinking, not of what is necessary, but of what is profitable, we have a different situation. The range of goods a merchant carries is limited largely by a process of natural economic selection, by weeding out the "stickers," whose turnover is too slow to pay for keeping them in stock. With a quickened demand there are fewer "stickers." Some goods which were just below the line of toleration will become profitable to handle on the basis of the increased rate at which they can be sold, and the natural result is the carrying of a greater variety of goods as well as of more goods of each kind. If the dealer is in doubt whether or not to keep a certain line in stock at all, a brisk state of demand will be likely to decide him to keep it.

When we begin considering what is profitable, rather than merely what is physically necessary, we open up a wide range of considerations. The size of the stock is one element in the quality of service rendered by any dealer, which means that it is something in which he is likely to economize when business is poor, and to be liberal when he can afford it. When demand is expanding, merchants are in general prosperous enough to be able to afford to spend money for the purpose of improving the quality of their service. If the increase in demand is part of a general growth of business activity, the customers themselves will be in just such a prosperous state of mind as would put petty economics at a discount. They would be less influenced by a slight saving in price, which can only be made sure of after close study of the qualities of the goods, than by an obvious superiority in quality of service and range of selection. When the buyer's mind swings in this direction the merchant is invited to respond in kind if he wishes to attract his share of the increase in business, rather than to attempt to do it merely by keeping prices down and seeing that the quality of the goods themselves is maintained. A time of general activity in business is a time when large stocks are good tactics commercially.

One other fact which may make merchants more willing to invest in considerable stocks is that a time of growing demand for some one commodity, or a time of general increase in activity, are both times of rising prices for the intermediate products called for in the business affected. This makes these commodities a profitable investment [17] so long as credit can be had on easy terms with which to enlarge

[17] Mitchell, *Business Cycles*, p. 459.

one's holdings. Merchants tend to assure their future supplies by buying either outright or for future delivery. Buying for future delivery is usually a cheaper way in which
to combine certainty of future supplies with a chance of a
speculative gain if prices go up, but it is chiefly used by contractors, and by shops and factories, rather than by merchants
dealing with finished products.

Each of these two ways of meeting the situation has its
own effect on the demand as felt by the manufacturer. Buying outright intensifies it, while buying for future delivery
has an effect which may at times prove even more disturbing.
While not increasing the immediate effect of an upward
swing, it puts the market in a condition in which, if the
demand from consumers slackens or stops its growth, the
demand for the same goods on the part of dealers cannot
immediately shrink in full response. The boom is artificially
prolonged for the manufacturer at the expense of the middleman, only to fall all the more suddenly when the future
contracts have been filled. At such a time the same factory
often sells the same goods at prices wide apart, the price on
new contracts being cut to the barest minimum while good
prices are still being received from middlemen unfortunate
enough to have bought too far ahead.[18] Taking all these
things into consideration, one is justified in concluding that
an increase in demand naturally tends toward an increased
investment in dealers' stocks, which is, if anything, more
than in proportion to the increase in sales, unless limited
by: (1) difficulty in getting added credit to carry the extra
"working capital," (2) an extremely sharp rise in supply
prices, (3) the fear that the prosperity is temporary, or (4)
the inability of manufacturers to make deliveries.

[18] *Ibid.*, p. 488.

7. CONCLUSIONS. SOME DYNAMIC LAWS OF DEMAND

So far we have considered only one big division of the process. If we imagine the effect of all this on those industries which produce the tools and machinery used in the construction industry itself, we have a further possibility of multiplying the effects of a change in demand. In fact, the possibilities multiply with every step backward, for every industry which produces the means of production for some other industry has its own demand for its own tools and machinery to be filled. These possibilities of intensification are soon mitigated, however, by the fact that as we get farther and farther back we reach industries which produce machinery and tools for a large number of other industries at once, so that they register the effect of the average of a great many changes in a great many particular lines of production. Thus we finally reach the steel industry, which produces the chief of all the raw materials used in making capital goods. This industry is so large that a change in the demand for any comparatively unimportant product, however much it may be intensified in the way we have just studied, has no appreciable effect on the great mass of steel production of the country. Only the largest industries buy enough steel to have a decided effect on the demand for this basic material. Railroading, which itself is to a very large extent engaged in the production of intermediate products, furnishes the steel industry with an outlet for its products which is so large as to be quite decisive and at the same time so fluctuating as to be a constant barometer of prosperity or of depression. And the steel industry itself is an equally important barometer, reporting in intensified form all general movements which originate with businesses closer to the final sale of the product.

In summary, the chief attempt of this study has been to give an exact formulation to the relationship, in quantity and in time, between demand for products and demand for the means of production; a relationship which plays a large part in several different theories of business cycles, and the results of which are so obvious that almost all descriptions of business cycles display them. The main principles contended for are as follows:

1. The demand for enlarging the means of production (including stocks of finished goods on the way to the consumer) varies, not with the volume of the demand for the finished product, but rather with the acceleration of that demand, allowance being made for the fact that the equipment cannot be adjusted as rapidly as demand changes, and so may be unusually scarce or redundant to start with in any given period. The demand for equipment may decrease as a result of this law even though the demand for the finished product is still growing.

2. The total demand for producers' goods tends to vary more sharply than the demand for finished products, the intensification being in proportion to the average life of the goods in question.[19]

3. The maximum and minimum points in the demand for producers' goods tend to precede the maximum and minimum points in the demand for the finished products, the effect being that the change may appear to precede its own cause.

These are but a few of the dynamic laws of demand. Two others may be mentioned which have been brought incidentally into the current of the argument and which have been discussed by other writers. We have seen that the

---

[19] The "life" of a finished product in this statement means the length of time it remains unsold.

demand for durable goods depends not merely on the price, but on the direction in which the price is expected to move in the near future, as judged chiefly by the direction in which it has been moving in the immediate past.[20] As this has been worked out by other writers, it need not be elaborated here, but may be listed as one of the dynamic laws of demand. Another fact clearly brought out by Mitchell's study is that the demand for materials is sometimes hindered from reacting promptly to a change in the demand for the finished product by the existence of standing contracts, which divide the market into open and closed sections. The result may be under certain conditions to accentuate the suddenness of changes.

ADDITIONAL NOTE ON "BUSINESS ACCELERATION AND THE LAW OF DEMAND" *

The foregoing essay is the writer's earliest treatment of this theme. Later treatments develop additional aspects. See *Studies in the Economics of Overhead Costs,* University of Chicago Press, 1923, pp. 389–94; and *Strategic Factors in Business Cycles,* National Bureau of Economic Research, 1934, pp 33–44, 170–182. In the latter volume the theory was extended to durable goods in general, and emphasis was laid on the way in which the effect of changes in activity in the durable-goods industries returns upon general consumer-demand, and so on, in a theoretically endless series of cycles. Thus the originating movement (which *may* occur at any point in the system) tends to be overlaid by these after-effects, so that its original character cannot be traced statistically. This point is important for the discussion that follows. The principle at work is essentially the same as that treated in the essay: "Aggregate

[20] This fact is mentioned by Senior, *Political Economy,* 6th ed., pp. 17-20, esp. p. 18, as well as by Mitchell, *op. cit.,* p. 459. Cf. also G. B. Dibblee, *The Laws of Supply and Demand,* pp. 139-40.

* This note was inserted in final revision, 1936.

Spending by Public Works," which appears elsewhere in this volume. The original theory became the subject of a controversy with Professor Ragnar Frisch, *Journal of Political Economy*, Oct., Dec., 1931, Apr., 1932. More recently it has been discussed at length by Dr. Simon Kuznets, "Relation Between Capital Goods and Finished Products in the Business Cycle," in *Economic Essays in Honor of Wesley Clair Mitchell*, Columbia University Press, 1935, pp. 209–267.

Dr. Kuznets' challenging and penetrating discussion invites comment and commendation at many points; but I think I shall be doing as he would wish by going to the heart of his conclusions and bringing out the extent of our agreement and the nature and source of our differences, if any. At the end of an extended and laborious statistical verification, he finds that: "The statistical analysis shows a striking disparity between the expectations based on the hypothesis and the actual changes revealed by the quantitative evidence. In the data studied, the amplitude of cyclical changes in the demand for capital goods is far short of that indicated on the basis of net changes in the demand for services of these goods. Similarly, the lead of the cycles in the demand for capital goods is far short of that suggested by the turning points in the net changes in the demand for finished products." Now it happens that the first of these findings agrees with that of my own more rudimentary statistical test; and also with my expressed expectations (See footnote, pp. 333-4). And the second finding also agrees with my expressed expectations (See line cc′ in chart, p. 336 and text commenting on it) although in my limited statistical sample, this line appeared to move more promptly than I should have expected.

The fact seems to be that the hypothesis which Dr. Kuznets is testing is, in those features which are essential for the present purpose, the one which I introduced by saying: "The nature of the mechanical law at work can be emphasized by imagining the industry reduced to a mere machine. . . . Finished goods are turned out as fast as wanted, and materials and means of production are instantly supplied as fast as the process of finishing requires them. On this simplified basis we can predict accurately how the speed of the different parts of the machine must needs vary,[1] and the results will furnish an index of the varying strains that are put on the much

---

[1] This refers to the *hypothetical* machine.

less mechanical system that does these things in real life" (p. 331). Again: "The assumption has been made that the new construction actually keeps pace with the demand for it, simply in order to have some figures that would not be too complicated. In fact, the supply is almost certain to fall behind the demand——" (p. 333, footnote). I should have added that actual demand in the shape of orders would also be morally certain in most cases to fall behind the hypothetically-indicated demand. Again: "Making all due allowances for mitigating factors in translating the illustration back into real life, it is still difficult to see how the building and machine-making industries can possibly avoid the disagreeable experience of outgrowing themselves in time of prosperity" (p. 334).

These citations may serve to show how the hypothesis in question was intended to be used. If taken as a picture of what must happen in real life, it would involve the absurd condition that producers of finished goods never have any excess or shortage of capacity (except when demand has shrunk faster than productive equipment can shrink by wearing out), while producers of productive equipment have always enough excess capacity to handle instantly any demand that may be put upon them. There is, of course, no reason for supposing that these two groups of producers behave in such diametrically opposite ways. Actually, each group has normally some excess capacity, part of which at least is likely to be of inferior quality and worth replacing or modernising if it comes into more constant demand. In respect to this and other matters Dr. Kuznets has contributed so substantially to elaborating the necessary qualifications and modifications of this provisional hypothesis that it causes some surprise to see him reverting to it to apply his statistical test and setting up as my theory what I had called "the impossibly fluid condition of industry that was previously assumed" (p. 337).

His use of this hypothesis affects his test in one way which might escape the casual reader. It controls the way in which the "theoretical demand" of his tables is constructed, and I should not accept this as unqualifiedly valid (to say the least) for the purpose in hand. He works out a slowly moving normal ratio of equipment to traffic—one freight car to so many million net ton-miles—and applies this to the excess of traffic in any year over traffic the previous year (with allowance for the fact that new equipment has more-than-average capacity) to determine the number of new cars theoretically needed, above replacements. This amounts to assuming for each year that the ratio of equipment to traffic was normal the preceding year; in spite of the fact that the figures themselves show that production of new equipment did not fluctuate nearly enough, nor promptly enough, to keep this ratio normal; and each year would actually start with an excess or shortage left over from the preceding year. This initial excess or shortage should play a part in determining "theoretical demand" for new equipment, as well as the change in volume of traffic during the current year.

One method which would do this would be to apply the equipment-ratio to the total volume of traffic in the second of a pair of years, subtract the actual volume of equipment in existence the first year, and so get the volume of new construction needed to bring the ratio to normal (with allowance for increased unit capacity of new equipment as before). The result would be to shift the timing of movements in theoretical demand for new equipment, bringing it nearer to that of movements in total volume of traffic, and thus shifting the base-line of Dr. Kuznets' comparisons. It would incidentally introduce an allowance, of a sort, for the factor of overcapacity to which Dr. Kuznets has called attention. (Cf. also Sec. 4, pp. 341-2.)

However, I have no intention of contending that my original treatment is perfect. I find it especially faulty in its handling of maintenance and replacements, which should be distinguished from each other and more emphasis given to replacements which should not, for long-lived equipment, be assumed to vary with current rate of output of the finished product. On this point Dr. Kuznets has brought out what seem to be the chief factors to be taken into account, and has developed one of them mathematically. For one of them, credit should be given also to Thomas M. McNiece—cf. "Rhythmic Variations in Industry," *Mechanical Engineering*, Nov., 1933, pp. 659 ff.

The important thing is, of course, what behavior should be expected with the principle in question operating under actual conditions. For this purpose the behavior of replacements should be carefully reconsidered. But more important is the fact that the interaction between consumers' purchases and the production of capital goods runs in both directions; and that the greater part of the fluctuations in the total amount of consumers' spendings or purchases are the result of fluctuations in their incomes, in which fluctuations in the production of durable goods play an important or controlling part. (Cf. footnote 15, p. 341.) An original disturbing impulse may come from either side; in either case it can start a series of interactions, mutually reinforcing one another. In the case of the production of durable capital goods, some six to eight months might be expected to elapse after an original impulse before the activity of production showed anything like the full effects. It would presumably take a shorter time for the resulting income to be distributed and to take effect on movements of consumers' purchases—let us say, on the average, two or three months. This picture is still highly simplified, but may contain enough of the important elements to afford a basis for prediction of an approximate normal pattern of behavior. What would such a pattern be?

If we start with an upward inflection of consumers' purchases, then the first period of six to eight months would witness an upward curve in production of capital goods, reaching a substantial amount by the end of the period, while the first effects of the reaction on consumers' purchases would have begun to show themselves in a slight reinforcement of the original rise. In the second period, consumers' purchases would continue to rise, and production of capital goods also; but the latter might now be rising in something like a straight line. The natural result would be a straight-line rise in consumers' purchases, with a slight lag. As this continued, the production of capital goods might soon reach a point at which it would taper off and cease to increase, though remaining at a higher level than at first, the result would be to put an end to the derived increase in consumers' purchases; and bring about a downward (relative) inflection of this curve. The result of this, with a lag, would be to start a decline in production of capital goods, which would in turn result in a decline of consumers' purchases, relative to their secular trend, and probably a positive decline unless the secular trend is very strongly upward. This would in turn drive the production of capital goods below its initial level. This downward movement would then ultimately reverse itself as a result of a similar series of interactions in the reverse direction. The whole cycle might be expected to take an amount of time approximately equal to four times the sum of the two lags (from thirty-two to forty-four months), or possibly longer. The high points of production of capital goods would lag behind the mid-points of the rises in consumers' purchases by six to eight months (possibly more) and would lead the high points of consumers' purchases by two to three months, or more if the upward secular trend of the latter is substantial.

If the initial movement came from the production of capital goods, these would lead in the first period, but after that the pattern would be substantially the same. Or if at any time some fresh originating impulse entered from either side, it would temporarily alter the timing of the pattern. It would also be modified by the fluctuations in the need for replacements resulting from previous fluctuations in production of equipment, and by any unusual surplus or shortage of productive capacity left over from preceding periods. This last might cause additional lags or prolongations of movements. A particular type of durable goods might have a natural cycle-period different from that of general business, with the result that its individual pattern would be a complex one.

When considering a single class of capital goods confined to the making of a product or products the demand for which moves to some extent independently of the general cyclical curve of consumer-demand, the problem will be different, because the secondary effects of changes in the production of such capital goods on consumers' demand for the particular products which these goods make, will be relatively slight. The observable effects will be almost entirely those running from consumer demand to demand for means of production. But if consumer-demand for these products moves in harmony with general consumer-demand, the resultant pattern should show the same features as the more general one.

This note has grown too long, without doing justice to all of Dr. Kuznets' points which invite comment. As to the possibility of statistical verification of the theoretical expectations here formulated, they are known in advance to agree with the general type of observed behavior of the shorter business cycles (the "forty-month" variety) and leave possibilities of longer movements. It would be interesting to study discrepancies and variations and their causes. One subtle and interesting question is whether the sum of the two lags figuring in the pattern just suggested has any causal bearing on the length of the "forty-month cycle." Since both are of the nature of distributed lags and presumably with their tails lopped off, the question presents its difficulties. The direct and obvious method of statistical attack would amount to verifying a tautology.

PRODUCTIVE CAPACITY AND
EFFECTIVE DEMAND*

THIS report addresses itself in the main to the problems
raised by the memorandum of Messrs. Barker,
Mitchell, and Person,† of productive capacity remaining chronically unutilized, even in good times. However, since one hypothesis as to the reason for this condition
attributes it to cyclical fluctuations in industrial activity, that
problem also necessarily enters into the discussion. The
central problem here taken up is, first, whether there exists
a condition which can be correctly described as a chronic
limitation of production owing to limitation of effective
demand, and second, if it does exist, what is the nature and
meaning of the condition which is commonly so described?
Underlying this is the analysis of the nature of the mechanism by which potential power to produce is transformed
into realized production, balanced and activated by an equivalent effective demand for the products turned out. No
definitive analysis of this sort has been made; and all that
can be done in a report of this character is to suggest
hypotheses bearing upon it, subject to verification by the
researches of many economists.

As to the facts, the memorandum of Barker, Mitchell,
and Person affords a starting point. It is presented only as

* Reprinted from MacIver: *Economic Reconstruction,* by permission of Columbia University Press.

† Report of Subcommittee on Production Capacity which inquired "whether
engineers generally share the view which has been expressed by several members
of their profession, that, given a free hand, technical experts could greatly increase income with existing industrial equipment."

355

a fragmentary sampling of the field; and the sample is probably to some extent a biased one. In manufacturing, one expects to find such conditions as are suggested by this memorandum; while agriculture, housing construction, mining, transportation, mercantile distribution, and various classes of services each have their own peculiar conditions, and the margin of unused productive capacity on the average of all these fields would, beyond reasonable doubt, be smaller than in manufacturing.

The impressions of engineers and executives as to the causes of limited output are also subject to some qualification. In particular, it is quite possible that if the factor which they feel as the present limiting one were to cease to act as a limitation, other limiting factors would come to bear and would limit output long before theoretical capacity was attained. Means of transportation and mercantile distribution might act in this way. But it is also fair to assume that if limitations due to "limited demand" were removed, these other limiting factors would be expanded, at a cost which would dilute the resulting gains but not completely cancel them. The present special report will assume that it has been reasonably well established that there exists a very considerable margin of unused productive capacity owing to the condition commonly thought of and spoken of as limted effective demand.

Another qualification is the moral certainty that if by a miracle there should be brought into existence a volume of effective demand equal to the existing unused productive power, that demand would not be directed to buying just those goods and services for which the economic system has unused capacity, and in precise proportion to the unused capacity existing. Therefore a complement to this study is the study of the standard of living which is attainable, so far as our power to produce is concerned. Only the most uncertain estimates could be made; but even these might be useful.

To indicate the difficult nature of the problem, one might start with a provisional assumption that a general increase of twenty-five per cent is possible, only to find that if increased income were largely concentrated in the hands of a few wealthy groups, so little of the increased demand would go to the mass-production industries where the chief untapped powers of production lie that the increase would be cut to ten per cent, even if an oversaving crisis could somehow be avoided. On the other hand, if the increase were accompanied by a radical equalizing of income, the resulting demand might be so concentrated on the mass-production industries that a twenty-five per cent increase would fall far short of exhausting the possibilities, if the motivation of industry were not impaired. The Chamber of Commerce of the United States has made a survey of the possible increase in demand growing out of a general standard of living of $2,500 per family. Such studies need to be correlated with possible increases in production and thinkable systems of distribution of the proceeds.

For instance, in New York the $2,500 family income would still fall just short of affording an effective demand for a modern four-room apartment built on a commercial basis, unless the family spends a larger percentage of its income for rent than is considered good budgeting. At present there is a wide gap between the highest rent the great mass of the people can pay and the lowest rent at which new commercial construction is practicable. But if incomes were to increase and construction costs to come down, somewhere there would be reached a critical point at which a vast new effective demand would be tapped; and

the resulting economies of larger-scale building would justify lower prices; and might free the mass of the people
from the necessity of living in obsolete and unfit quarters.

Lacking such studies of potential demand and supply,
we still know beyond a doubt that our system has actually
assimilated great increases in productive power since the
beginning of the Industrial Revolution, converting them
into actual realized increases in production. This is a basic
fact to be placed alongside the proposition that the system
has not assimilated its productive power as fast as that
power has come into being. And the question "Why has
the system not assimilated all its productive power?" might
as well be reversed. Why and how has it assimilated as
much as it has? Why should we expect that it would assimilate it all? Why should not considerable groups of laborers,
for instance, be pushed outside the circle of production,
reward, and power to buy goods and not be able to make
their way in again?

It may help us in attempting to analyze the mechanism
for assimilating progress to look at some of the adjustments which this mechanism has to make, if it is to do its
work successfully. In the first place, one of the things to
be assimilated is an ever-increasing supply of capital per
worker. This goes into more and more automatic machinery,
whereby one worker controls more and more spindles, or
more and more working power in other forms, with a
correspondingly increased output per worker. If the new
capital goes into needless duplication of existing types of
plant, then to that extent it is being wasted, and the productive power it contains is not being successfully used.
Since this actually happens to a considerable extent, the conclusion is that a full use of our supply of capital would
call for a more rapid development of labor-saving equip-

ment than we have actually witnessed, if it is all to be absorbed without useless duplications.

The resulting increase of output cannot take the shape simply of an even expansion in all lines. Foodstuffs cannot increase very much without glutting the market, manufactured goods in general have vastly more elastic possibilities, while services of an intangible sort have the greatest possibilities of all. To absorb the rising standard of living made possible by improvements in steel-making and the textile industries, we may be called on to employ a smaller percentage of our labor force there and a larger percentage in caring for our health and recreation. But it is not precisely those individuals who would be thrown out of work in steel and textiles whom we should want to employ in these much more responsible service capacities. Evidently the shift involved is a highly complex one. It becomes a trifle more simple to the extent that we enlarge our demands for tangible goods. But this requires the continual development of new commodities, which typically begin as luxuries for the well-to-do and finally make their way into quantity production at lowered costs which bring them within the reach of increasing numbers. Another item in the adjustment is a shortening of the hours of labor, whereby the workers get part of the benefit of increased productive power in the shape of leisure, and part in the shape of more goods.

Finally, we have to reckon with a tendency toward saving a progressively increasing proportion of our income as our income itself gets larger. Thus the whole process may need to go faster and faster, if the whole of the increasing productive power is to be utilized. And it is really very little wonder if some parts of this very complicated process do not proceed fast enough or accurately enough. A competent socialist government with the best possible planning board would not be able to avoid all mistakes and misfits. It might easily be reduced to the expedient of cutting down working hours, perhaps from eight to six, in spite of the fact that the workers might prefer to work nine hours if they could get correspondingly more goods.

The main items in the mechanism by which private business takes care of this process seem to be the following: (1) the willingness of business enterprise to produce in anticipation of demand either (*a*) some new commodity or (*b*) new equipment to produce a familiar commodity more economically; (2) an elastic credit system which can furnish business enterprise funds for expansion without waiting for individuals to pile up original savings enough to finance the projects in hand (The savings can come afterward, out of the earnings of the new equipment or the new enterprises, if they are successful. This carries with it a corollary which may not be so fortunate, namely that there is an increase in the volume of our real medium of exchange, all of which goes to finance producers' goods. There are other forms of credit used to finance consumers' goods, but there is no assurance that they expand and contract in such a way as to maintain a healthy balance between consumers' and producers' purchasing power); (3) reduced prices, to dispose of increased amounts of goods turned out at decreased unit costs; (4) decreased wage demands on the part of any workers who have been displaced, as a means of making it worth while for some employer to take them on again; (5) lower interest charges to make it worth while for employers to use capital fairly lavishly in order to economize labor; (6) increased consumer purchasing power resulting from the expenditures which producers have made in expanding production or doing other kinds of pioneering, or the disbursement of the earnings which have come to the successful ones.

Another factor in the situation is the stock market, which intervenes between people who save funds and businesses which put them into buildings, machines, and working capital. The stock market is one of the agencies for expanding production, but its operations too often lead to speculative booms which do not help the sound progress of the whole system.

If the circulating medium remained fixed in quantity, and its circuit velocity unchanged, no increased quantity of goods could find a market except at a proportionately lowered average price level. If some goods find a market in increased volume without corresponding decrease in price, they take up purchasing power formerly going into other goods, with the result that these other goods must sell either at a lower price or in smaller volume. If prices cannot or will not make all these adjustments in the way which permits increased output, then another factor must take up the burden of adjustment. If business cannot endure a falling price level, then the circulating medium or its circuit velocity must increase. Increase in volume of production is limited to the increase in the product of the volume of the circulating medium by its circuit velocity.

Neither the circulating medium nor prices are absolutely rigid; but our system is apparently more and more closely approximating the last condition mentioned: i.e., that of an economy which tolerates no general declines in prices of considerable magnitude, in the sense that it resists them so strongly at many points that they can never be carried through as balanced *general* movements, and never without precipitating a depression. And as the "circuit velocity" of money is largely an independent factor, this amounts to saying that in a general and approximate way, increased output is limited by increase in the circulating medium, modified by a certain tolerance of the system for relatively slow and mild declines in prices.

While these conditions as to volume of the medium of exchange and general price movements are necessary to absorption of potential productive power, they are not alone sufficient. There may be enough purchasing power in the economic system to take anything a given business man may produce with a part of the country's disengaged resources; but that is no guarantee that this purchasing power will actually be used to take off the market whatever this particular business man may see fit to produce. And if it is not used in this way, then the continuous flow of purchasing power which should result from this business man's operations will never come into being.

Purchasing power is not merely volume of circulating medium times its circuit velocity divided by the index of the price level. If this expression be analyzed, it reduces itself to a much simpler one: physical quantity of goods produced. Purchasing power and physical output are two aspects of the same thing, and real purchasing power can be increased only by measures which result in increasing physical output: measures which end by reducing physical output can only reduce real purchasing power and not increase it.

But this does not mean all it may seem to mean on the surface. It does not mean, for example, that all that is needed to increase purchasing power is to produce more of anything, no matter what. Only goods that sell in the market constitute purchasing power for other goods; and only goods that sell for enough to cover the minimum or "variable" or direct costs of production will continue to sell at all. Whenever goods are selling for less than cost, it means that the resources used to produce these goods are not bringing into being as much purchasing power to buy other products as is latent in these resources. But in this statement the assumption is made that the money costs of the productive resources are adjusted at what is supposed to be the normal level. The upshot of the matter is that while output of one salable product constitutes purchasing power for other products, a producer may be bringing into being more or less purchasing power, or in limiting cases none at all, according as he makes something which will sell for more or less than the resources used to produce it could have yielded elswhere, or something which the market will not take at any price which the seller is willing to accept.

The bearings of this discussion on the question at issue can be summed up by saying that adequate purchasing power is not merely a matter of volume of the circulating medium, or even of the total flow of money incomes, divorced from what happens to prices. The ultimate basis of purchasing power is production itself; and adequate purchasing power depends on the successful making of all the far-reaching adjustments already mentioned as necessary to the assimilation of increased power to produce goods.

The volume of media of exchange can be increased by credit inflation, bringing about an immediate increase in purchasing power not dependent on prior increase of production—and this is an important factor; but apart from a rather moderate long-run upward trend such increases are temporary. If they do not result in an increase in production, so adjusted as to be lasting, they produce only a momentary increase in real purchasing power.

Shifts of income from one group to another may involve

momentary increases or decreases in the active flow of purchasing power, if the income is shifted from groups who
receive it and use it more promptly to those who receive and
use it more slowly, and *vice versa*. Such shifts may also affect
the balance of the economic system by altering demand as
between different kinds of goods, or altering the relative
amounts of consumers' spending and saving. If such shifts
have the effect of improving the whole adjustment of the
economic system, in terms of all the elements already discussed, they may increase real purchasing power; but not
otherwise.

We may now pass on to the question of why potential
productive powers are not fully used, and consider those
causes whose immediate and visible symptom appears in
the form of an inadequate market for the products. Here
two hypotheses stand out. The first has to do with long-
run trends, and assumes that there is some limitation on the
increase of purchasing power, or on the rate at which
the economic system can make the adjustments which have
been outlined, such that this rate falls short of the rate of
increase in our powers of production. The second hypothesis
is that good times always start from a depression, and are
attained by methods and processes of such a sort that they
can go only a limited distance before they come to an
end and create a condition bringing on a reaction, without
ever reaching the point of full utilization of our powers of
production.

Both hypotheses may be true; but if the second is true, it
means that industrial fluctuations are the first obstacle to
full use of our productive powers, and until they are
measurably dealt with, we can hardly test the truth of the
first hypothesis, or grapple very usefully with the problems
which it raises. The present writer inclines to the view that

the second hypothesis is true, with the consequences just pointed out.

The mechanism of expansion from depression to boom may be divided into sources of the original impulse to expansion and sources of its cumulative effects. Leaving out of account the original initiating impulses, which may be of a great variety of sorts, the sources of cumulative expansion center chiefly in the class of durable goods, in which by far the greatest percentage of expansion and contraction is found. This includes capital equipment and durable consumers' goods, among which the dominant items are housing and automobiles. These goods have one common characteristic of vital importance: namely that an upward deflection of, let us say, five per cent in the course of the total supply of capital equipment or of housing space calls for much more than a five per cent increase in the current output of these goods.

If the production of these goods had to wait until people accumulated enough actual income to buy the houses for cash, or enough original personal savings to furnish funds for the capital expansion, these features tending toward intensified fluctuations would have little chance to operate. But such goods are bought on credit, and credit is elastic and makes it possible to buy the goods first and accumulate the income or savings afterwards, with the result that capital equipment can be paid for out of its own ultimate earnings, if these are sufficient. It is often installed without waiting for realized demand for the products.

But the process of installing it creates demand: that is, it brings about a diffusion of spending power among all who share in the income derived from making and installing the equipment; and this is the central fact in the general diffusion of the effects of such an expansion. The revival in the work of making capital equipment is an intensified reflection of the forces that gave rise to it; and it brings about a further revival in demand for things in general. This in turn is reflected back in a still stronger increase in demand for capital equipment; and the movement is further intensified by the speculative effects of rising prices, and by a general feeling of optimism.

Such a self-reinforcing expansion cannot go on forever, if only because it must at some point reach the limits of expansion of the credit system. It reaches the limits of safe expansion even sooner, since the basis of the credit is the earning power of the productive equipment which is being brought into being; and this rests on a shaky foundation. The rapid expansion in the durable goods industries is not an enduring thing, but a concentration, let us say, of two years' growth in one. There must some time come a tapering off in the rate of expansion, and when it comes, the buying power of consumers in general tapers off as a direct result. The further result in these durable goods industries is an absolute decline in the rate of production needed to satisfy the demand. This means an absolute decline in the amounts distributed as spending power to those who share in the income from these branches of production, and a corresponding decline in the effective demand for things in general. The cumulative effects of the movement are now reversed.

A further fact is that at the peak, people with more income than usual are saving a larger percentage of it than usual, and spending a smaller percentage for consumers' goods. Thus demand for consumers' goods in general does not increase as fast as productive power, so that the tapering-off process which starts the reversal is an inevitable thing. The expansion is bound to find a limit. Another source of instability is the fact that credit is debt, and the elastic type of credit is short-time or callable debt, the expansion of which introduces an explosive element into the situation.

The central facts may be put arithmetically. If an original increase of five per cent in demand for consumers' goods calls forth an increase of thirty per cent in the current output of durable means of production, as is fairly probable, the increased activity in producing capital equipment, spread over the whole field of industry, would amount to something like an additional five per cent increase in total production. If the original impulse were of a temporary sort, and had disappeared by the time the secondary effects came into being, the thing would end there. The thirty per cent expansion in the work of making capital equipment might be maintained until the total amount of productive capacity was adjusted to a five per cent increase in output, but then it would come to an end and a general contraction would result unless something else had in the meantime started another upward impulse of the cumulative sort.

If the original impulse did not vanish as soon as the secondary effects came into being, there would be a ten per cent increase in demand for things in general, which might quite possibly result in a sixty per cent increase in the demand for capital equipment, which in turn would lead to a still further increase in general demand for consumers' goods, and so on until some neutralizing factor appeared, or until the credit system could expand no farther.

If we take the process at the point where the output of capital equipment has expanded sixty per cent, this may mean possibly only a six per cent increase in productive capacity during the first year, which is less than the expansion in general demand. Thus there is a sellers' market with rising prices, and the other usual accompaniments. But if this condition keeps on, productive capacity will soon increase beyond the increase in general demand which the equipment boom is itself sustaining, by an inherent mathematical necessity.

This condition may be described in terms of failure of purchasing power to keep pace with power to produce, but the discrepancy seems inherent in the concentrated spurt of expansion in productive facilities. It is difficult to see how, in the nature of the case, purchasing power for goods in general can keep pace indefinitely with productive power when the increase of the latter has behind it the whole force, or the main force, of credit expansion. And when the expansion of capital equipment tapers off, general purchasing power declines. Thus the behavior of the production of durable goods seems to lie behind the shortage of purchasing power.

One further fact seems to be that the conditions of a boom in capital equipment act as an obstacle to the making of one of the adjustments which are necessary in the long run to the absorption of increased productive power. A general increase in the supply of capital per worker needs to be put in new forms of an increasingly automatic sort, rather than in mere duplication of plants of the existing types. If this were wisely done, it would reduce costs of production, though the output per thousand dollars of capital would not be as great as before. Then a condition of excess capacity would not come so quickly, and, when it did, the industries would be in a position to meet it by lowering prices and marketing an enlarged output in the face of a limited volume of dollar purchasing power.

But the condition of a capital-equipment boom is hostile to such a development. Expanding productive capacity, rather than reduced cost, is the thing sought, and the urgency is so great that conditions of future efficiency tend to be neglected. A limited supply of labor may still act as an incentive to developing more labor-saving types of equipment, as may also high wages maintained by strong unions in particular industries; but the typical outcome seems to be an undue amount of duplication of facilities of generally familiar types, rather than a change in the type adequate to absorb the full increase in the supply of capital per worker which is coming into being.

Lower interest rates would facilitate the proper adjustment, but in a time of expansion interest rates tend to be increased rather than reduced. They exceed the social productivity of added capital when that capital is being put into wasteful duplication and excess capacity. This condition acts as an obstacle to lower-grade uses of capital which could be made to yield a moderate, but real, social product.

Changing the forms of capital equipment would not solve all the problems of assimilating increased power to produce goods; it would merely be one step in the right direction. In fact, in the long run it would actually speed up the increase in per capita productive power, at the same time that it put industry in a somewhat better position to absorb such increases. It would not solve all the questions of what to produce, how to distribute income, how much to shorten hours of labor, and so forth. The short-run problems of the business cycle would be somewhat mitigated, but not cured, while the long-run problems of absorbing increased productive power would remain.

As to the short-run problems, the natural remedy would surely not be to try to pump enough extra dollar purchasing power into the economic system to take care of all the increase of productive power which a credit boom can finance, and to do it without any reduction in the level of prices. There seems to be no sound way of doing that. The more appropriate remedy would be to regularize the expansion of capital facilities, and so far as possible of durable goods in general, so that it will not go by spurts which cannot in the nature of things be maintained. This is no easy task, but it is vitally necessary, and it would be premature to say that it is impossible. Some suggestions bearing on it are contained in the concluding paragraphs of an article by the present writer, in the March, 1934, number of the *American Economic Review*.[1]

Another appropriate measure, and one which seems necessary and inevitable, is to make the flow of available purchasing power more stable than the flow of productive activity, by the use of stabilizing reserves. Dividend reserves are already common practice, and unemployment reserves would be a logical complement. But there are dangers to be avoided. The financial handling of the reserves, and the methods of realizing on them when benefits are to be paid, may defeat any purpose of stabilizing general purchasing power, and merely result in concentrating the fluctuations on the things in which the reserve funds are invested. Buying securities during booms and making forced sales during recessions will not be wise financing or helpful to the general situation; but other and better methods can be devised.

Another danger is that, if the benefits are too liberal, the result may be to stiffen unduly the wage rates below which workers would rather remain idle than accept employment. This, by reducing the flow of goods, would reduce real purchasing power instead of increasing it. In short, this device

---

[1] The article is entitled "Economics and the National Recovery Administration."

of unemployment reserves is a delicate instrument, which may do harm as well as good, and requires careful and courageous handling to produce the benefits of which it is capable.

If and when, by these means or others, we make substantial progress toward greater stability, we can face the further problem whether people spend too little for consumption, and save too much, for a balanced supply of capital in the forms into which we know how to convert it; and whether changes in the distribution of income can do something to improve the balance. It is, of course, a desirable thing that real purchasing power should expand as fast as possible. And it seems a primary consideration that it will, over a term of years, expand faster if it does so continuously and without the setbacks that follow our periods of concentrated expansion. On the other hand, this process would actually sharpen some of the problems that face us; particularly that of casual and semicasual labor. Regularization might mean permanent unemployment for considerable numbers of those who are able to get along under customary conditions with irregular or occasional jobs.

If, under regularization, the natural expansion of means of payment does not go on fast enough to absorb our possible output without reduced prices, the soundest way of expanding real purchasing power, on the whole, is to lower prices. This may or may not be necessary as a long-run tendency, depending on how fast the means of payment expand. If it should prove to be necessary, its disturbing effects on industry would be much reduced if it went on gradually and steadily, rather than being superimposed upon the customary cyclical expansions and contractions. Under the latter conditions, a long-term downward trend of prices serves to make expansions shorter and contractions longer, and probably more severe. Industry could more easily adjust itself to a slow and fairly regular downward trend.

The increase in product per worker which seems to be potentially available represents lowered unit costs of production, making some reduction of prices quite possible without crippling industry, even if real wages rise, as they naturally would do. The probability is that with the setbacks resulting from depressions largely removed, this process would go on quite as fast as we could find out what to produce in order to make effective use of our increased productive power.

This brings us to the more permanent question of our power to absorb increased productive power in the long run. Here it seems clear that there is no fixed limit to this power, but that, under present conditions, our power to absorb has not kept pace with our power to produce. Power to absorb is in part a matter of purchasing power, but only in part. Real purchasing power is governed not merely by the flow of media of exchange, but also by the prices of goods and services; and its effective character is governed not only by its total amount but by the things for which it is used—its distribution between consumption and savings, between mass-production goods and other goods and services, and between familiar goods and new goods. Equally important is the distribution of potential producing and purchasing power as between more goods and more leisure, and the distribution of the leisure.

But over and above all these questions involved in purchasing power is the problem of producing the right goods in the right proportions, at prices which will cause them to be bought and with adjustments between prices and payments for the factors of production which will enable the producers to go on producing goods in amounts which will utilize all existing factors of production. Production of capital goods has to be adjusted not only to the flow of savings, but to the volume of output for which there is an attainable demand.

It is not merely a question of industry distributing enough purchasing power to buy its current product at a price consistent with continued production. There must be capacity of increase in the system, and increase at a substantial rate which can be sustained and will not lead to reaction and depression. Out of the current cycle of production and consumption there must flow a volume of purchasing power which will initiate and sustain a larger succeeding cycle, and so on indefinitely. Such an increase can hardly be furnished by endless credit expansion on a fixed currency base, or by any kind of credit expansion flowing mainly to producers. If the expansion of the currency base is not sufficient, lowered prices are required.

It is an unquestionable fact that the present system does not accomplish this task of adjustment successfully; and it is hardly open to question that the mere removal of booms and depressions would not furnish automatic solutions for all the problems of adjustment which would remain. Would the problem be solved if we could by some miracle establish the completely fluid, freely-competitive system of individualistic theory?

To this question no scientifically proven answer can be given. But it seems overwhelmingly probable that under such a system there would still be booms and depressions, though the depressions might be shorter and less serious on the whole than those produced by the present hybrid system. The booms might still never reach our full potential power of production before they exhausted themselves. The net rate of long-run expansion might be faster than the

present system permits; but there seems to be no guarantee
that it would be as fast as the increase in our power to
produce. The processes of adjustment, even under the freest
competition imaginable, would still take time and involve
uncertainties, errors, and losses.

It should be clearly recognized, also, that "free competition" in this connection means competition which stands
ready to go to unlimited cutthroat lengths whenever necessary to find a market for productive resources which would
otherwise go unused. What this would mean to modern
industry is not entirely easy to visualize; but it would mean
a great many things which the National Recovery Administration and the codes adopted under it are deliberately trying
to do away with, regarding them as "unfair competition."
It would mean revolutionizing the status of public utility
rates and other rigid areas of prices, remaking financial
structures to eliminate fixed charges (and fixed incomes),
and introducing some sort of elasticity into union wage scales,
which to organized labor represent the fruits of many bitter
and costly struggles, not to be given up without still more
bitter resistance.

Moves in all these directions are desirable or even necessary to introduce much-needed elasticity into our system;
but that they should go the full lengths required to achieve
the free-competitive ideal is hardly thinkable; especially in
the absence of more definite assurance than can be given
that the net result would be to make us richer in the aggregate instead of poorer.

This brings us face to face with one of the basic faults
in the "price system" as it actually operates: namely, recourse to idleness if production will not cover "costs," when
these "costs" represent not what the productive resources
are worth under existing conditions but what they would be

worth under more favorable conditions than actually exist. A wage rate of three dollars per day for making shoes ought to mean that there are other opportunities for using this labor to produce something worth three dollars per day. If the worker stands idle because he is not worth three dollars per day at making shoes, that means that the three-dollar alternative does not exist, or at least is not available within the limits of existing knowledge. Under these conditions, to act on the assumption that shoes are not worth producing unless they will cover the three-dollar wage is false social accounting, flying in the face of the elementary fact that anything produced is that much more than nothing. It stands in the way of our making the best available use of our productive resources, whatever that use may be, by insisting that they shall not be used at all unless their use will cover "costs" which changed conditions may have rendered, for this purpose, arbitrary and misleading. This is a large subject, which the writer has discussed at greater length in his volume entitled *Studies in the Economics of Overhead Costs.*

Under these conditions, it is inevitable that productive resources should go to waste, with the further result that they create no purchasing power to buy the products of other productive resources. And it is quite possible for productive resources to be permanently expelled from the circle of active production and purchase, which becomes adjusted to the shrunken purchasing power resulting from their expulsion and cannot reabsorb them.

Somewhat different is the case of producers who go on producing for next to nothing, and whose purchasing power approaches the zero limit too closely for economic health. Here society at least has the goods they have produced, but it still suffers from a lack of normal balance between its different parts.

At the other extreme from the free-competitive ideal is the completely collectivist system, in which all persons would have a claim to some share of the society's income without reference to whether they were able to contribute to its creation or not. This would dispose of the worst feature of the limited market as a limitation on production, not so much by the money it would give everyone to buy goods with, as by another angle of its effects, which is not so often thought of. It would mean that the extra cost to the employer (the community) of hiring a worker to produce goods as compared to the cost of letting him stand idle would be reduced either to nothing at all or to such a small amount that almost any market demand would suffice to make production worth while. The employer would have little or nothing to gain by limiting output, in the same situation in which the commercial employer is forced to limit it because further producton would not cover "out-of-pocket expenses." There would remain, of course, the question of incentives to the workers and to managerial efficiency, the avoidance of bureaucratic stagnation, the method of accumulating adequate capital, and other similar problems familiar enough in the literature of this subject.

Between these two extremes lie those smaller modifications of the existing system which may constitute useful steps of an evolutionary sort, mitigating some of the specific faults in the system. Among these faults are the undue concentration of incomes and probably a resulting tendency to oversaving, though the latter point needs fuller investigation. Any move in the direction of more equal distribution would mean an increased market for the things industry knows how to produce and for which it has spare capacity. If this were achieved mainly at the expense of reducing a volume of savings so swollen that a considerable part of it goes to waste, the change would be very nearly a clear gain.

But methods of working toward this end present dilemmas. A compulsory increase of wages, by increasing costs of production, might lead to restriction of output in the attempt to protect profits—in short, to just the opposite of the desired effect. This is one of the serious dangers to be guarded against in the operation of the National Industrial Recovery Act. It is possible that the wage system in its conventional form cannot solve the dilemma between wage costs low enough to be consistent with full employment, and sufficient progress toward more equal distribution to furnish the type of market which a system of mass production requires, and to avoid the danger of oversaving.

One mitigating factor might be the increase of free social services of various sorts. And one change which could do no harm, and which is necessary if industry is to adjust itself to any real shift which gives wage earners a larger fraction of the social dividend, is a reduction of the spread in costs of production between the most efficient and the least efficient producers.[2] This presents sufficient difficulties, but may not be wholly impossible.

The present writer has a strong prejudice in favor of proceeding by evolutionary methods. If this is to be done, it is not necessary at this time to solve all the problems of long-run adjustment to increased productive power. Measures looking toward stabilization of industrial fluctuations have first claim on our attention. An industrial system

[2] See the concluding paragraphs of the article "Economics and the National Recovery Administration," already referred to.

which can make substantial progress in this direction will
necessarily have developed techniques of co-operative
action which may open up possibilities not now in sight for
attack on the longer-run problems.

XII

AGGREGATE SPENDING BY PUBLIC WORKS*†

I. INTRODUCTION

THE above title has been worded with some care to define the subject of this study. The principle is not confined to public spending, though public works constitute the instance commanding most attention at present; and it is public expenditures, of course, which can be positively controlled and so used as an instrument for the maintaining of general purchasing power. On the other hand, the principle *is* confined to expenditures which involve a change in the national aggregate and not a mere shift from one kind of spending to another—from spending for capital goods to spending for consumers' goods or *vice versa*, or from private to public spending or the reverse. If the government, either by borrowing or taxation, acquires funds which would otherwise have been spent privately, the public spending of those funds is a mere shifting, not an increase in the aggregate. But if government acquires funds which would not otherwise have been spent (and borrowing is the more likely method of doing this), then when it spends these funds it does increase the aggregate. Such expenditures I shall call "expansionary." They may or may not involve literal monetary inflation.

We have here to deal with the theoretical problem of the

* Reprinted by permission from the *American Economic Review*, Vol. XXV (Mar., 1935), pp. 14-20.

† This paper presents in abbreviated form material which is dealt with at greater length in *Economics of Planning Public Works*, Chap. IX, Government Printing Office, Washington, 1935.

cumulative effect of such aggregate changes. Such cumulative effects do a certain amount of violence to common-sense theories under which two plus two always equals four. In this realm of common sense, if more is spent on one thing, there is less to spend on something else; and if more is to be spent on capital goods, more must be saved and less spent for consumption. But quantitative studies show us that we reach our largest consumption at the same time when we are also making the largest investments in tangible capital goods, and they strongly suggest that, by spending more for one thing, the economy as a whole may have more left to spend on other things and not less, at least in the short run. It is on this hypothesis that the government has been attempting to stimulate business by a tremendous program of public works.

Corroboration of a general and tentative sort is found in the main facts of business cycles. Here (without probing for ultimate causes) there seems to be a primary change in aggregate spendings, usually by businesses, with resulting changes in incomes and in individual spendings, which react again upon business spendings in cumulative fashion. The course of cycles also suggests that these cumulative effects do not go on without limit, but exhaust themselves. These facts may have served to suggest the theory of dwindling successive impulses with a limited aggregate sum, which is discussed below. This theory in itself does not account for the final reversal of the movement, but it might form a part of a theory accounting for this reversal.

It is not easy to find a case in which a measurable primary change in spending can be isolated as a dominant active cause of the observed results; but possibly these conditions may be approximately fulfilled by the effect of Allied purchases in the United States during 1915–1916. These purchases were presumably the main primary cause of an enormous increase of production and national income. We were able to send abroad several billions of dollars' worth of goods, to make large additions to our industrial plant, and in addition to have more real income left for domestic consumption than ever before. The fact that our national economy received no real or ultimate payment for the goods sent abroad sharpens the paradox and may have been an essential feature of the case, from the standpoint of the immediate forces at work. The goods were sold on credit, and immediate dollar payment was forthcoming by expansionary methods. According to the theory we are considering, our real domestic spending power was increased, not in spite of sending more goods abroad, but because of it. The goods sent abroad were diverted from the domestic market for private consumption, and in that respect the case was similar to that of public works.

The real problem of cumulative effects must be distinguished from the simpler fact that, for every ten workers engaged, for example in actually building a dam, there are others engaged in making cement and excavating machinery and steel, and in hauling materials to the site of the dam and in numberless incidental services. These are all classed as *primary* activities, those on the site being *direct*, the others *indirect*, and all together accounting for the dollars the government actually spends for its dam. When those who receive this money as net income spend it again for food, clothes or automobiles, we have a new cycle, producing values beyond those of the dam the government has paid for. This and all subsequent cycles are classed as *secondary* activities. It is in the secondary activities that the cumulative effects of spending are to be found.

2. INDIRECT PRIMARY ACTIVITIES

Indirect primary activity raises no difficult theoretical questions, but is mainly a matter of statistical estimate. For the construction industry as a whole, direct primary labor appears to absorb about 40 per cent of gross income, this amount being fairly steady.[1] The profits of the construction industry are highly variable, but may on the average absorb about 10 per cent of the gross income. Of the 50 per cent which is passed on to indirect activities, something over seven-tenths appears to go to labor, at somewhat lower average wage-rates than are paid in construction itself, with the result that numbers employed in indirect primary activities are probably not far from equal to those employed directly. Of these, actual manufacture of construction materials absorbs only a part, and not a preponderant part.

But for our present purpose the question is, not average ratios of total activity, but the increase caused by an increase in volume of construction. From this standpoint one must reckon with the fact that the industries involved in the indirect activities have considerable amounts of overhead costs which are relatively constant. For example, depreciation represents ultimate activities of replacement; but such activities may be long deferred, especially in a time of deep depression. Furthermore, a policy of minimizing the use of machinery in construction tends to increase the ratio of direct labor and reduce the ratio of indirect. Thus the *additional* indirect labor immediately employed as a result of increased public works should be conservatively reckoned as less than the volume of direct primary employment.

[1] The study of *National Income, 1929-32*, issued by the Bureau of Foreign and Domestic Commerce, shows 38.6 per cent for 1929 and 40.5 per cent for 1932.

3. SECONDARY ACTIVITIES

We come now to the problem of secondary activities, in which the actual cumulative effects are to be found. Attempts to deal systematically with this problem are in their infancy, especially in the United States. There are two approaches, one *via* successive cycles of income and spendings by ultimate recipients of income, the other *via* the volume of money and its velocity of circulation. The first has been best developed (though not yet exhaustively) by Mr. R. F. Kahn of Cambridge and Professor J. M. Keynes; the second has, so far as I am aware, not found its way into print.[2] Exponents of these two approaches hardly speak the same langauge, nor do their minds meet on the basic concepts used. Therefore the best service a study like the present can render is to make clear the implications of the two approaches, and especially the assumptions on which each depends. Each affords a first approximation and each, when completed, must take into account the facts dealt with by the

[2] See J. M. Keynes, *The Means to Prosperity*, London, 1933. See also R. F. Kahn, "The Relation of Home Investment to Unemployment," *Econ. Jour.*, June, 1931; "Public Works and Inflation," *Jour. Amer. Statistical Assoc.*, Mar., 1933. See also M. Mitnitzky in *Social Research*, May, 1934. Studies have been made within narrowly limiting assumptions by W. N. Loucks and Frank G. Dickinson. See Loucks, *The Stabilization of Employment in Philadelphia*, Philadelphia, 1931, pp. 161 ff., especially p. 166; and Dickinson, "Public Construction and Cyclical Unemployment," *Annals Suppl.*, Sept., 1928. Mr. Loucks is dealing with effects in Philadelphia of local works only; hence the diffused effects on business outside Philadelphia constitute a very large leakage, and others are ignored. Dickinson deals with the effects of the spending of wages only, for the first secondary cycle only, on the assumption that they all go to manufacturing industries (these being the only ones with suitable payroll statistics). Neither of these two methods is appropriate to a comprehensive study.

A somewhat mixed method is used by Vernon A. Mund ("Prosperity Reserves of Public Works," *Annals*, May, 1930, Part II, pp. 15-19). He deals with wages only, assumes half are spent in retail stores, and a time-factor of 5 cycles per year, which is apparently taken as the circuit velocity of deposits. The "leakage" of 50 per cent is not compounded, with the result that the stimulus to business is figured at 50 per cent of primary wages paid, repeated 5 times in a year.

other; therefore in the end the conclusions from the two methods should not disagree. Discrepancies between the first approximations are due, among other things, to provisionally assuming as constant, factors which are actually variable.

One feature is common to both approaches. They deal in the first instance with monetary magnitudes, leaving for separate consideration the question how much of the resulting expansion is absorbed by rising prices and how much takes the form of increased physical production and increased real incomes.

4. THE KAHN-KEYNES APPROACH

The Kahn-Keynes approach involves, when fully carried out, some eight essential elements, of which the first four have been systematically developed by these writers, the next three left largely to implication and the last passed over.

(1) Expansionary expenditures. Since there is no simple and obvious way, short of printing new money, in which government can be sure that the funds it acquires would otherwise have remained wholly idle, an estimate becomes necessary of the percentage of the public expenditures which is really expansionary, considering methods of financing and the state of the capital markets. In a depression, public borrowing can easily secure funds which private industry would not otherwise use, but as revival proceeds, this becomes more difficult.

(2) A resultant increase in incomes, leading to increased spending (secondary) by the recipients.

(3) "Leakages," mainly contractionary uses of part of this increased income, for example, by paying off accumulated debts. This does not mean, as sometimes assumed, a cumulative piling up of unspent funds for the economy as

a whole, since it is merely a partial neutralizing of the opposite effect produced by the public financing itself.

(4) A resultant dwindling series of successive increments of income and expenditure. If the "leakages" remain constant, this series to infinity would have a finite sum, most of which would be realized in from four to six or more cycles, according to the size of the "leakages." If the leakages are ½, the sum of the series ($1 + ½ + ¼$ . . .) will be double the original expansionary outlay; if the leakages are ⅓, the series will amount to three times the original amount, and so on. The effect of one original expenditure will thus exhaust itself fairly soon (except as the "leakages" may return to circulation).

If the original expenditures are continued for some time, there will be present simultaneously one original expenditure, the first resulting from the previous expenditure, the second responding from the one before that, and so on: in short, a series of the same character as that representing the successive effects of a single original outlay and, if the factors remained constant, amounting to the same sum. Thus if "leakages" were ⅓, there would ultimately by $2 of secondary expenditures added to every dollar of original expansionary outlay by the government.

(5) The time element, representing the number of such cycles which may be assumed to take place in a year. This time element has not been worked out, so far as I am aware. It is not simple and in particular it is not identical with either the transaction velocity or the circuit velocity of money. Wage earners may actually get their extra wages before the employer receives his pay from the government, and presumably spend most of them in a week or two. Dividends are received more slowly, and possibly spent more slowly. The spendings may lead to further wage pay-

ments almost at once; indeed after the process is once started, its effects may be anticipated. This part of the time-factor, at least, is not an ordinary velocity concept at all, but rather a concept of the speed with which an increase of velocity is transmitted. To illustrate the difference, it may take a year for goods to move through a chain of production-processes; but an increase of sales may result in a speeding-up of the whole chain in a matter of weeks, and in these days of telephones it is not physically impossible for the effect to be transmitted in a matter of hours.

For our problem, I have tentatively assumed an average time-factor of six cycles per year, or a rate of transmission slower than the transaction-velocity of money but considerably faster than its circuit velocity. This may imply an increase in the existing average circuit velocity, in case there is not literal inflation of the amount of money sufficient to handle the increase in business without an increase in velocity.

(6) The result is a rising curve, tapering off toward a horizontal asymptote, the rate of rise being governed by the time-factor and the height of the limiting asymptote by the percentage of "leakages." With "leakages" at ⅓ and the time-factor at two months, continuing and truly expansionary expenditures of a million dollars a day should result within a year in about 2¾ millions a day added to the flow of production.

(7) Allowance for variation in the factors. Such a process cannot go on forever. If it succeeds in stimulating business, this will limit the possibility of expansionary borrowing by calling idle funds into use. If it does not succeed, debt charges will pile up, soon calling for taxation to meet them and again limiting the possibilities of expansionary borrow-

ing. Thus, it is hardly useful to carry the approximation represented by the formula beyond one year.

(8) Counteracting factors. Beside the elements acting on the factors in the formula, other outside elements are important, chiefly bearing on the effect of such a program on private business. Unlimited deficit financing does impair business confidence. And a public works program may bid up costs of construction against private enterprise, or prevent them from falling low enough to be attractive. Moreover, if an increase of business is known to be due to public deficit-spending, which presumably must come to an end before long, business may for that reason fail to respond with increased expenditures on its durable productive equipment, such as it would make if the same increase in business came from purely private sources.

A fair conclusion seems to be that public deficit-spending cannot bear the whole burden of lifting production from the level of a serious depression without going so far as to bring about these deterring effects on private business. For that reason, estimates of stimulative effects, based on such an approach as the Kahn-Keynes formula, are hardly worth carrying beyond, let us say, one year, even as rough approximations. In a longer pull the net effects will be decided by factors which cannot be brought within the formula.

5. THE APPROACH VIA MONEY AND ITS CIRCUIT VELOCITY

If circuit velocity remains constant, public spending can increase the total dollar volume of production and of incomes only by increasing the volume of "money," using that term in the broad sense which includes all means of direct dollar payment. The increase would be equal to the volume of added "money," times its circuit velocity. This is the first assumption of the more rigorous monetary theories.

Even an increase in circuit velocity tends to be construed by some as a circuit velocity for the added money greater than that of the rest. This might be hard to adapt to the limiting case where the amount of added money is zero.

The fact is that circuit velocity fluctuates enormously from prosperity to depression, and that at the trough of the present depression it was probably not more than two-thirds of normal. Thus there was ample leeway for expansion by mere speeding-up, if forces could be set at work tending in this direction. This shifts the issue to the ground of whether the forces described in the Kahn-Keynes analysis afford adequate causes for an increase in circuit velocity. Will velocity be increased by forces acting on volume of spendings, or must there be forces acting in some way more directly on velocity itself? This goes back to the question what velocity is and what governs its changes.

The long-run trends of velocity appear to depend on the organization of production (governing the number of exchanges required to carry through a given flow of production and income) and on people's habits and preferences as to the cash balances they carry. But monetary velocity is, after all, not an independent physical quantity like the velocities of sound or light: it is a ratio between volume of money and flow of income or production; and its short-run fluctuations can be affected directly by changes in that flow. Even the outside limits of its fluctuations are elastic in responding to extreme fluctuations in the volume of income and production. The World War brought about an extraordinary increase, the present depression an extraordinary decrease. Thus the forces analyzed, however imperfectly, in the Kahn-Keynes formula, because they act on the volume of spending, seem to be among the forces governing changes in velocity, and thus to be among the data of the problem, even from the monetary approach.

6. CONCLUSIONS

To sum up, the Kahn-Keynes formula, construed with due allowance for variations in the factors, appears to be a valid method of handling a portion of this problem, especially applicable to results within a limited period. But the whole effect depends on such elements as the influence of the program on construction costs and on business confidence in general, and these elements do not lend themselves to inclusion in the formula. In the long pull, these latter elements will dominate the outcome.

XIII

WESLEY C. MITCHELL'S CONTRI- BUTION TO THE THEORY OF BUSINESS CYCLES*

I. INTRODUCTION

IF a single study can be selected as the "formative type" of the present movement of quantitative research in American economics, that distinction undoubtedly belongs to Wesley C. Mitchell's study of business cycles. It has already had a transforming effect on our ways of conceiving and approaching one major economic phenomenon, while it has implications for general economic theory and method which may be even more far reaching.

The material embodiment of this research is already voluminous. In 1913 appeared the quarto volume *Business Cycles*, published by the University of California. The method used is set forth and carried through its various stages to the culminating interpretation. The book carries no claims of completeness, but is permeated with a sense of the need for better and more comprehensive data; it is a logical preface to the author's subsequent work as research director of the National Bureau of Economic Research. The studies of this bureau may be largely oriented by the problem of cycles; but, if so, their scope indicates that this problem is hardly narrower than the whole of economic life. (Witness the studies of national income and of trade-union membership.) A rewriting of Mitchell's own work is in preparation, and the first volume has appeared, correspond-

* Reprinted from *Methods in the Social Sciences*, edited by S. A. Rice, by permission of the University of Chicago Press.

ing to the first of the three main divisions of the original treatise.[1] To this revision the Bureau has contributed, not only its studies already made, but additional data, analyses, and expert advice in the technique of statistical treatment.[2] For added light on Mitchell's conceptions of method, one must turn to other papers, especially his presidential address to the American Economic Association,[3] and his essay in the collaborative volume, *The Trend of Economics*, edited by R. G. Tugwell.

In discussing research such as this, our major concern will naturally be with the larger matters of scientific strategy, rather than with details of statistical technique which might well constitute a separate study. It is noteworthy that such an outstanding statistical economist has developed his technique in the actual handling of problems, not by formal classroom training in the craft. The first edition makes little use of the more elaborate technical devices of statistical rendering. The second edition contains a fairly extended exposition of these methods, indicating a much larger use of them in the forthcoming volume. But Mitchell is no slave of these techniques, and repeatedly refrains from refinements of analysis and presentation where these are not justified by the adequacy and the accuracy of the data. In the original volume he makes free use of the theories, the data, and the organized indices produced by other students and agencies. Indeed, he gathers in an unprecedentedly wide range of material, both factual and theoretical. In the second edition the material is greatly enriched by the studies of the Bureau. The aid it has rendered in the actual preparation

[1] *Business Cycles: The Problem and Its Setting* (New York: National Bureau of Economic Research, 1927); referred to hereafter as "2d ed."

[2] Preface, *ibid.*

[3] "Quantitative Analysis in Economic Theory," *American Economic Review*, XV (March, 1925), 1-12.

of the book is described as having been volunteered; nevertheless the outcome is a product, not of individual research, nor of the collaboration of independent students, but of organized staff work. As a result the statistical material is rounded out in a more systematic way than would otherwise be possible and contributes much to the comprehensiveness of the treatment; though for this result, considerable credit must also be given to the general development of statistics in the past fifteen years.

In spite of the fact that the original volume was the most comprehensively grounded treatise in its field, its statistical basis was limited. Its "annals of business," [4] as well as its thoroughgoing statistical analyses, were confined to the period 1890–1911, and to the four countries: England, France, Germany, and the United States. International comparisons, even in the well-explored field of price movements, were handicapped by lack of comparability of data; and the elimination of noncomparable data reduced the size of the sample. In numerous fields other than that of prices, little international comparison was possible. In some matters, notably in physical production, consumption, and savings, the data were extremely scant, or of an indirect character requiring much resort to inference.

For the first volume of the second edition far more complete data are available. Use is made of the Bureau's own series of business annals, compiled by Dr. Willard Thorp.[5] This series covers the United States and England from

[4] The term "business annals" is applied to connected summaries of general business conditions built upon the summaries of contemporary financial writers. They are condensed into time-charts which simply designate the periods of prosperity, recession, depression, and recovery. Their only strictly quantitative feature is the duration of the periods.

[5] Willard Long Thorp, *Business Annals* (New York: National Bureau of Economic Research, Inc., 1926). The volume contains an Introduction, "Business Cycles as Revealed by Business Annals," by Wesley C. Mitchell, pp. 15-100.

1790, France from 1840, Germany from 1853, Austria from 1867, and twelve other countries from 1890, all concluding with the year 1925. These data provide observations upon a sufficiently large number of different cycles to permit the use of statistical methods in studying the annals themselves. They permit a sort of second-power statistical study which arrays the cycles and studies their characteristics by accepted methods of group analysis, including frequency curves of the main characteristics. The typical length and the departures therefrom are shown in frequency tables, both for the whole cycle and for its different phases; and notice is taken of the long-run trend of change in length, the relation of long-run price trends to the lengths of the different phases of the cycle, the relation of the length of the cycle to the relative length of its different phases, etc. International relationships are studied by the aid of a large chart of parallel spectrum-like bands.[6] The reliability of the "annals" is checked by comparisons with statistical indices of business conditions running back to 1875 for the United States, and to 1855 for England.[7] Use is made of the annals compiled by Dr. W. R. Scott, of St. Andrews, covering the period 1558–1720, to shed light on the question as to when the modern type of business cycles originated—those recorded by Scott being clearly a different variety.

On the statistical side, various indices of physical production are now available; and the Bureau itself has compiled, and is soon to publish, a series of social statistics for England, France, Germany, and the United States. In short, clear promise is given that the factual basis of the second edition will be far more complete than that of the first.

The end sought in the continuance of such inquiries is to

---

[6] 2d ed., pp. 444-45.
[7] *Ibid.*, pp. 367-74.

make negligible the probability that the limitation of data
has any material effect on the conclusions drawn. In some
cases, this probability can perhaps be treated by quantitative
methods; in others, it can only be estimated in general terms
by the exercise of "judgment." In the field of prices the
goal is either attained or closely approximated, while much
improvement has been made in other directions. By its contribution to this result, staff research appears to have justified
itself; while the work of independent investigators is also
justified by the assistance they have rendered toward the
same end.

2. THE DEVELOPMENT OF MITCHELL'S IDEAS OF METHOD

For an understanding of this study from the standpoint
of method one fact is so vital as to call for somewhat detailed development. This is not, like so many superficially
similar studies, a detached investigation of a special problem
representing an exception to the general theory held by the
author or devoid of important implications as to the existence or the truth of such a general theory. The method is
not chosen merely because it seems appropriate to the handling of this type of special problem without reference to
the methods appropriate to general theory. This may have
been the case with Mitchell's earliest descriptive studies,
but he was even then a rebel against deductive method in
theory. Long before the writing of *Business Cycles* he had
reached the conviction that general theory should be built
on the results of the quantitative-descriptive type of method.

One may say that the interest which was focused in his
early descriptive studies broadened—the problem of the
business cycle playing an important part in the broadening
process—until it grappled with the problems of general
theory. With the resulting perspective, the factual interest

narrowed again to the business cycle as a problem of practicable scope forming an integral part of the groundwork of the general structure. The fact that he set a new standard in the treatment of this problem is definitely an outcome of this broadening and subsequent refocusing. Because he has viewed the business cycle in its broadest relationships and lent a hospitable ear to all of the rival theories, he has in mind an unusually wide range of categories, in terms of which the business cycle may be described. Because his general theory is not a simple explanation of equilibrium, he could not be content with a simple conception of business cycles as departures from equilibrium (usually vaguely and inadequately conceived), but he is moved to drive toward as full a description as possible.

But enough of such generalizing! A more vivid picture is afforded by Mitchell's own words in a letter which he has, against his inclination, permitted to be published with this essay. In passing, one may note that his recollections cast doubt on some of the positions taken by Professor Homan in his very competent study.[8] Some modification is clearly called for in Homan's assumption that Mitchell brought to college only the common mental equipment of a well-brought-up, middle western boy of superior intelligence. The influence of Dewey and Veblen seems to have fallen in with and developed his previous leanings rather than to have planted the first seeds. Witness further the fact that, of various influences he might have received from Laughlin, he appears to have selected those which paralleled his own bent toward objectivity, rejecting others equally prominent. The evidence indicates that Mitchell felt himself to be influenced at least as much by those things he

---

[8] Paul Thomas Homan, *Contemporary Economic Thought* (New York: Harper & Bros., 1928), essay on Mitchell, pp. 375-436.

reacted against as by those with which he was in sympathy. And his statement that he regarded his first edition as an approach to general theory negatives Homan's surmise on this point.[9] Homan's suggestion that Mitchell's method of work has colored his conclusions [10] can hardly be other than true, but it does not follow that the basic character of his views is a mere rationalization of the bent of statistical workmanship.

The pyrotechnics of Veblen's battle with the orthodox left Mitchell not simply dazzled and confused, but grappling with the stubborn question: How important were the factors which Veblen emphasized and orthodox theory circumnavigated, compared to those which orthodox theory emphasized and Veblen slighted? A question of quantitative potentialities! One may conjecture that Mitchell's natural leanings received aid and comfort from Veblen's doctrine of replacing assumed harmonies by an observed sequence of matter-of-fact cause and effect. For, while Veblen preached this doctrine, Mitchell practices it—as nearly as may be and with reservations as to the meaning attached to "cause and effect" which will appear later.

It is quite natural that Mitchell refuses to subordinate quantitative economics to the function of verifying the conclusions of traditional deductive theory, or to be worried by the fact that, as yet, quantitative economics has not gotten far with this task.[11] In his view, traditional theory suggests problems and hypotheses, but they are likely to be recast in the process of adapting them to the test of observed behavior; while observation will itself suggest other problems whose standing is in no way inferior merely because tradi-

---

9 *Ibid.*, p. 393.
10 *Ibid.*, pp. 428-29.
11 Cf. "Quantitative Analysis in Economic Theory," *op. cit.*, esp. 3.

tional "theory" may ignore them. "Traditional theory," in this connection, means primarily the central theory of value and distribution, or the general theory of economic equilibrium; but the same proposition holds true in less degree of the special theories which have been set forth to explain, for instance, the business cycle. We shall see in a moment how these theories are utilized in Mitchell's study.

3. THE ORGANIZATION OF THE TREATISE

In organization and order of presentation, the method of the first edition is substantially followed in the second. Both studies start with a review of existing theories, the chief difference being that climatic theories are mentioned only in footnotes in the first edition, and receive more adequate attention in the second. There follows a survey of general features of the economic order, so far as they bear on the problem in hand. This is the author's closest approach to a formulation of his own economic philosophy. Next comes, in the first edition, a survey of "economic annals," or accounts of the sequences of prosperity and depression of business in general, by expert observers writing in financial journals and similar publications. Then follows a detailed statistical analysis of the behavior of different phenomena: prices of different classes of commodities, wages, interest rates of different classes, stock prices, physical production and consumption, unemployment, currency, banking conditions, savings, and profits. (Only the average amount of savings is studied, data being inadequate to reveal their variations.) In the second edition, this material is reserved for a later volume; but the first volume includes, with its lengthy exposition of methods of statistical analysis, enough sample tables and charts to give a very fair picture of the general form of the phenomenon as revealed by this method of attack.[12] Finally comes the author's own interpretation, which he characterizes as "analytic description" rather than causal explanation. He concludes that the modern type of business cycle is a phase of a well-developed "money economy," defined as a system in which the bulk of the people live by getting and spending money incomes, and production is guided by the pursuit of money profits.[13] In the second edition, this conclusion is based in part on a historical sketch of the development of the money economy (which reveals Mitchell as vastly more than a statistical analyst) but mainly on a detailed study of the "annals" reaching back to a period in which the present form of the phenomenon was clearly absent. This study constitutes a well-marked bit of "evolutionary economics," and is fulfilled by the conclusion that further changes are to be expected. The bulk of the "analytic description" is a picture of the typical course of cycles based on the common features of those observed but recognizing different degrees of variation from type.

4. THE TREATMENT OF EXISTING THEORIES

In the Preface to the first edition one finds the phrase: "To determine which of these [current] explanations are really valid. . . ." This is to be taken, not as a formulation of the central problem, but as a device to aid the mind in approaching it. The various theories are not separately verified.[14] They suggest classifications of data as significant for the statistical part of the study, for instance, the distinction between producers' and consumers' goods, or between "organic" and "inorganic" products. They suggest causal relationships at numerous points in the ultimate interpreta-

---

[12] 2d ed., pp. 66-82.
[13] *Ibid.*, pp. 63 ff.
[14] *Business Cycles*, p. 20; 2d ed., p. 58.

tion; but clearly none contains the sole cause and none by itself contains a sufficient cause of all the features of the phenomena. Mitchell entertains the question whether practical reasons justify singling out one or more conditions as "the cause" or "the causes," but he himself makes no such selection.[15] If made, it would seem almost necessarily to imply as a point of departure some theory of normal behavior, lapses from which may then be explained by single (additional) causes; and this Mitchell might well regard as hypothetical rather than realistic economics.

While recognizing the value of the various theories, he finds them open to the general criticism that they take too readily for granted the nature of the phenomenon they undertake to explain, and that they tend to view cycles as special problems of abnormal behavior, by focusing attention on "explanations of" the crisis—Why need anyone explain prosperity? [16] Mitchell's fuller description of the cycle, aided as it is by the special theories, in turn develops and alters the nature of the problem which the special theories attack. Incidentally, in the second edition he takes up the definition of the term "cycle" and defends his use of it, distinguishing between periodicity, which implies regular intervals, and cycles, which may be of varying length.[17]

5. MITCHELL'S CONSPECTUS OF THE ECONOMIC ORDER

In summarizing the leading features of the economic order, Mitchell selects those which seem significant for the purpose in hand. As to the methods used in making this selection, the author himself would probably have difficulty in formulating them on paper. He deals in part with eco-

---

[15] Cf. 2d ed., pp. 54-55.
[16] *Ibid.*, pp. 2, 451-55.
[17] *Ibid.*, pp. 464-69.

nomic motives, but mainly with the economic machinery which forms the framework in which these motives work. In the first edition, he deals mainly with such matters of common knowledge as the ordinary economic theorist has at his disposal; while in the second edition, considerable quantitative matter is introduced, utilizing the results of his own statistical researches. Even without this indication, it seems clear that the order in which this part appears in the published volume is not necessarily the order in which the work was done.[18] Presumably this section was formulated and reformulated as the statistical studies and interpretation progressed, the author having consciously undertaken to include such things, and only such things, as played a part in his final interpretation.

It is no contradiction of this statement to say that one finds symptoms of Veblenian influence: particularly in the distinction between technical and pecuniary occupations, in the subordination of technical to profit-making considerations, in the emphases on the motive of profit-making and the planlessness of production, without corresponding emphasis on the checks and the ordering influences of the "natural economic laws" of the traditional economics. Competition is mentioned, but not "normal competitive price," and the "law of supply and demand" is conspicuously absent.[19] There is also a decided kinship with the type of theoretical approach originated by Walras and used at present by Cassel, insofar as they substitute the idea of a multitude of interacting functional relationships for that of single or ultimate "causes" but Mitchell, of course, does

[18] Contrast Homan's assumption that this section was first in formulation as in presentation (op. cit., p. 399).

[19] 2d ed., pp. 154-57.

not follow them in focusing attention on the conditions of a theoretical equilibrium in these relationships.

6. ANNALS AND STATISTICS

In the second edition, Mitchell pays careful attention to the relative advantages and limitations of business annals and statistics, attempting to gain whatever light can be secured from each. The main uses of the annals have already been indicated. Statistical studies play the larger part, since it is through them that he is able to trace the complicated order of events of which the cycle is made up. He finds, for instance, that retail prices vary more than wholesale; those of production goods more than those of consumption goods (even at wholesale); those of raw materials more than those of finished products; and wage rates less than any class of prices.[20]

With reference to the timing of different related phenomena, the indications are for the most part less clear and more difficult of interpretation. Perhaps the clearest cases are those of bond yields in relation to short-time interest rates, and the loans, the deposits, and the reserves of banks. The conclusion is also reached that the physical volume of production revives ahead of prices, sometimes by as much as two years.[21] The preliminary material included in the first volume of the second edition indicates that these time-sequences are to be treated far more elaborately, with the aid of statistical methods of gauging leads and lags, using the results of recent studies in this field.[22] Some of the indications in the first volume—for example, as to coal and iron production and wages—are complicated by the

[20] *Business Cycles*, p. 458; cf. charts of coal and iron production (pp. 231-36) in connection with price charts (pp. 97-126).

[21] 2d ed., p. 115.

[22] *Ibid.*, p. 233.

merging of cyclical and secular trends, and raise the question whether the earlier upturn of production is due to the secular trend rather than to the purely cyclical movement. Yet the isolation of secular trends and cyclical-irregular movements may raise more problems than it settles—as Mitchell clearly realizes. Indeed, he has already formulated a series of penetrating queries as to the interactions of secular and cyclical trends.

He may be counted on to determine whether the isolation makes any difference in the timing of the cyclical-irregular upturn. He will probably assume that for certain purposes—perhaps for explaining effects on prices and related processes—the actual upturn is the significant thing, while for other purposes analysis into components is necessary. His factual bent would naturally lead him to recognize that these components are theoretical abstractions and cause him to be on his guard against assignments of causal responsibility to such abstractions—assignments which might be as doubtful in their way as those of traditional deductive theory.

7. THE FINAL INTERPRETATION

Perhaps the most interesting questions as to Mitchell's method arise in connection with his final synthesis, or "analytic description," of the typical business cycle. Certain features of this are obvious enough. The facts revealed by his statistical studies are recombined in the order in which they occur, showing what is happening at each stage of the cycle and how each stage leads to the next. The emphasis is on "how" rather than "why," and the whole result is not characterized as a causal explanation; yet the description is not merely empirical—it must accord with reason.[23] In the

23 Cf. *ibid.*, p. 470.

same spirit is his cautious treatment of coefficients of correlation. Yet he is willing to speak of causal relations at particular points—this being the form in which the mind habitually frames some of its most fruitful hypotheses; but he insists on the recognition that these relationships are manifold and interacting—that causes are at the same time effects and effects are also causes. Apparently the things to which he chiefly objects are: (1) the idea of an absolutely necessary sequence where modifying conditions are too numerous to justify such an inference,[24] and (2) the conception of causation as a single chain running in one direction and anchored somewhere to a cause which is ultimate—"the" cause—rather than one of an indefinitely large network of conditioning factors. And Mitchell's work should do much to help consign this obsolete chain-and-anchorage notion of cause to the museum of historical antiquities.

But what is meant by a description which accords with reason? An example or two may help us here. If dealers buy more goods (in physical terms) than they are selling, their stocks must increase; conversely, if they increase their stocks, they must be buying more than they sell; and if they increase their stocks at a time when their sales are increasing, their purchases—and the sales of those who supply them—must increase more than their sales. Here we have the quasi-mathematical "reason" that deals with physical quantities. But when do dealers increase their stocks? It is natural for them, in the pursuit of maximum profits and minimum losses, to attempt to reduce them when they expect dull trade, and increase them when there is prospect of increased sales, and especially of increased prices; and the most available sign of such a prospect is the beginning of an actual upward movement. But here we are in the

24 *Ibid.*, pp. 262-70.

realm of human expectations and reactions whose behavior is notoriously variable even when most of the significant conditions are apparently the same. A movement toward "hand-to-mouth buying" might start for reasons outside the business cycle, or for reasons arising from it, and in either case might alter permanently the typical habits of stock-keeping. Here it is unsafe to reason from conditions to conduct and make a priori predictions; but given the conduct, one may see that it accords with the customary operation of known motives as conditioned by the given circumstances, and is, in this sense, "explained."

The most obvious difference between this method and that of traditional theory is that Mitchell reasons from conduct to conditioning motive and circumstance, while traditional theory, in appearance at least, reasons from motive and circumstance to "normal" conduct. Mitchell insists that he would not trust himself to use his analysis of motive and circumstance as a basis for predicting conduct without constant check by observations of actual behavior. Theory, being interested in "normal" behavior, has no such hesitation; variations of behavior from normal are merely the results of other than normal causes. The normal behavior of equilibrium theory is highly simplified and differs from actual behavior. But is not Mitchell simplifying also, to a less extent, in picturing the normal cycle and giving separate recognition to variations from it? At certain points in his analytic description he notes alternative versions of behavior, while every cycle has some features which are unique. His picture of determining conditions is comprehensive, including many of the "disturbing factors" of traditional theory. It is also too complex to permit the mind to deduce a result which is uniquely determined and exact. And it is the lack of this quality, in all probability, which causes some readers to miss the feeling of definite explanation which they get from more traditional methods.

Here is a very great difference. Relying on the deductive methods, traditional theory simplifies to the point at which this method can secure definite results; and this definiteness, though abstract rather than actual, is apparently held by John Stuart Mill to be the criterion of scientific character in economic thinking. Such thinking proceeds ostensibly from premises to resulting behavior.

Much could be said on both sides as to whether this is the order in which the thinking is actually done, or whether the (hypothetical) results are themselves assumptions actually determining the "premises" selected to explain them. Since the method is limited to such premises as are capable of yielding definite deductive results, there is ground for holding that the available premises of this character really limit and determine the results it can attain. On the other hand, from the fact that the whole structure is the outgrowth of the search for the "natural levels" of price and its "component parts" (shares in distribution), one may make at least a reasonable claim that the assumed result— normal prices and distributive shares—comes first and the apparent premises are derived from it, a selection of conditioning motives and circumstances which are sufficient to "explain" the result. To the inductive student, the whole structure is one hypothesis, with its implications somewhat elaborated and the emphasis on its own internal consistency, as Mitchell points out, rather than on the resemblance of the whole to the observed facts.

And it is this whole hypothetical state of normal equilibrium, of which Mitchell finds no evidence in the facts as he observes them.[25] There is no level of prosperity of which

[25] *Business Cycles*, p. 86; 2d ed., p. 376.

he can say: "Whenever business is above this level, economic forces are acting to bring it down, and whenever it is below, they are acting to bring it up." Economic forces act upward from trough to crest, downward from crest to trough; near the turning-points a conflict of forces may appear, but hardly at the mid-point. Each stage tends to bring its successor into being and not to return to an equilibrium level. Yet even Mitchell speaks of profits in a way which implies a long-run normal relation of prices to costs on the average of the ups and downs.[26] So far as there are forces that act in this way, some approach to the theorist's "normal" seems to find justification. On the other hand, the theorist's abstract normal implies no unemployment; and such a normal is obviously not the average of the periods of prosperity and depression, in the same way that the normal price may represent the average of high and low periods. Evidently different parts of the static norm bear different relations to reality.

An assimilation of Mitchell's results should certainly challenge the most orthodox theorist to produce some modifications in the traditional analysis, other than a slight lengthening of the chapter on business cycles in that part of the theorist's treatise labeled "special problems" or "applied economics." Shall we ever see the general economic theory which would be the logical outcome of an approach to the whole subject via Mitchells study of cycles? Or will the effects of Mitchell's study be merged with the results of growing knowledge in many other realms of economic phenomena and motives? [27]

[26] *Ibid.*, pp. 182, 187-88.

[27] [This analysis was first written in September, 1928. After some negotiations concerning the inclusion of the correspondence between the analyst and Mr. Mitchell, it was given final revision by the former in April, 1929.—EDITOR.]

APPENDIX: THE AUTHOR'S OWN ACCOUNT OF HIS METHODOLOGICAL INTERESTS

EDITOR'S NOTE

In making their interpretations of an author's methods, analysts were encouraged to secure the co-operation of the author himself whenever circumstances permitted. In the present instance, Professor Clark was singularly fortunate in eliciting from Professor Mitchell an intimate and revealing account of the development of his research interests and methods. This was contained in a personal communication, unaffected by thought of publication. In addition to its value for Mr. Clark's analysis, it was found to represent a type of methodological inquiry which would otherwise not appear in the volume,[28] and Mr. Mitchell was asked to permit its publication in connection with Mr. Clark's analysis. The proposal was personally distasteful, but he gave reluctant consent, yielding to an appeal to his loyalty to the Council [29] and its project, and to the editor's contention that an illustration of this kind of methodological analysis was needed in the volume.

Professor Clark concurred in the proposal to publish the correspondence, and commented as follows:

It may not be out of place to express my gratitude to my friend and colleague [Professor Mitchell] for the thought and effort embodied in the very revealing letter he produced; as well as to assure the reader that the sole reason for suggesting its publication is its value as a document bearing on the development of Mitchell's basic ideas and methods. From that standpoint there is reason to regret the amount of space occupied by a purely technical discussion of the minor

[28] Cf. the Introduction, pp. 6-7.
[29] Mr. Mitchell has been chairman of the Social Science Research Council since August, 1927.

matter of the index of price dispersion. If the inclusion of this technical discussion is justified (aside from presenting the correspondence as it was), it is because it exhibits one of the qualities which helps explain Mitchell's achievements: namely, a scientific humility and readiness to assimilate criticism. It may thus serve as an offset to his own avowal of youthful "intellectual arrogance," an avowal which an arrogant man would hardly have made!

The two letters below are reproduced as written, except for the omission from both of the technical discussion of price dispersion, to which Clark refers in the preceding paragraph.

LETTER FROM JOHN M. CLARK TO WESLEY C. MITCHELL

41 WRIGHT ST., WESTORT, CONN.
Aug. 2, 1928

DEAR MITCHELL:

I have been persuaded to undertake one of these case studies of method in the social sciences, about which you undoubtedly know. Having side-stepped one assignment, I find myself committed to trying to handle your study of business cycles. I hesitate to discuss a colleague's work; and if you see any impropriety in my doing it, perhaps it is not too late to change. If not, there are some things I should like to discuss with you.

First as to the choice of the problem. Is there any use in raising the question whether you are drawn to this problem because you prefer the methods of quantitative and analytic description to those of abstract theorizing, or whether you develop these methods because you are interested in problems that require them? At any rate, others have dealt with the same problem of cycles in the abstract way. It seems reasonable to me to suppose that you are naturally interested in problems of concrete behavior; that you reacted against your early theoretical teaching because it did not come to grips with many such problems, among which that of business cycles stood out like the proverbial sore thumb. But your reaction is more fundamental than most in that it extends to the whole matter of method. And your choice of a problem seems part of a method of attacking the general interpretation of economic life, as the problem of equilibrium is to a different school.

In this I suppose it is fair to say that you were influenced by Veblen, despite obvious differences. I learn from Homan's book that Veblen's earliest study was more like your type of work than anything he has done since.

Your general survey of leading features of economic life involves, of course, the selection of those that are significant for the problem in hand. Can one say anything about the method by which this selection was made or guided? In some cases you are using facts of common knowledge, and your selection *could* be the result of the same kind of mental processes as produced the special theories of earlier writers. But, even if that is the case, I naturally assume that you would check the significance of such facts by the part they play in the final analytic description. Other facts are more detailed and quantitative in character (especially in the second edition) and seem clearly the outgrowth of your quantitative studies, as well as of at least a partial working out of your ultimate interpretation. Could you say anything as to the order in which the various parts of the work were done? Or am I trying to dissect mental processes that are unanalyzable or "intuitive"?

As to your final interpretation, I have often wondered, to no great purpose, over the difference between this kind of treatment and others more definitely "causal." As it looks to me now, the key of your treatment seems to consist in presenting each situation so that the behavior leading to the next step appears as the natural result of business motives under the given situation of market prospects, behavior of costs, etc. That seems to be the crucial part of the proposition that the description must square with reason, and distinguishes it from mere empiricism. Perhaps there are other features that have escaped me.

[Here follow two paragraphs devoted to details of the method of measuring price-dispersions.]

Pardon me for inflicting this on you. Possibly this letter will fail to reach you, in which case you will escape.

With best wishes;

JOHN M. CLARK

LETTER FROM WESLEY C. MITCHELL TO JOHN M. CLARK

HUCKLEBERRY ROCKS, GREENSBORO, VT.
August 9, 1928

DEAR MAURICE:

I know no reason why you should hesitate to dissect a colleague for the instruction, or amusement, of mankind. Your interest in ideas rather than in personalities will be clear to any intelligent reader. Nor is the admiration I feel for your skill as an analyst likely to grow less warm if you take me apart to see how I work. Indeed, I should like to know myself!

Whether I can really help you is doubtful. The questions you put are questions I must answer from rather hazy recollections of what went on inside me thirty and forty and more years ago. Doubtless my present impressions of how I grew up are largely rationalizations. But perhaps you can make something out of the type of rationalizations in which I indulge.

Concerning the inclination you note to prefer concrete problems and methods to abstract ones, my hypothesis is that it got started, perhaps manifested itself would be more accurate, in childish theological discussions with my grand aunt. She was the best of Baptists, and knew exactly how the Lord had planned the world. God is love; he planned salvation; he ordained immersion; his immutable word left no doubt about the inevitable fate of those who did not walk in the path he had marked. Hell is no stain upon his honor, no inconsistency with love. . . . I adored the logic and thought my grand aunt flinched unworthily when she expressed hopes that some back stairs method might be found of saving from everlasting flame the ninety and nine who are not properly baptized. But I also read the Bible and began to cherish private opinions about the character of the potentate in Heaven. Also I observed that his followers on earth did not seem to get what was promised them here and now. I developed an impish delight in dressing up logical difficulties which my grand aunt could not dispose of. She always slipped back into the logical scheme, and blinked the facts in which I came to take a proprietary interest.

I suppose there is nothing better as a teething-ring for a child who likes logic than the garden variety of Christian theology. I cut my eye-teeth on it with gusto and had not entirely lost interest in that exercise when I went to college.

There I began studying philosophy and economics about the same time. The similarity of the two disciplines struck me at once. I found no difficulty in grasping the differences between the great philosophical systems as they were presented by our text-books and our teachers. Economic theory was easier still. Indeed, I thought the successive systems of economics were rather crude affairs compared with the subtleties of the metaphysicians. Having run the gamut from Plato to T. H. Green (as undergraduates do) I felt the gamut from Quesnay to Marshall was a minor theme. The technical part of the theory was easy. Give me premises and I could spin speculations by the yard. Also I knew that my "deductions" were futile. It seemed to me that people who took seriously the sort of articles which were then appearing in the *Q. J. E.* might have a better time if they went in for metaphysics proper.

Meanwhile I was finding something really interesting in philosophy and in economics. John Dewey was giving courses under all sorts of titles and every one of them dealt with the same problem—how we think. I was fascinated by his view of the place which logic holds in human behavior. It explained the economic theorists. The thing to do was to find out how they came to attack certain problems; why they took certain premises as a matter of course; why they did not consider all the permutations and variants of those problems which were logically possible; why their contemporaries thought their conclusions were significant. And, if one wanted to try his own hand at constructive theorizing, Dewey's notion pointed the way. It is a misconception to suppose that consumers guide their course by ratiocination—they don't think except under stress. There is no way of deducing from certain principles what they will do, just because their behavior is not itself rational. One has to find out what they do. That is a matter of observation, which the economic theorists had taken all too lightly. Economic theory became a fascinating subject—the orthodox types particularly—when one began to take the mental operations of the theorists as the problem, instead of taking their theories seriously.

Of course Veblen fitted perfectly into this set of notions. What drew me to him was his artistic side. I had a weakness for paradoxes —Hell set up by the God of love. But Veblen was a master developing beautiful subtleties, while I was a tyro emphasizing the obvious. He did have such a good time with the theory of the leisure class and then with the preconceptions of economic theory! And the economists reacted with such bewildered soberness! There was a man who really could play with ideas! If one wanted to indulge in the game of spinning theories who could match his skill and humor? But if anything were needed to convince me that the standard procedure of orthodox economics could meet no scientific tests, it was that Veblen got nothing more certain by his dazzling performances with another set of premises. His working conceptions of human nature might be a vast improvement; he might have uncanny insights; but he could do no more than make certain conclusions plausible—like the rest. How important were the factors he dealt with and the factors he scamped was never established.

That was a sort of problem which was beginning to concern me. William Hill set me a course paper on "Wool Growing and the Tariff." I read a lot of the tariff speeches and got a new side-light on the uses to which economic theory is adapted, and the ease with which it is brushed aside on occasion. Also I wanted to find out what really had happened to wool growers as a result of protection. The obvious thing to do was to collect and analyze the statistical data. If at the end I had demonstrated no clear-cut conclusion, I at least knew how superficial were the notions of the gentlemen who merely debated the tariff issue, whether in Congress or in academic quarters. That was my first "investigation"—I did it in the way which seemed obvious, following up the available materials as far as I could, and reporting what I found to be the "facts." It's not easy to see how any student assigned this topic could do much with it in any other way.

A brief introduction to English economic history by A. C. Miller, and unsystematic readings in anthropology instigated by Veblen reenforced the impressions I was getting from other sources. Everything Dewey was saying about how we think, and when we think, made these fresh materials significant. Men had always deluded themselves, it appeared, with strictly logical accounts of the world and their own origin; they had always fabricated theories for their spiritual comfort and practical guidance which ran far beyond the realm of fact without straining their powers of belief. My grand aunt's theology; Plato and Quesnay; Kant, Ricardo and Karl Marx;

Cairnes and Jevons, even Marshall were much of a piece. Each system was tolerably selfconsistent—as if that were a test of "truth"! There were realms in which speculation on the basis of assumed premises achieved real wonders; but they were realms in which one began frankly by cutting loose from the phenomena we can observe. And the results were enormously useful. But that way of thinking seemed to get good results only with reference to the simplest of problems, such as numbers and spatial relations. Yet men practiced this type of thinking with reference to all types of problems which could not be treated readily on a matter-of-fact basis—creation, God, "just" prices in the middle ages, the Wealth of Nations in Adam Smith's time, the distribution of incomes in Ricardo's generation, the theory of equilibrium in my own day.

There seemed to be one way of making real progress, slow, very slow, but tolerably sure. That was the way of natural science. I really knew nothing of science and had enormous respect for its achievements. Not the Darwinian type of speculation which was then so much in the ascendant—that was another piece of theology. But chemistry and physics. They had been built up not in grand systems like soap bubbles; but by the patient processes of observation and testing—always critical testing—of the relations between the working hypotheses and the processes observed. There was plenty of need for rigorous thinking, indeed of thinking more precise than Ricardo achieved; but the place for it was *inside* the investigation, so to speak —the place that mathematics occupied in physics as an indispensable tool. The problems one could really do something with in economics were problems in which speculation could be controlled.

That's the best account I can give off hand of my predilection for the concrete. Of course, it seems to me rather a predilection for problems one can treat with some approach to scientific method. The abstract is to be made use of at every turn, as a handmaiden to help hew the wood and draw the water. I loved romances—particularly William Morris's tales of lands that never were—and utopias, and economic systems, of which your father's, when I came to know it, seemed the most beautiful; but these were objects of art, and I was a workman who wanted to become a scientific worker, who might enjoy the visions which we see in mountain mists but who trusted only what we see in the light of common day.

Besides the spice of rationalizing which doubtless vitiates my recollections—uncontrolled recollections at that—this account worries me by the time it is taking, yours as well as mine. I'll try to answer the other questions concisely.

Business cycles turned up as a problem in the course of the studies which I began with Laughlin. My first book on the greenbacks dealt only with the years of rapid depreciation and spasmodic wartime reaction. I knew that I had not gotten to the bottom of the problems and wanted to go on. So I compiled that frightful second book as an apparatus for a more thorough analysis. By the time it was finished I had learned to see the problems in a larger way. Veblen's paper on "Industrial and Pecuniary Employments" had a good deal to do with opening my eyes. Presently I found myself working on the system of prices and its place in modern economic life. Then I got hold of Simmel's *Théorie des Geldes*—a fascinating book. But Simmel, no more than Veblen, knew the relative importance of the factors he was working with. My manuscript grew—it lies unpublished to this day. As it grew in size it became more speculative. I was working away from any solid foundation—having a good time, but sliding gayly over abysses I had not explored. One of the most formidable was the recurring readjustments of prices, which economists treated apart from their general theories of value, under the caption "Crises." I had to look into the problem. It proved to be susceptible of attack by methods which I thought reliable. The result was the big California monograph. I thought of it as an introduction to economic theory.

This conception is responsible for the chapter on "Modern Economic Organization." I don't remember precisely at what stage the need of such a discussion dawned upon me. But I have to do everything a dozen times. Doubtless I wrote parts of that chapter fairly early and other parts late as I found omissions in the light of the chapters on "The Rhythm of Business Activity." Of course, I put nothing in which did not seem to me strictly pertinent to the understanding of the processes with which the volume dealt. That I did not cover the field very intelligently, even from my own viewpoint, appears from a comparison of the books published in 1913 and 1927. Doubtless before I am done with my current volume, I shall be passing a similar verdict upon the chapter as I left it last year.

As to the relation between my analytic description and "causal" theory I have no clear ideas—though I might develop some at need. To me it seems that I try to follow through the interlacing processes involved in business expansion and contraction by the aid of everything I know, checking my speculations just as far as I can by the data of observation. Among the things I "know" are the way in which economic activity is organized in business enterprises, and the way these enterprises are conducted for money profits. But that is not a simple matter which enables me to deduce certain results— or rather, to deduce results with certainty. There is much in the workings of business technique which I should never think of if I were not always turning back to observation. And I should not trust even my reasoning about what business men will do if I could not check it up. Some unverifiable suggestions do emerge; but I hope it is always clear that they are unverified. Very likely what I try to do is merely carrying out the requirements of John Stuart Mill's "complete method." But there is a great deal more passing back and forth between hypotheses and observation, each modifying and enriching the other, than I seem to remember in Mill's version. Perhaps I do him injustice as a logician through default of memory; but I don't think I do classical economics injustice when I say that it erred sadly in trying to think out a deductive scheme and then talked of verifying *that*. Until a science has gotten to the stage of elaborating the details of an established body of theory—say finding a planet from the aberrations of orbits, or filling a gap in the table of elements— it is rash to suppose one can get an hypothesis which stands much chance of holding good except from a process of attempted verification, modification, fresh observation, and so on. (Of course, there is a good deal of commerce between most economic theorizing and personal observation of an irregular sort—that is what has given our theories their considerable measure of significance. But I must not go off into that issue.) . . .

[Here follow two paragraphs on the measurement of price-dispersions, dealing with the points raised by Mr. Clark and referring to a discussion of the same points in F. C. Mill's *Behavior of Prices*, pp. 279 ff, esp. p. 283 n.]

I did not intend to inflict such a screed upon you when I started. Now that I have read it over, I feel compunctions about sending it.

Also some hesitations. I don't like the intellectual arrogance which I developed as a boy, which stuck by me in college, and which I shall never get rid of wholly. My only defence is that I was made on a certain pattern and had to do the best I could—like everybody else. Doubtless I am at bottom as simple a theologian as my grand aunt. The difference is that I have made my view of the world out of the materials which were available in the 1880's and '90's, whereas she built, with less competent help than I had, out of the materials available in the farming communities of the 1840's and '50's. Perhaps you have been able to develop an outlook on the world which gives you a juster view than I had of the generations which preceded me and of the generation to which I belong. If I did not think so, I should not be sending you a statement so readily misunderstood.

Ever yours,
Wesley C. Mitchell *

* Mr. Mitchell was kind enough to permit republication of this letter.

PAST ACCOMPLISHMENTS AND PRESENT PROSPECTS OF AMERICAN ECONOMICS * †

THIS is a time for reviewing fifty years of accomplishment in our science; and much accomplishment there has been, in which we may well take pride. But while this is fitting and proper, we shall not do well to dwell too much on the mood of selfcongratulation. For this is also a time for rather deep humility, and searching examination of our results, our methods and our standards. We know much more than we did fifty years ago, but in another sense there is much less of which we are certain. And it remains true that in a time of desperate need, economics has not furnished the unified and authoritative guidance which many have thought, rightly or wrongly, that they had a right to expect. The story I must try to tell is an unfinished one, and there is no guarantee of a happy ending.

I. A REVIEW OF FIFTY YEARS: THE STARTING-POINT

"Speaking generally, . . . the men best qualified to stand in the front rank of American Economists are not the authors of systems or general theories, or textbooks of principles, but writers on special subjects. . . . The num-

---

* Reprinted by permission from the *American Economic Review*, Vol. XXVI (Mar., 1936), pp. 1-11. Presidential address delivered at the Forty-eighth Annual Meeting of the American Economic Association, New York City, December 27, 1935.

† I have dealt with certain aspects of this subject in more detail in "Recent Developments in Economics" contributed to a volume entitled, *Recent Developments in the Social Sciences*, edited by E. C. Hayes, 1927, pp. 213-307.

ber of powerful intellects it has brought to bear on them is a remarkable phenomenon. . . . In the perfection of its economic statistics America leaves England behind." This was not written in 1935, but in 1880, by Cliffe Leslie; and the men he names as writers on special subjects include David A. Wells, Francis A. Walker, William G. Sumner, C. F. Dunbar and Simon Newcomb. A few years later, Walker and Newcomb joined the ranks of the authors of general treatises; and later still, the tone of the picture changed radically.

The great revival and expansion of American economics dates, not from the founding of the American Economic Association, but from the end of the Civil War. The founding of the Association marks, however, a profound reorientation of the utmost importance. To understand it, one must go back to the state of college teaching of economics half a generation previous. The subject was typically treated as an adjunct to philosophy; and simple and absolute "natural laws" were presented as final truths about the economic world. Out of this schooling came a small group of young and able students, independent enough to react against it, conscious of defects of traditional method and shortcomings of traditional doctrine, and ambitious to build a better structure on sounder foundations. They went to Germany for advanced study; and we now delight to honor them as the Pilgrim Fathers of the new movement.

The period of over sixty years which followed may be roughly marked off into four main movements, coming into dominance at successive periods of time, but overlapping one another as all such movements in history are bound to do. First came a period of preparation, orientation and gestation, lasting until approximately 1890, and including the formation of the Economic Association. Second came the development and consolidation of an indigenous form of the marginal economics; paralleling the development of the Austrian economics and of Alfred Marshall's economics in England. Third came a critical movement; and fourth, the rise to dominance of positive types of study of diverse sorts, among which our efforts are divided—shall I say dispersed? —at the present time.

2. PREPARATION, ORIENTATION, GESTATION

The process of orientation contained much that was superficially paradoxical. It was part of a transition of which one might flippantly say that it gradually transformed American economists from *laissez-faire* protectionists to free-traders who believed strongly in the positive function of the State in economic life. This paradox, however, is easily explained by the changing issues of the times. More seriously one might ponder over a movement, largely animated by a spirit of breaking away from traditional system theories and apparently well launched in the direction of the Historical School, yet the outstanding fruit of which in its first twenty years and more was a most luxuriant crop of system theories of a new sort. If there was one thing that American economics did not do during that period, it was to become dominantly historical.

To explain this fact it may be sufficient to recall that these Pilgrim Fathers were individuals, independent-minded, differing from one another, and no more prepared to accept uncritically the more extreme forms of German doctrines than those of their own country. They brought back with them a social type of ethical background, but not a particularistic type of nationalism. Their conception of the increased rôle of the State was at the service of this social ethics, not of narrow nationalistic ends. They genuinely wished a broader groundwork of historical fact to put system theory on a proper basis, but not to displace it entirely. On the whole, they were, and remained, more nearly in the current of the English tradition than in that of Germany.

While the younger members of the group were laying their foundations, the commanding figure of Francis A. Walker dominated the field; his *Political Economy*, appearing in 1883, took rank as the outstanding American treatise, and bridged the interval between the earlier classical period and the later marginalism. Soon after, the younger group began to put forth their works. As might be expected, there were many special studies; but far more revealing were a few that expressed the writers' general points of view—my father's *Philosophy of Wealth*, Patten's *Premises of Political Economy* and his *Consumption of Wealth*, and Henry C. Adams's classic monograph on *The State in Relation to Industrial Action*. Here was an unmistakable reorientation, neither classical nor purely historical. By the end of the eighties, Ely's *Introduction to Political Economy* had appeared; and two papers by my father and one by Stuart Wood had staked out the marginal productivity theory of distribution. The phase of preparation was at an end.

3. SYSTEMATIC MARGINAL ECONOMICS

Of the various forms of systematic marginal economics which had their independent origin in this country, there is little I can profitably attempt to say in the time available, save that they caused this country to take rank with the leading foreign countries in the development of theoretical economics which was directed to analyzing the conditions of a stable or a static equilibrium. The few comments I shall make are not so much on the marginal economics as on our attitude toward it.

One is that the marginal or differential method is and remains perhaps the greatest single tool of economic analysis; and its usefulness is by no means confined to the study of the simple conditions of perfect and stable equilibrium. Another is that these studies of equilibrium are not end-products; and not to be construed as finished pictures of the actual world; in my father's case at least great care was taken not to present them as such. They are themselves tools of analysis and methods of approach to a picture too complicated ever to be finished. A third point is that while a picture of perfect equilibrium deals in its way with forces which are at work in the actual world, the form in which it presents these forces will almost inevitably need to be modified when we move on to the task of studying them as they actually operate. The terms of a static demand schedule need to be changed in order to fashion it into a verifiable concept; and the tendency of prices toward cost of production does not operate unqualifiedly under all conditions. Some of these changes are likely to be of the sort which John Stuart Mill described as chemical rather than mechanical, leading to results not deducible by the method of composition of forces. And a fourth point is that the problems with which these theories of marginal equilibrium deal are not the whole of economics.

In the period when the economics of marginal equilibrium held the field as the supreme orthodoxy, these qualifications tended to be forgotten to a greater or less extent; and the result was really an injustice to the theory. Too much was expected of it.

4. THE CRITICAL MOVEMENT

At no time was the marginal economics free from disagreement and controversy; in fact, some of its family quarrels were famous. More serious criticism began to come from Thorstein Veblen even before the publication of my father's *Distribution of Wealth*; but for some time he made little impression on those inside the citadel, save one of irritated puzzlement as to what he was driving at and why. But for some years before the outbreak of the World War there was an increasing spirit of scepticism mixed with active iconoclasm, which before long came to seem the characteristic mood.

There were attacks on the hedonistic psychology under-lying marginal utility, leading some to withdraw into psychological agnosticism. Some managed miraculously to keep a semblance of the doctrine while attempting to withdraw from all vulnerable psychological positions. There were attacks on the ethical implications of marginal productivity, attacks on the logic of marginal imputation and on the founding of the factors which underlay it. There were attacks on statics for not being dynamics, or more pertinently for not affording an adequate approach to dynamics. There were attacks going no deeper than verbal questions of the formulation of theories, and attacks apparently aiming to uproot all theory as such. In caliber, the attacks ranged from mediocrity cavilling at what it did not understand to genius declining to classify its intuitive insights in the customary pigeonholes.

It is obviously out of the question to estimate the validity of all this body of criticism. Instead, I shall content myself with suggesting the way in which it seems probable that this question will work itself out—namely, in the theories and assumptions which the oncoming generation will find useful and necessary in the positive work which they will do. Judging by present indications, the effect in the long run will not be one of complete destruction.

Modern inductive and quantitative studies are already making use of bits of the equilibrium theory as hypotheses, although they have usually had to be reformulated to adapt them to the requirements of verification. Even in the study of disturbances themselves, pictures of the conditions necessary to equilibrium often furnish a starting-point in the analysis of why equilibrium is not reached. This method has its dangers; for the investigator is prone to rest content when he has found one cause which seems sufficient to explain the general fact of disturbance, and emerges with a one-sided and inadequate theory. Such reasoning should be based on an adequate factual picture; but the factual picture alone is not sufficient.

An interesting case is afforded by the question whether statistical studies reveal evidence of a tendency of price toward "normal." Construing this for the moment in the limited sense of a normal relation of price to expense of production, the figures show a tendency of price to fluctuate around some kind of typical or average relation to cost, and in this sense a normal price persists. What the figures do not show is a separate force tending to cause prices to return to this normal relation to costs whenever they have departed from it in the smallest degree, beginning to act as soon as any discrepancy shows itself, continuing until prices have returned to normal, and then ceasing. This latter concept of the tendency to normal, which is appropriate to a static state, is too simple to represent the forces acting under dynamic conditions. Instead, it seems probable that the self-limiting and the cumulative forces are not neatly separated from each other, but may represent the same forces or factors acting differently under different conditions.

Another aspect of the static normal is the tendency to full utilization of the productive factors. It is obvious that actual conditions cannot fluctuate around this as an average, since they can depart from it in only one direction. Hence the typical or average condition is necessarily below the static norm; and a "normal" percentage of utilization derived from the average of observed behavior is necessarily a dynamic factor and not anything pertinent to a static state of perfect and stable equilibrium.

When equilibrium theories are used as devices to analyze actual conditions which do not follow the equilibrium model, one curious and interesting result sometimes follows— namely, a fuller development of the equilibrium theory itself. The conditions *necessary* to equilibrium often have to be more carefully and rigorously stated than ever before, in order to show how actual conditions differ and why they lead to a different result. In this way the theory of imperfect competition has forced economists to pay serious and searching attention to the definition of the conditions necessary to perfect competition—something which had previously been strangely neglected. The same principle applies to the theory of marginal productivity, in whose mathematical implications some renewed interest has lately been shown by mathematico-quantitative investigators. One may anticipate a considerable development and refinement of this theory in following out the different ways and degrees in which the underlying principle applies to different kinds of concrete situations.

Negative criticism did not drive out "orthodoxy" from the field of theory, partly because nature abhors a vacuum— if such a pre-scientific expression may be indulged in. What happened during this period was that other fields of study expanded enormously and drew more and more apart from the central core of theory. These special fields involved much factual study and had their own special histories, and were constantly dealing with problems of expanding governmental action. In this way American economics was approaching more closely to the character announced in the early manifesto of the Economic Association. With the entry of this country into the World War, interest in negative theoretical criticism was overshadowed by more urgent positive needs.

5. POSITIVE INQUIRY OF DIVERSE TYPES

With this change in emphasis, the foreground came to be occupied by various types of positive studies, some of which were already well under way. First, and perhaps most characteristic, was the quantitative analysis of economic behavior, with its chief interest centered on the problem of economic fluctuations.

This branch of study had previously been regarded as hardly respectable for a scientific economist to take seriously, owing largely to three handicaps. One was the lack of adequate statistical material. This left the study of booms and depressions in the realm of speculative theories, and the assumptions underlying them necessarily ran counter to the preconceptions of the dominant equilibrium theory, and hence were worse than suspect as being unscientific. Worst of all, these theories were associated with socialistic doctrines which were beyond the pale. The first handicap has been overcome by the development of statistics. If the problem is not solved, there is now at least plenty of material to set one's teeth into. The other obstacles have been worn away by a sort of attrition, aided by the waning of the prestige of equilibrium theory and the decline of the general spirit of optimistic faith in the spontaneous workings of the competitive system which characterized the nineteenth century. But the most active element has probably been the growing seriousness of the problem itself, which could not forever be dismissed by a defense reaction based mainly on the classical proof of the impossibility of general over-production.

The appearance of Mitchell's first volume on business cycles in 1913 marks a new epoch in this field of study, replacing abstract speculation by a detailed quantitative investigation of the phenomenon itself. And now, after a lapse of twenty years, this problem has at last suddenly forced its way into the front rank of issues of public policy; and thereby has marked a new epoch in the relation of government to business.

Along with this development went the growth of the rather elusive movement known as "Institutionalism," which means so many different things to so many different people that doubt has arisen whether it has any definable meaning at all. It covers certain fields of study, such as Veblen's evolutionary theories and the investigations of legal institutions by Ely and Commons. But it may be more important as an underlying point of view orienting many different kinds of specific studies and lending changed significance to the day-to-day routine operations of the business system. It may be that we cannot fully understand these day-to-day operations without understanding them as parts of an evolutionary movement going back before the present forms of property rights and containing forces destined to make the present forms obsolete. This is something vastly different from the nineteenth century conception of progress within an institutional framework which was expected to remain fixed because it had found its final terminus in the system of individualism and free contract, modified only by piecemeal control of specific abuses.

Another major development of late years is that of mathematical economics, using new and powerful techniques and bringing its results in touch with quantitative verification. The recent founding of the Econometric Society is a landmark in this movement. It faces great and inherent difficulties in the framing of assumptions simple enough to lend themselves to mathematical formulas yet flexible enough to grapple effectively with the problems of dynamic economics. Even the measurement of a demand schedule for a manufactured product is a surprisingly baffling problem. In the face of these difficulties, important achievements have been made, and more are to be looked for in the future.

Much has been done lately by mathematical and quantitative methods with the theory of general price levels and their changes. Here the most notable recent contributions have come from the other side of the water; but all appear to be in a decidedly controversial stage at present. Another subject recently attacked by mathematical methods, both here and in England, is imperfect competition. The results so far are of great interest; but they illustrate the difficulty already mentioned, of framing usable assumptions adequate to interpreting the complexities of actual conditions. The time element in demand and supply schedules is particularly baffling, while the relation between these abstract curves and the mental processes governing the actual reactions of business men bids fair to defy systematic analysis. We shall probably be wrestling with these difficulties for some time to come.

The fact is that as we enter the realm of dynamic and quantitative problems, we face more and more exacting demands. The certainties of equilibrium theory, hypothetical though they were, are replaced by stubborn uncertainties; and the most careful students are the least ready to present final answers. The mills of quantitative research grind slowly, and may never produce certainties on many of the larger issues. Hence, the humility which the responsible student must needs feel, even after footing up a large total of achievement by his science of economics during the past fifty years.

Equilibrium theory assumed that what is saved is spent; that purchasing power arising from production is used and flows back into further production. Now we ask if this is true, and find evidence of discrepancies. If we spend more for some one thing, shall we have less left to spend on other things, or more? The answer begins with: "It depends." Are imports an addition to our national dividend and exports a subtraction, or *vice versa?* We have no ready-made answer. We cannot combat old heresies with the same whole-hearted confidence as our predecessors—there may be something in them. And in this mood of doubtful potency we entered the gravest crisis of economic policy which this country has faced since the slavery question.

6. ECONOMICS AND THE WORLD CRISIS

If we try to assess the part economists have played in this crisis, the result is likely to be confusing. If our criterion is the part they have played in shaping policy, we find that a few economists have played a strategic part, while many more have rendered able and conscientious service in subordinate positions, below the levels at which policies were formed. If we ask instead whether economists have been able to reach substantial agreement on proposed measures, we find that there has been a considerable measure of agreement, though far short of unanimity; but this agreement has quite commonly been contrary to the policies actually followed. The greatest approach to unanimity probably came in the condemnation of a high tariff. This was a standard reaction on the part of the economists; and the politicians countered with their own standard reaction—by ignoring it.

The unfortunate fact seems to be that the consensus of economists has no absolute authority, and no right to claim it. Scientific truth is not to be certified by a general counting of noses, even the noses of economists. The results of new and untried measures can seldom if ever be predicted with scientific certainty. Within the margin of doubt, economists, like others, will follow their preconceptions; the minority view may happen to be right; and the government will be free to select those theories and proposals which best fit the tone of the administrative mind.

This difficulty will probably always be with us. In the face of it, what is the best we can do? Few would nowadays attempt to draw solutions ready-made from traditional theories. I can think of instances which approximate this, but they are rare. And the economist who does this is hardly less risky a guide than the one who follows the more popular course, throwing all received theories overboard and trying to work out every problem as a fresh and disconnected exercise. What is needed is a readiness to use accepted theories, and the methods by which they were derived, as tools of analysis, with a clear eye for the limitations of their applicability to the specific conditions of the problem in hand, and a readiness to make the theories over, if need be, on a basis of changed assumptions. In short, what is needed is thinking which is free, but disciplined. A few of us are like soldiers going through the manual of arms in the face of the enemy; more of us are throwing away our guns because we see no use in the manual. Neither of these is the way to win battles.

I have already said that this present crisis marks an epoch in the relation of government to business. Earlier controls dealt with localized sections of industry, applying standards derived from the unregulated field; or they dealt with particular incidental aspects other than the central question what and how much to produce and at what price. Now we are dealing with industry as a whole and going to the core of the matter. Earlier controls dealt mainly in restraints on particular abuses; the present problem is not one of restraints on abuses of vigorous private activities, but one of supplying motive force itself where motive force is lacking. Earlier attacks left unquestioned the main redeeming feature of private industry—its power to produce goods plentifully and efficiently; now this main redeeming feature is called in question. And apparently few leaders of private industry yet realize the seriousness of the situation.

The issue seems to be wrongly put by many, who ask whether in the face of the weakness of private industry and our fumbling attempts to deal with it, the *present system of private industry* can be maintained. The answer seems clear. If the system persists, its character will be changed until it will no longer be the *present* system. If change does not come through governmental action, it will come through inevitable developments in industry itself. The system has been changing its character constantly during the last hundred and fifty years, and as much through the action of industry as that of government. More changes are in store; and we can set no ultimate limit on their extent.

The present system is failing to use the productive powers it has so plentifully developed, and to give everyone an opportunity to produce and to earn a living. Can a system which will do these things be fashioned out of the present system by methods which will preserve the continuity of our development; or will a violent break be unavoidable? This seems to be the real question; and the world will not give us unlimited time to work out the answer.

Those who, like myself, have been brought up in the liberal tradition of gradual change, will approach this question with a strong leaning—call it a prejudice if you will— in favor of evolutionary rather than revolutionary methods of change, urging that the former be given the benefit of every reasonable doubt. Personally, I hope most earnestly that evolutionary methods will prove sufficient; but I recognize that this is hope, not prophecy. To make it come true will be one of the most difficult things a nation ever undertook; but it is not yet proved impossible.

If this is a true estimate of the probabilities, it places the future work of the economist in a very different setting from the atmosphere of relative stability and certainty in which our predecessors operated. It points to the likelihood of a world full of trial-and-error experimentation, in which the more deliberate studies may seem fated to reach their goal, if at all, too late to render service. That chance some of us must take, while others grapple with the more immediate issues.

7. PROBLEMS FOR ECONOMISTS

As to the technical problems facing us as economists, many have been dealt with at these meetings, and I shall mention only three groups by way of illustration.

In the field of economics of wage levels, what is the character of the demand schedule for labor under different conditions? What are the effects of wage changes on the three-fold function of wages (a) as incentive to the worker, (b) as cost of production to the employer, and (c) as purchasing power furnishing demand for goods? Are the requirements of these three functions in harmony, or if not, can they be brought into harmony?

In the theoretical field, there is a whole class of questions arising where a given economic change may have either self-limiting or cumulative effects or both, the question being to distinguish the fields within which these two opposite effects occur—in short, to give us a better systematized basis for judging which kind of effect to expect in any given case. For example, under what conditions, or over what periods of time, will spending more for radios leave the country less to spend on other things, and under what conditions will it leave more? Under what conditions are imports a loss to our national economy and under what conditions are they a gain?

Another large class of theoretical questions has to do with introducing time elements which have not yet been introduced into familiar concepts. Take, for example, a demand schedule. Will a given change in the price of electric refrigerators, relative to other things, have different effects in a day, a month, a year, five years? Would other commodities show substantially the full effect more quickly or more slowly? Can this time element be represented by a curve approaching a saturation-point in time, or by some other type of curve? Will sales at a price of $100 be different one week after a reduction from $120 from what they would be one week after an increase from $80? This problem seems especially pertinent to the concept of the demand schedule for the output of a single productive enterprise, of which so much use is now being made in the theory of imperfect competition.

The list of problems is endless; but these examples may suffice. It is clear that there is no lack of tasks for economists, and tasks which have important bearings on policy, aside from catch-as-catch-can wrestling with the expediencies of particular proposed measures.

8. CONCLUSION

It is not certain how much time the world will give us for finding answers to questions such as these; indeed, it is not certain that free scientific inquiry itself has a perpetual undisturbed lease on life. These also are chances we must take. It may not be wise to embark on inquiries which presuppose that the present system will remain substantially unchanged for generations to come. But it is still less wise to be stampeded by the critical state of the world into abandonment of all systematic inquiry; of all definitely scientific researches which do not bear on the instant solution of the question of a processing tax or a coal-control bill. And back of these researches lies the thing which makes them possible: free scientific inquiry. This, rather than particular conclusions and doctrines, is the most precious heritage left us by our honored predecessors. It still has its place in the world, so long as the world will tolerate it; and of all our possessions as economists, this is the one best worth conserving, and defending if the need should arise, with every effort in our power.

BIBLIOGRAPHY

A bibliography of the writings of Professor Clark, substantially complete up to and including the year 1929, is to be found in *A Bibliography of the Faculty of Political Science of Columbia University 1880–1930*, pp. 301–304. *University Bibliography, 1930*, pp. 28, 29, and *University Bibliography, 1931*, p. 34, list his publications during these two years. Since that date, a record of Professor Clark's writings is on file in the *Columbiana* Office of Columbia University.

Professor Clark's major works follow:

Standards of Reasonableness in Local Freight Discrimination. New York, 1910.

The Control of Trusts. Rewritten and Enlarged Edition. With John Bates Clark. New York, 1912.

Readings in the Economics of the War. Editor, with Walton Hale Hamilton and Howard Glenn Moulton. Chicago, 1918.

Studies in the Economics of Overhead Costs. Chicago, 1923.

The Social Control of Business. Chicago, 1926.

The Costs of the World War to the American People. New Haven, 1931.

Strategic Factors in Business Cycles. New York, 1934.

Economics of Planning Public Works. Washington, 1935.

INDEX OF NAMES